Christian Classics

Timeless Wisdom That Will Enrich Your Life

Compiled by
Pasco A. Manzo

Christian Classics
Timeless Wisdom That Will Enrich Your Life
Compiled by Pasco A. Manzo

Teen Challenge New England, Inc.
1311 Main Street
Brockton, MA 02301

Cover and Layout Design by Eric Castonguay

ISBN: 978-0-578-75191-7

Printed in the United States of America
2020 - First Edition

Christian Classics

Timeless Wisdom That Will Enrich Your Life

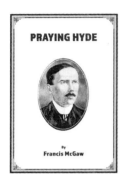
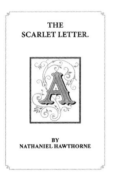
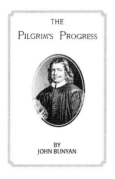

Foreward

Oscar Cruz
Vice President of Finance
Teen Challenge New England & New Jersey

$\mathfrak{T}$hese timeless Christian works are a must-read for

every believer. These books have stood the test of time as they each strike a chord of deep conviction in Christian leaders and laypeople alike. Christian thinking has been profoundly impacted by these pieces since their original publication long ago. It is natural for us, as believers, to become complacent in our faith amid our busy lives. These influential benchmarks of Christian literature were meant to stretch and expand our understanding of both who God is and who we are in Him.

The first of these works was written by Francis A. McGaw he tells the remarkable story of John Hyde, who overcame crushing physical and psychological challenges to save countless souls in India. Despite being partially deaf, he was determined to learn difficult native languages. He endured unimaginable persecution to win his first converts. No matter what he faced, he was a tireless evangelist who worked all day and prayed all night. This book encourages the reader to pursue the spiritual breakthroughs that come from a life fully surrendered to God. No better place to learn about effective prayer than the life of John Hyde.

The Scarlet Letter is considered a masterpiece of American literature. It is as relevant today as it was in 1850. A spine-chilling story filled with hypocrisy, revenge, guilt, repentance, adultery, and the power of confession. This tale explores the pain and internal anguish caused by secret sin. It is also an indictment on self-righteousness, and a testament to the power of humility. We find an unlikely protagonist in Hester Prynne, who overcomes the stigma and shame of sinful mistakes to find a life of contentment and salvation. This story amazingly has a lesson for everyone, wherever they find themselves on their faith journey.

The Pilgrim's Progress is one of the most compelling allegories of the Christian life ever written. This captivating drama chronicles the trials and temptations facing every Christian. In a world full of temptation and distraction, this story provides a sobering reminder of how easy it is to get off the straight and narrow path. Bunyan masterfully conveys how perseverance will overcome sin and compromise in our Christian walk.

In this information age, we can often find ourselves craving shortcuts in every area of our lives. We want what we want, and we want it now! We are so eager to finish one thing, just to rush to the next. These amazing works are meant to reveal the spiritual value of taking our time on our spiritual journey and investing some sweat equity into our relationship with Jesus. You will not be disappointed!

PRAYING HYDE

Glimpses of the amazing prayer-
life of a missionary in India whose
intercession "changed things" for
the Sialkot Revival.

BY

FRANCIS A. McGAW

The fact that John Hyde came by universal accord
of his intimates to be known as "Praying Hyae"
dates back to a day on the deck of the steamer which
was taking him out to his twenty-year missionary
service in India, when he crumpled up in anger a
letter from a friend urging him "to seek for the baptism of the Holy Spirit as the great qualification for
mission work." How he thought better of his hasty
ac*, and how not only India but the world at large
was blessed by this man's amazing prayer-life, is
lovingly set forth in this brief record.

CHICAGO
THE BIBLE INSTITUTE COLPORTAGE ASS'N
843-845 North Wells Street

Christ in the Home

Jesus said, "Today I must' abide at thy house" (Luke 19:5). What a blessed day that was in the home of Zacchaeus-Christ in the home!

John Hyde,"The Apostle of Prayer," as he was often called, was reared in a home where Jesus was an abiding guest, and where the dwellers in that home breathed an atmosphere of prayer. I was well acquainted with John's father, Smith Harris Hyde, D.D., during the seventeen years he was pastor of the Presbyterian Church at Carthage, Illinois. Dr. Herrick Johnson, of Chicago, shortly before he died wrote these words: "Hyde's father was of rare proportion and balance, a healthful soul, genial and virile, firm of conviction, of good scholarly attainment, of abundant cheer and bent on doing for God to the best of his ability."

Personally I knew him in his home to be a courteous, loving husband. I knew him to be a firm yet sympathetic father, "commanding his household after him." I knew the sweet spirited, gentle, music loving, Christ like Mrs. Hyde. I knew each one of the three boys and three girls who grew up in that home. Often I have eaten at their table. Twice I have been with the family when the crepe was on the door; once when Mrs. Hyde was taken away, and again when dear John's body was brought home and lovingly laid to rest in Moss Ridge Cemetery. Often I have kneeled with them and have, as a young minister, been strangely moved when dear Dr. Hyde poured out his heart to God as he prayed at the family altar. I knew him in his church and in the Presbyterial meetings. He was a noble man of God. Under God, his congregation was built up, and he was a leader among his ministerial brethren. I have frequently heard Dr. Hyde pray the Lord of the harvest to thrust out laborers into his harvest. He would pray this prayer both at the family altar and from his pulpit. It is therefore no strange thing that God called two of his sons into the Gospel ministry, and one of his daughters for a time into active Christian work.

A minister once said in my hearing, "My son will never follow me into the ministry. He knows too well the treatment a minister receives at the hands of the people." Dr. Hyde magnified his office and rejoiced to give his sons up to a life of hardship and trial. Why are there thousands of churches in our country without pastors today? A prominent pastor recently said to me: "Our denomination is facing a tremendous shortage of pastors." Why are the millions in the foreign field yet waiting for the human voice to proclaim to them the everlasting Gospel of the Son of God?

Today I read in "Far North in India" the statement by a former missionary in India, Dr. W. B. Anderson, that a hundred million people in India today have not heard of Jesus Christ, and as things are now have not the remotest chance to hear about him. There are other millions in Africa and other countries in the same Christless ignorance. Why is it so? Because prayer closets are deserted, family altars are broken down, and pulpit prayers are formal and dead!

Bible schools and seminaries can never supply the workers needed. My own sainted mother prayed as a young girl that the doors of the heathen countries might be opened. Afterwards as the mother of ten children (eight of whom grew to manhood and womanhood), she prayed for laborers to enter these open doors, and God sent one of her sons to India and two of her daughters to China.

Grandmother Lois and mother Eunice prayed, and when the Great Apostle to the Gentiles was about to take his departure he could lay his hands on son Timothy and commission him to "Preach the Word!"

John Hyde was an answer to prayer, and when in other years he prayed in Indian, God raised up scores of native workers in answer to his prayers. The Great Head of the Church has provided one method for securing laborers. He said: "Look on the fields... they are white... the laborers are few... PRAY!"

Holy Ground

In the Tabernacle of Moses there was one room so sacred that only one man of all the thousands of Israel was ever permitted to enter it; and he on one day only of all the three hundred and sixty-five days of the year. That room was the Holy of Holies. The place where John Hyde met God was holy ground. The scenes of his life are too sacred for common eyes. I shrink from placing them before the public. But when I remember Jacob at the Brook, Elijah on Carmel, Paul in his agony for Israel, and especially the Dear Man in the Garden, then I am impressed by the Spirit of God that the experiences of this Man of God should be published for the learning and admonition (God grant) of thousands. So we take our stand near the prayer closet of John Hyde, and are permitted to hear the sighing and the groaning, and to see the tears coursing down his dear face, to see his frame weakened by foodless days and sleepless nights, shaken with sobs as he pleads, "O God, give me souls or I die!"

Settled

His decision to go to the foreign field came about in this way; his oldest brother, Edmund, was in seminary preparing to preach, and was also a Student Volunteer for the foreign field. During vacation one summer Edmund was engaged in Sunday-school mission work in Montana. He contracted the mountain fever. The doctor advised his speedy return to his home in Illinois; so with his railroad ticket and instructions to the different conductors pinned to the lapel of his coat, he started. He became delirious before reaching home, but arrived safely. After a few days he passed away. John, who was already expecting to preach, was deeply impressed by his brother's death. There would be a break in the ranks on the foreign field, and he wondered if it were not God's will for him to step into the gap.

The decision was not finally reached till the next year, his last in seminary. Late one Saturday night he went to a classmate's room and asked him for all the arguments he could furnish on the question of the foreign field. His classmate told him that it was not argument he needed; what he should do was to go to his room, get on his knees before God, and stay there till the question was settled. The next morning at Chapel he said to his classmate, "It is settled," and his shining face was enough to show which way the decision had been made.

Sailing Day and the Voyage

The mighty deep, the great rolling waves, the days on days of water, water, only water, the feet lifted up from off the dear homeland and not yet planted on the new homeland, all these furnish suggestion and opportunity for thoughtful meditation. To our John this voyage in the autumn of 1892 was a time of heart searching and prayer. He received a letter to which he afterwards makes reference in an Indian publication. He says, "My father had a friend who greatly desired to be a foreign missionary, but was not permitted to go. This man wrote me a letter directed in care of the ship. I received it a few hours out of New York harbor. He urged me to seek for the baptism of the Holy Spirit as the great

10

qualification for mission work. When I had read the letter I crumpled it up in anger and threw it on the deck.

Did this friend think that I had not received the baptism of the Spirit, or that I would think of going to India without this equipment? I was angry. But by and by better judgment prevailed and I picked up the letter and read it again. Possibly I did need something which I had not yet received. The result was that during the rest of that voyage I gave myself much to prayer that I might indeed be filled with the Spirit and know by an actual experience what Jesus meant when he said, "Ye shall receive power, when the Holy Ghost is come upon you: and ye shall be my witnesses both in Jerusalem, and in all Judea and Samaria, and unto the uttermost part of the earth" (Acts 1:8 R.V.). These prayers on ship board were finally answered in a marvelous way.

First Years in India

At the first John Hyde was not a remarkable missionary. He was slow of speech. When a question or a remark was directed to him he seemed not to hear, or if he heard he seemed a long time in framing a reply. His hearing was slightly defective and this it was feared would hinder him in acquiring the language. His disposition was gentle and quiet, he seemed to be lacking in the enthusiasm and zeal which a young missionary should have. He had a wonderful pair of blue eyes. They seemed to search into the very depth of your inmost being, and they seemed also to shine out of the soul of a prophet.

On arriving in India, he was assigned the usual language study. At first he went to work on this, but later neglected it for Bible study. He was reprimanded by the committee, but he replied: "First things first." He argued that he had come to India to teach the Bible, and he needed to know it before he could teach it. And God by his Spirit wonderfully opened up the Scriptures to him. Nor did he neglect language study. "He became a correct and easy speaker in Urdu, Punjabi, and English; but away and above that, he learned the language of heaven, and he so learned to speak that he held audiences of hundreds of Indians spellbound while he opened to them the truths of God's Word."

The Punjab Prayer Union

In every revival there is a divine side and a human side. In the Welsh revival the divine element comes out prominently. Evan Roberts, the leader under God, seems in a sense to have been a passive agent, mightily moved upon in the night seasons by the Holy Spirit. There was no organization and very little preaching comparatively little of the human element. The Sialkot revival, while just as certainly sent down from heaven, seems not so spontaneous. There was, under God, organization; there was a certain amount of definite planning, and there were seasons of long continued prayer.

Just here as showing where human agency avails I wish to mention the Punjab Prayer Union. This was started about the time (1904), of the first Sialkot Convention. The principles of this union are stated in the form of questions which were signed by those becoming members.

1. Are you praying for quickening in your own life, in the life of your fellow-workers, and in the Church?
2. Are you longing for greater power of the Holy Spirit in your own life and work, and are you convinced that you cannot go on without this power?
3. Will you pray that you may not be ashamed of Jesus?
4. Do you believe that prayer is the great means for securing this spiritual awakening?
5. Will you set apart one-half hour each day as soon after noon as possible to pray for this awaken ing, and are you willing to pray till the uwakening comes!

John Hyde was associated with this prayer union from its beginning and also had a definite part in the Sialkot convention. The members of the prayer union lifted up their eyes according to Christ's command and saw the fields, white to the harvest. In the Book they read the immutable promises of God. They saw the one method of obtaining this spiritual awakening, even by prayer. They set themselves deliberately, definitely, and desperately to use the means till they secured the result. The Sialkot revival was not an accident nor an unsought breeze from heaven.

Charles G. Finney says: "A revival is no more a miracle than a crop of wheat." In any community revival can be secured from heaven when heroic souls enter the conflict determined to win or die or if need be to win and die!" The kingdom of heaven suffereth violence, and the violent take it by force" (Matt. 11:12).

Three Men

David's mighty men are catalogued in the Scriptures; there were the first three, then the second three, and afterwards the thirty; Jesus had many unnamed disciples. He had the Twelve, but in the inner circle nearest to himself were the special three: Peter, James, and John. Hundreds came to Sialkot and helped mightily by prayer and praise. But God honored a few men as leaders. This sketch is not given to flattery or fulsome praise, but God's Word says, "Honor to whom honor is due." God laid a great burden of prayer upon the heart of John N. Hyde, R. McCheyne Paterson, and George Turner for this wonderful convention. There was need for a yearly meeting for Bible study and prayer, where the spiritual life of the workers-pastors, teachers, and evangelists, both foreign and native, could be deepened. The church life in the Punjab (as indeed in all India) was far below the Bible standard; the Holy Spirit was so little honored in these ministries that few were being saved from among the Christless millions. Sialkot was the place selected for this meeting and 1904 became memorable as the date of the First Sialkot Convention.

Before one of the first conventions Hyde and Paterson waited and tarried one whole month before the opening day. For thirty days and thirty nights these godly men waited before God in prayer. Do we wonder that there was power in the convention? Turner joined them after nine days, so that for twenty-one days and twenty-one nights these three men prayed and praised God for a mighty outpouring of His power! Three human hearts that beat as one and that One the heart of Christ yearning, pleading, crying, and agonizing over the church of India and the myriads of lost souls. Three renewed human wills that by faith linked themselves as with hooks of steel to the omnipotent will of God. Three pairs of fire-touched lips that out of believing hearts shouted, "It shall be done!"

Do you who read these words look at those long continued vigils, those days of fasting and prayer, those nights of wakeful watching and intercessions, and do you say: "What a price to pay!" Then I point you to scores and hundreds of workers quickened and fitted for the service of Christ; I point you to literally thousands prayed into the kingdom and I say unto you, "Behold, the purchase of such a price!"

Surely Calvary represents a fearful price. But your soul and mine and the millions thus far redeemed and other millions yet to be redeemed, a wrecked earth restored back to Eden perfection, the kingdoms of this world wrested from the grasp of the usurper and delivered over to the reign of their rightful King! When we shall see all this shall we not gladly say, "Behold the purchase!"

1904 The First Sialkot Convention

One of his dearest friends in India writes about the great change that came to John Hyde's spiritual life at this convention in 1904. He writes that though John was a missionary and a child of God, for he had been born of God, he was yet a babe in Christ. He had never been compelled to tarry at his Jerusalem till he was endued with power from on high. But God in his love spoke to him and showed him his great need. At this convention, while he was speaking to his brother missionaries on the work of the Holy Spirit, God spoke to his own soul and opened up to him the divine plan of sanctification by faith. Such a touch of God, such a light from heaven came to him, that he said at the close of the convention: "I must not lose this vision." And he never did lose it, but rather obtained grace for grace, and the vision brightened as he went obediently forward.

Another missionary tells how John came to this convention to lead the Bible studies. During those days he spoke on the length and breadth and height and depth of the love of God. That mighty love seemed to reach out through him and grip the hearts of men and women and draw them closer to God. This brother writes:

"One night he came into my study about half-past nine and began to talk to me about the value of public testimony. We had an earnest discussion until long after midnight and I think until after one o'clock, and as I remember it, quite an interesting argument.

"We had asked him on the next evening to lead a meeting for men which was being held in the tabernacle out on the compound, while the women of the convention were holding a meeting of their own in the missionary bungalow.

"When the time for the meeting arrived the men of us were seated there on the mats in the tent, but Mr. Hyde the leader had not arrived. We began to sing, and sang several numbers before he did come in, quite late.

"I remember how he sat down on the mat in front of us, and sat silently for a considerable time after the singing stopped. Then he arose and said to us very quietly, "Brothers, I did not sleep any last night and I have not eaten anything today. I have been having a great controversy with God. I feel that he has wanted me to come here and testify to you concerning some things that he has done for me, and I have been arguing with him that I should not do this. Only this evening a little while ago have I got peace concerning the matter and have I agreed to obey him, and now I have come to tell you just some things that he has done for me."

"After making this brief statement, he told us very quietly and simply some of the desperate conflicts that he had had with sin and how God had given him victory. I think he did not talk more than fifteen or twenty minutes and then sat down and bowed his head for a few minutes, and then said, "Let us have a season of prayer." I remember how the little company prostrated themselves upon the mats on their faces in the Oriental manner, and then how for a long time, how long I do not know, man after man rose to his feet to pray, how there was such confession of sin as most of us had never heard before and such crying out to God for mercy and help.

"It was very late that night when the little gathering broke up and some of us know definitely of several lives that were wholly transformed through the influence of that meeting."

Evidently that one message opened the doors of men's hearts for the incoming of the great revival in the Indian Church.

1905 Convention
"Brokenheartedness for Sin"

In the spring of each year the Punjab Prayer Union holds its annual meeting. But as preparation for this meeting the leaders spend much time in prayers and fastings and all night watching. Then when the Union comes together we look to God for guidance during the coming year. "Early in 1905, at that annual meeting, God laid on our hearts," writes a brother, "the burden of a world plunged in sin. We were permitted to share to some extent in the sufferings of Christ. It was a glorious preparation for the convention in the fall of 1905."

At this convention John Hyde was constantly in the prayer room day and night; he lived there as on the Mount of Transfiguration. The words were burned into his brain as a command from God: "I have set watchmen upon thy walls, O Jerusalem, which shall never hold their peace day nor night: ye that are the Lord's remembrancers take ye no rest and give him no rest till he establish, and till he make Jerusalem a praise in the earth" (Isa. 62:6, 7).

There can be no doubt that he was sustained by divine strength, for are we not told to "endure hardness according to the power of God," not in our own weakness but in his strength? It was not the quantity but the quality of sweet childlike sleep that our Father gave his servant which enabled him to continue so long watching unto prayer. One could see from his face that it was the presence of Christ himself that strengthened his weak body. John Hyde was the principal speaker, but it was from communion with God that he derived his power.

His prayer life was one of absolute obedience to God. I remember once the lunch-bell sounded when we were in the prayer room. I heard him whisper: "Father, is it thy will that I go?" There was a pause, the answer came, he said: "Thank you, Father," and rose with a smile and went to lunch. Needless to say, he recognized his Lord as seated at the table with them, and oh, how many hungry souls were refreshed by his talks.

He was leader of the morning Bible readings, his subject being John 15:26, 27, "He shall bear witness of me, and ye also shall bear witness of me." "Is the Holy Spirit first in your pulpits, pastors?" Do you consciously put him in front and keep yourselves behind him, when preaching? Teachers, when you are asked hard. questions do you ask his aid as a witness of all Christ's life? He alone was a witness of the incarnation, the miracles, the death and the resurrection of Christ. So he is the only witness!" It was a heart-searching message, and many were bowed down under the convicting power. The next morning Mr. Hyde was not allowed to give any further teaching. The chairman came down from his seat and declared the meeting to be in the hands of God's Spirit. How wonderfully He witnessed of Christ and his power to cleanse all who repent. The next morning once again his servant said that he had no fresh message from God. It was pointed out that God would not be mocked till we had all learned this lesson as to putting the Holy Spirit first at all times God would not give any fresh message. Who can forget that day? How wonderfully those prayers were answered! The watchmen that night in the prayer room were filled with joy unspeakable and they ushered in the dawn with shouts of triumph. And why not, for we are "more than conquerors through him who loves us."

At one time John Hyde was told to do something and he went and obeyed, but returned to the prayer room weeping, confessing that he had obeyed God unwillingly. "Pray for me, brethren, that I may do this joyfully." We soon learned after he went out that he had been led to obey triumphantly. Then he received the promise that he would be the (spiritual) father of many children, an Abraham indeed. He entered the hall with great joy, and as he came before the people, after having obeyed God, he spoke three words in Urdu and three in English, repeating them three times, "Ai Asmani Bak," "O Heavenly Father." What followed who can describe? It was as if a great ocean came sweeping into that assembly, and "suddenly there came a sound from heaven as of a rushing mighty wind, and it filled all the house where they were sitting." Hearts were bowed before that divine presence as the trees of the wood before a mighty tempest. It was the ocean of God's love being outpoured through one man's obedience. Hearts were broken before it. There were confessions of sins with tears that were soon changed to joy and then to shouts of rejoicing. Truly, we were filled with new wine, the new wine of Heaven!

Here is the experience of one missionary: "Hours alone with God, with no one to see or hear but God were customary; but the fellowship of others in prayer or praise, for hours, could it be downright real? On entering that room the problem was solved. At once you knew you were in the holy presence of God, where there could be only awful reality. Others in the room were forgotten except when the combined prayers and praises made you realize the strength and power and sympathy of such fellowship. The hours of waiting on God in communion with others were precious times, when together we waited on God to search us and to speak to us, together interceded for others, together praised him for himself and for his wonderworking power. There was a breadth and freedom during those ten days that I never imagined existed on earth. Surely it was for freedom such as this that Christ has set us free. Each one did exactly as he or she felt led to do. Some went to bed early, some prayed for hours, some prayed all night long, some went to the meetings and some to the prayer room and some to their own rooms; some prayed, some praised, some sat to pray, some kneeled, some lay prostrate on their faces before God, just as the Spirit of God bade them. There was no criticism, no judging of what was being done or said. Each one realized that all superficialities were put away, that each one was in the awful presence of the Holy God."

The same missionary referred to John Hyde when she wrote, "There were some who knew that God had chosen and ordained them to be 'watchmen.' There were some who had lived for long so near Jehovah that they heard his voice and received orders direct from him about everything, even as to when they were to watch and pray and when they were to sleep. Some watched all night long for nights because God told them to do so, and he kept sleep from them that they might have the privilege and honor of watching with him over the affairs of his kingdom.'

1906 The Lamb on His Throne

Again at this convention in answer to prayer God poured out on us by his Spirit a burden for lost souls. We saw the same "brokenheartedness" for the sins of others. None felt this more than John Hyde. God was deepening his prayer life. He was permitted of God to have the privilege of drinking of the Master's cup and of being baptized with his baptism - the second baptism of fire, suffering with him that we may reign with him here and now, the life of true Kings for the sake of others.

About this time John Hyde began to have visions of the glorified Christ as a Lamb on his throne suffering such infinite pain for and with his suffering Body on earth, as it is so often revealed in God's Word. As the Divine Head, he is the nerve center of all the body. He is indeed living today a life of intercession for us. Prayer for others is as it were the very breath of our Lord's life in heaven. "He ever liveth to make intercession for us." It was becoming increasingly true of John Hyde. How often in the prayer room he would break out into tears over the sins of the world, and especially of God's children. Even then his tears would be changed into shouts of praise according to the divine promise repeated by our Lord on that last night when he talked freely with his own. "Ye shall be sorrowful, but your sorrow shall be turned into joy" (John 16:20-22).

A brother writes about the Convention of 1906, "Thank God, he has heard our prayers and poured out the Spirit of Grace and intercession upon so many of his children. For example I saw a Punjabi brother convulsed and sobbing as if his heart would break. I went up to him and put my arms about him and said, 'The blood of Jesus Christ cleanseth us from all sin.' A smile lit up his face. 'Thank God, Sahib,' he cried, 'but oh, what an awful vision I have had! Thousands of souls in this land of India being carried away by the dark river of sin! They are in hell now. Oh, to snatch them from the fire before it is too late!"

See another example of how this agony of soul in John Hyde was reflected in one who was a daughter in Christ to him. An Indian Christian girl was at this convention. Her father had compelled her to neglect Christ's claims upon her. In the prayer room she was convicted of her sin and told how her heart was being torn away from her father to Christ. One could almost see the springing tendrils of her heart as the power of the love of Christ came upon her. It was a terrible time. Then she asked us to pray for her father. We began to pray and suddenly the great burden for that soul was cast upon us, and the room was filled with sobs and cries for one whom most of us had never seen or heard of before. Strong men lay on the ground groaning in agony for that soul. There was not a dry eye in that place until at last God gave us the assurance that prayer had been heard and out of Gethsemane we came into the Pentecostal joy of being able to praise him that he heard our cry.

"That meeting was one," writes this brother, "that will never leave my memory. It went on all night. It was a time when God's power was felt as I never had felt it before."

This brother continues, "God wants those who are willing to bear the burden of the souls of these millions without God to go with Jesus into Gethsemane. He wants us to do this. It is a blessed experience to feel that in some measure we can enter into the fellowship of Christ's sufferings. It brings us into a precious nearness to the Son of God. And not only this, but it is God's appointed way of bringing the lost sheep back to the fold. He is saying, 'Who will go for us, and whom shall I send?' Are you who read these words willing to be intercessors? If we are willing to put ourselves into God's hands, then God is willing to use us. But there are two conditions: obedience and purity. Obedience in everything, even in the least, surrendering up our wills and taking the will of God. And the next step is purity. God wants pure vessels for his service, clean channels through which to pour forth his grace. He wants purity in the very center of the soul, and unless God can have a pure vessel, purified by the fire of the Holy Spirit, he cannot use that vessel. He is asking you now if you will let him cleanse away part of your very life. God must have a vessel he can use!

1907 Holy Laughter

In the summer of 1907 John went to a friend's house for a holiday. It was in the M- Hills. The friend writes about it thus: "The crowning act of God's love to us personally was the wonderful way in which he brought Mr. Hyde up to stay with us. I also had to come up to do duty among some English troops here. So Hyde and I have been having glorious times together. There were seasons of great conflict and at times I thought Hyde would break down completely. But after all nights of prayer and praise he would appear fresh and smiling in the morning. God has been teaching us wonderful lessons when he calls us to seasons of such wrestling. It is that command in 2 Timothy 1:8, "Suffer hardship with the gospel according to the power of God." So that we have the power of God to draw upon for all our need. Ever since Mr. Hyde realized this he says he has scarcely ever felt tired, though he has had at times little sleep for weeks. No man need ever break down through overstrain in this ministry of intercession."

"Another element of power: 'The joy of the Lord is your strength.' Ah G-, a poor Punjabi brother of low caste origin, has been used of God to teach us all how to make such times of prayer a very heaven upon earth, how to prevent the pleasure of praying and even of wrestling ever descending into a toil. How often has G- after most awful crying seemed to break through the hosts of evil and soar up into the presence of the Father! You could see the smile of God reflected in his face. Then he would laugh aloud in the midst of his prayer. It was the joy of a son revelling in the delight of his Father's smile. God has been teaching John and me that his name is the God of Isaac-laughter. Have you observed that picture of heaven in Proverbs 8:30? 'I was daily in his delight.' This is the Father's love being showered upon his own Son. No wonder that in such a home the Son should say that he was 'always rejoicing before him.' 'Rejoicing,' laughing, the same word as Isaac. This holy laughter seemed to relieve the tension and give heaven's own refreshment to wrestling spirits.

"I must tell you of dear Hyde's last message before he returned to Ludhiana. It was a special revelation to Paul, and one which the Spirit forced him to give out to the Romans, that he had unceasing pain, for he could wish that he himself were ana thema from Christ for his kinsmen according to the flesh (Rom. 9 : 1-3). Surely this was more than Paul's love for Christ. When he could wish that he should be what Christ had become for us - a curse! Fancy having to give up all hope in Christ! Fancy going back to the old sins and their domination over us! The thought is unbearable! Yet such was the divine pity in Paul's heart that he was willing to be anathema from Christ, if it were possible in this way to save his kinsmen the Jews. Such in a few words was God's message by his messenger, John Hyde.

How we all broke down! Ah, God's love was indeed shed abroad in the hearts of those present. All this was leading to the great crisis in John Hyde's prayer life, which I had the privilege of seeing."

Summer 1908

"This summer we persuaded him to come up to the Hills with us. His room was a separate one upon the hill and to one side of our house. Here he came. but came for a very real intercession with his Master. This intercession was fraught with mighty issues for the kingdom of God amongst us. It was evident to all that he was bowed down with sore travail of soul. He missed many meals, and when I went to his room I would find him lying as in great agony, or walking up and down as if an inward fire were burning in his bones. And so there was that fire of which our Lord spoke when he said: 'I came to cast fire upon the earth, and how would I that it were already kindled! But I have a baptism to be baptized with, and how I am straitened till it be accomplished.' John did not fast in the ordinary sense of the word, yet often at that time when I begged him to come for a meal he would look at me and smile and say, 'I am not hungry.' No! there was a far greater hunger eating up his very soul, and prayer alone could satisfy that. Before the spiritual hunger the physical disappeared. He had heard our Lord's voice saying to him: 'Abide ye here and watch with ME." So he abode there with his Lord, who gave him the privilege of entering Gethsemane with himself.

One thought was constantly uppermost in his mind, that

our Lord still agonizes for souls. Many times he used to quote from the Old and New Testaments, especially as to the privilege of 'filling up that which was lacking of the afflictions of Christ.' He would speak of the vow made by our Lord devoting a long drawn out travail of soul till all his own were safely folded. 'For! say unto you that I shall not drink henceforth of the fruit of the vine till that day when I drink it new with you in my Father's kingdom.' 'Saul, Saul, why persecutest thou Me?' These were some of the verses used of God to open his eyes to the fellowship of Christ's sufferings. These were days when the clouds were often pierced and the glorified life that our Lord now leads shone through, revealing many mysteries of travail and pain. It was truly a following of him who is the Lamb, suffering still with us as he once did for us on earth, though now himself on the throne. John Hyde found that he still carries our crosses-the heavy end of our crosses, 'for he ever liveth to make intercession for us.'

"It was into the life of prayer and watching and agonizing for others that he was being led step by step. All this time, though he ate little and slept less, he was bright and cheerful. Our children had ever been a great joy to him. Uncle John, who had so often played with them, was always welcomed with smiles of love. Yet now, even the little ones appeared to realize that this was no time for play! They were wonderfully subdued and quiet in his presence in those days, for there was a light on his face that told of communion with another world. Yet there was nothing of the hermit about him, in fact people were more than ever attracted to him, and freely asked for his prayers. He always had leisure to speak to them of spiritual things, and entered even more patiently than ever into their trials and disappointments. We will not speak in detail of those days of watching and praying and fasting when he appeared to enter into our Lord's great yearning for his sheep. We feared his poor weak body would sink under the strain; but how marvelously he was sustained all the time! At times that agony was dumb, at times it was a crying out for the millions perishing before our eyes; yet it was always lit up with hope. Hope in the love of God - Hope in the God of Love."

With all that depth of love which he seemed to be sounding with his Lord, there were glimpses of its heights-moments of heaven upon earth, when his soul was flooded with songs of praise, and he would enter into the joy of his Lord. Then he would break into song but they were always "Songs in the night." In those days he never seemed to lose sight of those thousands in his own district without God and without hope in the world. How he pleaded for them with sobs-dry choking sobs, that showed how the depths of his soul were being stirred. "Father, give me these souls or I die!" was the burden of his prayers. His own prayer that he might rather burn out than rust out was already being answered.

Let me introduce here a gem from the pen of Paterson: "What was the secret of that prayer-life of John Hyde's?" he asks. This, that it was a life of prayer. Who is the source of all life? The glorified Jesus. How do I get this life from him? Just as I receive his righteousness to begin with. I own that I have no righteousness of my own only filthy rags and I in faith claim his righteousness. Now, a twofold result follows: - As to our Father in heaven, He sees Christ's righteousness - not my unrighteousness. A second result as to ourselves: Christ's righteousness not merely clothes us outwardly, but enters into our very being, by his Spirit, received in faith as with the disciples (see John 20:22) and works out sanctification in us.

Why not the same with our prayer life? Let us remember the word "for." "Christ died for us," and "He ever liveth to make intercession 'for' us," that is, in our room and stead. So I confess my ever failing prayers (it dare not be called a life), and plead his never failing intercession. Then it affects our Father, for he looks upon Christ's prayer-life in us, and answers accordingly. So that the answer is far "above all we can ask or think." Another great result follows: it affects us. Christ's prayer life enters into us and he prays in us. This is prayer in the Holy Spirit. Only thus can we pray without ceasing. This is the life more abundant which our Lord gives. Oh, what peace, what comfort! No more working up a life of prayer and failing constantly. Jesus enters the boat and the toiling ceases, and we are at the land whither we would be. Now, we need to be still before him, so as to hear his voice and allow him to pray in us-nay, allow him to pour into our souls his overflowing life of intercession, which means literally: FACE TO FACE meeting with God-real UNION and COMMUNION."

1908 Convention One Soul a Day

It was about this time that John Hyde laid hold of God in a very definite covenant. This was for one soul a day-not less, not enquirers simply but a soul saved-ready to confess Christ in public and be baptized in his name. Then the stress and strain was relieved. His heart was filled with the peace of full assurance. All who spoke to him perceived a new life and a new life-work which this life can never end.

He returned to his district with this confidence nor was he disappointed. It meant long journeys, nights of watching unto prayer and fasting, pain and conflict, yet victory always crowning this. What though the dews chilled him by night and the drought exhausted him by day? His sheep were being gathered into the fold and the Good Shepherd was seeing of the travail of his soul and being satisfied. By the end of that year more than four hundred were gathered in.

Was he satisfied? Far from it. How could he possibly be so long as his Lord was not? How could our Lord be satisfied, so long as one single sheep was yet outside his fold? But John Hyde was learning the secret of Divine Strength: "The joy of the Lord." For, after all, the greater our capacity for joy the greater our capacity also for sorrow. Thus it was with the Man of Sorrows, he who could say: "These words have I spoken unto you that my joy may be in you and that your joy may be full."

John Hyde seemed always to be hearing the Good Shepherd's voice saying, "Other sheep I have--other sheep I have." No matter if he won the one a day or two a day or four a day, he had an unsatisfied longing, an undying passion for lost souls. Here is a picture given by one of his friends in India: "As a personal worker he would engage a man in a talk about his salvation. By and by he would have his hands on the man's shoulders looking him very earnestly in the eye. Soon he would get the man on his knees confessing his sins and seeking salvation. Such a one he would baptize in the village, by the roadside, or anywhere."

I once attended one of his conventions for Christians. He would meet his converts as they came in and embrace them in Oriental style, laying his hand first on one shoulder and then on the other. Indeed, his embraces were so loving that he got nearly all to give like embraces to Christians and those too of the lowest caste.

This was his strong point. Love won him victories.

1909 Convention Two Souls a Day

Again John Hyde laid hold of God with a definite and importunate request. This time it was for two souls a day. At this convention God used him even more mightily than ever before. God spoke through his servant John Hyde.

We speak with bated breath of the most sacred lesson of

all-glimpses that he gave us into the divine heart of Christ broken for our sins. He did not overwhelm us with this sight all at once. He revealed these glimpses gently and lovingly according to our ability to endure it. Ah, who can forget how he showed us his great heart of love pierced by that awful sorrow at the wickedness of the whole world, "which grieved him at his heart."

Deeper and deeper we were allowed to enter into the agony of God's soul, till like the prophet of sorrow, Jeremiah, we heard his anguish, desiring that his eyes might become a fountain of tears, that he might weep day and night for the slain of the daughter of his people. There the divine longing was realized in Gethsemane and Calvary! We were led to see the awful suffering of the Son of God, and the still more awful suffering of the Father and of the Eternal Spirit, through whom He offered up himself without spot unto God.

How can we enter into the fellowship of such sufferings? "Ask, and it shall be given you, seek and ye shall find, knock, and it shall be opened unto you." Observe the progress in intensified desire,great, greater, greatest, and the corresponding reward till, to crown it all, the Father's heart is thrown open to us. Yes, to all and sundry we tell our joys; it is the privileged few very near our hearts to whom we tell our sorrows! So it is with the love of God. It was to John the beloved as he lay close to the heart of the Master, and then drew closer still, that Jesus revealed the awful anguish that was breaking his heart, that one of them should betray him. The closer we draw to his heart, the more we shall share his sorrows. All this we obtain only by faith. It is not our broken heart, it is God's we need. It is not our sufferings, it is Christ's we are partakers of. It is not our tears with which we should admonish night and day - it is all Christ's. The fellowship of his sufferings is his free gift-free for the taking in simple faith, never minding our feelings.

"Lord, give me Thy heart of love for sinners, Thy broken heart for their sins. Thy tears with which to admonish night and day," cried a dear child of God at the end of this contention. Then he went on: "But, O Lord, I feel so cold. My heart is so hard and dead. I am so lukewarm!" A friend had to interrupt him. "Why are you looking down at your poor self, brother? Of course your heart is cold and dead. But you have asked for the broken heart of Jesus, his love, his burden for sin, his tears. Is he a liar? Has he not given what you asked for? Then why look away from his heart to your own?" John used to say, "When we keep near to Jesus it is he who draws souls to himself through us, but he must be lifted up in our lives; that is, we must be crucified with him. It is 'self' in some shape that comes between us and him, so self must be dealt with as he was dealt with. Self must be crucified, dead and buried with Christ. If not 'buried' the stench of the old man will frighten souls away. If these three steps downwards are taken as to. the old man, then the new man will be revived, raised, and seated - the corresponding steps upward which God permits us to take. Then indeed Christ is lifted up in our lives, and he cannot fail to attract souls to himself. All this is the result of a close union and communion, that is 'fellowship' with him in his sufferings!"

1910 Convention Four Souls a Day

The eight hundred souls gathered in since last year's convention did not satisfy John Hyde. God was enlarging his heart with his love. Once again he laid hold on God with holy desperation. How many weeks it was I do not remember, but he went deeper still with Christ into the shadows of the Garden! Praying took the form now of confessing the sins of others and taking the place of those sinners, as so many of the prophets did in old time. He was bearing the sins of others alone with his Lord and Master. "Bear ye one another's burdens, and so fulfill the law of Christ." According to that law we ought to lay down our lives for the brethren. This, John Hyde was doing. He was "dying daily."

What was that burden referred to in Galatians 6:2? The previous verse reveals it. It was bearing the sins of others. He at length got the assurance of four souls a day.

Yet this was the year that God used him all over India. He was called to help in revivals and conferences in Calcutta, Bombay, and many of the larger cities. Surely he was being prepared for an eternity-wide mission. Yet he was never more misjudged and misunderstood. But that too was part of the fellowship of Christ's pain. "He came unto his own, and his own received him not."

We who were so privileged saw in John Hyde's life the deepening horror of sin during that year of 1910, though it was all but a pale reflection of the awful anguish over sin that at length broke our Saviour's heart. Before this year's convention he spent long nights in prayer to God. This burden had lain now for five years on 'his heart- each year pressing heavier and heavier. How it had eaten into his very soul! One saw the long sleepless nights and weary days of watching with prayer written on every feature of his face. Yet his figure was almost transformed as he gave forth God's own words to his people with such fire and such force that many hardly recognized the changed man with the glory of God lighting up every feature. It was Jehovah's messenger speaking Jehovah's message, and we who had shared some of its burden in prayer knew that it was God's own burden spoken to his Church in India,- yes, to his Church throughout the whole world.

We were transported to Mount Sinai and to the sin of Israel in worshiping the golden calf. Up till that time Moses had not interceded for God's people. Why? Because he had not yet entered into the sufferings of God's heart over sin. So he is sent down among the sinners. Sin cost him the presence of God. Was he not being made a partaker of the sufferings of the Lamb slain from the foundation of the world?

Then he fasts a second forty days and forty nights (Deut. 9:19). "For I was afraid of the anger and hot displeasure, wherewith Jehovah was wroth against you to destroy you. But Jehovah hearkened unto me that time also." Moses reports this in 9:25, doubly emphasized by the Holy Spirit. Surely the Great White Throne in its awful purity shone among us from that time right on through the convention-no wonder we were filled with shame and confusion of face as were so many of God's Intercessors of old-Moses, Job, Ezra, Nehemiah, Isaiah, Jeremiah, Ezekiel and Daniel. When God said to Moses, "Let me alone," he revealed the power of intercession. No! Moses "stood in the breach," and the wrath of God was stayed. He gave up the honor and glory of his own name and family for the sake of God's people. "The Church in the wilderness" was saved by one who shadowed forth our Great Divine Intercessor and partook of his Spirit.

The confession of the sins of others laid hold of John Hyde's heart. It was about that time he was taught a very solemn lesson-the sin of fault-finding even in prayer for others. He was once weighed down with the burden of prayer for a certain Indian pastor. So he retired to his "inner chamber," and thinking of the pastor's coldness and the consequent deadness of his church, he began to pray: "O Father, thou knowest how cold" he was going to say; but a finger seemed to be laid on his lips, so that the word was not uttered and a voice said in his ear, "He that toucheth him toucheth the apple of mine eye." Mr. Hyde cried out in sorrow: "Forgive me, Father, in that I have been an accuser of the brethren before thee!" He realized that in God"s sight he must look at "'Whatsoever things are lovely." Yet he wanted also to look at "Whatsoever things are true." He was shown that the "true" of this verse are limited to what are both lovely and true, that the sin of God's children is fleeting, it is not the true nature of God's children. For we should see them as they are in Christ Jesus-"complete,"' what they shall be when he has finished the good work he has begun in them. "And it is right for me to be thus minded concerning you all, because I have you in my heart." Then John asked the Father to show him all that was to be praised ("if there be any virtue and if there be any praise take account of these things") in that pastor's life. He was reminded of much for which he could heartily thank God, and spent his time in praise ! This was the way to victory. The result? He shortly afterwards heard that the pastor had at that very time received a great reviving and was preaching with fire. It is this way of praise which is appointed of God for preparing the Bride and the putting on her beautiful garments. In Revelation 19:6-8 it is praise that leads to the glorious results.

I remember John telling me that in those days if on any day four souls were not brought into the fold, at night there would be such a weight on his heart that it was positively painful, and he could not eat nor sleep. Then in prayer he would ask his Lord to show him what was the obstacle in him to this blessing. He invariably found that it was the want of praise in his life. This command, which has been repeated in God's Word hundreds of times-surely it is all important! He would then confess his sin, and accept the forgiveness by the Blood. Then he would ask for the spirit of praise as for any other gift of God. So he would exchange his ashes for Christ's garland, his mourning for Christ's oil of joy, his spirit of heaviness for Christ's garment of praise (the Song of the Lamb-praising God beforehand for what he was going to do), and as he praised God souls would come to him, and the numbers lacking would be made up.

Here is a picture of his work in those days: Two evangelists went out with Mr. Hyde to a distant village; before leaving they were assured of ten souls being won for Christ. They reached the village, they preached, they sang, the day wore on, not a sign of any soul being interested. They became hungry and thirsty. No man gave unto them. The evangelists became impatient to get home for rest and food. John Hyde would not move. He was waiting for those ten souls. At last, at a common cottage they asked for a drink of water. The man offered them milk, too. They went into his humble home and were refreshed. As they talked to him, he showed a most intelligent knowledge of Jesus Christ. Yes, he had entertained them in his name. Would the family not become his followers? Why not now? He agreed, and called his wife and children. They certainly realized what they were doing, and were determined as a family to come out on the Lord's side. One can picture how tenderly John Hyde ushered them into the family of God. Nine in all were baptized.

But it was now growing dark, and a dangerous road lay ahead of them. The evangelists made haste. The father began to urge it, too. Unwillingly John Hyde left that house. The cart was sent for by one, and the other tried to hasten John's steps. Then they wanted to lift him into the cart. But no, his eyes rested pleadingly on one of his men: "What about that one that is wanting?" The evangelist (he told me this with a hot flush of shame) lost his temper. It is all very well for the Sahib if he broke his neck; he had no wife or family to think of. But it was a very different story for them both. But John stood there waiting for that one soul, the tenth was yet wanting. He knew the Good. Shepherd was himself searching for that one, and would search "until he find it." The two evangelists used almost force to get him to move. There burst one cry from his lips: "What about that one?" By and by the father of the family came up. Why was the Padre Sahib waiting? John told him of the one not yet in the fold. "Why, there he is!" cried the man. "He has just come back. My nephew, whom I have adopted." He brought the boy forward. Mr. Hyde went back to the house and asked him of his faith in Christ. He was clear and intelligent. So the tenth was gathered into the fold. He gave a sigh of heart's ease and weary content as he climbed into the cart. Of course, they were kept and reached home safely-with a heart full of rest such as the Good Shepherd gives his faithful under-shepherds. Yes, and that is the rest of the soul they give him, for through such he shall yet see of the travail of his soul and be satisfied.

And now, farewell to Sialkot ! As far as this sketch is concerned, we are leaving those hallowed scenes. Others there are who will assemble on those holy grounds; others care for the great company that annually assembles in those audiences; others will keep watch in the prayer-room; but as for our dear brother Hyde, 1910 was his last year at Sialkot. We may wonder why it should be so. Only forty-seven, surely his taking away seemed untimely. But God in heaven knows how wonderfully rounded out were the years of dear John Hyde. Seven Sialkot conventions, and seven wonderful years of prayer. Surely God saw in John Hyde a well rounded out experience and character. Surely God and the recording angel know that the fruitage will be bountiful at the ingathering at the great harvest home. "He that soweth bountifully shall also reap bountifully."

But before we leave Sialkot I am led to record my appreciation of our brother, McCheyne Paterson. Paterson, I have fallen in love with you in the Lord. Because you loved Hyde I love you. Often, dear brother, I have prayed for you, and shall yet pray. And will not all who read this sketch join me in praying for the convention at Sialkot, and for this precious man of God, still praying and preaching and praising there?

Calcutta and the Doctor

John Hyde was only one of many men who have hazarded life for God's service. Nehemiah was warned of the plotting of Sanballat and Tobiah. He was advised to go into the house of God and shut the doors. He answered, "Should such a man as I flee? and who is there that, being such as I, would go into the temple to save his life? I will not go in."

Of Jesus it is written, "And it came to pass, when the days

were well-nigh come that he should be received up, he steadfastly set his face to go to Jerusalem" (Luke 9:51).

When Mr. Moody was in England the last time, he is having trouble with his heart. He was examined by an eminent physician, who told him that his excessive labors were costing him his life. He was killing himself. He promised that he would not work so hard.

On the voyage back to America, an awful storm struck his ship, the Spree. She was partly sub merged, and in great distress the people appealed to Mr. Moody. He exhorted and prayed. He told the Lord at that time that if he would get them out of this trouble he would never let up in his labors for lost souls.

That summer was the time of the World's Fair in Chicago. Mr. Moody gathered such a band of preachers, evangelists, workers, and singers as probably never was assembled for such work before or since. Halls, storerooms, theaters, churches, and even circus tents, were utilized for Gospel meetings, Mr. Moody worried with all his old-time vigor. They "put over" a magnificent campaign. A few months later, at Kansas City, while on the platform preaching with all his tremendous energy, the great evangelists heart gave way, his voice ceased, and his labors on earth were over. A few days later, among his friends at Northfield, he passed over to join that heroic band who counted not their lives dear unto themselves that they might win precious souls to Jesus.

A friend of John Hyde's, living in Calcutta, who now knows what it means to be despised and rejected of men, gives the following testimony as to John's prayer life. "I remember W. T. speaking of dear Hyde's having spent thirty days and nights in prayer for the great Sialkot Convention (that was in 1900), when the Convention was opened for the first time to all Christians.

"This news made a deep impression on me, as it stood out in such contrast to my own prayerless life at that time. When he and I were alone, I pressed Turner for more details, particulars of which he was very reluctant to give (as he himself had stayed twenty-one days with the little prayer band). 'I cannot go into details,' he said, 'but it was a time in the Mount with God.'

Soon after the 1910 Sialkot Convention, John Hyde held a meeting in Calcutta. His friend in that city writes about him: "He stayed with us nearly a fortnight, and during the whole time he had fever. Yet he took the meetings regularly, and how God spoke to us, though he was bodily unfit to do any work! At that time I was unwell for several days. The pain in my chest kept me awake for several nights. It was then that I noticed what Mr. Hyde was doing in his room opposite. The room where I was being in darkness, I could see the flash of the electric light when he got out of bed and turned it on. I watched him do it at twelve and at two and at four, and then at five. From that time the light stayed on till sunrise. By this I know that in spite of his night watches and illness, he began his day at five.

"I shall never forget the lessons I learned at that time. I had always claimed exemption from night watches, as I felt too tired at bed time. Had I ever prayed for the privilege of waiting upon God in the hours of night? No ! This led me to claim that privilege then and there. The pain which had kept me awake night after night was turned into joy and praise because of this new ministry which I had suddenly discovered, of keeping watch in the night with the Lord's 'Remembrancers.' At length the pain quite left my chest, sleep returned, but with it the fear came upon me lest I should miss my hours of communion with God. I prayed, 'Lord, wake me when the hour comes' (see Isa. 50:4). At first it was at two A.M., and afterwards at four with striking regularity. At five every morning I heard a Mohammedan priest at the Mosque nearby call out for prayers in a ringing, melodious voice. The thought that I had been up an hour before him filled me with joy.

"But Mr. Hyde grew worse, and the annual meeting of his Mission was calling him. Being anxious, I induced him to come with me to a doctor. The next morning the doctor said: 'The heart is in an awful condition. I have never come across such a bad case as this. It has been shifted out of its natural position on the left side to a place over on the right side. Through stress and strain it is in such a bad condition that it will require months and months of strictly quiet life to bring it back again to anything like its normal state. What have you been doing with yourself?' Dear Hyde said nothing; he only smiled. But we who knew him knew the cause: his life of incessant prayer day and night, praying exceedingly with many tears for his converts, for his fellow-laborers, for his friends, and for the church in India!"

Then the friend writes how God taught him to live a life of prayer through Mr. Hyde's example, and how afterwards he too, like John Hyde, was led into the fellowship of Christ's sufferings down, down, down, farther and farther into the very recesses of Gethsemane, till he too seemed to tread the winepress of the wrath of God against sin all alone.

"The spirit jealously desires us for his own" (Jas. 4:5; Alford). It is his highest desire that there be in us a life of fellowship with himself. For this supreme wish of his heart he rises early, seeking, knocking, unasked, uninvited (Isa. 50:4). How much more if asked and invited! Does not this fact make the Morning Watch unspeakably precious and glorious?

He seeks communion with us because it is his right and our benefit. He seeks this communion at the beginning of the day. He would claim the best, the very best hour of the day. With so great a privilege pressed upon us, does it not mean a solemn obligation on our part to cultivate this life of fellowship? If we are willing, he will quicken and empower.

Remember Gethsemane! Our Lord's appeal to his disciples in his hour of supreme crisis was: "Could ye not watch with me one hour?" The appeal, though thrice repeated, fell upon deaf ears, because the enemy's power had overmastered the disciples through sleep. Do we not hear the Lamb upon his throne, "standing as though it had been slain," make the same appeal again at this hour of world-crisis, at this hour of church-crisis, "Could ye not watch with me one hour?" The renewal of the church will depend on the renewal of our prayer life. The powers of the world to come are at our disposal if we will make time for quiet hours for fellowship and communion, which is our Lord's supreme, yearning desire."

> "Oh, ye who sigh and languish,
> And mourn your lack of power,
> Heed ye this gentle whisper:
> 'Could ye not watch one hour?'
> For fruitfulness and blessing,
> Thece is no royal road;
> The power for holy service
> Is intercourse with God.
>
> "Or e'er a word or action
> Hath stained its snowy scroll
> Bring the new day to Jesus,
> And consecrate the whole.
> Then fear not for the record;
> He surely will indite,
> Whatever may betide thee,
> It shall be, must be, right.
>
> "Soon the last golden sunrise,

Shall deck the eastern sky;
Soon the last "Watch" be ended,
Redemption draweth nigh.
Then may this bright incentive.
Within our spirits burn.
It may be that this morning
The Bridegroom shall return!"

The Calcutta friend concludes: "We have heard of martyrs who were kept in prison, and in the end were put to death. But have we ever heard of one who was so given up to the ministry of prayer that the strain of a daily burden brought him to a premature grave?" "No, friend," answers another brother in India, "not a premature grave; it was the grave of Jesus Christ. John Hyde laid down his life calmly and deliberately for the Church of God in India." Who follows in his train?"

Transformed Lives

Behold how much was wrought in the life and work of one lady missionary. She had worked hard for many years in her district and none of the work there was bearing real fruit. She read the account of Mr. Hyde's prayer-life and resolved to devote the best hours of her time to prayer and waiting on God in the study of his word and will. She would make prayer primary, and not secondary as she had been doing. She would begin to live a prayer-life in God's strength. God had said to her: "Call upon Me, and I will show thee great and mighty things. You have not called upon me and therefore you do not see these things in your work." She writes: "I felt that at any cost I must know him and this prayer-life, and so at last the battle of my heart was ended and I had the victory." One thing she prayed for was that God would keep her hidden. She had to face being misunderstood and being dumb and not opening her mouth in self-defense if she was to be a follower of the Lamb.

In less than a year she wrote a letter, and oh, what a change! New life everywhere-the wilderness being transformed into a garden. Fifteen were baptized at first and one hundred and twenty-five adults during the first half of the following year!

"The most of the year has been a battle to keep to my resolution, I have always lived so active a life, accustomed to steady work all day long, and my new life called for much of the best part of the day to be spent in prayer and Bible study. Can you not imagine what it was and what it is sometimes now? To hear others going around hard at work while I stayed quietly in my room, as it were inactive. Many a time I have longed to be out again in active work among the people in the rush of life, but God would not let me go. His hand held me with as real a grip as any human hand and I knew that I could not go. Only the other day I felt this again and God seemed to say to me, 'What fruit had ye in those things whereof ye are now ashamed?' Yes, I knew I was ashamed of the years of almost prayerless missionary life. "Every department of the work now is in a more prosperous condition than I have ever known it to be. The stress and the strain have gone out of my life. The joy of feeling that my life is evenly balanced, the life of communion on the one hand and the life of work on the other, brings constant rest and peace. I could not go back to the old life, and God grant that it may always be impossible."

Another year passed, and she wrote again: "The spirit of earnest inquiry is increasing in the villages and there is every promise of a greater movement in the future than we have ever yet had. Our Christians now number six hundred in contrast with one sixth of that number two years ago [before she began the prayer-life and gave herself to it]. 'I believe we may expect soon to see great things in India. Praise for his nourly presence and fellowship!"

The pastor of a congregation in Illinois writes, "We have

lost a strong and noble brother, who has not only done the Lord's work in the far-off land but has been an inspiration to us as well and the means of awakening at least one from this congregation to such an interest in the foreign work that today she is in China." 'Who can measure John Hyde's influence and power in India, in England, and in America?

"J.N. Hyde was like his father. When duty called, the call was imperative. He answered it not with skyrocket exploitation and great ado, but with unalterableness of purpose that meant this or death! It seems God meant this and death. In the last class letter he wrote to his seminary classmates he says: 'For three full years now God has given us decisions and baptisms every day when we have been out in our district-over a thousand the past two years. ... never a day if we were right with God without souls." 'They that turn many to righteousness shall shine as the stars forever and ever. Is there anything in this old world worthwhile except seeking and saving that which was lost?" (Herrick Johnson.)

Read of these experiences, as recorded by a missionary in India who wrote "An American Girl's Struggle and Surrender."

"On the wall in my room in India hung a motto card. It is the picture of a stony hill with a little green grass here and there. On the top of the hill is a tree; most of the branches on one side have been entirely swept away by the wind and only a few scraggly limbs remain on the other side. On this card is printed: 'Endure when there is every external reason not to endure.' And this verse: 'He endured... seeing him who is invisible.'

"A dear young friend seeing this card said to me; 'Memsahib, that motto card is to me your photograph. God has been cutting from your life one branch after another and again and again has removed earthly supports.'"

She and her husband were very happy in their going out to India and during the first year. But there were shadows over the pathway. The next year God gave and soon took to himself a dear little life. From the first her husband would ask God to fill him with the Spirit at any cost to himself. At first she could not pray this prayer. After the babe was taken she would join her husband in this prayer, and as they would rise from their knees she would say, "But, oh, I am afraid of the cost." Then next her husband was taken with fever. How she pleaded and prayed and even commanded God. But he passed away. For months she was dazed and seemed oblivious to everything but her unutterable loss. It was a year of great darkness. But in the spring God sent a messenger (Mr. Reginald Studd, a man from whom John Hyde learned much) through whom God revealed what He desired to be to each of his children, their all in all, the chiefest among ten thousand, their heartfriend.

Christ possessed this man's life. Christ was to him all that the dearest earthly friend could be, and infinitely more. Not only was his life centered in Christ, Christ was his very life. He communed with him as with a friend, spending hours with him, his inmost being was made radiant with Christ's abiding presence, and wherever he went "Christ was revealed." Soon after meeting this messenger of Christ she relates further, "In a written consecration I gave myself, my child [born shortly after her husband's death], all I had and all I ever would have, to the Lord, to be his forever. It was an unconditional surrender and the Holy Spirit entered in his fulness and began to lead me into the love and joy and peace a knowledge surpassing the love and joy and peace for which I had long been yearning. There came to my heart a deep quietness. The Word of God opened up to me in marvelous richness, becoming food for the soul.

"In the years that have followed I have again and again been brought to places where two ways opened; one the way of the ordinary Christian life, the other the way on which one seemed to see the bloodstained marks of the Saviour's footsteps; and he called me to follow him-the slain Lamb. It has meant the way of the cross; but it has also meant fellowship with Christ."

She writes further about "the Messenger" whom God had sent to the Punjab who showed such a Christ-possessed life. She writes: "I do not remember that he ever talked about prayer; he prayed. Speaking sometimes four and five times a day, he would then spend half the night in prayer, sometimes alone, sometimes with others. He prayed."

She gives us modestly some glimpses of how wonderfully God worked through her. Sometimes it was among the Mohammedans, sometimes among the native Hindus, and sometimes among the foreign missionaries. She was associated with the Punjab Prayer Union and the Sialkot Convention.

She says, "There have been many failures, times when the self-life hindered God. I am more and more amazed that God has been able, notwithstanding my failures, to work in such wondrous ways, and has given me the joy of seeing him work.

"God offers," she continues, "to bring all who are willing into the secret place, within the vail, the place of sweetest refuge, where 'all is peace and quiet stillness.'"

> "Within the vait. Be this, beloved, thy portion.
> Within the secret of thy Lord to dwelt.
> Beholding him, until thy face his Glory,
> Thy life his love, thy lips his praise shall tell.
>
> "Within the vail - for only as thou gazest

Upon the matchless beauty of his face
Canst thou become a living revelation
Of his great heart of love, his untold grace.

"Within the vail - his fragrance poured upon thee;
Without the vait, fhat fragrance shed abroad:
Within the vail his hand shall tune the music,
Which sounds on earth the praises of the Lord."

When I was a boy there was a pond near my father's house. I would stand on the shore of that pond and throw a stone out into the water and then watch the waves in ever widening circles move out from that center, till every part of the surface of the pond would be in motion. The waves would come to the shore at my very feet and every little channel and inlet would be moved by the ripples.

Sialkot started circles and waves of blessing that are even now beating in the secret recesses and inlets of many human hearts. And I am led to believe that every atom and molecule of water in that pond felt the impact of that stone. Only God and the recording angel can determine how much the whole body of Christ has been moved upon and benefited by the tremendous prayer force generated by the Holy Spirit in that prayer room at Sialkot.

Native pastors, teachers and evangelists have gone home from these conventions with new zeal for Jesus Christ and have influenced thousands of lives in their many fields of labor.

Foreign missionaries have had their lives deepened by visions of God. Letters and printed pages, like the aprons and handkerchiefs from Paul's body, have been sent probably to every country on earth to bring healing to the faint-hearted, and direction and encouragement to those desiring to enter the prayer-life. I am assured that tens of thousands have been born into the kingdom because of the soul travail at Sialkot. Myriads will one day rise up to thank God that two or three men in North India in the name of Jehovah said, "Let us have a convention at Sialkot!"

England Again

The meeting and visit in Calcutta occurred in the fall or winter following the 1910 Sialkot Convention. The next spring, March, 1911, John Hyde started home as the physicians would say a "dying man." He had arrived in India in the autumn of 1892, less than twenty years before. But surely they were nineteen beautiful years!

When he arrived in England, he went to visit some friends in Wales, intending later to attend the Keswick Convention. While in Wales he heard that Dr. J. Wilbur Chapman and Mr. Charles M. Alexander, on their world-wide evangelistic tour, were holding a meeting at Shrewsbury. With two of his friends he went to the opening of this campaign. During the first stay of three days a friend writes: "We greatly enjoyed the services, but we realized that there was some great hindrance, and this was felt especially at the meeting for ministers."

"After that service we saw that the burden had come upon Mr. Hyde, and as we were leaving the next day he asked whether we could engage his room at the hotel for the following week. He was preaching on the Sunday at another place; but he intended returning early Monday morning to take up the burden of prayer for Shrewsbury. To those who knew him, it was apparent that the load was weighing very heavily upon him. The faraway gaze, the remarkably sweet pathetic pained expression, the loss of appetite, the sleepless nights, all went to prove this."

Here is Dr. Chapman's letter:

"God has been graciously near to us in all these long journeys around the world, and we have learned some things which have increased our faith. First, more than ever before we believe in the Bible as the authentic Word of God.

"Second: We believe in prayer as never before. I have learned some great lessons concerning prayer. I know that all great revivals are born of prayer. At one of our missions in England the audience was extremely small-results seemed impossible-but I received a note saying that an American missionary was coming to the town and was going to pray God's blessing down upon our work. He was known as 'The Praying Hyde.' Almost instantly the tide turned. The hall was packed, and my first invitation meant fifty men for Jesus Christ. As we were leaving I said: 'Mr. Hyde, I want you to pray for me.' He came to my room, turned the key in the door, dropped on his knees, waited five minutes without a single syllable coming from his lips. I could hear my own heart thumping and his beating. I felt the hot tears running down my face. I knew I was with God. Then with upturned face, down which the tears were streaming, he said: 'Oh God!' Then for five minutes at least, he was still again, and then when he knew he was talking with God his arm went around my shoulder and there came up from the depth of his heart such petitions for men as I had never heard before. I rose from my knees to know what real prayer was. We believe that prayer is mighty and we believe it as we never did before."

Mr. Charles M. Alexander related to Mr. Hyde's sister Mary further particulars about this meeting. Not only did Dr. Chapman meet John Hyde, but Mr. Alexander was present also. And the three of them spent almost the whole day in conference about the· meeting. Then later the other workers were called in, and a long time was spent in prayer. After that the Spirit was present in the meetings in such power that all barriers were broken down and sinners were crying for mercy and being saved all over the house.

Mr. Hyde had a helper in intercession furnished him in the person of Mr. Davis of the Pocket Testament League, and the two, being kindred spirits, became very friendly.

Mr. Hyde remained there for a whole week and then went back to his friends in Wales. The following day he was seriously ill and could scarcely speak, but he smiled and whispered: "The burden of Shrewsbury was very heavy, but my Saviour's burden took him down to the grave."

The manner in which John Hyde prayed as referred to in the above quotation-that is of pausing between petitions or expressions is also referred to by another writer: "Right on his face on the ground is 'Praying Hyde' this was his favorite attitude for prayer. Listen! he is praying, he utters a petition, and then waits, in a little time he repeats it, and then waits, and this many times until we feel that that petition has penetrated every fibre of our nature and we feel assured that God has heard and without doubt He will answer. How well I remember him praying that we might open our mouth wide that He might fill it (Psa. 81:10). I think he repeated the word 'wide' scores of times with long pauses between. 'Wide, Lord, wide, open wide, wide.' How effectual it was to hear him address God, 'O Father, Father.'"

A lady who was for years a missionary in India writes to The Remembrancer, "I remember, during one of the Jubbulpore Conventions at the noontime prayer meeting I was kneeling near to him, and can never forget how I was thrilled with a feeling I cannot describe as he pleaded in prayer: 'Jesus Jesus-Jesus!' It seemed as if a baptism of love and power came over me, and my soul was humbled in the dust before the Lord. I had the privilege of meeting Mr. Hyde again in England, when on his way to America. How his influence still lives."

𝕳ome at 𝕷ast

"And the toils of the road will seem nothing, When we come
to the end of the way."

John Hyde arrived in New York, August 8, 1911. He went at once to Clifton Springs, N.Y. His purpose was to obtain relief from a severe headache from which he had suffered much before leaving India. A tumor soon developed which when operated on became malignant and was pronounced by the physician to be sarcoma, for which as yet medical science has found no remedy. He rallied from this operation, and on December 19 went to his sister the wife of Prof. E.H. Mensel at Northampton, Mass.

But soon after New Year's he began to have pains in his back and side. He thought it was rheumatism, but the physician knew it was the dreaded sarcoma again.

He passed away February 17, 1912. His body was taken by his brother Will Hyde and his sister Mary back to the old home at Carthage, Illinois, and the funeral was held in the church where his father was for seventeen years the pastor. At the time of John's funeral the Rev. J.F. Young, his classmate, was pastor of the home church and preached at the funeral. It was my privilege to assist in the service and to stand on the platform and look down into the casket at that dear, dear face. He was greatly emaciated, but it was the same sweet, peaceful, gentle yet strong, resolute face that I had known in 1901, the last time I saw him alive.

That February the 20th was cloudy and chill and gloomy as out in beautiful Moss Ridge we tenderly laid him beside his father and his mother and his brother Edmund. But I know that by and by the clouds and the shadows will flee away, the chill and

49

gloom of the grave be dispelled, and that man of prayer and praise come forth in the likeness of the Risen Son of God!

Ḥoliness Unto the Lord

As I have carefully and prayerfully gone over the facts and incidents and experiences in the life of my dear friend, I am impressed that the one great characteristic of John Hyde was holiness. I do not mention prayerfulness now, for prayer was his lifework. I do not especially call attention to soul-winning, for his power as a soul-winner was due to his Christlikeness. God says, "Without holiness no man shall see the Lord," and we may scripturally say without holiness no man shall be a great soul winner. Mr. Hyde himself said in substance, "Self must not only be dead but buried out of sight, for the stench of the unburied self-life will frighten souls away from Jesus."

It does not seem that John Hyde preached much about his own personal experience of sanctification, but he lived the sanctified life. His life preached. Just as he did not say very much about prayer. He prayed. His life was a witness to the power of Jesus' Blood to cleanse from all sin.

Read these testimonies that have come to me from a number of sources. Further search would no doubt reveal scores of other witnesses to the saintliness of this beloved servant of Jesus Christ, and man of prayer.

From a publication in this country: "The Bishop of Oxford says of personal holiness: 'There is no power in the world so irrepressible as the power of personal holiness. A man's gifts may lack opportunity, his efforts be misunderstood and resisted, but the spiritual power of a consecrated will needs no opportunity and can enter where doors are shut. In this strange and tangled business of human life there is no energy that so steadily does its work as the mysterious, unconscious, silent, unobtrusive, impenetrable influence which comes from a man who has done with all self-seeking. And herein lay John Hyde's mystical power and great influence. Multitudes have been brought to their knees by prayer he uttered when filled with the Spirit."

This from a letter written to Mr. Hyde's sister, "If ever there was a godly man, forgetful of himself and devoted to the Master's service, your brother was that one."

A native of India, "The marvelous spirituality of Mr. Hyde had for some time been so great that all who saw it were filled with wonder." These words are by a missionary in India: "His loss will be sadly felt in this country, especially by the Indian Christians. He was one of the holiest men I have ever known, and his life exerted a great influence."

One of his classmates writes, "No saint of the church was ever beyond him in holiness. He verily gave his life for Christ and India."

Another missionary in India wrote, "He revealed a Christ-possessed prayer-life. He talked with Christ as with a friend, spending hours with him. His inmost being was made radiant by Christ's abiding presence, and wherever he went Christ was revealed."

The Indian Witness says this: "He has had a very remarkable influence in the Indian Church. A year ago last autumn his addresses at the Sialkot Convention produced a profound impression. He was an acceptable speaker in Urdu, Punjabi and in English and it was always the man of holiness and power back of an address which made it indeed a message." Another India missionary writes, "He had become a real prophet of God. He was truly one who spoke for God. Thoughtful men would sit for hours during a day listening to his wonderful exposition of truth, as he slowly, quietly, and clearly set forth what the

Spirit of God had taught him from His Word." Not only was his the word of a prophet, but his life had been sanctified by the truth. One day a missionary was talking to a young Hindu who had become acquainted with Mr. Hyde, when the Hindu said: "Do you know, Sir, that Mr. Hyde seems to me like God." He was not far from the truth, for in a sense unknown to his Hindu understanding this man had become an incarnation. I quote from a postal card written by John to his sister while he was at Clifton Springs, N.Y., dated October 27th, 1911, "Am still in bed or wheel chair getting a fine rest and doing a lot of the ministry of intercession, and having not a few opportunities of personal work. How the radiance of holiness shone out in Jesus' every word and deed!" Yes, dear heart, and we can truthfully and reverently say, "How the radiance of holiness shone out in John Hyde's every word and deed." A cry of anguish and a song of praise.

The Twenty Second Psalm

I am grateful to God that in a letter to John's sister Mary has been preserved the following exposition and comment on this wonderful Messianic psalm. I am adding the full text of the Psalm where he has given only the reference to verses. I have changed a little the arrangement, but the notes are from the hand of dear John himself.

Psalm 22:
Verses 1-2: "My God, my God, why hast thou forsaken me? Why art thou so far from helping me, and from the words of my groaning? O my God, I cry in the daytime, but thou hearest not; and in the night season, and am not silent."

David is here praying in some deep and terrible trial, but the prayer is of agony--experience so real and awful as to reveal to David Christ's prayer. Jesus in the awful agony and desolation on the cross used the words of the first verse. God seemed to answer in these words: "For a small moment have I hid my face from thee, but with everlasting kindness will I gather thee." Here in these verses are the sufferings of the lost and the victory of the saved. The Spirit of Christ in David witnessed clearly the sufferings of Christ and the glory that should follow.

This prayer in verse 1 is the cry, the voice of the sufferings of hell, but by a person with the praise of heaven in his heart.

Verses 3-5: "But thou art holy, 0 thou that inhabitest the praises. of Israel. Our fathers trusted in thee : They trusted, and thou didst deliver them. They cried unto thee, and were delivered. They trusted in thee, and were not put to shame." This man was a Jew, and said "Our fathers."

Verses 6-8: "But I am a worm, and no man, A reproach of men, and despised of the people. All they that see me laugh me to scorn. They shoot out the lip, they shake the head, saying, Commit thyself unto Jehovah, let him deliver him. Let him rescue him, seeing he delighteth in him.

Here he is taking the sinner's place and enduring what came to him on the Cross of Calvary. The sinner's place and reproach, yet himself without sin.

Verses 9-11: "But thou art he that took me out of the womb; Thou didst make me to trust when I was upon my mother's breasts. - I was cast upon thee from the womb. Thou art my God since my mother bare me. Be not far from me ; for trouble is near. For there is none to help." Here is "trust." He says, "My God." Here is the right in himself to be helped-no cry for mercy-just help which is his by right-the sinless Christ. Yet in his greatest sufferings, "There is none to help."

Verses 12-1: "Many bulls have compassed me ; strong bulls of Bashan have beset me round. They gape upon me with their mouth, as a ravening and a roaring lion. I am poured out like water, and all my bones are out of joint. My heart is like wax, it is melted within me. My strength is dried up like a potsherd, and my tongue cleaveth to my jaws, and thou hast brought me into the dust of death." Surrounded by enemies and by fiercest adversaries brought into "the dust of death"- still unhelped, God has become as it were his adversary : "Yet it pleased the Lord to bruise him, he hath put him to grief." (Isa. 53:10.)

Verses 16-18: "For dogs have compassed me: A company of evil-doers inclosed me. They pierced my hands and my feet. I may count all my bones. They look and stare upon me. They part my garments among them, and upon my vesture do they cast lots." What a picture of the cross! "I may tell all my bones." How this tells of three years-yes, a lifetime, but especially of three years of sorrow over our, my, sin, of prayer and fasting and watching, sometimes whole nights; and then days and nights of work-teaching, healing, preaching, and of grief as he saw sin and its hold and havoc as he saw the weaknesses and sins of God's own disciples!

"They look and stare upon me." How this tells of a human soul, sensitive and shrinking from the gaze of men. This tells of the indignities heaped upon him which only the most refined and holy can feel in all their power!"

It tells too of astonishment: "Many were astonished at thee- his visage was so marred more than any man, and his form more than the sons of men" (Isa. 52:14). They were surprised, he was so emaciated and worn. How this all tells of his sorrow over sin. "Whose sorrow is like unto my sorrow?" "Oh! thou Man of Sorrow!"

Verses 19-21: "But be not thou far off, O Jehovah: O thou my succor, haste thee to help me. Deliver my soul from the sword, my darling from the power of the dog. Save me from the lion's mouth. Yea, from the horns of the wild oxen thou hast answered me."

Here again is a cry for help unheard, yet in faith heard. Thou hast "answered me." "It is finished," "Into thy hands I commend my spirit."

Here end these wonderful notes except that he points out that in the remaining verses, 23-31, are revealed "The glory that shall follow."

These words have been wonderfully blessed of God in giving me a new vision of the Lamb slain from the foundation of the world, who is worthy "to receive power, and riches, and wisdom and might, and honor, and glory, and blessing" (Rev. 5:12).

And then it has seemed to me that in no other writings have I seen such a likeness of the dear brother himself. I have said, "John Hyde has here unconsciously given us a portrait of John Hyde."

Victory

"The last enemy that shall be destroyed is Death', (1 Cor. 15:26). John Hyde had faced the enemy too many times in going over into "No Man's Land" to rescue the dying to be frightened when the last awful encounter took place that February day in 1912. When John Hyde was in England Mr. Charles M. Alexander took him to his own doctor and then a consultation with two other physicians was held. The doctor then endeavored to impress Mr. Hyde with the seriousness of his condition. Mr. Alexander listened to the conversation. Surely Mr. Hyde understood that really he was then in a dying condition. Both Mr. Alexander and the doctor were amazed at Mr. Hyde's perfect composure. He had long ago ceased to fear death, and for him to depart and be with Christ was far better.

I am persuaded that no words of mine could fittingly bring this sketch to a close. But the description I am using is from the pen of Dr. W. B. Anderson in The Men's Record and Missionary Review (United Presbyterian.) Dr. Anderson was for some years himself a missionary in India and was chairman of the committee that established the Sialkot Convention. He was well acquainted with dear John Hyde. He writes: "He went a long way into the suffering of India and he had desperate encounters with her foe for her deliverance. To him who dares much in this warfare God seems to give a wonderful vision of victory.

"One day about four years ago he was talking of an experience he had on a day of prayer that was being observed for India. He was speaking intimately to intimate friends. He said: 'On the day of prayer God gave me a new experience. I seemed to be away above our conflict here in the Punjab and I saw God's great battle in all India, and then away out beyond in China, Japan, and Africa. I saw how we had been thinking in narrow circles of our own countries and in our own denominations, and how God was now rapidly joining force to force and line to line and all was beginning to be one great struggle. That, to me, means the great triumph of Christ. We do not dare any longer to fight without the consciousness of this great world battle in which we are engaged.

'We must exercise the greatest care to be utterly obedient to Him who sees all the battlefield all the time. It is only He who can put each man in the place where his life can count for the most." Above all the strife of battle he could see the great Commander whom he was following so implicitly.

"When the word came to us in India that after severe suffering in America, he had been called Home, it seemed to me that I could hear something of an echo of the shout of victory as he entered into the King's presence. Then the next word that came was that he had died with the words upon his lips: 'Bol, Yisu' Masili, Ki Jail' ('Shout, the victory of Jesus Christ!)

"When I heard that I thought of that awful time in the life of our Lord when his foes were closing in about him. He knew that the time of his sacrifice was near. Just before him lay the desertion of his disciples, and Gethsemane and Calvary. Yet in that hour he said, 'Be of good cheer, I have overcome the world.' Then I remembered the days and nights when Mr. Hyde had struggled in India for those bound by sin, and that after hours of agony he had often risen with those about him to shout: 'Bol, Yisu' Masili ki jai,' until this has become the great war cry of the Punjab Church. As he sent that shout back to us from the presence of the great Victor, let us see to it that it rings throughout the whole world:

'Shout, the victory of Jesus Christ.'" In Jehovah's Name, Amen!

THE
SCARLET LETTER.

BY
NATHANIEL HAWTHORNE

BOSTON:
JAMES R. OSGOOD AND COMPANY,
Late Ticknor & Fields, and Fields, Osgood, & Co.
1878.

Chapter 1

A throng of bearded men, in sad-colored garments, and gray, steeple-crowned hats, intermixed with women, some wearing hoods and others bareheaded, was assembled in front of a wooden edifice, the door of which was heavily timbered with oak, and studded with iron spikes.

The founders of a new colony, whatever Utopia of human virtue and happiness they might originally project, have invariably recognized it among their earliest practical necessities to allot a portion of the virgin soil as a cemetery, and another portion as the site of a prison. In accordance with this rule, it may safely be assumed that the forefathers of Boston had built the first prison-house somewhere in the vicinity of Cornhill, almost as seasonably as they marked out the first burial-ground, on Isaac Johnson's lot, and round about his grave, which subsequently became the nucleus of all the congregated sepulchres in the old churchyard of King's Chapel. Certain it is, that, some fifteen or twenty years after the settlement of the town, the wooden jail was already marked with weather-stains and other indications of age, which gave a yet darker aspect to its beetle-browed and gloomy front. The rust on the ponderous iron-work of its oaken door looked more antique than anything else in the New World. Like all that pertains to crime, it seemed never to have known a youthful era. Before this ugly edifice, and between it and the wheel-track of the street, was a grass-plot, much overgrown with burdock, pigweed, apple-peru, and such unsightly vegetation, which evidently found something congenial in the soil that had so early borne the black flower of civilized society, a prison. But on one side of the portal, and rooted almost at the threshold, was a wild rose-bush, covered, in this month of June, with its delicate gems, which might be imagined to offer their fragrance and fragile beauty to the prisoner as he went in, and to the condemned criminal as he came forth to his doom, in token that the deep heart of Nature could pity and be kind to him.

This rose-bush, by a strange chance, has been kept alive in history; but whether it had merely survived out of the stern old wilderness, so long after the fall of the gigantic pines and oaks that originally overshadowed it,—or whether, as there is fair authority for believing, it had sprung up under the footsteps of the sainted Ann Hutchinson, as she entered the prison-door,—we shall not take upon us to determine. Finding it so directly on the threshold of our narrative, which is now about to issue from that inauspicious portal, we could hardly do otherwise than pluck one of its flowers, and present it to the reader. It may serve, let us hope, to symbolize some sweet moral blossom, that may be found along the track, or relieve the darkening close of a tale of human frailty and sorrow.

Chapter 2

$\mathfrak{T}$he grass-plot before the jail, in Prison Lane, on a certain summer morning, not less than two centuries ago, was occupied by a pretty large number of the inhabitants of Boston; all with their eyes intently fastened on the iron-clamped oaken door. Amongst any other population, or at a later period in the history of New England, the grim rigidity that petrified the bearded physiognomies of these good people would have augured some awful business in hand. It could have betokened nothing short of the anticipated execution of some noted culprit, on whom the sentence of a legal tribunal had but confirmed the verdict of public sentiment. But, in that early severity of the Puritan character, an inference of this kind could not so indubitably be drawn. It might be that a sluggish bond-servant, or an undutiful child, whom his parents had given over to the civil authority, was to be corrected at the whipping-post. It might be, that an Antinomian, a Quaker, or other heterodox religionist was to be scourged out of the town, or an idle and vagrant Indian, whom the white man's fire-water had made riotous about the streets, was to be driven with stripes into the shadow of the forest. It might be, too, that a witch, like old Mistress Hibbins, the bitter-tempered widow of the magistrate, was to die upon the gallows. In either case, there was very much the same solemnity of demeanor on the part of the spectators; as befitted a people amongst whom religion and law were almost identical, and in whose character both were so thoroughly interfused, that the mildest and the severest acts of public discipline were alike made venerable and awful. Meagre, indeed, and cold was the sympathy that a transgressor might look for, from such bystanders, at the scaffold. On the other hand, a penalty, which, in our days, would infer a degree of mocking infamy and ridicule, might then be invested with almost as stern a dignity as the punishment of death itself.

It was a circumstance to be noted, on the summer morning when our story begins its course, that the women, of whom there were several in the crowd, appeared to take a peculiar interest in whatever penal infliction might be expected to ensue. The age had not so much refinement, that any sense of impropriety restrained the wearers of petticoat and farthingale from stepping forth into the public ways, and wedging their not unsubstantial persons, if occasion were, into the throng nearest to the scaffold at an execution. Morally, as well as materially, there was a coarser fibre in those wives and maidens of old English birth and breeding, than in their fair descendants, separated from them by a series of six or seven generations; for, throughout that chain of ancestry, every successive mother has transmitted to her child a fainter bloom, a more delicate and briefer beauty, and a slighter physical frame, if not a character of less force and solidity, than her own. The women who were now standing about the prison-door stood within less than half a century of the period when the man-like Elizabeth had been the not altogether unsuitable representative of the sex. They were her countrywomen; and the beef and ale of their native land, with a moral diet not a whit more refined, entered largely into their composition. The bright morning sun, therefore, shone on broad shoulders and well-developed busts, and on round and ruddy cheeks, that had ripened in the far-off island, and had hardly yet grown paler or thinner in the atmosphere of New England. There was, moreover, a boldness and rotundity of speech among these matrons, as most of them seemed to be, that would startle us at the present day, whether in respect to its purport or its volume of tone.

"Goodwives," said a hard-featured dame of fifty, "I'll tell ye a piece of my mind. It would be greatly for the public behoof, if we women, being of mature age and church-members in good repute, should have the handling of such malefactresses as this Hester Prynne. What think ye, gossips? If the hussy stood up for judgment before us five, that are now here in a knot together, would she come off with such a sentence as the worshipful magistrates have awarded? Marry, I trow not!"

"People say," said another, "that the Reverend Master Dimmesdale, her godly pastor, takes it very grievously to heart that such a scandal should have come upon his congregation."

"The magistrates are God-fearing gentlemen, but merciful overmuch,—that is a truth," added a third autumnal matron. "At the very least, they should have put the brand of a hot iron on Hester Prynne's forehead. Madam Hester would have winced at that, I warrant me. But she,—the naughty baggage,—little will she care what they put upon the bodice of her gown! Why, look you, she may cover it with a brooch, or such like heathenish adornment, and so walk the streets as brave as ever!"

"Ah, but," interposed, more softly, a young wife, holding a child by the hand, "let her cover the mark as she will, the pang of it will be always in her heart."

"What do we talk of marks and brands, whether on the bodice of her gown, or the flesh of her forehead?" cried another female, the ugliest as well as the most pitiless of these self-constituted judges. "This woman has brought shame upon us all, and ought to die. Is there not law for it? Truly, there is, both in the Scripture and the statute-book. Then let the magistrates, who have made it of no effect, thank themselves if their own wives and daughters go astray!"

"Mercy on us, goodwife," exclaimed a man in the crowd, "is there no virtue in woman, save what springs from a wholesome fear of the gallows? That is the hardest word yet! Hush, now, gossips! for the lock is turning in the prison-door, and here comes Mistress Prynne herself."

The door of the jail being flung open from within, there appeared, in the first place, like a black shadow emerging into sunshine, the grim and grisly presence of the town-beadle, with a sword by his side, and his staff of office in his hand. This personage prefigured and represented in his aspect the whole dismal severity of the Puritanic code of law, which it was his business to administer in its final and closest application to the offender. Stretching forth the official staff in his left hand, he laid his right upon the shoulder of a young woman, whom he thus drew forward; until, on the threshold of the prison-door, she repelled him, by an action marked with natural dignity and force of character, and stepped into the open air, as if by her own free will. She bore in her arms a child, a baby of some three months old, who winked and turned aside its little face from the too vivid light of day; because its existence, heretofore, had brought it acquainted only with the gray twilight of a dungeon, or other darksome apartment of the prison.

When the young woman—the mother of this child—stood fully revealed before the crowd, it seemed to be her first impulse to clasp the infant closely to her bosom; not so much by an impulse of motherly affection, as that she might thereby conceal a certain token, which was wrought or fastened into her dress. In a moment, however, wisely judging that one token of her shame would but poorly serve to hide another, she took the baby on her arm, and, with a burning blush, and yet a haughty smile, and a glance that would not be abashed, looked around at her towns-people and neighbors. On the breast of her gown, in fine red cloth, surrounded with an elaborate embroidery and fantastic flourishes of gold-thread, appeared the letter A. It was so artistically done, and with so much fertility and gorgeous luxuriance of fancy, that it had all the effect of a last and fitting decoration to the apparel which she wore; and which was of a splendor in accordance with the taste of the age, but greatly beyond what was allowed by the sumptuary regulations of the colony.

The young woman was tall, with a figure of perfect elegance on a large scale. She had dark and abundant hair, so glossy that it threw off the sunshine with a gleam, and a face which, besides being beautiful from regularity of feature and richness of complexion, had the impressiveness belonging to a marked brow and deep black eyes. She was lady-like, too, after the manner of the feminine gentility of those days; characterized by a certain state and dignity, rather than by the delicate, evanescent, and indescribable grace, which is now recognized as its indication. And never had Hester Prynne appeared more lady-like, in the antique interpretation of the term, than as she issued from the prison. Those who had before known her, and had expected to behold her dimmed and obscured by a disastrous cloud, were astonished, and even startled, to perceive how her beauty shone out, and made a halo of the misfortune and ignominy in which she was enveloped. It may be true, that, to a sensitive observer, there was something exquisitely painful in it. Her attire, which, indeed, she had wrought for the occasion, in prison, and had modelled much after her own fancy, seemed to express the attitude of her spirit, the desperate recklessness of her mood, by its wild and picturesque peculiarity. But the point which drew all eyes, and, as it were, transfigured the wearer,—so that both men and women, who had been familiarly acquainted with

Hester Prynne, were now impressed as if they beheld her for the first time, — was that Scarlet Letter, so fantastically embroidered and illuminated upon her bosom. It had the effect of a spell, taking her out of the ordinary relations with humanity, and enclosing her in a sphere by herself.

"She hath good skill at her needle, that's certain," remarked one of her female spectators; "but did ever a woman, before this brazen hussy, contrive such a way of showing it! Why, gossips, what is it but to laugh in the faces of our godly magistrates, and make a pride out of what they, worthy gentlemen, meant for a punishment?"

"It were well," muttered the most iron-visaged of the old dames, "if we stripped Madam Hester's rich gown off her dainty shoulders; and as for the red letter, which she hath stitched so curiously, I'll bestow a rag of mine own rheumatic flannel, to make a fitter one!"

"O, peace, neighbors, peace!" whispered their youngest companion; "do not let her hear you! Not a stitch in that embroidered letter but she has felt it in her heart."

The grim beadle now made a gesture with his staff.

"Make way, good people, make way, in the King's name!" cried he. "Open a passage; and, I promise ye, Mistress Prynne shall be set where man, woman, and child may have a fair sight of her brave apparel, from this time till an hour past meridian. A blessing on the righteous Colony of the Massachusetts, where iniquity is dragged out into the sunshine! Come along, Madam Hester, and show your scarlet letter in the market-place!"

A lane was forthwith opened through the crowd of spectators. Preceded by the beadle, and attended by an irregular procession of stern-browed men and unkindly visaged women, Hester Prynne set forth towards the place appointed for her punishment. A crowd of eager and curious school-boys, understanding little of the matter in hand, except that it gave them a half-holiday, ran before her progress, turning their heads continually to stare into her face, and at the winking baby in her arms, and at the ignominious letter on her breast. It was no great distance, in those days, from the prison-door to the market-place. Measured by the prisoner's experience, however, it might be reckoned a journey of some length; for, haughty as her demeanor was, she perchance underwent an agony from every footstep of those that thronged to see her, as if her heart had been flung into the street for them all to spurn and trample upon. In our nature, however, there is a provision, alike marvellous and merciful, that the sufferer should never know the intensity of what he endures by its present torture, but chiefly by the pang that rankles after it. With almost a serene deportment, therefore, Hester Prynne passed through this portion of her ordeal, and came to a sort of scaffold, at the western extremity of the market-place. It stood nearly beneath the eaves of Boston's earliest church, and appeared to be a fixture there.

In fact, this scaffold constituted a portion of a penal machine, which now, for two or three generations past, has been merely historical and traditionary among us, but was held, in the old time, to be as effectual an agent, in the promotion of good citizenship, as ever was the guillotine among the terrorists of France. It was, in short, the platform of the pillory; and above it rose the framework of that instrument of discipline, so fashioned as to confine the human head in its tight grasp, and thus hold it up to the public gaze. The very ideal of ignominy was embodied and made manifest in this contrivance of wood and iron. There can be no outrage, methinks, against our common nature,—whatever be the delinquencies of the individual,—no outrage more flagrant than to forbid the culprit to hide his face for shame;

as it was the essence of this punishment to do. In Hester Prynne's instance, however, as not unfrequently in other cases, her sentence bore, that she should stand a certain time upon the platform, but without undergoing that gripe about the neck and confinement of the head, the proneness to which was the most devilish characteristic of this ugly engine. Knowing well her part, she ascended a flight of wooden steps, and was thus displayed to the surrounding multitude, at about the height of a man's shoulders above the street.

Had there been a Papist among the crowd of Puritans, he might have seen in this beautiful woman, so picturesque in her attire and mien, and with the infant at her bosom, an object to remind him of the image of Divine Maternity, which so many illustrious painters have vied with one another to represent; something which should remind him, indeed, but only by contrast, of that sacred image of sinless motherhood, whose infant was to redeem the world. Here, there was the taint of deepest sin in the most sacred quality of human life, working such effect, that the world was only the darker for this woman's beauty, and the more lost for the infant that she had borne.

The scene was not without a mixture of awe, such as must always invest the spectacle of guilt and shame in a fellow-creature, before society shall have grown corrupt enough to smile, instead of shuddering, at it. The witnesses of Hester Prynne's disgrace had not yet passed beyond their simplicity. They were stern enough to look upon her death, had that been the sentence, without a murmur at its severity, but had none of the heartlessness of another social state, which would find only a theme for jest in an exhibition like the present. Even had there been a disposition to turn the matter into ridicule, it must have been repressed and overpowered by the solemn presence of men no less dignified than the Governor, and several of his counsellors, a judge, a general, and the ministers of the town; all of whom sat or stood in a balcony of the meeting-house, looking down upon the platform. When such personages could constitute a part of the spectacle, without risking the majesty or reverence of rank and office, it was safely to be inferred that the infliction of a legal sentence would have an earnest and effectual meaning. Accordingly, the crowd was sombre and grave. The unhappy culprit sustained herself as best a woman might, under the heavy weight of a thousand unrelenting eyes, all fastened upon her, and concentrated at her bosom. It was almost intolerable to be borne. Of an impulsive and passionate nature, she had fortified herself to encounter the stings and venomous stabs of public contumely, wreaking itself in every variety of insult; but there was a quality so much more terrible in the solemn mood of the popular mind, that she longed rather to behold all those rigid countenances contorted with scornful merriment, and herself the object. Had a roar of laughter burst from the multitude,—each man, each woman, each little shrill-voiced child, contributing their individual parts,—Hester Prynne might have repaid them all with a bitter and disdainful smile. But, under the leaden infliction which it was her doom to endure, she felt, at moments, as if she must needs shriek out with the full power of her lungs, and cast herself from the scaffold down upon the ground, or else go mad at once.

Yet there were intervals when the whole scene, in which she was the most conspicuous object, seemed to vanish from her eyes, or, at least, glimmered indistinctly before them, like a mass of imperfectly shaped and spectral images. Her mind, and especially her memory, was preternaturally active, and kept bringing up other scenes than this roughly hewn street of a little town, on the edge of the Western wilderness; other faces than were lowering upon her from beneath the brims of those steeple-crowned hats. Reminiscences the most trifling and immaterial, passages of infancy and school-days, sports, childish quarrels, and the little domestic traits of her maiden years, came swarming back upon her, intermingled with recollections of whatever was gravest in her subsequent life; one picture precisely as vivid as another; as if all were of similar importance, or all alike a play. Possibly, it was an instinctive device of her spirit, to relieve itself, by the exhibition of these phantasmagoric forms, from the cruel weight and hardness of the reality.

Be that as it might, the scaffold of the pillory was a point of view that revealed to Hester Prynne the entire track along which she had been treading, since her happy infancy. Standing on that miserable eminence, she saw again her native village, in Old England, and her paternal home; a decayed house of gray stone, with a poverty-stricken aspect, but retaining a half-obliterated shield of arms over the portal, in token of antique gentility. She saw her father's face, with its bald brow, and reverend white beard, that flowed over the old-fashioned Elizabethan ruff; her mother's, too, with the look of heedful and anxious love which it always wore in her remembrance, and which, face, glowing with girlish beauty, and illuminating all the interior even since her death, had so often laid the impediment of a gentle remonstrance in her daughter's pathway. She saw her own of the dusky mirror in which she had been wont to gaze at it. There she beheld another countenance, of a man well stricken in years, a pale, thin, scholar-like visage, with eyes dim and bleared by the lamplight that had served them to pore over many ponderous books. Yet those same bleared optics had a strange, penetrating power, when it was their owner's purpose to read the human soul. This figure of the study and the cloister, as Hester Prynne's womanly fancy failed not to recall, was slightly deformed, with the left shoulder a trifle higher than the right. Next rose before her, in memory's picture-gallery, the intricate and narrow thoroughfares, the tall, gray houses, the huge cathedrals, and the public edifices, ancient in date and quaint in architecture, of a Continental city; where a new life had awaited her, still in connection with the misshapen scholar; a new life, but feeding itself on time-worn materials, like a tuft of green moss on a crumbling wall. Lastly, in lieu of these shifting scenes, came back the rude market-place of the Puritan settlement, with all the towns-people assembled and levelling their stern regards at Hester Prynne,—yes, at herself,—who stood on the scaffold of the pillory, an infant on her arm, and the letter A, in scarlet, fantastically embroidered with gold-thread, upon her bosom!

Could it be true? She clutched the child so fiercely to her breast, that it sent forth a cry; she turned her eyes downward at the scarlet letter, and even touched it with her finger, to assure herself that the infant and the shame were real. Yes!—these were her realities,—all else had vanished!

Chapter 3

From this intense consciousness of being the object of severe and universal observation, the wearer of the scarlet letter was at length relieved, by discerning, on the outskirts of the crowd, a figure which irresistibly took possession of her thoughts. An Indian, in his native garb, was standing there; but the red men were not so infrequent visitors of the English settlements, that one of them would have attracted any notice from Hester Prynne, at such a time; much less would he have excluded all other objects and ideas from her mind. By the Indian's side, and evidently sustaining a companionship with him, stood a white man, clad in a strange disarray of civilized and savage costume.

He was small in stature, with a furrowed visage, which, as yet, could hardly be termed aged. There was a remarkable intelligence in his features, as of a person who had so cultivated his mental part that it could not fail to mould the physical to itself, and become manifest by unmistakable tokens. Although, by a seemingly careless arrangement of his heterogeneous garb, he had endeavored to conceal or abate the peculiarity, it was sufficiently evident to Hester Prynne, that one of this man's shoulders rose higher than the other. Again, at the first instant of perceiving that thin visage, and the slight deformity of the figure, she pressed her infant to her bosom with so convulsive a force that the poor babe uttered another cry of pain. But the mother did not seem to hear it.

At his arrival in the market-place, and some time before she saw him, the stranger had bent his eyes on Hester Prynne. It was carelessly, at first, like a man chiefly accustomed to look inward, and to whom external matters are of little value and import, unless they bear relation to something within his mind. Very soon, however, his look became keen and penetrative. A writhing horror twisted itself across his features, like a snake gliding swiftly over them, and making one little pause, with all its wreathed intervolutions in open sight. His face darkened with some powerful emotion, which, nevertheless, he so instantaneously controlled by an effort of his will, that, save at a single moment, its expression might have passed for calmness. After a brief space, the convulsion grew almost imperceptible, and finally subsided into the depths of his nature. When he found the eyes of Hester Prynne fastened on his own, and saw that she appeared to recognize him, he slowly and calmly raised his finger, made a gesture with it in the air, and laid it on his lips.

Then, touching the shoulder of a townsman who stood next to him, he addressed him, in a formal and courteous manner.

"I pray you, good Sir," said he, "who is this woman?—and wherefore is she here set up to public shame?"

"You must needs be a stranger in this region, friend," answered the townsman, looking curiously at the questioner and his savage companion, "else you would surely have heard of Mistress Hester Prynne, and her evil doings. She hath raised a great scandal, I promise you, in godly Master Dimmesdale's church."

"You say truly," replied the other. "I am a stranger, and have been a wanderer, sorely against my will. I have met with grievous mishaps by sea and land, and have been long held in bonds among the heathen-folk, to the southward; and am now brought hither by this Indian, to be redeemed out of my captivity. Will it please you, therefore, to tell me of Hester Prynne's,—have I her name rightly?—of this woman's offences, and what has brought her to yonder scaffold?"

"Truly, friend; and methinks it must gladden your heart, after your troubles and sojourn in the wilderness," said the townsman, "to find yourself, at length, in a land where iniquity is searched out, and punished in the sight of rulers and people; as here in our godly New England. Yonder woman, Sir, you must know, was the wife of a certain learned man, English by birth, but who had long dwelt in Amsterdam, whence, some good time agone, he was minded to cross over and cast in his lot with us of the Massachusetts. To this purpose, he sent his wife before him, remaining himself to look after some necessary affairs. Marry, good Sir, in some two years, or less, that the woman has been a dweller here in Boston, no tidings have come of this learned gentleman, Master Prynne; and his young wife, look you, being left to her own misguidance—"

"Ah!—aha!—I conceive you," said the stranger, with a bitter smile. "So learned a man as you speak of should have learned this too in his books. And who, by your favor, Sir, may be the father of yonder babe—it is some three or four months old, I should judge—which Mistress Prynne is holding in her arms?"

"Of a truth, friend, that matter remaineth a riddle; and the Daniel who shall expound it is yet a-wanting," answered the townsman. "Madam Hester absolutely refuseth to speak, and the magistrates have laid their heads together in vain. Peradventure the guilty one stands looking on at this sad spectacle, unknown of man, and forgetting that God sees him."

"The learned man," observed the stranger, with another smile, "should come himself, to look into the mystery."

"It behooves him well, if he be still in life," responded the townsman. "Now, good Sir, our Massachusetts magistracy, bethinking themselves that this woman is youthful and fair, and doubtless was strongly tempted to her fall,—and that, moreover, as is most likely, her husband may be at the bottom of the sea,—they have not been bold to put in force the extremity of our righteous law against her. The penalty thereof is death. But in their great mercy and tenderness of heart, they have doomed Mistress Prynne to stand only a space of three hours on the platform of the pillory, and then and thereafter, for the remainder of her natural life, to wear a mark of shame upon her bosom."

"A wise sentence!" remarked the stranger, gravely bowing his head. "Thus she will be a living sermon against sin, until the ignominious letter be engraved upon her tombstone. It irks me, nevertheless, that the partner of her iniquity should not, at least, stand on the scaffold by her side. But he will be known!—he will be known!—he will be known!"

He bowed courteously to the communicative townsman, and, whispering a few words to his Indian attendant, they both made their way through the crowd.

While this passed, Hester Prynne had been standing on her pedestal, still with a fixed gaze towards the stranger; so fixed a gaze, that, at moments of intense absorption, all other objects in the visible world seemed to vanish, leaving only him and her. Such an interview, perhaps, would have been more terrible than even to meet him as she now did, with the hot, mid-day sun burning down upon her face, and lighting up its shame; with the scarlet token of infamy on her breast; with the sin-born infant in her arms; with a whole people, drawn forth as to a festival, staring at the features that should have been seen only in the quiet gleam of the fireside, in the happy shadow of a home, or beneath a matronly veil, at church. Dreadful as it was, she was conscious of a shelter in the presence of these thousand witnesses. It was better to stand thus, with so many betwixt him and her, than to greet him, face to face, they two alone. She fled for refuge, as it were, to the public exposure, and dreaded the moment when its protection should be withdrawn from her. Involved in these thoughts, she scarcely heard a voice behind her, until it had repeated her name more than once, in a loud and solemn tone, audible to the whole multitude.

"Hearken unto me, Hester Prynne!" said the voice.

It has already been noticed, that directly over the platform on which Hester Prynne stood was a kind of balcony, or open gallery, appended to the meeting-house. It was the place whence proclamations were wont to be made, amidst an assemblage of the magistracy, with all the ceremonial that attended such public observances in those days. Here, to witness the scene which we are describing, sat Governor Bellingham himself, with four sergeants about his chair, bearing halberds, as a guard of honor. He wore a dark feather in his hat, a border of embroidery on his cloak, and a black velvet tunic beneath; a gentleman advanced in years, with a hard experience written in his wrinkles. He was not ill fitted to be the head and representative of a community, which owed its origin and progress, and its present state of development, not to the impulses of youth, but to the stern and tempered energies of manhood, and the sombre sagacity of age; accomplishing so much, precisely because it imagined and hoped so little. The other eminent characters, by whom the chief ruler was surrounded, were distinguished by a dignity of mien, belonging to a period when the forms of authority were felt to possess the sacredness of Divine institutions. They were, doubtless, good men, just and sage. But, out of the whole human family, it would not have been easy to select the same number of wise and virtuous persons, who should be less capable of sitting in judgment on an erring woman's heart, and disentangling its mesh of good and evil, than the sages of rigid aspect towards whom Hester Prynne now turned her face. She seemed conscious, indeed, that whatever sympathy she might expect lay in the larger and warmer heart of the multitude; for, as she lifted her eyes towards the balcony, the unhappy woman grew pale and trembled.

The voice which had called her attention was that of the reverend and famous John Wilson, the eldest clergyman of Boston, a great scholar, like most of his contemporaries in the profession, and withal a man of kind and genial spirit. This last attribute, however, had been less carefully developed than his intellectual gifts, and was, in truth, rather a matter of shame than self-congratulation with him. There he stood, with a border of grizzled locks beneath his skull-cap; while his gray eyes, accustomed to the shaded light of his study, were winking, like those of Hester's infant, in the unadulterated sunshine. He looked like the darkly engraved portraits which we see prefixed to old volumes of sermons; and had no more right than one of those portraits would have, to step forth, as he now did, and meddle with a question of human guilt, passion, and anguish.

"Hester Prynne," said the clergyman, "I have striven with my young brother here, under whose preaching of the word you have been privileged to sit," — here Mr. Wilson laid his hand on the shoulder of a pale young man beside him, — "I have sought, I say, to persuade this godly youth, that he should deal with you, here in the face of Heaven, and before these wise and upright rulers, and in hearing of all the people, as touching the vileness and blackness of your sin. Knowing your natural temper better than I, he could the better judge what arguments to use, whether of tenderness or terror, such as might prevail over your hardness and obstinacy;

insomuch that you should no longer hide the name of him who tempted you to this grievous fall. But he opposes to me (with a young man's over-softness, albeit wise beyond his years), that it were wronging the very nature of woman to force her to lay open her heart's secrets in such broad daylight, and in presence of so great a multitude. Truly, as I sought to convince him, the shame lay in the commission of the sin, and not in the showing of it forth. What say you to it, once again, Brother Dimmesdale? Must it be thou, or I, that shall deal with this poor sinner's soul?"

There was a murmur among the dignified and reverend occupants of the balcony; and Governor Bellingham gave expression to its purport, speaking in an authoritative voice, although tempered with respect towards the youthful clergyman whom he addressed.

"Good Master Dimmesdale," said he, "the responsibility of this woman's soul lies greatly with you. It behooves you, therefore, to exhort her to repentance, and to confession, as a proof and consequence thereof."

The directness of this appeal drew the eyes of the whole crowd upon the Reverend Mr. Dimmesdale; a young clergyman, who had come from one of the great English universities, bringing all the learning of the age into our wild forest-land. His eloquence and religious fervor had already given the earnest of high eminence in his profession. He was a person of very striking aspect, with a white, lofty, and impending brow, large brown, melancholy eyes, and a mouth which, unless when he forcibly compressed it, was apt to be tremulous, expressing both nervous sensibility and a vast power of self-restraint. Notwithstanding his high native gifts and scholar-like attainments, there was an air about this young minister,—an apprehensive, a startled, a half-frightened look,—as of a being who felt himself quite astray and at a loss in the pathway of human existence, and could only be at ease in some seclusion of his own. Therefore, so far as his duties would permit, he trod in the shadowy by-paths, and thus kept himself simple and childlike; coming forth, when occasion was, with a freshness, and fragrance, and dewy purity of thought, which, as many people said, affected them like the speech of an angel.

Such was the young man whom the Reverend Mr. Wilson and the Governor had introduced so openly to the public notice, bidding him speak, in the hearing of all men, to that mystery of a woman's soul, so sacred even in its pollution. The trying nature of his position drove the blood from his cheek, and made his lips tremulous.

"Speak to the woman, my brother," said Mr. Wilson. "It is of moment to her soul, and therefore, as the worshipful Governor says, momentous to thine own, in whose charge hers is. Exhort her to confess the truth!"

The Reverend Mr. Dimmesdale bent his head, in silent prayer, as it seemed, and then came forward.

"Hester Prynne," said he, leaning over the balcony and looking down steadfastly into her eyes, "thou hearest what this good man says, and seest the accountability under which I labor. If thou feelest it to be for thy soul's peace, and that thy earthly punishment will thereby be made more effectual to salvation, I charge thee to speak out the name of thy fellow-sinner and fellow-sufferer! Be not silent from any mistaken pity and tenderness for him; for, believe me, Hester, though he were to step down from a high place, and stand there beside thee, on thy pedestal of shame, yet better were it so than to hide a guilty heart through life. What can thy silence do for him, except it tempt him— yea, compel him, as it were—to add hypocrisy to sin? Heaven hath granted thee an open ignominy, that thereby thou mayest work out an open triumph over the evil within thee, and the sorrow without. Take heed how thou deniest to him—who, perchance, hath not the courage to grasp it for himself—the bitter, but wholesome, cup that is now presented to thy lips!"

The young pastor's voice was tremulously sweet, rich, deep, and broken. The feeling that it so evidently manifested, rather than the direct purport of the words, caused it to vibrate within all hearts, and brought the listeners into one accord of sympathy. Even the poor baby, at Hester's bosom, was affected by the same influence; for it directed its hitherto vacant gaze towards Mr. Dimmesdale, and held up its little arms, with a half-pleased, half-plaintive murmur. So powerful seemed the minister's appeal, that the people could not believe but that Hester Prynne would speak out the guilty name; or else that the guilty one himself, in whatever high or lowly place he stood, would be drawn forth by an inward and inevitable necessity, and compelled to ascend to the scaffold.

Hester shook her head.

"Woman, transgress not beyond the limits of Heaven's mercy!" cried the Reverend Mr. Wilson, more harshly than before. "That little babe hath been gifted with a voice, to second and confirm the counsel which thou hast heard. Speak out the name! That, and thy repentance, may avail to take the scarlet letter off thy breast."

"Never!" replied Hester Prynne, looking, not at Mr. Wilson, but into the deep and troubled eyes of the younger clergyman. "It is too deeply branded. Ye cannot take it off. And would that I might endure his agony, as well as mine!"

"Speak, woman!" said another voice, coldly and sternly, proceeding from the crowd about the scaffold. "Speak; and give your child a father!"

"I will not speak!" answered Hester, turning pale as death, but responding to this voice, which she too surely recognized. "And my child must seek a heavenly Father; she shall never know an earthly one!"

"She will not speak!" murmured Mr. Dimmesdale, who, leaning over the balcony, with his hand upon his heart, had awaited the result of his appeal. He now drew back, with a long respiration. "Wondrous strength and generosity of a woman's heart! She will not speak!"

Discerning the impracticable state of the poor culprit's mind, the elder clergyman, who had carefully prepared himself for the occasion, addressed to the multitude a discourse on sin, in all its branches, but with continual reference to the ignominious letter. So forcibly did he dwell upon this symbol, for the hour or more during which his periods were rolling over the people's heads, that it assumed new terrors in their imagination, and seemed to derive its scarlet hue from the flames of the infernal pit. Hester Prynne, meanwhile, kept her place upon the pedestal of shame, with glazed eyes, and an air of weary indifference. She had borne, that morning, all that nature could endure; and as her temperament was not of the order that escapes from too intense suffering by a swoon, her spirit could only shelter itself beneath a stony crust of insensibility, while the faculties of animal life remained entire. In this state, the voice of the preacher thundered remorselessly, but unavailingly, upon her ears. The infant, during the latter portion of her ordeal, pierced the air with its wailings and screams; she strove to hush it, mechanically, but seemed scarcely to sympathize with its trouble. With the same hard demeanor, she was led back to prison, and vanished from the public gaze within its iron-clamped portal. It was whispered, by those who peered after her, that the scarlet letter threw a lurid gleam along the dark passage-way of the interior.

Chapter 4

After her return to the prison, Hester Prynne was found to be in a state of nervous excitement that demanded constant watchfulness, lest she should perpetrate violence on herself, or do some half-frenzied mischief to the poor babe. As night approached, it proving impossible to quell her insubordination by rebuke or threats of punishment, Master Brackett, the jailer, thought fit to introduce a physician. He described him as a man of skill in all Christian modes of physical science, and likewise familiar with whatever the savage people could teach, in respect to medicinal herbs and roots that grew in the forest. To say the truth, there was much need of professional assistance, not merely for Hester herself, but still more urgently for the child; who, drawing its sustenance from the maternal bosom, seemed to have drank in with it all the turmoil, the anguish and despair, which pervaded the mother's system. It now writhed in convulsions of pain, and was a forcible type, in its little frame, of the moral agony which Hester Prynne had borne throughout the day.

Closely following the jailer into the dismal apartment appeared that individual, of singular aspect, whose presence in the crowd had been of such deep interest to the wearer of the scarlet letter. He was lodged in the prison, not as suspected of any offence, but as the most convenient and suitable mode of disposing of him, until the magistrates should have conferred with the Indian sagamores respecting his ransom. His name was announced as Roger Chillingworth. The jailer, after ushering him into the room, remained a moment, marvelling at the comparative quiet that followed his entrance; for Hester Prynne had immediately become as still as death, although the child continued to moan.

"Prithee, friend, leave me alone with my patient," said the practitioner. "Trust me, good jailer, you shall briefly have peace in your house; and, I promise you, Mistress Prynne shall hereafter be more amenable to just authority than you may have found her heretofore."

"Nay, if your worship can accomplish that," answered Master Brackett, "I shall own you for a man of skill indeed! Verily, the woman hath been like a possessed one; and there lacks little, that I should take in hand to drive Satan out of her with stripes."

The stranger had entered the room with the characteristic quietude of the profession to which he announced himself as belonging. Nor did his demeanor change, when the withdrawal of the prison-keeper left him face to face with the woman, whose absorbed notice of him, in the crowd, had intimated so close a relation between himself and her. His first care was given to the child; whose cries, indeed, as she lay writhing on the trundle-bed, made it of peremptory necessity to postpone all other business to the task of soothing her. He examined the infant carefully, and then proceeded to unclasp a leathern case, which he took from beneath his dress. It appeared to contain medical preparations, one of which he mingled with a cup of water.

"My old studies in alchemy," observed he, "and my sojourn, for above a year past, among a people well versed in the kindly properties of simples, have made a better physician of me than many that claim the medical degree. Here, woman! The child is yours, — she is none of mine, — neither will she recognize my voice or aspect as a father's. Administer this draught, therefore, with thine own hand."

Hester repelled the offered medicine, at the same time gazing with strongly marked apprehension into his face.

"Wouldst thou avenge thyself on the innocent babe?" whispered she.

"Foolish woman!" responded the physician, half coldly, half soothingly. "What should ail me, to harm this misbegotten and miserable babe? The medicine is potent for good; and were it my child, — yea, mine own, as well as thine! — I could do no better for it."

As she still hesitated, being, in fact, in no reasonable state of mind, he took the infant in his arms, and himself administered the draught. It soon proved its efficacy, and redeemed the leech's pledge. The moans of the little patient subsided; its convulsive tossings gradually ceased; and, in a few moments, as is the custom of young children after relief from pain, it sank into a profound and dewy slumber. The physician, as he had a fair right to be termed, next bestowed his attention on the mother. With calm and intent scrutiny he felt her pulse, looked into her eyes, — a gaze that made her heart shrink and shudder, because so familiar, and yet so strange and cold, — and, finally, satisfied with his investigation, proceeded to mingle another draught.

"I know not Lethe nor Nepenthe," remarked he; "but I have learned many new secrets in the wilderness, and here is one of them, — a recipe that an Indian taught me, in requital of some lessons of my own, that were as old as Paracelsus. Drink it! It may be less soothing than a sinless conscience. That I cannot give thee. But it will calm the swell and heaving of thy passion, like oil thrown on the waves of a tempestuous sea."

He presented the cup to Hester, who received it with a slow, earnest look into his face; not precisely a look of fear, yet full of doubt and questioning, as to what his purposes might be. She looked also at her slumbering child.

"I have thought of death," said she, — "have wished for it, — would even have prayed for it, were it fit that such as I should pray for anything. Yet if death be in this cup, I bid thee think again, ere thou beholdest me quaff it. See! It is even now at my lips."

"Drink, then," replied he, still with the same cold composure. "Dost thou know me so little, Hester Prynne? Are my purposes wont to be so shallow? Even if I imagine a scheme of vengeance, what could I do better for my object than to let thee live, — than to give thee medicines against all harm and peril of life, — so that this burning shame may still blaze upon thy bosom?" As he spoke, he laid his long forefinger on the scarlet letter, which forthwith seemed to scorch into Hester's breast, as if it had been red-hot. He noticed her involuntary gesture, and smiled. "Live, therefore, and bear about thy doom with thee, in the eyes of men and women, — in the eyes of him whom thou didst call thy husband, — in the eyes of yonder child! And, that thou mayest live, take off this draught."

Without further expostulation or delay, Hester Prynne drained the cup, and, at the motion of the man of skill, seated herself on the bed where the child was sleeping; while he drew the only chair which the room afforded, and took his own seat beside her. She could not but tremble at these preparations; for she felt that—having now done all that humanity or principle, or, if so it were, a refined cruelty, impelled him to do, for the relief of physical suffering—he was next to treat with her as the man whom she had most deeply and irreparably injured.

"Hester," said he, "I ask not wherefore, nor how, thou hast fallen into the pit, or say, rather, thou hast ascended to the pedestal of infamy, on which I found thee. The reason is not far to seek. It was my folly, and thy weakness. I,—a man of thought,—the bookworm of great libraries,—a man already in decay, having given my best years to feed the hungry dream of knowledge,—what had I to do with youth and beauty like thine own! Misshapen from my birth-hour, how could I delude myself with the idea that intellectual gifts might veil physical deformity in a young girl's fantasy! Men call me wise. If sages were ever wise in their own behoof, I might have foreseen all this. I might have known that, as I came out of the vast and dismal forest, and entered this settlement of Christian men, the very first object to meet my eyes would be thyself, Hester Prynne, standing up, a statue of ignominy, before the people. Nay, from the moment when we came down the old church steps together, a married pair, I might have beheld the bale-fire of that scarlet letter blazing at the end of our path!"

"Thou knowest," said Hester,—for, depressed as she was, she could not endure this last quiet stab at the token of her shame,—"thou knowest that I was frank with thee. I felt no love, nor feigned any."

"True," replied he. "It was my folly! I have said it. But, up to that epoch of my life, I had lived in vain. The world had been so cheerless! My heart was a habitation large enough for many guests, but lonely and chill, and without a household fire. I longed to kindle one! It seemed not so wild a dream,—old as I was, and sombre as I was, and misshapen as I was,—that the simple bliss, which is scattered far and wide, for all mankind to gather up, might yet be mine. And so, Hester, I drew thee into my heart, into its innermost chamber, and sought to warm thee by the warmth which thy presence made there!"

"I have greatly wronged thee," murmured Hester.

"We have wronged each other," answered he. "Mine was the first wrong, when I betrayed thy budding youth into a false and unnatural relation with my decay. Therefore, as a man who has not thought and philosophized in vain, I seek no vengeance, plot no evil against thee. Between thee and me the scale hangs fairly balanced. But, Hester, the man lives who has wronged us both! Who is he?"

"Ask me not!" replied Hester Prynne, looking firmly into his face. "That thou shalt never know!"

"Never, sayest thou?" rejoined he, with a smile of dark and self-relying intelligence. "Never know him! Believe me, Hester, there are few things,—whether in the outward world, or, to a certain depth, in the invisible sphere of thought,—few things hidden from the man who devotes himself earnestly and unreservedly to the solution of a mystery. Thou mayest cover up thy secret from the prying multitude. Thou mayest conceal it, too, from the ministers and magistrates, even as thou didst this day, when they sought to wrench the name out of thy heart, and give thee a partner on thy pedestal. But, as for me, I come to the inquest with other senses than they possess. I shall seek this man, as I have sought truth in books; as I have sought gold in alchemy. There is a sympathy that will make me conscious of him. I shall see him tremble. I shall feel myself shudder, suddenly and unawares. Sooner or later, he must needs be mine!"

The eyes of the wrinkled scholar glowed so intensely upon her, that Hester Prynne clasped her hands over her heart, dreading lest he should read the secret there at once.

"Thou wilt not reveal his name? Not the less he is mine," resumed he, with a look of confidence, as if destiny were at one with him. "He bears no letter of infamy wrought into his garment, as thou dost; but I shall read it on his heart. Yet fear not for him! Think not that I shall interfere with Heaven's own method of retribution, or, to my own loss, betray him to the gripe of human law. Neither do thou imagine that I shall contrive aught against his life; no, nor against his fame, if, as I judge, he be a man of fair repute. Let him live! Let him hide himself in outward honor, if he may! Not the less he shall be mine!"

"Thy acts are like mercy," said Hester, bewildered and appalled. "But thy words interpret thee as a terror!"

"One thing, thou that wast my wife, I would enjoin upon thee," continued the scholar. "Thou hast kept the secret of thy paramour. Keep, likewise, mine! There are none in this land that know me. Breathe not, to any human soul, that thou didst ever call me husband! Here, on this wild outskirt of the earth, I shall pitch my tent; for, elsewhere a wanderer, and isolated from human interests, I find here a woman, a man, a child, amongst whom and myself there exist the closest ligaments. No matter whether of love or hate; no matter whether of right or wrong! Thou and thine, Hester Prynne, belong to me. My home is where thou art, and where he is. But betray me not!"

"Wherefore dost thou desire it?" inquired Hester, shrinking, she hardly knew why, from this secret bond. "Why not announce thyself openly, and cast me off at once?"

"It may be," he replied, "because I will not encounter the dishonor that besmirches the husband of a faithless woman. It may be for other reasons. Enough, it is my purpose to live and die unknown. Let, therefore, thy husband be to the world as one already dead, and of whom no tidings shall ever come. Recognize me not, by word, by sign, by look! Breathe not the secret, above all, to the man thou wottest of. Shouldst thou fail me in this, beware! His fame, his position, his life, will be in my hands. Beware!"

"I will keep thy secret, as I have his," said Hester.

"Swear it!" rejoined he.

And she took the oath.

"And now, Mistress Prynne," said old Roger Chillingworth, as he was hereafter to be named, "I leave thee alone; alone with thy infant, and the scarlet letter! How is it, Hester? Doth thy sentence bind thee to wear the token in thy sleep? Art thou not afraid of nightmares and hideous dreams?"

"Why dost thou smile so at me?" inquired Hester, troubled at the expression of his eyes. "Art thou like the Black Man that haunts the forest round about us? Hast thou enticed me into a bond that will prove the ruin of my soul?"

"Not thy soul," he answered, with another smile. "No, not thine!"

Chapter 5

Hester Prynne's term of confinement was now at an end. Her prison-door was thrown open, and she came forth into the sunshine, which, falling on all alike, seemed, to her sick and morbid heart, as if meant for no other purpose than to reveal the scarlet letter on her breast. Perhaps there was a more real torture in her first unattended footsteps from the threshold of the prison, than even in the procession and spectacle that have been described, where she was made the common infamy, at which all mankind was summoned to point its finger. Then, she was supported by an unnatural tension of the nerves, and by all the combative energy of her character, which enabled her to convert the scene into a kind of lurid triumph. It was, moreover, a separate and insulated event, to occur but once in her lifetime, and to meet which, therefore, reckless of economy, she might call up the vital strength that would have sufficed for many quiet years. The very law that condemned her—a giant of stern features, but with vigor to support, as well as to annihilate, in his iron arm—had held her up, through the terrible ordeal of her ignominy. But now, with this unattended walk from her prison-door, began the daily custom; and she must either sustain and carry it forward by the ordinary resources of her nature, or sink beneath it. She could no longer borrow from the future to help her through the present grief. To-morrow would bring its own trial with it; so would the next day, and so would the next; each its own trial, and yet the very same that was now so unutterably grievous to be borne. The days of the far-off future would toil onward, still with the same burden for her to take up, and bear along with her, but never to fling down; for the accumulating days, and added years, would pile up their misery upon the heap of shame. Throughout them all, giving up her individuality, she would become the general symbol at which the preacher and moralist might point, and in which they might vivify and embody their images of woman's frailty and sinful passion. Thus the young and pure would be taught to look at her, with the scarlet letter flaming on her breast,—at her, the child of honorable parents,—at her, the mother of a babe, that would hereafter be a woman,—at her, who had once been innocent,—as the figure, the body, the reality of sin. And over her grave, the infamy that she must carry thither would be her only monument.

It may seem marvellous, that, with the world before her,— kept by no restrictive clause of her condemnation within the limits of the Puritan settlement, so remote and so obscure,— free to return to her birthplace, or to any other European land, and there hide her character and identity under a new exterior, as completely as if emerging into another state of being,—and having also the passes of the dark, inscrutable forest open to her, where the wildness of her nature might assimilate itself with a people whose customs and life were alien from the law that had condemned her,—it may seem marvellous, that this woman should still call that place her home, where, and where only, she must needs be the type of shame. But there is a fatality, a feeling so irresistible and inevitable that it has the force of doom, which almost invariably compels human beings to linger around and haunt, ghost-like, the spot where some great and marked event has given the color to their lifetime; and still the more irresistibly, the darker the tinge that saddens it. Her sin, her ignominy, were the roots which she had struck into the soil. It was as if a new birth, with stronger assimilations than the first, had converted the forest-land, still so uncongenial to every other pilgrim and wanderer, into Hester Prynne's wild and dreary, but life-long home. All other scenes of earth—

even that village of rural England, where happy infancy and stainless maidenhood seemed yet to be in her mother's keeping, like garments put off long ago—were foreign to her, in comparison. The chain that bound her here was of iron links, and galling to her inmost soul, but could never be broken.

It might be, too,—doubtless it was so, although she hid the secret from herself, and grew pale whenever it struggled out of her heart, like a serpent from its hole,—it might be that another feeling kept her within the scene and pathway that had been so fatal. There dwelt, there trode the feet of one with whom she deemed herself connected in a union, that, unrecognized on earth, would bring them together before the bar of final judgment, and make that their marriage-altar, for a joint futurity of endless retribution. Over and over again, the tempter of souls had thrust this idea upon Hester's contemplation, and laughed at the passionate and desperate joy with which she seized, and then strove to cast it from her. She barely looked the idea in the face, and hastened to bar it in its dungeon. What she compelled herself to believe—what, finally, she reasoned upon, as her motive for continuing a resident of New England—was half a truth, and half a self-delusion. Here, she said to herself, had been the scene of her guilt, and here should be the scene of her earthly punishment; and so, perchance, the torture of her daily shame would at length purge her soul, and work out another purity than that which she had lost; more saint-like, because the result of martyrdom.

Hester Prynne, therefore, did not flee. On the outskirts of the town, within the verge of the peninsula, but not in close vicinity to any other habitation, there was a small thatched cottage. It had been built by an earlier settler, and abandoned because the soil about it was too sterile for cultivation, while its comparative remoteness put it out of the sphere of that social activity which already marked the habits of the emigrants. It stood on the shore, looking across a basin of the sea at the forest-covered hills, towards the west. A clump of scrubby trees, such as alone grew on the peninsula, did not so much conceal the cottage from view, as seem to denote that here was some object which would fain have been, or at least ought to be, concealed. In this little, lonesome dwelling, with some slender means that she possessed, and by the license of the magistrates, who still kept an inquisitorial watch over her, Hester established herself, with her infant child. A mystic shadow of suspicion immediately attached itself to the spot. Children, too young to comprehend wherefore this woman should be shut out from the sphere of human charities, would creep nigh enough to behold her plying her needle at the cottage-window, or standing in the doorway, or laboring in her little garden, or coming forth along the pathway that led townward; and, discerning the scarlet letter on her breast, would scamper off with a strange, contagious fear.

Lonely as was Hester's situation, and without a friend on earth who dared to show himself, she, however, incurred no risk of want. She possessed an art that sufficed, even in a land that afforded comparatively little scope for its exercise, to supply food for her thriving infant and herself. It was the art—then, as now, almost the only one within a woman's grasp—of needlework. She bore on her breast, in the curiously embroidered letter, a specimen of her delicate and imaginative skill, of which the dames of a court might gladly have availed themselves, to add the richer and more spiritual adornment of human ingenuity to their fabrics of silk and gold. Here, indeed, in the sable simplicity that generally characterized the Puritanic modes of dress, there might be an infrequent call for the finer productions of her handiwork. Yet the taste of the age, demanding whatever was elaborate in compositions of this kind, did not fail to extend its influence over our stern progenitors, who had cast behind them so many fashions which it might seem harder to dispense with. Public ceremonies, such as ordinations, the installation of magistrates, and all that could give majesty to the forms in which a new government manifested itself to the people, were, as a matter of policy, marked by a stately and well-conducted ceremonial, and a sombre, but yet a studied magnificence. Deep ruffs, painfully wrought bands, and gorgeously embroidered gloves, were all deemed necessary to the official state of men assuming the reins of power; and were readily allowed to individuals dignified by rank or wealth, even while sumptuary laws forbade these and similar extravagances to the plebeian order. In the array of funerals, too, — whether for the apparel of the dead body, or to typify, by manifold emblematic devices of sable cloth and snowy lawn, the sorrow of the survivors, — there was a frequent and characteristic demand for such labor as Hester Prynne could supply. Baby-linen—for babies then wore robes of state—afforded still another possibility of toil and emolument.

By degrees, nor very slowly, her handiwork became what would now be termed the fashion. Whether from commiseration for a woman of so miserable a destiny; or from the morbid curiosity that gives a fictitious value even to common or worthless things; or by whatever other intangible circumstance was then, as now, sufficient to bestow, on some persons, what others might seek in vain; or because Hester really filled a gap which must otherwise have remained vacant; it is certain that she had ready and fairly requited employment for as many hours as she saw fit to occupy with her needle. Vanity, it may be, chose to mortify itself, by putting on, for ceremonials of pomp and state, the garments that had been wrought by her sinful hands. Her needlework was seen on the ruff of the Governor; military men wore it on their scarfs, and the minister on his band; it decked the baby's little cap; it was shut up, to be mildewed and moulder away, in the coffins of the dead. But it is not recorded that, in a single instance, her skill was called in aid to embroider the white veil which was to cover the pure blushes of a bride. The exception indicated the ever-relentless rigor with which society frowned upon her sin.

Hester sought not to acquire anything beyond a subsistence, of the plainest and most ascetic description, for herself, and a simple abundance for her child. Her own dress was of the coarsest materials and the most sombre hue; with only that one ornament, — the scarlet letter, — which it was her doom to wear. The child's attire, on the other hand, was distinguished by a fanciful, or, we might rather say, a fantastic ingenuity, which served, indeed, to heighten the airy charm that early began to develop itself in the little girl, but which appeared to have also a deeper meaning. We may speak further of it hereafter. Except for that small expenditure in the decoration of her infant, Hester bestowed all her superfluous means in charity, on wretches less miserable than herself, and who not unfrequently insulted the hand that fed them. Much of the time, which she might readily have applied to the better efforts of her art, she employed in making coarse garments for the poor. It is probable that there was an idea of penance in this mode of occupation, and that she offered up a real sacrifice of enjoyment, in devoting so many hours to such rude handiwork. She had in her nature a rich, voluptuous, Oriental characteristic, — a taste for the gorgeously beautiful, which, save in the exquisite productions of her needle, found nothing else, in all the possibilities of her life, to exercise itself upon. Women derive a pleasure, incomprehensible to the other sex, from the delicate toil of the needle. To Hester Prynne it might have been a mode of expressing, and therefore soothing, the passion of her life. Like all other joys, she rejected it as sin. This morbid meddling of conscience with an immaterial matter betokened, it is to be feared, no genuine and steadfast penitence, but something doubtful, something that might be deeply wrong, beneath.

In this manner, Hester Prynne came to have a part to perform in the world. With her native energy of character, and rare capacity, it could not entirely cast her off, although it had set a mark upon her, more intolerable to a woman's heart than that which branded the brow of Cain. In all her intercourse with society, however, there was nothing that made her feel as if she belonged to it. Every gesture, every word, and even the silence of those with whom she came in contact, implied, and often expressed, that she was banished, and as much alone as if she inhabited another sphere, or communicated with the common nature by other organs and senses than the rest of human kind. She stood apart from moral interests, yet close beside them, like a ghost that revisits the familiar fireside, and can no longer make itself seen or felt; no more smile with the household joy, nor mourn with the kindred sorrow; or, should it succeed in manifesting its forbidden sympathy, awakening only terror and horrible repugnance. These emotions, in fact, and its bitterest scorn besides, seemed to be the sole portion that she retained in the universal heart. It was not an age of delicacy; and her position, although she understood it well, and was in little danger of forgetting it, was often brought before her vivid self-perception, like a new anguish, by the rudest touch upon the tenderest spot. The poor, as we have already said, whom she sought out to be the objects of her bounty, often reviled the hand that was stretched forth to succor them. Dames of elevated rank, likewise, whose doors she entered in the way of her occupation, were accustomed to distil drops of bitterness into her heart; sometimes through that alchemy of quiet malice, by which women can concoct a subtle poison from ordinary trifles; and sometimes, also, by a coarser expression, that fell upon the sufferer's defenceless breast like a rough blow upon an ulcerated wound. Hester had schooled herself long and well; she never responded to these attacks, save by a flush of crimson that rose irrepressibly over her pale cheek, and again subsided into the depths of her bosom. She was patient,—a martyr, indeed,—but she forbore to pray for her enemies; lest, in spite of her forgiving aspirations, the words of the blessing should stubbornly twist themselves into a curse.

Continually, and in a thousand other ways, did she feel the innumerable throbs of anguish that had been so cunningly contrived for her by the undying, the ever-active sentence of the Puritan tribunal. Clergymen paused in the street to address words of exhortation, that brought a crowd, with its mingled grin and frown, around the poor, sinful woman. If she entered a church, trusting to share the Sabbath smile of the Universal Father, it was often her mishap to find herself the text of the discourse. She grew to have a dread of children; for they had imbibed from their parents a vague idea of something horrible in this dreary woman, gliding silently through the town, with never any companion but one only child. Therefore, first allowing her to pass, they pursued her at a distance with shrill cries, and the utterance of a word that had no distinct purport to their own minds, but was none the less terrible to her, as proceeding from lips that babbled it unconsciously. It seemed to argue so wide a diffusion of her shame, that all nature knew of it; it could have caused her no deeper pang, had the leaves of the trees whispered the dark story among themselves,—had the summer breeze murmured about it,—had the wintry blast shrieked it aloud! Another peculiar torture was felt in the gaze of a new eye. When strangers looked curiously at the scarlet letter,—and none ever failed to do so,—they branded it afresh into Hester's soul; so that, oftentimes, she could scarcely refrain, yet always did refrain, from covering the symbol with her hand. But then, again, an accustomed eye had likewise its own anguish to inflict. Its cool stare of familiarity was intolerable. From first to last, in short, Hester Prynne had always this dreadful agony in feeling a human eye upon the token; the spot never grew callous; it seemed, on the contrary, to grow more sensitive with daily torture.

But sometimes, once in many days, or perchance in many months, she felt an eye—a human eye—upon the ignominious brand, that seemed to give a momentary relief, as if half of her agony were shared. The next instant, back it all rushed again, with still a deeper throb of pain; for, in that brief interval, she had sinned anew. Had Hester sinned alone?

Her imagination was somewhat affected, and, had she been of a softer moral and intellectual fibre, would have been still more so, by the strange and solitary anguish of her life. Walking to and fro, with those lonely footsteps, in the little world with which she was outwardly connected, it now and then appeared to Hester,—if altogether fancy, it was nevertheless too potent to be resisted,—she felt or fancied, then, that the scarlet letter had endowed her with a new sense. She shuddered to believe, yet could not help believing, that it gave her a sympathetic knowledge of the hidden sin in other hearts. She was terror-stricken by the revelations that were thus made. What were they? Could they be other than the insidious whispers of the bad angel, who would fain have persuaded the struggling woman, as yet only half his victim, that the outward guise of purity was but a lie, and that, if truth were everywhere to be shown, a scarlet letter would blaze forth on many a bosom besides Hester Prynne's? Or, must she receive those intimations— so obscure, yet so distinct—as truth? In all her miserable experience, there was nothing else so awful and so loathsome as this sense. It perplexed, as well as shocked her, by the irreverent inopportuneness of the occasions that brought it into vivid action. Sometimes the red infamy upon her breast would give a sympathetic throb, as she passed near a venerable minister or magistrate, the model of piety and justice, to whom that age of antique reverence looked up, as to a mortal man in fellowship with angels. "What evil thing is at hand?" would Hester say to herself. Lifting her reluctant eyes, there would be nothing human within the scope of view, save the form of this earthly saint! Again, a mystic sisterhood would contumaciously assert itself, as she met the sanctified frown of some matron, who, according to the rumor of all tongues, had kept cold snow within her bosom throughout life. That unsunned snow in the matron's bosom, and the burning shame on Hester Prynne's, — what had the two in common? Or, once more, the electric thrill would give her warning, — "Behold, Hester, here is a companion!" — and, looking up, she would detect the eyes of a young maiden glancing at the scarlet letter, shyly and aside, and quickly averted with a faint, chill crimson in her cheeks; as if her purity were somewhat sullied by that momentary glance. O Fiend, whose talisman was that fatal symbol, wouldst thou leave nothing, whether in youth or age, for this poor sinner to revere? — such loss of faith is ever one of the saddest results of sin. Be it accepted as a proof that all was not corrupt in this poor victim of her own frailty, and man's hard law, that Hester Prynne yet struggled to believe that no fellow-mortal was guilty like herself.

The vulgar, who, in those dreary old times, were always contributing a grotesque horror to what interested their imaginations, had a story about the scarlet letter which we might readily work up into a terrific legend. They averred, that the symbol was not mere scarlet cloth, tinged in an earthly dye-pot, but was red-hot with infernal fire, and could be seen glowing all alight, whenever Hester Prynne walked abroad in the night-time. And we must needs say, it seared Hester's bosom so deeply, that perhaps there was more truth in the rumor than our modern incredulity may be inclined to admit.

Chapter 6

We have as yet hardly spoken of the infant; that little creature, whose innocent life had sprung, by the inscrutable decree of Providence, a lovely and immortal flower, out of the rank luxuriance of a guilty passion. How strange it seemed to the sad woman, as she watched the growth, and the beauty that became every day more brilliant, and the intelligence that threw its quivering sunshine over the tiny features of this child! Her Pearl!—For so had Hester called her; not as a name expressive of her aspect, which had nothing of the calm, white, unimpassioned lustre that would be indicated by the comparison. But she named the infant "Pearl," as being of great price,—purchased with all she had,—her mother's only treasure! How strange, indeed! Man had marked this woman's sin by a scarlet letter, which had such potent and disastrous efficacy that no human sympathy could reach her, save it were sinful like herself. God, as a direct consequence of the sin which man thus punished, had given her a lovely child, whose place was on that same dishonored bosom, to connect her parent forever with the race and descent of mortals, and to be finally a blessed soul in heaven! Yet these thoughts affected Hester Prynne less with hope than apprehension. She knew that her deed had been evil; she could have no faith, therefore, that its result would be good. Day after day, she looked fearfully into the child's expanding nature, ever dreading to detect some dark and wild peculiarity, that should correspond with the guiltiness to which she owed her being.

Certainly, there was no physical defect. By its perfect shape, its vigor, and its natural dexterity in the use of all its untried limbs, the infant was worthy to have been brought forth in Eden; worthy to have been left there, to be the plaything of the angels, after the world's first parents were driven out. The child had a native grace which does not invariably coexist with faultless beauty; its attire, however simple, always impressed the beholder as if it were the very garb that precisely became it best. But little Pearl was not clad in rustic weeds. Her mother, with a morbid purpose that may be better understood hereafter, had bought the richest tissues that could be procured, and allowed her imaginative faculty its full play in the arrangement and decoration of the dresses which the child wore, before the public eye. So magnificent was the small figure, when thus arrayed, and such was the splendor of Pearl's own proper beauty, shining through the gorgeous robes which might have extinguished a paler loveliness, that there was an absolute circle of radiance around her, on the darksome cottage floor. And yet a russet gown, torn and soiled with the child's rude play, made a picture of her just as perfect. Pearl's aspect was imbued with a spell of infinite variety; in this one child there were many children, comprehending the full scope between the wild-flower prettiness of a peasant-baby, and the pomp, in little, of an infant princess. Throughout all, however, there was a trait of passion, a certain depth of hue, which she never lost; and if, in any of her changes, she had grown fainter or paler, she would have ceased to be herself,—it would have been no longer Pearl!

This outward mutability indicated, and did not more than fairly express, the various properties of her inner life. Her nature appeared to possess depth, too, as well as variety; but—or else Hester's fears deceived her—it lacked reference and adaptation to the world into which she was born. The child could not be made amenable to rules. In giving her existence, a great law had been broken; and the result was a being whose elements were perhaps beautiful and brilliant, but all in disorder; or with an order peculiar to themselves, amidst which the point of variety and arrangement was difficult or impossible to be discovered. Hester could only account for the child's character—and even then most vaguely and imperfectly—by recalling what she herself had been, during that momentous period while Pearl was imbibing her soul from the spiritual world, and her bodily frame from its material of earth. The mother's impassioned state had been the medium through which were transmitted to the unborn infant the rays of its moral life; and, however white and clear originally, they had taken the deep stains of crimson and gold, the fiery lustre, the black shadow, and the untempered light of the intervening substance. Above all, the warfare of Hester's spirit, at that epoch, was perpetuated in Pearl. She could recognize her wild, desperate, defiant mood, the flightiness of her temper, and even some of the very cloud-shapes of gloom and despondency that had brooded in her heart. They were now illuminated by the morning radiance of a young child's disposition, but later in the day of earthly existence might be prolific of the storm and whirlwind.

The discipline of the family, in those days, was of a far more rigid kind than now. The frown, the harsh rebuke, the frequent application of the rod, enjoined by Scriptural authority, were used, not merely in the way of punishment for actual offences, but as a wholesome regimen for the growth and promotion of all childish virtues. Hester Prynne, nevertheless, the lonely mother of this one child, ran little risk of erring on the side of undue severity. Mindful, however, of her own errors and misfortunes, she early sought to impose a tender, but strict control over the infant immortality that was committed to her charge. But the task was beyond her skill. After testing both smiles and frowns, and proving that neither mode of treatment possessed any calculable influence, Hester was ultimately compelled to stand aside, and permit the child to be swayed by her own impulses. Physical compulsion or restraint was effectual, of course, while it lasted. As to any other kind of discipline, whether addressed to her mind or heart, little Pearl might or might not be within its reach, in accordance with the caprice that ruled the moment. Her mother, while Pearl was yet an infant, grew acquainted with a certain peculiar look, that warned her when it would be labor thrown away to insist, persuade, or plead. It was a look so intelligent, yet inexplicable, so perverse, sometimes so malicious, but generally accompanied by a wild flow of spirits, that Hester could not help questioning, at such moments, whether Pearl were a human child. She seemed rather an airy sprite, which, after playing its fantastic sports for a little while upon the cottage floor, would flit away with a mocking smile. Whenever that look appeared in her wild, bright, deeply black eyes, it invested her with a strange remoteness and intangibility; it was as if she were hovering in the air and might vanish, like a glimmering light, that comes we know not whence, and goes we know not whither. Beholding it, Hester was constrained to rush towards the child,— to pursue the little elf in the flight which she invariably began,—to snatch her to her bosom, with a close pressure and earnest kisses,—not so much from overflowing love, as to assure herself that Pearl was flesh and blood, and not utterly delusive. But Pearl's laugh, when she was caught, though full of merriment and music, made her mother more doubtful than before.

Heart-smitten at this bewildering and baffling spell, that so often came between herself and her sole treasure, whom she had bought so dear, and who was all her world, Hester sometimes burst into passionate tears. Then, perhaps,— for there was no foreseeing how it might affect her,— Pearl would frown, and clench her little fist, and harden her small features into a stern, unsympathizing look of discontent. Not seldom, she would laugh anew, and louder than before, like a thing incapable and unintelligent of human sorrow. Or—but this more rarely happened—she would be convulsed with a rage of grief, and sob out her love for her mother, in broken words, and seem intent on proving that she had a heart, by breaking it. Yet Hester was hardly safe in confiding herself to that gusty tenderness; it passed, as suddenly as it came. Brooding over all these matters, the mother felt like one who has evoked a spirit, but, by some irregularity in the process of conjuration, has failed to win the master-word that should control this new and incomprehensible intelligence. Her only real comfort was when the child lay in the placidity of sleep. Then she was sure of her, and tasted hours of quiet, sad, delicious happiness; until—perhaps with that perverse expression glimmering from beneath her opening lids little Pearl awoke!

How soon—with what strange rapidity, indeed!—did Pearl arrive at an age that was capable of social intercourse, beyond the mother's ever-ready smile and nonsense-words! And then what a happiness would it have been, could Hester Prynne have heard her clear, bird-like voice mingling with the uproar of other childish voices, and have distinguished and unravelled her own darling's tones, amid all the entangled outcry of a group of sportive children! But this could never be. Pearl was a born outcast of the infantile world. An imp of evil, emblem and product of sin, she had no right among christened infants. Nothing was more remarkable than the instinct, as it seemed, with which the child comprehended her loneliness; the destiny that had drawn an inviolable circle round about her; the whole peculiarity, in short, of her position in respect to other children. Never, since her release from prison, had Hester met the public gaze without her. In all her walks about the town, Pearl, too, was there; first as the babe in arms, and afterwards as the little girl, small companion of her mother, holding a forefinger with her whole grasp, and tripping along at the rate of three or four footsteps to one of Hester's. She saw the children of the settlement, on the grassy margin of the street, or at the domestic thresholds, disporting themselves in such grim fashion as the Puritanic nurture would permit; playing at going to church, perchance; or at scourging Quakers; or taking scalps in a sham-fight with the Indians; or scaring one another with freaks of imitative witchcraft. Pearl saw, and gazed intently, but never sought to make acquaintance. If spoken to, she would not speak again. If the children gathered about her, as they sometimes did, Pearl would grow positively terrible in her puny wrath, snatching up stones to fling at them, with shrill, incoherent exclamations, that made her mother tremble, because they had so much the sound of a witch's anathemas in some unknown tongue.

The truth was, that the little Puritans, being of the most intolerant brood that ever lived, had got a vague idea of something outlandish, unearthly, or at variance with ordinary fashions, in the mother and child; and therefore scorned them in their hearts, and not unfrequently reviled them with their tongues. Pearl felt the sentiment, and requited it with the bitterest hatred that can be supposed to rankle in a childish bosom. These outbreaks of a fierce temper had a kind of value, and even comfort, for her mother; because there was at least an intelligible earnestness in the mood, instead of the fitful caprice that so often thwarted her in the child's manifestations. It appalled her, nevertheless, to discern here, again, a shadowy reflection of the evil that had existed in herself. All this enmity and passion had Pearl inherited, by inalienable right, out of Hester's heart. Mother and daughter stood together in the same circle of seclusion from human society; and in the nature of the child seemed to be perpetuated those unquiet elements that had distracted Hester Prynne before Pearl's birth, but had since begun to be soothed away by the softening influences of maternity.

At home, within and around her mother's cottage, Pearl wanted not a wide and various circle of acquaintance. The spell of life went forth from her ever-creative spirit, and communicated itself to a thousand objects, as a torch kindles a flame wherever it may be applied. The unlikeliest materials—a stick, a bunch of rags, a flower—were the puppets of Pearl's witchcraft, and, without undergoing any outward change, became spiritually adapted to whatever drama occupied the stage of her inner world. Her one baby-voice served a multitude of imaginary personages, old and young, to talk withal. The pine-trees, aged, black and solemn, and flinging groans and other melancholy utterances on the breeze, needed little transformation to figure as Puritan elders; the ugliest weeds of the garden were their children, whom Pearl smote down and uprooted, most unmercifully. It was wonderful, the vast variety of forms into which she threw her intellect, with no continuity, indeed, but darting up and dancing, always in a state of preternatural activity,—soon sinking down, as if exhausted by so rapid and feverish a tide of life,—and succeeded by other shapes of a similar wild energy. It was like nothing so much as the phantasmagoric play of the northern lights. In the mere exercise of the fancy, however, and the sportiveness of a growing mind, there might be little more than was observable in other children of bright faculties; except as Pearl, in the dearth of human playmates, was thrown more upon the visionary throng which she created. The singularity lay in the hostile feelings with which the child regarded all these offspring of her own heart and mind. She never created a friend, but seemed always to be sowing broadcast the dragon's teeth, whence sprung a harvest of armed enemies, against whom she rushed to battle. It was inexpressibly sad—then what depth of sorrow to a mother, who felt in her own heart the cause!—to observe, in one so young, this constant recognition of an adverse world, and so fierce a training of the energies that were to make good her cause, in the contest that must ensue.

Gazing at Pearl, Hester Prynne often dropped her work upon her knees, and cried out with an agony which she would fain have hidden, but which made utterance for itself, betwixt speech and a groan,—"O Father in Heaven,—if Thou art still my Father,—what is this being which I have brought into the world!" And Pearl, overhearing the ejaculation, or aware, through some more subtile channel, of those throbs of anguish, would turn her vivid and beautiful little face upon her mother, smile with sprite-like intelligence, and resume her play.

One peculiarity of the child's deportment remains yet to be told. The very first thing which she had noticed in her life was—what?—not the mother's smile, responding to it, as other babies do, by that faint, embryo smile of the little mouth, remembered so doubtfully afterwards, and with such fond discussion whether it were indeed a smile. By no means! But that first object of which Pearl seemed to become aware was—shall we say it?—the scarlet letter on Hester's bosom! One day, as her mother stooped over the cradle, the infant's eyes had been caught by the glimmering of the gold embroidery about the letter; and, putting up her little hand, she grasped at it, smiling, not doubtfully, but with a decided gleam, that gave her face the look of a much older child. Then, gasping for breath, did Hester Prynne clutch the fatal token, instinctively endeavoring to tear it away; so infinite was the torture inflicted by the intelligent touch of Pearl's baby-hand. Again, as if her mother's agonized gesture were meant only to make sport for her, did little Pearl look into her eyes, and smile! From that epoch, except when the child was asleep, Hester had never felt a moment's safety; not a moment's calm enjoyment of her. Weeks, it is true, would sometimes elapse, during which Pearl's gaze might never once be fixed upon the scarlet letter; but then, again, it would come at unawares, like the stroke of sudden death, and always with that peculiar smile, and odd expression of the eyes.

Once, this freakish, elvish cast came into the child's eyes, while Hester was looking at her own image in them, as mothers are fond of doing; and, suddenly,—for women in solitude, and with troubled hearts, are pestered with unaccountable delusions,—she fancied that she beheld, not her own miniature portrait, but another face, in the small black mirror of Pearl's eye. It was a face, fiend-like, full of smiling malice, yet bearing the semblance of features that she had known full well, though seldom with a smile, and never with malice in them. It was as if an evil spirit possessed the child, and had just then peeped forth in mockery. Many a time afterwards had Hester been tortured, though less vividly, by the same illusion.

In the afternoon of a certain summer's day, after Pearl grew big enough to run about, she amused herself with gathering handfuls of wild-flowers, and flinging them, one by one, at her mother's bosom; dancing up and down, like a little elf, whenever she hit the scarlet letter. Hester's first motion had been to cover her bosom with her clasped hands. But, whether from pride or resignation, or a feeling that her penance might best be wrought out by this unutterable pain, she resisted the impulse, and sat erect, pale as death, looking sadly into little Pearl's wild eyes. Still came the battery of flowers, almost invariably hitting the mark, and covering the mother's breast with hurts for which she could find no balm in this world, nor knew how to seek it in another. At last, her shot being all expended, the child stood still and gazed at Hester, with that little, laughing image of a fiend peeping out—or, whether it peeped or no, her mother so imagined it—from the unsearchable abyss of her black eyes.

"Child, what art thou?" cried the mother.

"O, I am your little Pearl!" answered the child.

But, while she said it, Pearl laughed, and began to dance up and down, with the humorsome gesticulation of a little imp, whose next freak might be to fly up the chimney.

"Art thou my child, in very truth?" asked Hester.

Nor did she put the question altogether idly, but, for the moment, with a portion of genuine earnestness; for, such was Pearl's wonderful intelligence, that her mother half doubted whether she were not acquainted with the secret spell of her existence, and might not now reveal herself.

"Yes; I am little Pearl!" repeated the child, continuing her antics.

"Thou art not my child! Thou art no Pearl of mine!" said the mother, half playfully; for it was often the case that a sportive impulse came over her, in the midst of her deepest suffering. "Tell me, then, what thou art, and who sent thee hither."

"Tell me, mother!" said the child, seriously, coming up to Hester, and pressing herself close to her knees. "Do thou tell me!"

"Thy Heavenly Father sent thee!" answered Hester Prynne.

But she said it with a hesitation that did not escape the acuteness of the child. Whether moved only by her ordinary freakishness, or because an evil spirit prompted her, she put up her small forefinger, and touched the scarlet letter.

"He did not send me!" cried she, positively. "I have no Heavenly Father!"

"Hush, Pearl, hush! Thou must not talk so!" answered

the mother, suppressing a groan. "He sent us all into this world. He sent even me, thy mother. Then, much more, thee! Or, if not, thou strange and elfish child, whence didst thou come?"

"Tell me! Tell me!" repeated Pearl, no longer seriously, but laughing, and capering about the floor. "It is thou that must tell me!"

But Hester could not resolve the query, being herself in a dismal labyrinth of doubt. She remembered—betwixt a smile and a shudder—the talk of the neighboring towns-people; who, seeking vainly elsewhere for the child's paternity, and observing some of her odd attributes, had given out that poor little Pearl was a demon offspring; such as, ever since old Catholic times, had occasionally been seen on earth, through the agency of their mother's sin, and to promote some foul and wicked purpose. Luther, according to the scandal of his monkish enemies, was a brat of that hellish breed; nor was Pearl the only child to whom this inauspicious origin was assigned, among the New England Puritans.

Chapter 7

Hester Prynne went, one day, to the mansion of Governor Bellingham, with a pair of gloves, which she had fringed and embroidered to his order, and which were to be worn on some great occasion of state; for, though the chances of a popular election had caused this former ruler to descend a step or two from the highest rank, he still held an honorable and influential place among the colonial magistracy.

Another and far more important reason than the delivery of a pair of embroidered gloves impelled Hester, at this time, to seek an interview with a personage of so much power and activity in the affairs of the settlement. It had reached her ears, that there was a design on the part of some of the leading inhabitants, cherishing the more rigid order of principles in religion and government, to deprive her of her child. On the supposition that Pearl, as already hinted, was of demon origin, these good people not unreasonably argued that a Christian interest in the mother's soul required them to remove such a stumbling-block from her path. If the child, on the other hand, were really capable of moral and religious growth, and possessed the elements of ultimate salvation, then, surely, it would enjoy all the fairer prospect of these advantages, by being transferred to wiser and better guardianship than Hester Prynne's. Among those who promoted the design, Governor Bellingham was said to be one of the most busy. It may appear singular, and indeed, not a little ludicrous, that an affair of this kind, which, in later days, would have been referred to no higher jurisdiction than that of the selectmen of the town, should then have been a question publicly discussed, and on which statesmen of eminence took sides. At that epoch of pristine simplicity, however, matters of even slighter public interest, and of far less intrinsic weight, than the welfare of Hester and her child, were strangely mixed up with the deliberations of legislators and acts of state. The period was hardly, if at all, earlier than that of our story, when a dispute concerning the right of property in a pig not only caused a fierce and bitter contest in the legislative body of the colony, but resulted in an important modification of the framework itself of the legislature.

Full of concern, therefore,—but so conscious of her own right that it seemed scarcely an unequal match between the public, on the one side, and a lonely woman, backed by the sympathies of nature, on the other,—Hester Prynne set forth from her solitary cottage. Little Pearl, of course, was her companion. She was now of an age to run lightly along by her mother's side, and, constantly in motion, from morn till sunset, could have accomplished a much longer journey than that before her. Often, nevertheless, more from caprice than necessity, she demanded to be taken up in arms; but was soon as imperious to be set down again, and frisked onward before Hester on the grassy pathway, with many a harmless trip and tumble. We have spoken of Pearl's rich and luxuriant beauty; a beauty that shone with deep and vivid tints; a bright complexion, eyes possessing intensity both of depth and glow, and hair already of a deep, glossy brown, and which, in after years, would be nearly akin to black. There was fire in her and throughout her; she seemed the unpremeditated offshoot of a passionate moment. Her mother, in contriving the child's garb, had allowed the gorgeous tendencies of her imagination their full play; arraying her in a crimson velvet tunic, of a peculiar cut, abundantly embroidered with fantasies and flourishes of gold-thread. So much strength of coloring, which must have given a wan and pallid aspect to cheeks of a fainter bloom, was admirably adapted to Pearl's beauty, and made her the very brightest little jet of flame that ever danced upon the earth.

But it was a remarkable attribute of this garb, and, indeed, of the child's whole appearance, that it irresistibly and inevitably reminded the beholder of the token which Hester Prynne was doomed to wear upon her bosom. It was the scarlet letter in another form; the scarlet letter endowed with life! The mother herself—as if the red ignominy were so deeply scorched into her brain that all her conceptions assumed its form—had carefully wrought out the similitude; lavishing many hours of morbid ingenuity, to create an analogy between the object of her affection and the emblem of her guilt and torture. But, in truth, Pearl was the one, as well as the other; and only in consequence of that identity had Hester contrived so perfectly to represent the scarlet letter in her appearance.

As the two wayfarers came within the precincts of the town, the children of the Puritans looked up from their play,—or what passed for play with those sombre little urchins,—and spake gravely one to another:—

"Behold, verily, there is the woman of the scarlet letter; and, of a truth, moreover, there is the likeness of the scarlet letter running along by her side! Come, therefore, and let us fling mud at them!"

But Pearl, who was a dauntless child, after frowning, stamping her foot, and shaking her little hand with a variety of threatening gestures, suddenly made a rush at the knot of her enemies, and put them all to flight. She resembled, in her fierce pursuit of them, an infant pestilence,—the scarlet fever, or some such half-fledged angel of judgment,—whose mission was to punish the sins of the rising generation. She screamed and shouted, too, with a terrific volume of sound, which, doubtless, caused the hearts of the fugitives to quake within them. The victory accomplished, Pearl returned quietly to her mother, and looked up, smiling, into her face.

Without further adventure, they reached the dwelling of Governor Bellingham. This was a large wooden house, built in a fashion of which there are specimens still extant in the streets of our older towns; now moss-grown, crumbling to decay, and melancholy at heart with the many sorrowful or joyful occurrences, remembered or forgotten, that have happened, and passed away, within their dusky chambers. Then, however, there was the freshness of the passing year on its exterior, and the cheerfulness, gleaming forth from the sunny windows, of a human habitation, into which death had never entered. It had, indeed, a very cheery aspect; the walls being overspread with a kind of stucco, in which fragments of broken glass were plentifully intermixed; so that, when the sunshine fell aslant-wise over the front of the edifice, it glittered and sparkled as if diamonds had been flung against it by the double handful. The brilliancy might have befitted Aladdin's palace, rather than the mansion of a grave old Puritan ruler. It was further decorated with strange and seemingly cabalistic figures and diagrams, suitable to the quaint taste of the age, which had been drawn in the stucco when newly laid on, and had now grown hard and durable, for the admiration of after times.

Pearl, looking at this bright wonder of a house, began to caper and dance, and imperatively required that the whole breadth of sunshine should be stripped off its front, and given her to play with.

"No, my little Pearl!" said her mother. "Thou must gather thine own sunshine. I have none to give thee!"

They approached the door; which was of an arched form,

and flanked on each side by a narrow tower or projection of the edifice, in both of which were lattice-windows, with wooden shutters to close over them at need. Lifting the iron hammer that hung at the portal, Hester Prynne gave a summons, which was answered by one of the Governor's bond-servants; a free-born Englishman, but now a seven years' slave. During that term he was to be the property of his master, and as much a commodity of bargain and sale as an ox, or a joint-stool. The serf wore the blue coat, which was the customary garb of serving-men of that period, and long before, in the old hereditary halls of England.

"Is the worshipful Governor Bellingham within?" inquired Hester.

"Yea, forsooth," replied the bond-servant, staring with wide-open eyes at the scarlet letter, which, being a new-comer in the country, he had never before seen. "Yea, his honorable worship is within. But he hath a godly minister or two with him, and likewise a leech. Ye may not see his worship now."

"Nevertheless, I will enter," answered Hester Prynne, and the bond-servant, perhaps judging from the decision of her air, and the glittering symbol in her bosom, that she was a great lady in the land, offered no opposition.

So the mother and little Pearl were admitted into the hall of entrance. With many variations, suggested by the nature of his building-materials, diversity of climate, and a different mode of social life, Governor Bellingham had planned his new habitation after the residences of gentlemen of fair estate in his native land. Here, then, was a wide and reasonably lofty hall, extending through the whole depth of the house, and forming a medium of general communication, more or less directly, with all the other apartments. At one extremity, this spacious room was lighted by the windows of the two towers, which formed a small recess on either side of the portal. At the other end, though partly muffled by a curtain, it was more powerfully illuminated by one of those embowed hall-windows which we read of in old books, and which was provided with a deep and cushioned seat. Here, on the cushion, lay a folio tome, probably of the Chronicles of England, or other such substantial literature; even as, in our own days, we scatter gilded volumes on the centre-table, to be turned over by the casual guest. The furniture of the hall consisted of some ponderous chairs, the backs of which were elaborately carved with wreaths of oaken flowers; and likewise a table in the same taste; the whole being of the Elizabethan age, or perhaps earlier, and heirlooms, transferred hither from the Governor's paternal home. On the table—in token that the sentiment of old English hospitality had not been left behind—stood a large pewter tankard, at the bottom of which, had Hester or Pearl peeped into it, they might have seen the frothy remnant of a recent draught of ale.

On the wall hung a row of portraits, representing the forefathers of the Bellingham lineage, some with armor on their breasts, and others with stately ruffs and robes of peace. All were characterized by the sternness and severity which old portraits so invariably put on; as if they were the ghosts, rather than the pictures, of departed worthies, and were gazing with harsh and intolerant criticism at the pursuits and enjoyments of living men.

At about the centre of the oaken panels, that lined the hall, was suspended a suit of mail, not, like the pictures, an ancestral relic, but of the most modern date; for it had been manufactured by a skilful armorer in London, the same year in which Governor Bellingham came over to New England. There was a steel head-piece, a cuirass, a gorget, and greaves, with a pair of gauntlets and a sword hanging beneath; all, and especially the helmet and breastplate, so highly burnished as to glow with white radiance, and scatter an illumination everywhere about upon the floor. This bright panoply was not meant for mere idle show, but had been worn by the Governor on many a solemn muster and training field, and had glittered, moreover, at the head of a regiment in the Pequod war. For, though bred a lawyer, and accustomed to speak of Bacon, Coke, Noye, and Finch as his professional associates, the exigencies of this new country had transformed Governor Bellingham into a soldier, as well as a statesman and ruler.

Little Pearl—who was as greatly pleased with the gleaming armor as she had been with the glittering frontispiece of the house—spent some time looking into the polished mirror of the breastplate.

"Mother," cried she, "I see you here. Look! Look!"

Hester looked, by way of humoring the child; and she saw that, owing to the peculiar effect of this convex mirror, the scarlet letter was represented in exaggerated and gigantic proportions, so as to be greatly the most prominent feature of her appearance. In truth, she seemed absolutely hidden behind it. Pearl pointed upward, also, at a similar picture in the head-piece; smiling at her mother, with the elfish intelligence that was so familiar an expression on her small physiognomy. That look of naughty merriment was likewise reflected in the mirror, with so much breadth and intensity of effect, that it made Hester Prynne feel as if it could not be the image of her own child, but of an imp who was seeking to mould itself into Pearl's shape.

"Come along, Pearl," said she, drawing her away. "Come and look into this fair garden. It may be we shall see flowers there; more beautiful ones than we find in the woods."

Pearl, accordingly, ran to the bow-window, at the farther

end of the hall, and looked along the vista of a garden-walk, carpeted with closely shaven grass, and bordered with some rude and immature attempt at shrubbery. But the proprietor appeared already to have relinquished, as hopeless, the effort to perpetuate on this side of the Atlantic, in a hard soil and amid the close struggle for subsistence, the native English taste for ornamental gardening. Cabbages grew in plain sight; and a pumpkin-vine, rooted at some distance, had run across the intervening space, and deposited one of its gigantic products directly beneath the hall-window; as if to warn the Governor that this great lump of vegetable gold was as rich an ornament as New England earth would offer him. There were a few rose-bushes, however, and a number of apple-trees, probably the descendants of those planted by the Reverend Mr. Blackstone, the first settler of the peninsula; that half-mythological personage, who rides through our early annals, seated on the back of a bull.

Pearl, seeing the rose-bushes, began to cry for a red rose, and would not be pacified.

"Hush, child, hush!" said her mother, earnestly. "Do not cry, dear little Pearl! I hear voices in the garden. The Governor is coming, and gentlemen along with him!"

In fact, adown the vista of the garden avenue a number of persons were seen approaching towards the house. Pearl, in utter scorn of her mother's attempt to quiet her, gave an eldritch scream, and then became silent; not from any notion of obedience, but because the quick and mobile curiosity of her disposition was excited by the appearance of these new personages.

Chapter 8

Governor Bellingham, in a loose gown and easy cap,—such as elderly gentlemen loved to endue themselves with, in their domestic privacy,—walked foremost, and appeared to be showing off his estate, and expatiating on his projected improvements. The wide circumference of an elaborate ruff, beneath his gray beard, in the antiquated fashion of King James's reign, caused his head to look not a little like that of John the Baptist in a charger. The impression made by his aspect, so rigid and severe, and frost-bitten with more than autumnal age, was hardly in keeping with the appliances of worldly enjoyment wherewith he had evidently done his utmost to surround himself. But it is an error to suppose that our grave forefathers—though accustomed to speak and think of human existence as a state merely of trial and warfare, and though unfeignedly prepared to sacrifice goods and life at the behest of duty—made it a matter of conscience to reject such means of comfort, or even luxury, as lay fairly within their grasp. This creed was never taught, for instance, by the venerable pastor, John Wilson, whose beard, white as a snow-drift, was seen over Governor Bellingham's shoulder; while its wearer suggested that pears and peaches might yet be naturalized in the New England climate, and that purple grapes might possibly be compelled to nourish, against the sunny garden-wall. The old clergyman, nurtured at the rich bosom of the English Church, had a long-established and legitimate taste for all good and comfortable things; and however stern he might show himself in the pulpit, or in his public reproof of such transgressions as that of Hester Prynne, still the genial benevolence of his private life had won him warmer affection than was accorded to any of his professional contemporaries.

Behind the Governor and Mr. Wilson came two other guests: one the Reverend Arthur Dimmesdale, whom the reader may remember as having taken a brief and reluctant part in the scene of Hester Prynne's disgrace; and, in close companionship with him, old Roger Chillingworth, a person of great skill in physic, who, for two or three years past, had been settled in the town. It was understood that this learned man was the physician as well as friend of the young minister, whose health had severely suffered, of late, by his too unreserved self-sacrifice to the labors and duties of the pastoral relation.

The Governor, in advance of his visitors, ascended one or two steps, and, throwing open the leaves of the great hall-window, found himself close to little Pearl. The shadow of the curtain fell on Hester Prynne, and partially concealed her.

"What have we here?" said Governor Bellingham, looking with surprise at the scarlet little figure before him. "I profess, I have never seen the like, since my days of vanity, in old King James's time, when I was wont to esteem it a high favor to be admitted to a court mask! There used to be a swarm of these small apparitions, in holiday time; and we called them children of the Lord of Misrule. But how gat such a guest into my hall?"

"Ay, indeed!" cried good old Mr. Wilson. "What little bird of scarlet plumage may this be? Methinks I have seen just such figures, when the sun has been shining through a richly painted window, and tracing out the golden and crimson images across the floor. But that was in the old land. Prithee, young one, who art thou, and what has ailed thy mother to bedizen thee in this strange fashion? Art thou a Christian child,—ha? Dost know thy catechism? Or art thou one of those naughty elfs or fairies, whom we thought to have left behind us, with other relics of Papistry, in merry old England?"

"I am mother's child," answered the scarlet vision, "and my name is Pearl!"

"Pearl?—Ruby, rather!—or Coral!—or Red Rose, at the very least, judging from thy hue!" responded the old minister, putting forth his hand in a vain attempt to pat little Pearl on the cheek. "But where is this mother of thine? Ah! I see," he added; and, turning to Governor Bellingham, whispered, "This is the selfsame child of whom we have held speech together; and behold here the unhappy woman, Hester Prynne, her mother!"

"Sayest thou so?" cried the Governor. "Nay, we might have judged that such a child's mother must needs be a scarlet woman, and a worthy type of her of Babylon! But she comes at a good time; and we will look into this matter forthwith."

Governor Bellingham stepped through the window into the hall, followed by his three guests.

"Hester Prynne," said he, fixing his naturally stern regard on the wearer of the scarlet letter, "there hath been much question concerning thee, of late. The point hath been weightily discussed, whether we, that are of authority and influence, do well discharge our consciences by trusting an immortal soul, such as there is in yonder child, to the guidance of one who hath stumbled and fallen, amid the pitfalls of this world. Speak thou, the child's own mother! Were it not, thinkest thou, for thy little one's temporal and eternal welfare that she be taken out of thy charge, and clad soberly, and disciplined strictly, and instructed in the truths of heaven and earth? What canst thou do for the child, in this kind?"

"I can teach my little Pearl what I have learned from this!" answered Hester Prynne, laying her finger on the red token.

"Woman, it is thy badge of shame!" replied the stern magistrate. "It is because of the stain which that letter indicates, that we would transfer thy child to other hands."

"Nevertheless," said the mother, calmly, though growing more pale, "this badge hath taught me—it daily teaches me—it is teaching me at this moment—lessons whereof my child may be the wiser and better, albeit they can profit nothing to myself."

"We will judge warily," said Bellingham, "and look well what we are about to do. Good Master Wilson, I pray you, examine this Pearl,—since that is her name,—and see whether she hath had such Christian nurture as befits a child of her age."

The old minister seated himself in an arm-chair, and made an effort to draw Pearl betwixt his knees. But the child, unaccustomed to the touch or familiarity of any but her mother, escaped through the open window, and stood on the upper step, looking like a wild tropical bird, of rich plumage, ready to take flight into the upper air. Mr. Wilson, not a little astonished at this outbreak,—for he was a grandfatherly sort of personage, and usually a vast favorite with children,—essayed, however, to proceed with the examination.

"Pearl," said he, with great solemnity, "thou must take heed to instruction, that so, in due season, thou mayest wear in thy bosom the pearl of great price. Canst thou tell me, my child, who made thee?"

Now Pearl knew well enough who made her; for Hester Prynne, the daughter of a pious home, very soon after her talk with the child about her Heavenly Father, had begun to inform her of those truths which the human spirit, at whatever stage of immaturity, imbibes with such eager interest. Pearl, therefore, so large were the attainments of her three years' lifetime, could have borne a fair examination in the New England Primer, or the first column of the Westminster Catechisms, although unacquainted with the outward form of either of those celebrated works. But that perversity which all children have more or less of, and of which little Pearl had a tenfold portion, now, at the most inopportune moment, took thorough possession of her, and closed her lips, or impelled her to speak words amiss. After putting her finger in her mouth, with many ungracious refusals to answer good Mr. Wilson's question, the child finally announced that she had not been made at all, but had been plucked by her mother off the bush of wild roses that grew by the prison-door.

This fantasy was probably suggested by the near proximity of the Governor's red roses, as Pearl stood outside of the window; together with her recollection of the prison rose-bush, which she had passed in coming hither.

Old Roger Chillingworth, with a smile on his face, whispered something in the young clergyman's ear. Hester Prynne looked at the man of skill, and even then, with her fate hanging in the balance, was startled to perceive what a change had come over his features,—how much uglier they were,—how his dark complexion seemed to have grown duskier, and his figure more misshapen,—since the days when she had familiarly known him. She met his eyes for an instant, but was immediately constrained to give all her attention to the scene now going forward.

"This is awful!" cried the Governor, slowly recovering from the astonishment into which Pearl's response had thrown him. "Here is a child of three years old, and she cannot tell who made her! Without question, she is equally in the dark as to her soul, its present depravity, and future destiny! Methinks, gentlemen, we need inquire no further."

Hester caught hold of Pearl, and drew her forcibly into her arms, confronting the old Puritan magistrate with almost a fierce expression. Alone in the world, cast off by it, and with this sole treasure to keep her heart alive, she felt that she possessed indefeasible rights against the world, and was ready to defend them to the death.

"God gave me the child!" cried she. "He gave her in requital of all things else, which ye had taken from me. She is my happiness!—she is my torture, none the less! Pearl keeps me here in life! Pearl punishes me too! See ye not, she is the scarlet letter, only capable of being loved, and so endowed with a million-fold the power of retribution for my sin? Ye shall not take her! I will die first!"

"My poor woman," said the not unkind old minister, "the child shall be well cared for!—far better than thou canst do it!"

"God gave her into my keeping," repeated Hester Prynne, raising her voice almost to a shriek. "I will not give her up!"—And here, by a sudden impulse, she turned to the young clergyman, Mr. Dimmesdale, at whom, up to this moment, she had seemed hardly so much as once to direct her eyes.—"Speak thou for me!" cried she. "Thou wast my pastor, and hadst charge of my soul, and knowest me better than these men can. I will not lose the child! Speak for me! Thou knowest,—for thou hast sympathies which these men lack!—thou knowest what is in my heart, and what are a mother's rights, and how much the stronger they are, when that mother has but her child and the scarlet letter! Look thou to it! I will not lose the child! Look to it!"

At this wild and singular appeal, which indicated that Hester Prynne's situation had provoked her to little less than madness, the young minister at once came forward, pale, and holding his hand over his heart, as was his custom whenever his peculiarly nervous temperament was thrown into agitation. He looked now more care-worn and emaciated than as we described him at the scene of Hester's public ignominy; and whether it were his failing health, or whatever the cause might be, his large dark eyes had a world of pain in their troubled and melancholy depth.

"There is truth in what she says," began the minister, with a voice sweet, tremulous, but powerful, insomuch that the hall re-echoed, and the hollow armor rang with it, — "truth in what Hester says, and in the feeling which inspires her! God gave her the child, and gave her, too, an instinctive knowledge of its nature and requirements, — both seemingly so peculiar, — which no other mortal being can possess. And, moreover, is there not a quality of awful sacredness in the relation between this mother and this child?"

"Ay! — how is that, good Master Dimmesdale?" interrupted the Governor. "Make that plain, I pray you!"

"It must be even so," resumed the minister. "For, if we deem it otherwise, do we not thereby say that the Heavenly Father, the Creator of all flesh, hath lightly recognized a deed of sin, and made of no account the distinction between unhallowed lust and holy love? This child of its father's guilt and its mother's shame hath come from the hand of God, to work in many ways upon her heart, who pleads so earnestly, and with such bitterness of spirit, the right to keep her. It was meant for a blessing; for the one blessing of her life! It was meant, doubtless, as the mother herself hath told us, for a retribution too; a torture to be felt at many an unthought-of moment; a pang, a sting, an ever-recurring agony, in the midst of a troubled joy! Hath she not expressed this thought in the garb of the poor child, so forcibly reminding us of that red symbol which sears her bosom?"

"Well said, again!" cried good Mr. Wilson. "I feared the woman had no better thought than to make a mountebank of her child!"

"O, not so!—not so!" continued Mr. Dimmesdale. "She recognizes, believe me, the solemn miracle which God hath wrought, in the existence of that child. And may she feel, too,—what, methinks, is the very truth,—that this boon was meant, above all things else, to keep the mother's soul alive, and to preserve her from blacker depths of sin into which Satan might else have sought to plunge her! Therefore it is good for this poor, sinful woman that she hath an infant immortality, a being capable of eternal joy or sorrow, confided to her care,—to be trained up by her to righteousness,—to remind her, at every moment, of her fall,—but yet to teach her, as it were by the Creator's sacred pledge, that, if she bring the child to heaven, the child also will bring its parent thither! Herein is the sinful mother happier than the sinful father. For Hester Prynne's sake, then, and no less for the poor child's sake, let us leave them as Providence hath seen fit to place them!"

"You speak, my friend, with a strange earnestness," said old Roger Chillingworth, smiling at him.

"And there is a weighty import in what my young brother hath spoken," added the Reverend Mr. Wilson. "What say you, worshipful Master Bellingham? Hath he not pleaded well for the poor woman?"

"Indeed hath he," answered the magistrate, "and hath adduced such arguments, that we will even leave the matter as it now stands; so long, at least, as there shall be no further scandal in the woman. Care must be had, nevertheless, to put the child to due and stated examination in the catechism, at thy hands or Master Dimmesdale's. Moreover, at a proper season, the tithing-men must take heed that she go both to school and to meeting."

The young minister, on ceasing to speak, had withdrawn a few steps from the group, and stood with his face partially concealed in the heavy folds of the window-curtain; while the shadow of his figure, which the sunlight cast upon the floor, was tremulous with the vehemence of his appeal. Pearl, that wild and flighty little elf, stole softly towards him, and taking his hand in the grasp of both her own, laid her cheek against it; a caress so tender, and withal so unobtrusive, that her mother, who was looking on, asked herself, — "Is that my Pearl?" Yet she knew that there was love in the child's heart, although it mostly revealed itself in passion, and hardly twice in her lifetime had been softened by such gentleness as now. The minister, — for, save the long-sought regards of woman, nothing is sweeter than these marks of childish preference, accorded spontaneously by a spiritual instinct, and therefore seeming to imply in us something truly worthy to be loved, — the minister looked round, laid his hand on the child's head, hesitated an instant, and then kissed her brow. Little Pearl's unwonted mood of sentiment lasted no longer; she laughed, and went capering down the hall, so airily, that old Mr. Wilson raised a question whether even her tiptoes touched the floor.

"The little baggage hath witchcraft in her, I profess," said he to Mr. Dimmesdale. "She needs no old woman's broomstick to fly withal!"

"A strange child!" remarked old Roger Chillingworth. "It is easy to see the mother's part in her. Would it be beyond a philosopher's research, think ye, gentlemen, to analyze that child's nature, and, from its make and mould, to give a shrewd guess at the father?"

"Nay; it would be sinful, in such a question, to follow the clew of profane philosophy," said Mr. Wilson. "Better to fast and pray upon it; and still better, it may be, to leave the mystery as we find it, unless Providence reveal it of its own accord. Thereby, every good Christian man hath a title to show a father's kindness towards the poor, deserted babe."

The affair being so satisfactorily concluded, Hester Prynne, with Pearl, departed from the house. As they descended the steps, it is averred that the lattice of a chamber-window was thrown open, and forth into the sunny day was thrust the face of Mistress Hibbins, Governor Bellingham's bitter-tempered sister, and the same who, a few years later, was executed as a witch.

"Hist, hist!" said she, while her ill-omened physiognomy seemed to cast a shadow over the cheerful newness of the house. "Wilt thou go with us to-night? There will be a merry company in the forest; and I wellnigh promised the Black Man that comely Hester Prynne should make one."

"Make my excuse to him, so please you!" answered Hester, with a triumphant smile. "I must tarry at home, and keep watch over my little Pearl. Had they taken her from me, I would willingly have gone with thee into the forest, and signed my name in the Black Man's book too, and that with mine own blood!"

"We shall have thee there anon!" said the witch-lady, frowning, as she drew back her head.

But here—if we suppose this interview betwixt Mistress Hibbins and Hester Prynne to be authentic, and not a parable—was already an illustration of the young minister's argument against sundering the relation of a fallen mother to the offspring of her frailty. Even thus early had the child saved her from Satan's snare.

Chapter 9

$\mathcal{U}$nder the appellation of Roger Chillingworth, the reader will remember, was hidden another name, which its former wearer had resolved should never more be spoken. It has been related, how, in the crowd that witnessed Hester Prynne's ignominious exposure, stood a man, elderly, travel-worn, who, just emerging from the perilous wilderness, beheld the woman, in whom he hoped to find embodied the warmth and cheerfulness of home, set up as a type of sin before the people. Her matronly fame was trodden under all men's feet. Infamy was babbling around her in the public market-place. For her kindred, should the tidings ever reach them, and for the companions of her unspotted life, there remained nothing but the contagion of her dishonor; which would not fail to be distributed in strict accordance and proportion with the intimacy and sacredness of their previous relationship. Then why—since the choice was with himself—should the individual, whose connection with the fallen woman had been the most intimate and sacred of them all, come forward to vindicate his claim to an inheritance so little desirable? He resolved not to be pilloried beside her on her pedestal of shame. Unknown to all but Hester Prynne, and possessing the lock and key of her silence, he chose to withdraw his name from the roll of mankind, and, as regarded his former ties and interests, to vanish out of life as completely as if he indeed lay at the bottom of the ocean, whither rumor had long ago consigned him. This purpose once effected, new interests would immediately spring up, and likewise a new purpose; dark, it is true, if not guilty, but of force enough to engage the full strength of his faculties.

In pursuance of this resolve, he took up his residence in the Puritan town, as Roger Chillingworth, without other introduction than the learning and intelligence of which he possessed more than a common measure. As his studies, at a previous period of his life, had made him extensively acquainted with the medical science of the day, it was as a physician that he presented himself, and as such was cordially received. Skilful men, of the medical and chirurgical profession, were of rare occurrence in the colony. They seldom, it would appear, partook of the religious zeal that brought other emigrants across the Atlantic. In their researches into the human frame, it may be that the higher and more subtile faculties of such men were materialized, and that they lost the spiritual view of existence amid the intricacies of that wondrous mechanism, which seemed to involve art enough to comprise all of life within itself. At all events, the health of the good town of Boston, so far as medicine had aught to do with it, had hitherto lain in the guardianship of an aged deacon and apothecary, whose piety and godly deportment were stronger testimonials in his favor than any that he could have produced in the shape of a diploma. The only surgeon was one who combined the occasional exercise of that noble art with the daily and habitual flourish of a razor. To such a professional body Roger Chillingworth was a brilliant acquisition. He soon manifested his familiarity with the ponderous and imposing machinery of antique physic; in which every remedy contained a multitude of far-fetched and heterogeneous ingredients, as elaborately compounded as if the proposed result had been the Elixir of Life. In his Indian captivity, moreover, he had gained much knowledge of the properties of native herbs and roots; nor did he conceal from his patients, that these simple medicines, Nature's boon to the untutored savage, had quite as large a share of his own confidence as the European pharmacopœia, which so many learned doctors had spent centuries in elaborating.

This learned stranger was exemplary, as regarded, at least, the outward forms of a religious life, and, early after his arrival, had chosen for his spiritual guide the Reverend Mr. Dimmesdale. The young divine, whose scholar-like renown still lived in Oxford, was considered by his more fervent admirers as little less than a heaven-ordained apostle, destined, should he live and labor for the ordinary term of life, to do as great deeds for the now feeble New England Church, as the early Fathers had achieved for the infancy of the Christian faith. About this period, however, the health of Mr. Dimmesdale had evidently begun to fail. By those best acquainted with his habits, the paleness of the young minister's cheek was accounted for by his too earnest devotion to study, his scrupulous fulfilment of parochial duty, and, more than all, by the fasts and vigils of which he made a frequent practice, in order to keep the grossness of this earthly state from clogging and obscuring his spiritual lamp. Some declared, that, if Mr. Dimmesdale were really going to die, it was cause enough, that the world was not worthy to be any longer trodden by his feet. He himself, on the other hand, with characteristic humility, avowed his belief, that, if Providence should see fit to remove him, it would be because of his own unworthiness to perform its humblest mission here on earth. With all this difference of opinion as to the cause of his decline, there could be no question of the fact. His form grew emaciated; his voice, though still rich and sweet, had a certain melancholy prophecy of decay in it; he was often observed, on any slight alarm or other sudden accident, to put his hand over his heart, with first a flush and then a paleness, indicative of pain.

Such was the young clergyman's condition, and so imminent the prospect that his dawning light would be extinguished, all untimely, when Roger Chillingworth made his advent to the town. His first entry on the scene, few people could tell whence, dropping down, as it were, out of the sky, or starting from the nether earth, had an aspect of mystery, which was easily heightened to the miraculous. He was now known to be a man of skill; it was observed that he gathered herbs, and the blossoms of wild-flowers, and dug up roots, and plucked off twigs from the forest-trees, like one acquainted with hidden virtues in what was valueless to common eyes. He was heard to speak of Sir Kenelm Digby, and other famous men,—whose scientific attainments were esteemed hardly less than supernatural,—as having been his correspondents or associates. Why, with such rank in the learned world, had he come hither? What could he, whose sphere was in great cities, be seeking in the wilderness? In answer to this query, a rumor gained ground,—and, however absurd, was entertained by some very sensible people,—that Heaven had wrought an absolute miracle, by transporting an eminent Doctor of Physic, from a German university, bodily through the air, and setting him down at the door of Mr. Dimmesdale's study! Individuals of wiser faith, indeed, who knew that Heaven promotes its purposes without aiming at the stage-effect of what is called miraculous interposition, were inclined to see a providential hand in Roger Chillingworth's so opportune arrival.

This idea was countenanced by the strong interest which the physician ever manifested in the young clergyman; he attached himself to him as a parishioner, and sought to win a friendly regard and confidence from his naturally reserved sensibility. He expressed great alarm at his pastor's state of health, but was anxious to attempt the cure, and, if early undertaken, seemed not despondent of a favorable result. The elders, the deacons, the motherly dames, and the young and fair maidens, of Mr. Dimmesdale's flock, were alike importunate that he should make trial of the physician's frankly offered skill. Mr. Dimmesdale gently repelled their entreaties.

"I need no medicine," said he.

But how could the young minister say so, when, with every successive Sabbath, his cheek was paler and thinner, and his voice more tremulous than before,—when it had now become a constant habit, rather than a casual gesture, to press his hand over his heart? Was he weary of his labors? Did he wish to die? These questions were solemnly propounded to Mr. Dimmesdale by the elder ministers of Boston and the deacons of his church, who, to use their own phrase, "dealt with him" on the sin of rejecting the aid which Providence so manifestly held out. He listened in silence, and finally promised to confer with the physician.

"Were it God's will," said the Reverend Mr. Dimmesdale, when, in fulfilment of this pledge, he requested old Roger Chillingworth's professional advice, "I could be well content, that my labors, and my sorrows, and my sins, and my pains, should shortly end with me, and what is earthly of them be buried in my grave, and the spiritual go with me to my eternal state, rather than that you should put your skill to the proof in my behalf."

"Ah," replied Roger Chillingworth, with that quietness which, whether imposed or natural, marked all his deportment, "it is thus that a young clergyman is apt to speak. Youthful men, not having taken a deep root, give up their hold of life so easily! And saintly men, who walk with God on earth, would fain be away, to walk with him on the golden pavements of the New Jerusalem."

"Nay," rejoined the young minister, putting his hand to his heart, with a flush of pain flitting over his brow, "were I worthier to walk there, I could be better content to toil here."

"Good men ever interpret themselves too meanly," said the physician.

In this manner, the mysterious old Roger Chillingworth became the medical adviser of the Reverend Mr. Dimmesdale. As not only the disease interested the physician, but he was strongly moved to look into the character and qualities of the patient, these two men, so different in age, came gradually to spend much time together. For the sake of the minister's health, and to enable the leech to gather plants with healing balm in them, they took long walks on the sea-shore, or in the forest; mingling various talk with the plash and murmur of the waves, and the solemn wind-anthem among the tree-tops. Often, likewise, one was the guest of the other, in his place of study and retirement. There was a fascination for the minister in the company of the man of science, in whom he recognized an intellectual cultivation of no moderate depth or scope; together with a range and freedom of ideas, that he would have vainly looked for among the members of his own profession. In truth, he was startled, if not shocked, to find this attribute in the physician. Mr. Dimmesdale was a true priest, a true religionist, with the reverential sentiment largely developed, and an order of mind that impelled itself powerfully along the track of a creed, and wore its passage continually deeper with the lapse of time. In no state of society would he have been what is called a man of liberal views; it would always be essential to his peace to feel the pressure of a faith about him, supporting, while it confined him within its iron framework. Not the less, however, though with a tremulous enjoyment, did he feel the occasional relief of looking at the universe through the medium of another kind of intellect than those with which he habitually held converse. It was as if a window were thrown open, admitting a freer atmosphere into the close and stifled study, where his life was wasting itself away, amid lamplight, or obstructed day-beams, and the musty fragrance, be it sensual or moral, that exhales from books. But the air was too fresh and chill to be long breathed with comfort. So the minister, and the physician with him, withdrew again within the limits of what their church defined as orthodox.

Thus Roger Chillingworth scrutinized his patient carefully, both as he saw him in his ordinary life, keeping an accustomed pathway in the range of thoughts familiar to him, and as he appeared when thrown amidst other moral scenery, the novelty of which might call out something new to the surface of his character. He deemed it essential, it would seem, to know the man, before attempting to do him good. Wherever there is a heart and an intellect, the diseases of the physical frame are tinged with the peculiarities of these. In Arthur Dimmesdale, thought and imagination were so active, and sensibility so intense, that the bodily infirmity would be likely to have its groundwork there. So Roger Chillingworth—the man of skill, the kind and friendly physician—strove to go deep into his patient's bosom, delving among his principles, prying into his recollections, and probing everything with a cautious touch, like a treasure-seeker in a dark cavern. Few secrets can escape an investigator, who has opportunity and license to undertake such a quest, and skill to follow it up. A man burdened with a secret should especially avoid the intimacy of his physician. If the latter possess native sagacity, and a nameless something more,—let us call it intuition; if he show no intrusive egotism, nor disagreeably prominent characteristics of his own; if he have the power, which must be born with him, to bring his mind into such affinity with his patient's, that this last shall unawares have spoken what he imagines himself only to have thought; if such revelations be received without tumult, and acknowledged not so often by an uttered sympathy as by silence, an inarticulate breath, and here and there a word, to indicate that all is understood; if to these qualifications of a confidant be joined the advantages afforded by his recognized character as a physician;—then, at some inevitable moment, will the soul of the sufferer be dissolved, and flow forth in a dark, but transparent stream, bringing all its mysteries into the daylight.

Roger Chillingworth possessed all, or most, of the attributes above enumerated. Nevertheless, time went on; a kind of intimacy, as we have said, grew up between these two cultivated minds, which had as wide a field as the whole sphere of human thought and study, to meet upon; they discussed every topic of ethics and religion, of public affairs and private character; they talked much, on both sides, of matters that seemed personal to themselves; and yet no secret, such as the physician fancied must exist there, ever stole out of the minister's consciousness into his companion's ear. The latter had his suspicions, indeed, that even the nature of Mr. Dimmesdale's bodily disease had never fairly been revealed to him. It was a strange reserve!

After a time, at a hint from Roger Chillingworth, the friends of Mr. Dimmesdale effected an arrangement by which the two were lodged in the same house; so that every ebb and flow of the minister's life-tide might pass under the eye of his anxious and attached physician. There was much joy throughout the town, when this greatly desirable object was attained. It was held to be the best possible measure for the young clergyman's welfare; unless, indeed, as often urged by such as felt authorized to do so, he had selected some one of the many blooming damsels, spiritually devoted to him, to become his devoted wife. This latter step, however, there was no present prospect that Arthur Dimmesdale would be prevailed upon to take; he rejected all suggestions of the kind, as if priestly celibacy were one of his articles of church-discipline. Doomed by his own choice, therefore, as Mr. Dimmesdale so evidently was, to eat his unsavory morsel always at another's board, and endure the life-long chill which must be his lot who seeks to warm himself only at another's fireside, it truly seemed that this sagacious, experienced, benevolent old physician, with his concord of paternal and reverential love for the young pastor, was the very man, of all mankind, to be constantly within reach of his voice.

The new abode of the two friends was with a pious widow, of good social rank, who dwelt in a house covering pretty nearly the site on which the venerable structure of King's Chapel has since been built. It had the graveyard, originally Isaac Johnson's home-field, on one side, and so was well adapted to call up serious reflections, suited to their respective employments, in both minister and man of physic. The motherly care of the good widow assigned to Mr. Dimmesdale a front apartment, with a sunny exposure, and heavy window-curtains, to create a noontide shadow, when desirable. The walls were hung round with tapestry, said to be from the Gobelin looms, and, at all events, representing the Scriptural story of David and Bathsheba, and Nathan the Prophet, in colors still unfaded, but which made the fair woman of the scene almost as grimly picturesque as the woe-denouncing seer. Here the pale clergyman piled up his library, rich with parchment-bound folios of the Fathers, and the lore of Rabbis, and monkish erudition, of which the Protestant divines, even while they vilified and decried that class of writers, were yet constrained often to avail themselves. On the other side of the house old Roger Chillingworth arranged his study and laboratory; not such as a modern man of science would reckon even tolerably complete, but provided with a distilling apparatus, and the means of compounding drugs and chemicals, which the practised alchemist knew well how to turn to purpose. With such commodiousness of situation, these two learned persons sat themselves down, each in his own domain, yet familiarly passing from one apartment to the other, and bestowing a mutual and not incurious inspection into one another's business.

And the Reverend Arthur Dimmesdale's best discerning friends, as we have intimated, very reasonably imagined that the hand of Providence had done all this, for the purpose—besought in so many public, and domestic, and secret prayers—of restoring the young minister to health. But—it must now be said—another portion of the community had latterly begun to take its own view of the relation betwixt Mr. Dimmesdale and the mysterious old physician. When an uninstructed multitude attempts to see with its eyes, it is exceedingly apt to be deceived. When, however, it forms its judgment, as it usually does, on the intuitions of its great and warm heart, the conclusions thus attained are often so profound and so unerring, as to possess the character of truths supernaturally revealed. The people, in the case of which we speak, could justify its prejudice against Roger Chillingworth by no fact or argument worthy of serious refutation. There was an aged handicraftsman, it is true, who had been a citizen of London at the period of Sir Thomas Overbury's murder, now some thirty years agone; he testified to having seen the physician, under some other name, which the narrator of the story had now forgotten, in company with Doctor Forman, the famous old conjurer, who was implicated in the affair of Overbury. Two or three individuals hinted, that the man of skill, during his Indian captivity, had enlarged his medical attainments by joining in the incantations of the savage priests; who were universally acknowledged to be powerful enchanters, often performing seemingly miraculous cures by their skill in the black art. A large number—and many of these were persons of such sober sense and practical observation that their opinions would have been valuable, in other matters—affirmed that Roger Chillingworth's aspect had undergone a remarkable change while he had dwelt in town, and especially since his abode with Mr. Dimmesdale.

At first, his expression had been calm, meditative, scholar-like. Now, there was something ugly and evil in his face, which they had not previously noticed, and which grew still the more obvious to sight, the oftener they looked upon him. According to the vulgar idea, the fire in his laboratory had been brought from the lower regions, and was fed with infernal fuel; and so, as might be expected, his visage was getting sooty with the smoke.

To sum up the matter, it grew to be a widely diffused opinion, that the Reverend Arthur Dimmesdale, like many other personages of especial sanctity, in all ages of the Christian world, was haunted either by Satan himself, or Satan's emissary, in the guise of old Roger Chillingworth. This diabolical agent had the Divine permission, for a season, to burrow into the clergyman's intimacy, and plot against his soul. No sensible man, it was confessed, could doubt on which side the victory would turn. The people looked, with an unshaken hope, to see the minister come forth out of the conflict, transfigured with the glory which he would unquestionably win. Meanwhile, nevertheless, it was sad to think of the perchance mortal agony through which he must struggle towards his triumph.

Alas! to judge from the gloom and terror in the depths of the poor minister's eyes, the battle was a sore one and the victory anything but secure.

Chapter 10

Old Roger Chillingworth, throughout life, had been calm in temperament, kindly, though not of warm affections, but ever, and in all his relations with the world, a pure and upright man. He had begun an investigation, as he imagined, with the severe and equal integrity of a judge, desirous only of truth, even as if the question involved no more than the air-drawn lines and figures of a geometrical problem, instead of human passions, and wrongs inflicted on himself. But, as he proceeded, a terrible fascination, a kind of fierce, though still calm, necessity, seized the old man within its gripe, and never set him free again, until he had done all its bidding. He now dug into the poor clergyman's heart, like a miner searching for gold; or, rather, like a sexton delving into a grave, possibly in quest of a jewel that had been buried on the dead man's bosom, but likely to find nothing save mortality and corruption. Alas for his own soul, if these were what he sought!

Sometimes, a light glimmered out of the physician's eyes, burning blue and ominous, like the reflection of a furnace, or, let us say, like one of those gleams of ghastly fire that darted from Bunyan's awful doorway in the hillside, and quivered on the pilgrim's face. The soil where this dark miner was working had perchance shown indications that encouraged him.

"This man," said he, at one such moment, to himself, "pure as they deem him,—all spiritual as he seems,—hath inherited a strong animal nature from his father or his mother. Let us dig a little further in the direction of this vein!"

Then, after long search into the minister's dim interior, and turning over many precious materials, in the shape of high aspirations for the welfare of his race, warm love of souls, pure sentiments, natural piety, strengthened by thought and study, and illuminated by revelation,—all of which invaluable gold was perhaps no better than rubbish to the seeker,—he would turn back, discouraged, and begin his quest towards another point. He groped along as stealthily, with as cautious a tread, and as wary an outlook, as a thief entering a chamber where a man lies only half asleep,—or, it may be, broad awake,—with purpose to steal the very treasure which this man guards as the apple of his eye. In spite of his premeditated carefulness, the floor would now and then creak; his garments would rustle; the shadow of his presence, in a forbidden proximity, would be thrown across his victim. In other words, Mr. Dimmesdale, whose sensibility of nerve often produced the effect of spiritual intuition, would become vaguely aware that something inimical to his peace had thrust itself into relation with him. But old Roger Chillingworth, too, had perceptions that were almost intuitive; and when the minister threw his startled eyes towards him, there the physician sat; his kind, watchful, sympathizing, but never intrusive friend.

Yet Mr. Dimmesdale would perhaps have seen this individual's character more perfectly, if a certain morbidness, to which, sick hearts are liable, had not rendered him suspicious of all mankind. Trusting no man as his friend, he could not recognize his enemy when the latter actually appeared. He therefore still kept up a familiar intercourse with him, daily receiving the old physician in his study; or visiting the laboratory, and, for recreation's sake, watching the processes by which weeds were converted into drugs of potency.

One day, leaning his forehead on his hand, and his elbow

on the sill of the open window, that looked towards the graveyard, he talked with Roger Chillingworth, while the old man was examining a bundle of unsightly plants.

"Where," asked he, with a look askance at them, — for it was the clergyman's peculiarity that he seldom, nowadays, looked straightforth at any object, whether human or inanimate, — "where, my kind doctor, did you gather those herbs, with such a dark, flabby leaf?"

"Even in the graveyard here at hand," answered the physician, continuing his employment. "They are new to me. I found them growing on a grave, which bore no tombstone, nor other memorial of the dead man, save these ugly weeds, that have taken upon themselves to keep him in remembrance. They grew out of his heart, and typify, it may be, some hideous secret that was buried with him, and which he had done better to confess during his lifetime."

"Perchance," said Mr. Dimmesdale, "he earnestly desired it, but could not."

"And wherefore?" rejoined the physician. "Wherefore not; since all the powers of nature call so earnestly for the confession of sin, that these black weeds have sprung up out of a buried heart, to make manifest an unspoken crime?"

"That, good Sir, is but a fantasy of yours," replied the minister. "There can be, if I forebode aright, no power, short of the Divine mercy, to disclose, whether by uttered words, or by type or emblem, the secrets that may be buried with a human heart. The heart, making itself guilty of such secrets, must perforce hold them, until the day when all hidden things shall be revealed. Nor have I so read or interpreted Holy Writ, as to understand that the disclosure of human thoughts and deeds, then to be made, is intended as a part of the retribution. That, surely, were a shallow view of it. No; these revelations, unless I greatly err, are meant merely to promote the intellectual satisfaction of all intelligent beings, who will stand waiting, on that day, to see the dark problem of this life made plain. A knowledge of men's hearts will be needful to the completest solution of that problem. And I conceive, moreover, that the hearts holding such miserable secrets as you speak of will yield them up, at that last day, not with reluctance, but with a joy unutterable."

"Then why not reveal them here?" asked Roger Chillingworth, glancing quietly aside at the minister. "Why should not the guilty ones sooner avail themselves of this unutterable solace?"

"They mostly do," said the clergyman, griping hard at his breast as if afflicted with an importunate throb of pain. "Many, many a poor soul hath given its confidence to me, not only on the death-bed, but while strong in life, and fair in reputation. And ever, after such an outpouring, O, what a relief have I witnessed in those sinful brethren! even as in one who at last draws free air, after long stifling with his own polluted breath. How can it be otherwise? Why should a wretched man, guilty, we will say, of murder, prefer to keep the dead corpse buried in his own heart, rather than fling it forth at once, and let the universe take care of it!"

"Yet some men bury their secrets thus," observed the calm physician.

"True; there are such men," answered Mr. Dimmesdale. "But, not to suggest more obvious reasons, it may be that they are kept silent by the very constitution of their nature. Or,—can we not suppose it?—guilty as they may be, retaining, nevertheless, a zeal for God's glory and man's welfare, they shrink from displaying themselves black and filthy in the view of men; because, thenceforward, no good can be achieved by them; no evil of the past be redeemed by better service. So, to their own unutterable torment, they go about among their fellow-creatures, looking pure as new-fallen snow while their hearts are all speckled and spotted with iniquity of which they cannot rid themselves."

"These men deceive themselves," said Roger Chillingworth, with somewhat more emphasis than usual, and making a slight gesture with his forefinger. "They fear to take up the shame that rightfully belongs to them. Their love for man, their zeal for God's service,—these holy impulses may or may not coexist in their hearts with the evil inmates to which their guilt has unbarred the door, and which must needs propagate a hellish breed within them. But, if they seek to glorify God, let them not lift heavenward their unclean hands! If they would serve their fellow-men, let them do it by making manifest the power and reality of conscience, in constraining them to penitential self-abasement! Wouldst thou have me to believe, O wise and pious friend, that a false show can be better—can be more for God's glory, or man's welfare—than God's own truth? Trust me, such men deceive themselves!"

"It may be so," said the young clergyman, indifferently, as waiving a discussion that he considered irrelevant or unseasonable. He had a ready faculty, indeed, of escaping from any topic that agitated his too sensitive and nervous temperament.—"But, now, I would ask of my well-skilled physician, whether, in good sooth, he deems me to have profited by his kindly care of this weak frame of mine?"

Before Roger Chillingworth could answer, they heard the clear, wild laughter of a young child's voice, proceeding from the adjacent burial-ground. Looking instinctively from the open window,—for it was summer-time,—the minister beheld Hester Prynne and little Pearl passing along the footpath that traversed the enclosure. Pearl looked as beautiful as the day, but was in one of those moods of perverse merriment which, whenever they occurred, seemed to remove her entirely out of the sphere of sympathy or human contact. She now skipped irreverently from one grave to another; until, coming to the broad, flat, armorial tombstone of a departed worthy,—perhaps of Isaac Johnson himself,—she began to dance upon it. In reply to her mother's command and entreaty that she would behave more decorously, little Pearl paused to gather the prickly burrs from a tall burdock which grew beside the tomb. Taking a handful of these, she arranged them along the lines of the scarlet letter that decorated the maternal bosom, to which the burrs, as their nature was, tenaciously adhered. Hester did not pluck them off.

Roger Chillingworth had by this time approached the window, and smiled grimly down.

"There is no law, nor reverence for authority, no regard for human ordinances or opinions, right or wrong, mixed up with that child's composition," remarked he, as much to himself as to his companion. "I saw her, the other day, bespatter the Governor himself with water, at the cattle-trough in Spring Lane. What, in Heaven's name, is she? Is the imp altogether evil? Hath she affections? Hath she any discoverable principle of being?"

"None, save the freedom of a broken law," answered Mr. Dimmesdale, in a quiet way, as if he had been discussing the point within himself. "Whether capable of good, I know not."

The child probably overheard their voices; for, looking up to the window, with a bright, but naughty smile of mirth and intelligence, she threw one of the prickly burrs at the Reverend

Mr. Dimmesdale. The sensitive clergyman shrunk, with nervous dread, from the light missile. Detecting his emotion, Pearl clapped her little hands, in the most extravagant ecstasy. Hester Prynne, likewise, had involuntarily looked up; and all these four persons, old and young, regarded one another in silence, till the child laughed aloud, and shouted, — "Come away, mother! Come away, or yonder old Black Man will catch you! He hath got hold of the minister already. Come away, mother, or he will catch you! But he cannot catch little Pearl!"

So she drew her mother away, skipping, dancing, and frisking fantastically, among the hillocks of the dead people, like a creature that had nothing in common with a bygone and buried generation, nor owned herself akin to it. It was as if she had been made afresh, out of new elements, and must perforce be permitted to live her own life, and be a law unto herself, without her eccentricities being reckoned to her for a crime.

"There goes a woman," resumed Roger Chillingworth, after a pause, "who, be her demerits what they may, hath none of that mystery of hidden sinfulness which you deem so grievous to be borne. Is Hester Prynne the less miserable, think you, for that scarlet letter on her breast?"

"I do verily believe it," answered the clergyman. "Nevertheless, I cannot answer for her. There was a look of pain in her face, which I would gladly have been spared the sight of. But still, methinks, it must needs be better for the sufferer to be free to show his pain, as this poor woman Hester is, than to cover it all up in his heart."

There was another pause; and the physician began anew to examine and arrange the plants which he had gathered.

"You inquired of me, a little time agone," said he, at length, "my judgment as touching your health."

"I did," answered the clergyman, "and would gladly learn it. Speak frankly, I pray you, be it for life or death."

"Freely, then, and plainly," said the physician, still busy with his plants, but keeping a wary eye on Mr. Dimmesdale, "the disorder is a strange one; not so much in itself, nor as outwardly manifested,—in so far, at least, as the symptoms have been laid open to my observation. Looking daily at you, my good Sir, and watching the tokens of your aspect, now for months gone by, I should deem you a man sore sick, it may be, yet not so sick but that an instructed and watchful physician might well hope to cure you. But—I know not what to say—the disease is what I seem to know, yet know it not."

"You speak in riddles, learned Sir," said the pale minister, glancing aside out of the window.

"Then, to speak more plainly," continued the physician, "and I crave pardon, Sir,—should it seem to require pardon,—for this needful plainness of my speech. Let me ask,—as your friend,—as one having charge, under Providence, of your life and physical well-being,—hath all the operation of this disorder been fairly laid open and recounted to me?"

"How can you question it?" asked the minister. "Surely, it were child's play, to call in a physician, and then hide the sore!"

"You would tell me, then, that I know all?" said Roger Chillingworth, deliberately, and fixing an eye, bright with intense and concentrated intelligence, on the minister's face. "Be it so! But, again! He to whom only the outward and physical evil is laid open, knoweth, oftentimes, but half the evil which he is called upon to cure. A bodily disease, which we look upon as whole and entire within itself, may, after all, be but a symptom of some ailment in the spiritual part. Your pardon, once again, good Sir, if my speech give the shadow of offence. You, Sir, of all men whom I have known, are he whose body is the closest conjoined, and imbued, and identified, so to speak, with the spirit whereof it is the instrument."

"Then I need ask no further," said the clergyman, somewhat hastily rising from his chair. "You deal not, I take it, in medicine for the soul!"

"Thus, a sickness," continued Roger Chillingworth, going on, in an unaltered tone, without heeding the interruption, — but standing up, and confronting the emaciated and white-cheeked minister, with his low, dark, and misshapen figure, — "a sickness, a sore place, if we may so call it, in your spirit, hath immediately its appropriate manifestation in your bodily frame. Would you, therefore, that your physician heal the bodily evil? How may this be, unless you first lay open to him the wound or trouble in your soul?"

"No!—not to thee!—not to an earthly physician!" cried Mr. Dimmesdale, passionately, and turning his eyes, full and bright, and with a kind of fierceness, on old Roger Chillingworth. "Not to thee! But if it be the soul's disease, then do I commit myself to the one Physician of the soul! He, if it stand with his good pleasure, can cure; or he can kill! Let him do with me as, in his justice and wisdom, he shall see good. But who art thou, that meddlest in this matter?—that dares thrust himself between the sufferer and his God?"

With a frantic gesture he rushed out of the room.

"It is as well to have made this step," said Roger Chillingworth to himself, looking after the minister with a grave smile. "There is nothing lost. We shall be friends again anon. But see, now, how passion takes hold upon this man, and hurrieth him out of himself! As with one passion, so with another! He hath done a wild thing erenow, this pious Master Dimmesdale, in the hot passion of his heart!"

It proved not difficult to re-establish the intimacy of the two companions, on the same footing and in the same degree as heretofore. The young clergyman, after a few hours of privacy, was sensible that the disorder of his nerves had hurried him into an unseemly outbreak of temper, which there had been nothing in the physician's words to excuse or palliate. He marvelled, indeed, at the violence with which he had thrust back the kind old man, when merely proffering the advice which it was his duty to bestow, and which the minister himself had expressly sought. With these remorseful feelings, he lost no time in making the amplest apologies, and besought his friend still to continue the care, which, if not successful in restoring him to health, had, in all probability, been the means of prolonging his feeble existence to that hour. Roger Chillingworth readily assented, and went on with his medical supervision of the minister; doing his best for him, in all good faith, but always quitting the patient's apartment, at the close of a professional interview, with a mysterious and puzzled smile upon his lips. This expression was invisible in Mr. Dimmesdale's presence, but grew strongly evident as the physician crossed the threshold.

"A rare case!" he muttered. "I must needs look deeper into it. A strange sympathy betwixt soul and body! Were it only for the art's sake, I must search this matter to the bottom!"

It came to pass, not long after the scene above recorded, that the Reverend Mr. Dimmesdale, at noonday, and entirely unawares, fell into a deep, deep slumber, sitting in his chair, with a large black-letter volume open before him on the table. It must have been a work of vast ability in the somniferous school of literature. The profound depth of the minister's repose was the more remarkable, inasmuch as he was one of those persons whose sleep, ordinarily, is as light, as fitful, and as easily scared away, as a small bird hopping on a twig. To such an unwonted remoteness, however, had his spirit now withdrawn into itself, that he stirred not in his chair, when old Roger Chillingworth, without any extraordinary precaution, came into the room. The physician advanced directly in front of his patient, laid his hand upon his bosom, and thrust aside the vestment, that, hitherto, had always covered it even from the professional eye.

Then, indeed, Mr. Dimmesdale shuddered, and slightly stirred.

After a brief pause, the physician turned away.

But, with what a wild look of wonder, joy, and horror! With what a ghastly rapture, as it were, too mighty to be expressed only by the eye and features, and therefore bursting forth through the whole ugliness of his figure, and making itself even riotously manifest by the extravagant gestures with which he threw up his arms towards the ceiling, and stamped his foot upon the floor! Had a man seen old Roger Chillingworth, at that moment of his ecstasy, he would have had no need to ask how Satan comports himself, when a precious human soul is lost to heaven, and won into his kingdom.

But what distinguished the physician's ecstasy from Satan's was the trait of wonder in it!

Chapter 11

After the incident last described, the intercourse between the clergyman and the physician, though externally the same, was really of another character than it had previously been. The intellect of Roger Chillingworth had now a sufficiently plain path before it. It was not, indeed, precisely that which he had laid out for himself to tread. Calm, gentle, passionless, as he appeared, there was yet, we fear, a quiet depth of malice, hitherto latent, but active now, in this unfortunate old man, which led him to imagine a more intimate revenge than any mortal had ever wreaked upon an enemy. To make himself the one trusted friend, to whom should be confided all the fear, the remorse, the agony, the ineffectual repentance, the backward rush of sinful thoughts, expelled in vain! All that guilty sorrow, hidden from the world, whose great heart would have pitied and forgiven, to be revealed to him, the Pitiless, to him, the Unforgiving! All that dark treasure to be lavished on the very man, to whom nothing else could so adequately pay the debt of vengeance!

The clergyman's shy and sensitive reserve had balked this scheme. Roger Chillingworth, however, was inclined to be hardly, if at all, less satisfied with the aspect of affairs, which Providence—using the avenger and his victim for its own purposes, and, perchance, pardoning where it seemed most to punish—had substituted for his black devices. A revelation, he could almost say, had been granted to him. It mattered little, for his object, whether celestial, or from what other region. By its aid, in all the subsequent relations betwixt him and Mr. Dimmesdale, not merely the external presence, but the very inmost soul, of the latter, seemed to

151

be brought out before his eyes, so that he could see and comprehend its every movement. He became, thenceforth, not a spectator only, but a chief actor, in the poor minister's interior world. He could play upon him as he chose. Would he arouse him with a throb of agony? The victim was forever on the rack; it needed only to know the spring that controlled the engine;—and the physician knew it well! Would he startle him with sudden fear? As at the waving of a magician's wand, uprose a grisly phantom,—uprose a thousand phantoms,—in many shapes, of death, or more awful shame, all flocking round about the clergyman, and pointing with their fingers at his breast!

All this was accomplished with a subtlety so perfect, that the minister, though he had constantly a dim perception of some evil influence watching over him, could never gain a knowledge of its actual nature. True, he looked doubtfully, fearfully,—even, at times, with horror and the bitterness of hatred,—at the deformed figure of the old physician. His gestures, his gait, his grizzled beard, his slightest and most indifferent acts, the very fashion of his garments, were odious in the clergyman's sight; a token implicitly to be relied on, of a deeper antipathy in the breast of the latter than he was willing to acknowledge to himself. For, as it was impossible to assign a reason for such distrust and abhorrence, so Mr. Dimmesdale, conscious that the poison of one morbid spot was infecting his heart's entire substance, attributed all his presentiments to no other cause. He took himself to task for his bad sympathies in reference to Roger Chillingworth, disregarded the lesson that he should have drawn from them, and did his best to root them out. Unable to accomplish this, he nevertheless, as a matter of principle, continued his habits of social familiarity with the old man, and thus gave him constant opportunities for perfecting the purpose to which—poor, forlorn creature that he was, and more wretched than his victim—the avenger had devoted himself.

While thus suffering under bodily disease, and gnawed and tortured by some black trouble of the soul, and given over to the machinations of his deadliest enemy, the Reverend Mr. Dimmesdale had achieved a brilliant popularity in his sacred office. He won it, indeed, in great part, by his sorrows. His intellectual gifts, his moral perceptions, his power of experiencing and communicating emotion, were kept in a state of preternatural activity by the prick and anguish of his daily life. His fame, though still on its upward slope, already overshadowed the soberer reputations of his fellow-clergymen, eminent as several of them were. There were scholars among them, who had spent more years in acquiring abstruse lore, connected with the divine profession, than Mr. Dimmesdale had lived; and who might well, therefore, be more profoundly versed in such solid and valuable attainments than their youthful brother. There were men, too, of a sturdier texture of mind than his, and endowed with a far greater share of shrewd, hard, iron, or granite understanding; which, duly mingled with a fair proportion of doctrinal ingredient, constitutes a highly respectable, efficacious, and unamiable variety of the clerical species. There were others, again, true saintly fathers, whose faculties had been elaborated by weary toil among their books, and by patient thought, and etherealized, moreover, by spiritual communications with the better world, into which their purity of life had almost introduced these holy personages, with their garments of mortality still clinging to them. All that they lacked was the gift that descended upon the chosen disciples at Pentecost, in tongues of flame; symbolizing, it would seem, not the power of speech in foreign and unknown languages, but that of addressing the whole human brotherhood in the heart's native language. These fathers, otherwise so apostolic, lacked Heaven's last and rarest attestation of their office, the Tongue of Flame. They would have vainly sought—had they ever dreamed of seeking—to express the highest truths through the humblest medium of familiar words and images. Their voices came down, afar and indistinctly, from the upper heights where they habitually dwelt.

Not improbably, it was to this latter class of men that Mr. Dimmesdale, by many of his traits of character, naturally belonged. To the high mountain-peaks of faith and sanctity he would have climbed, had not the tendency been thwarted by the burden, whatever it might be, of crime or anguish, beneath which it was his doom to totter. It kept him down, on a level with the lowest; him, the man of ethereal attributes, whose voice the angels might else have listened to and answered! But this very burden it was, that gave him sympathies so intimate with the sinful brotherhood of mankind; so that his heart vibrated in unison with theirs, and received their pain into itself, and sent its own throb of pain through a thousand other hearts, in gushes of sad, persuasive eloquence. Oftenest persuasive, but sometimes terrible! The people knew not the power that moved them thus. They deemed the young clergyman a miracle of holiness. They fancied him the mouthpiece of Heaven's messages of wisdom, and rebuke, and love. In their eyes, the very ground on which he trod was sanctified. The virgins of his church grew pale around him, victims of a passion so imbued with religious sentiment that they imagined it to be all religion, and brought it openly, in their white bosoms, as their most acceptable sacrifice before the altar. The aged members of his flock, beholding Mr. Dimmesdale's frame so feeble, while they were themselves so rugged in their infirmity, believed that he would go heavenward before them, and enjoined it upon their children, that their old bones should be buried close to their young pastor's holy grave. And, all this time, perchance, when poor Mr. Dimmesdale was thinking of his grave, he questioned with himself whether the grass would ever grow on it, because an accursed thing must there be buried!

It is inconceivable, the agony with which this public veneration tortured him! It was his genuine impulse to adore the truth, and to reckon all things shadow-like, and utterly devoid of weight or value, that had not its divine essence as the life within their life. Then, what was he?—a substance?—or the dimmest of all shadows? He longed to speak out, from his own pulpit, at the full height of his voice, and tell the people what he was. "I, whom you behold in these black garments of the priesthood,—I, who ascend the sacred desk, and turn my pale face heavenward, taking upon myself to hold communion, in your behalf, with the Most High Omniscience,—I, in whose daily life you discern the sanctity of Enoch,—I, whose footsteps, as you suppose, leave a gleam along my earthly track, whereby the pilgrims that shall come after me may be guided to the regions of the blest,—I, who have laid the hand of baptism upon your children,—I, who have breathed the parting prayer over your dying friends, to whom the Amen sounded faintly from a world which they had quitted,—I, your pastor, whom you so reverence and trust, am utterly a pollution and a lie!"

More than once, Mr. Dimmesdale had gone into the pulpit, with a purpose never to come down its steps, until he should have spoken words like the above. More than once, he had cleared his throat, and drawn in the long, deep, and tremulous breath, which, when sent forth again, would come burdened with the black secret of his soul. More than once—nay, more than a hundred times—he had actually spoken! Spoken! But how? He had told his hearers that he was altogether vile, a viler companion of the vilest, the worst of sinners, an abomination, a thing of unimaginable iniquity; and that the only wonder was, that they did not see his wretched body shrivelled up before their eyes, by the burning wrath of the Almighty! Could there be plainer speech than this? Would not the people start up in their seats, by a simultaneous impulse, and tear him down out of the pulpit which he defiled? Not so, indeed! They heard it all, and did but reverence him the more. They little guessed what deadly purport lurked in those self-condemning words. "The godly youth!" said they among themselves. "The saint on earth! Alas, if he discern such sinfulness in his own white soul, what horrid spectacle would he behold in thine or mine!"

155

The minister well knew—subtle, but remorseful hypocrite that he was!—the light in which his vague confession would be viewed. He had striven to put a cheat upon himself by making the avowal of a guilty conscience, but had gained only one other sin, and a self-acknowledged shame, without the momentary relief of being self-deceived. He had spoken the very truth, and transformed it into the veriest falsehood. And yet, by the constitution of his nature, he loved the truth, and loathed the lie, as few men ever did. Therefore, above all things else, he loathed his miserable self!

His inward trouble drove him to practices more in accordance with the old, corrupted faith of Rome, than with the better light of the church in which he had been born and bred. In Mr. Dimmesdale's secret closet, under lock and key, there was a bloody scourge. Oftentimes, this Protestant and Puritan divine had plied it on his own shoulders; laughing bitterly at himself the while, and smiting so much the more pitilessly because of that bitter laugh. It was his custom, too, as it has been that of many other pious Puritans, to fast,—not, however, like them, in order to purify the body and render it the fitter medium of celestial illumination, but rigorously, and until his knees trembled beneath him, as an act of penance. He kept vigils, likewise, night after night, sometimes in utter darkness; sometimes with a glimmering lamp; and sometimes, viewing his own face in a looking-glass, by the most powerful light which he could throw upon it. He thus typified the constant introspection wherewith he tortured, but could not purify, himself. In these lengthened vigils, his brain often reeled, and visions seemed to flit before him; perhaps seen doubtfully, and by a faint light of their own, in the remote dimness of the chamber, or more vividly, and close beside him, within the looking-glass. Now it was a herd of diabolic shapes, that grinned and mocked at the pale minister, and beckoned him away with them; now a group of shining angels, who flew upward heavily, as sorrow-laden, but grew more ethereal as they rose. Now came the dead friends of his youth, and his white-bearded father, with a saint-like frown, and his mother, turning her face away as she passed by. Ghost of a mother,—thinnest fantasy of a mother,—methinks she might yet have thrown a pitying glance towards her son! And now, through the chamber which these spectral thoughts had made so ghastly, glided Hester Prynne, leading along little Pearl, in her scarlet garb, and pointing her forefinger, first at the scarlet letter on her bosom, and then at the clergyman's own breast.

None of these visions ever quite deluded him. At any moment, by an effort of his will, he could discern substances through their misty lack of substance, and convince himself that they were not solid in their nature, like yonder table of carved oak, or that big, square, leathern-bound and brazen-clasped volume of divinity. But, for all that, they were, in one sense, the truest and most substantial things which the poor minister now dealt with. It is the unspeakable misery of a life so false as his, that it steals the pith and substance out of whatever realities there are around us, and which were meant by Heaven to be the spirit's joy and nutriment. To the untrue man, the whole universe is false,—it is impalpable,—it shrinks to nothing within his grasp. And he himself, in so far as he shows himself in a false light, becomes a shadow, or, indeed, ceases to exist. The only truth that continued to give Mr. Dimmesdale a real existence on this earth, was the anguish in his inmost soul, and the undissembled expression of it in his aspect. Had he once found power to smile, and wear a face of gayety, there would have been no such man!

On one of those ugly nights, which we have faintly hinted at, but forborne to picture forth, the minister started from his chair. A new thought had struck him. There might be a moment's peace in it. Attiring himself with as much care as if it had been for public worship, and precisely in the same manner, he stole softly down the staircase, undid the door, and issued forth.

Chapter 12

Walking in the shadow of a dream, as it were, and perhaps actually under the influence of a species of somnambulism, Mr. Dimmesdale reached the spot where, now so long since, Hester Prynne had lived through her first hours of public ignominy. The same platform or scaffold, black and weather-stained with the storm or sunshine of seven long years, and foot-worn, too, with the tread of many culprits who had since ascended it, remained standing beneath the balcony of the meeting-house. The minister went up the steps.

It was an obscure night of early May. An unvaried pall of cloud muffled the whole expanse of sky from zenith to horizon. If the same multitude which had stood as eye-witnesses while Hester Prynne sustained her punishment could now have been summoned forth, they would have discerned no face above the platform, nor hardly the outline of a human shape, in the dark gray of the midnight. But the town was all asleep. There was no peril of discovery. The minister might stand there, if it so pleased him, until morning should redden in the east, without other risk than that the dank and chill night-air would creep into his frame, and stiffen his joints with rheumatism, and clog his throat with catarrh and cough; thereby defrauding the expectant audience of to-morrow's prayer and sermon. No eye could see him, save that ever-wakeful one which had seen him in his closet, wielding the bloody scourge. Why, then, had he come hither? Was it but the mockery of penitence? A mockery, indeed, but in which his soul trifled with itself! A mockery at which angels blushed and wept, while fiends rejoiced, with jeering laughter! He had been driven hither by the impulse of that Remorse which dogged him everywhere, and whose own sister and closely linked companion was that Cowardice which invariably drew him back, with her tremulous gripe, just when the other impulse had hurried him to the verge of a disclosure. Poor, miserable man! what right had infirmity like his to burden itself with crime? Crime is for the iron-nerved, who have their choice either to endure it, or, if it press too hard, to exert their fierce and savage strength for a good purpose, and fling it off at once! This feeble and most sensitive of spirits could do neither, yet continually did one thing or another, which intertwined, in the same inextricable knot, the agony of heaven-defying guilt and vain repentance.

And thus, while standing on the scaffold, in this vain show of expiation, Mr. Dimmesdale was overcome with a great horror of mind, as if the universe were gazing at a scarlet token on his naked breast, right over his heart. On that spot, in very truth, there was, and there had long been, the gnawing and poisonous tooth of bodily pain. Without any effort of his will, or power to restrain himself, he shrieked aloud; an outcry that went pealing through the night, and was beaten back from one house to another, and reverberated from the hills in the background; as if a company of devils, detecting so much misery and terror in it, had made a plaything of the sound, and were bandying it to and fro.

"It is done!" muttered the minister, covering his face with his hands. "The whole town will awake, and hurry forth, and find me here!"

But it was not so. The shriek had perhaps sounded with a far greater power, to his own startled ears, than it actually possessed. The town did not awake; or, if it did, the drowsy slumberers mistook the cry either for something frightful in a dream, or for the noise of witches; whose voices, at that period, were often heard to pass over the settlements or lonely cottages, as they rode with Satan through the air. The clergyman, therefore, hearing no symptoms of disturbance, uncovered his eyes and looked about him. At one of the chamber-windows of Governor Bellingham's mansion, which stood at some distance, on the line of another street, he beheld the appearance of the old magistrate himself, with a lamp in his hand, a white night-cap on his head, and a long white gown enveloping his figure. He looked like a ghost, evoked unseasonably from the grave. The cry had evidently startled him. At another window of the same house, moreover, appeared old Mistress Hibbins, the Governor's sister, also with a lamp, which, even thus far off, revealed the expression of her sour and discontented face. She thrust forth her head from the lattice, and looked anxiously upward. Beyond the shadow of a doubt, this venerable witch-lady had heard Mr. Dimmesdale's outcry, and interpreted it, with its multitudinous echoes and reverberations, as the clamor of the fiends and night-hags, with whom she was well known to make excursions into the forest.

Detecting the gleam of Governor Bellingham's lamp, the old lady quickly extinguished her own, and vanished. Possibly, she went up among the clouds. The minister saw nothing further of her motions. The magistrate, after a wary observation of the darkness, — into which, nevertheless, he could see but little further than he might into a mill-stone, — retired from the window.

The minister grew comparatively calm. His eyes, however, were soon greeted by a little, glimmering light, which, at first a long way off, was approaching up the street. It threw a gleam of recognition on here a post, and there a garden-fence, and here a latticed window-pane, and there a pump, with its full trough of water, and here, again, an arched door of oak, with an iron knocker, and a rough log for the doorstep. The Reverend Mr. Dimmesdale noted all these minute particulars, even while firmly convinced that the doom of his existence was stealing onward, in the footsteps which he now heard; and that the gleam of the lantern would fall upon him, in a few moments more, and reveal his long-hidden secret. As the light drew nearer, he beheld, within its illuminated circle, his brother clergyman,—or, to speak more accurately, his professional father, as well as highly valued friend,—the Reverend Mr. Wilson; who, as Mr. Dimmesdale now conjectured, had been praying at the bedside of some dying man. And so he had. The good old minister came freshly from the death-chamber of Governor Winthrop, who had passed from earth to heaven within that very hour. And now, surrounded, like the saint-like personages of olden times, with a radiant halo, that glorified him amid this gloomy night of sin,—as if the departed Governor had left him an inheritance of his glory, or as if he had caught upon himself the distant shine of the celestial city, while looking thitherward to see the triumphant pilgrim pass within its gates,—now, in short, good Father Wilson was moving homeward, aiding his footsteps with a lighted lantern! The glimmer of this luminary suggested the above conceits to Mr. Dimmesdale, who smiled,— nay, almost laughed at them,—and then wondered if he were going mad.

As the Reverend Mr. Wilson passed beside the scaffold, closely muffling his Geneva cloak about him with one arm, and holding the lantern before his breast with the other, the minister could hardly restrain himself from speaking.

"A good evening to you, venerable Father Wilson! Come up hither, I pray you, and pass a pleasant hour with me!"

Good heavens! Had Mr. Dimmesdale actually spoken? For

one instant, he believed that these words had passed his lips. But they were uttered only within his imagination. The venerable Father Wilson continued to step slowly onward, looking carefully at the muddy pathway before his feet, and never once turning his head towards the guilty platform. When the light of the glimmering lantern had faded quite away, the minister discovered, by the faintness which came over him, that the last few moments had been a crisis of terrible anxiety; although his mind had made an involuntary effort to relieve itself by a kind of lurid playfulness.

Shortly afterwards, the like grisly sense of the humorous again stole in among the solemn phantoms of his thought. He felt his limbs growing stiff with the unaccustomed chilliness of the night, and doubted whether he should be able to descend the steps of the scaffold. Morning would break, and find him there. The neighborhood would begin to rouse itself. The earliest riser, coming forth in the dim twilight, would perceive a vaguely defined figure aloft on the place of shame; and, half crazed betwixt alarm and curiosity, would go, knocking from door to door, summoning all the people to behold the ghost—as he needs must think it—of some defunct transgressor. A dusky tumult would flap its wings from one house to another. Then—the morning light still waxing stronger—old patriarchs would rise up in great haste, each in his flannel gown, and matronly dames, without pausing to put off their night-gear. The whole tribe of decorous personages, who had never heretofore been seen with a single hair of their heads awry, would start into public view, with the disorder of a nightmare in their aspects. Old Governor Bellingham would come grimly forth, with his King James's ruff fastened askew; and Mistress Hibbins, with some twigs of the forest clinging to her skirts, and looking sourer than ever, as having hardly got a wink of sleep after her night ride; and good Father Wilson, too, after spending half the night at a death-bed, and liking ill to be disturbed, thus early, out of his dreams about the glorified saints. Hither, likewise, would come the elders and deacons of Mr. Dimmesdale's church, and the young virgins who so idolized their minister, and had made a shrine for him in their white bosoms; which now, by the by, in their hurry and confusion, they would scantly have given themselves time to cover with their kerchiefs. All people, in a word, would come stumbling over their thresholds, and turning up their amazed and horror-stricken visages around the scaffold. Whom would they discern there, with the red eastern light upon his brow? Whom, but the Reverend Arthur Dimmesdale, half frozen to death, overwhelmed with shame, and standing where Hester Prynne had stood!

Carried away by the grotesque horror of this picture, the minister, unawares, and to his own infinite alarm, burst into a great peal of laughter. It was immediately responded to by a light, airy, childish laugh, in which, with a thrill of the heart,—but he knew not whether of exquisite pain, or pleasure as acute,—he recognized the tones of little Pearl.

"Pearl! Little Pearl!" cried he after a moment's pause; then, suppressing his voice,—"Hester! Hester Prynne! Are you there?"

"Yes; it is Hester Prynne!" she replied, in a tone of surprise; and the minister heard her footsteps approaching from the sidewalk, along which she had been passing. "It is I, and my little Pearl."

"Whence come you, Hester?" asked the minister. "What sent you hither?"

"I have been watching at a death-bed," answered Hester Prynne;—"at Governor Winthrop's death-bed, and have taken his measure for a robe, and am now going homeward to my dwelling."

"Come up hither, Hester, thou and little Pearl," said the Reverend Mr. Dimmesdale. "Ye have both been here before, but I was not with you. Come up hither once again, and we will stand all three together!"

She silently ascended the steps, and stood on the platform, holding little Pearl by the hand. The minister felt for the child's other hand, and took it. The moment that he did so, there came what seemed a tumultuous rush of new life, other life than his own, pouring like a torrent into his heart, and hurrying through all his veins, as if the mother and the child were communicating their vital warmth to his half-torpid system. The three formed an electric chain.

"Minister!" whispered little Pearl.

"What wouldst thou say, child?" asked Mr. Dimmesdale.

"Wilt thou stand here with mother and me, tomorrow noontide?" inquired Pearl.

"Nay; not so, my little Pearl," answered the minister; for, with the new energy of the moment, all the dread of public exposure, that had so long been the anguish of his life, had returned upon him; and he was already trembling at the conjunction in which—with a strange joy, nevertheless—he now found himself. "Not so, my child. I shall, indeed, stand with thy mother and thee one other day, but not tomorrow."

Pearl laughed, and attempted to pull away her hand. But the minister held it fast.

"A moment longer, my child!" said he.

"But wilt thou promise," asked Pearl, "to take my hand, and mother's hand, to-morrow noontide?"

"Not then, Pearl," said the minister, "but another time."

"And what other time?" persisted the child.

"At the great judgment day," whispered the minister,—and, strangely enough, the sense that he was a professional teacher of the truth impelled him to answer the child so. "Then, and there, before the judgment-seat, thy mother, and thou, and I must stand together. But the daylight of this world shall not see our meeting!"

Pearl laughed again.

But, before Mr. Dimmesdale had done speaking, a light gleamed far and wide over all the muffled sky. It was doubtless caused by one of those meteors, which the night-watcher may so often observe burning out to waste, in the vacant regions of the atmosphere. So powerful was its radiance, that it thoroughly illuminated the dense medium of cloud betwixt the sky and earth. The great vault brightened, like the dome of an immense lamp. It showed the familiar scene of the street, with the distinctness of mid-day, but also with the awfulness that is always imparted to familiar objects by an unaccustomed light. The wooden houses, with their jutting stories and quaint gable-peaks; the doorsteps and thresholds, with the early grass springing up about them; the garden-plots, black with freshly turned earth; the wheel-track, little worn, and, even in the market-place, margined with green on either side;—all were visible, but with a singularity of aspect that seemed to give another moral interpretation to the things of this world than they had ever borne before. And there stood the minister, with his hand over his heart; and Hester Prynne, with the embroidered letter glimmering on her bosom; and little Pearl, herself a symbol, and the connecting link between those two. They stood in the noon of that strange and solemn splendor, as if it were the light that is to reveal all secrets, and the daybreak that shall unite all who belong to one another.

There was witchcraft in little Pearl's eyes, and her face, as she glanced upward at the minister, wore that naughty smile which made its expression frequently so elvish. She withdrew her hand from Mr. Dimmesdale's, and pointed across the street. But he clasped both his hands over his breast, and cast his eyes towards the zenith.

Nothing was more common, in those days, than to interpret all meteoric appearances, and other natural phenomena, that occurred with less regularity than the rise and set of sun and moon, as so many revelations from a supernatural source. Thus, a blazing spear, a sword of flame, a bow, or a sheaf of arrows, seen in the midnight sky, prefigured Indian warfare. Pestilence was known to have been foreboded by a shower of crimson light. We doubt whether any marked event, for good or evil, ever befell New England, from its settlement down to Revolutionary times, of which the inhabitants had not been previously warned by some spectacle of this nature. Not seldom, it had been seen by multitudes. Oftener, however, its credibility rested on the faith of some lonely eye-witness, who beheld the wonder through the colored, magnifying, and distorting medium of his imagination, and shaped it more distinctly in his after-thought. It was, indeed, a majestic idea, that the destiny of nations should be revealed, in these awful hieroglyphics, on the cope of heaven. A scroll so wide might not be deemed too expansive for Providence to write a people's doom upon. The belief was a favorite one with our forefathers, as betokening that their infant commonwealth was under a celestial guardianship of peculiar intimacy and strictness. But what shall we say, when an individual discovers a revelation addressed to himself alone, on the same vast sheet of record! In such a case, it could only be the symptom of a highly disordered mental state, when a man, rendered morbidly self-contemplative by long, intense, and secret pain, had extended his egotism over the whole expanse of nature, until the firmament itself should appear no more than a fitting page for his soul's history and fate!

We impute it, therefore, solely to the disease in his own eye and heart, that the minister, looking upward to the zenith, beheld there the appearance of an immense letter,—the letter A,—marked out in lines of dull red light. Not but the meteor may have shown itself at that point, burning duskily through a veil of cloud; but with no such shape as his guilty imagination gave it; or, at least, with so little definiteness, that another's guilt might have seen another symbol in it.

There was a singular circumstance that characterized Mr. Dimmesdale's psychological state, at this moment. All the time that he gazed upward to the zenith, he was, nevertheless, perfectly aware that little Pearl was pointing her finger towards old Roger Chillingworth, who stood at no great distance from the scaffold. The minister appeared to see him, with the same glance that discerned the miraculous letter. To his features, as to all other objects, the meteoric light imparted a new expression; or it might well be that the physician was not careful then, as at all other times, to hide the malevolence with which he looked upon his victim. Certainly, if the meteor kindled up the sky, and disclosed the earth, with an awfulness that admonished Hester Prynne and the clergyman of the day of judgment, then might Roger Chillingworth have passed with them for the arch-fiend, standing there with a smile and scowl, to claim his own. So vivid was the expression, or so intense the minister's perception of it, that it seemed still to remain painted on the darkness, after the meteor had vanished, with an effect as if the street and all things else were at once annihilated.

"Who is that man, Hester?" gasped Mr. Dimmesdale, overcome with terror. "I shiver at him! Dost thou know the man? I hate him, Hester!"

She remembered her oath, and was silent.

"I tell thee, my soul shivers at him!" muttered the minister again. "Who is he? Who is he? Canst thou do nothing for me? I have a nameless horror of the man!"

"Minister," said little Pearl, "I can tell thee who he is!"

"Quickly, then, child!" said the minister, bending his ear close to her lips. "Quickly!—and as low as thou canst whisper."

Pearl mumbled something into his ear, that sounded, indeed, like human language, but was only such gibberish as children may be heard amusing themselves with, by the hour together. At all events, if it involved any secret information in regard to old Roger Chillingworth, it was in a tongue unknown to the erudite clergyman, and did but increase the bewilderment of his mind. The elvish child then laughed aloud.

"Dost thou mock me now?" said the minister.

"Thou wast not bold!—thou wast not true!"—answered the child. "Thou wouldst not promise to take my hand, and mother's hand, to-morrow noontide!"

"Worthy Sir," answered the physician, who had now advanced to the foot of the platform. "Pious Master Dimmesdale, can this be you? Well, well, indeed! We men of study, whose heads are in our books, have need to be straitly looked after! We dream in our waking moments, and walk in our sleep. Come, good Sir, and my dear friend,

I pray you, let me lead you home!"

"How knewest thou that I was here?" asked the minister, fearfully.

"Verily, and in good faith," answered Roger Chillingworth, "I knew nothing of the matter. I had spent the better part of the night at the bedside of the worshipful Governor Winthrop, doing what my poor skill might to give him ease. He going home to a better world, I, likewise, was on my way homeward, when this strange light shone out. Come with me, I beseech you, Reverend Sir; else you will be poorly able to do Sabbath duty to-morrow. Aha! see now, how they trouble the brain,—these books!—these books! You should study less, good Sir, and take a little pastime; or these night-whimseys will grow upon you."

"I will go home with you," said Mr. Dimmesdale.

With a chill despondency, like one awaking, all nerveless, from an ugly dream, he yielded himself to the physician, and was led away.

The next day, however, being the Sabbath, he preached a discourse which was held to be the richest and most powerful, and the most replete with heavenly influences, that had ever proceeded from his lips. Souls, it is said more souls than one, were brought to the truth by the efficacy of that sermon, and vowed within themselves to cherish a holy gratitude towards Mr. Dimmesdale throughout the long hereafter. But, as he came down the pulpit steps, the gray-bearded sexton met him, holding up a black glove, which the minister recognized as his own.

"It was found," said the sexton, "this morning, on the scaffold where evil-doers are set up to public shame. Satan dropped it there, I take it, intending a scurrilous jest against your reverence. But, indeed, he was blind and foolish, as he ever and always is. A pure hand needs no glove to cover it!"

"Thank you, my good friend," said the minister, gravely, but startled at heart; for, so confused was his remembrance, that he had almost brought himself to look at the events of the past night as visionary. "Yes, it seems to be my glove, indeed!"

"And since Satan saw fit to steal it, your reverence must needs handle him without gloves, henceforward," remarked the old sexton, grimly smiling. "But did your reverence hear of the portent that was seen last night?—a great red letter in the sky,—the letter A, which we interpret to stand for Angel. For, as our good Governor Winthrop was made an angel this past night, it was doubtless held fit that there should be some notice thereof!"

"No," answered the minister, "I had not heard of it."

Chapter 13

In her late singular interview with Mr. Dimmesdale, Hester Prynne was shocked at the condition to which she found the clergyman reduced. His nerve seemed absolutely destroyed. His moral force was abased into more than childish weakness. It grovelled helpless on the ground, even while his intellectual faculties retained their pristine strength, or had perhaps acquired a morbid energy, which disease only could have given them. With her knowledge of a train of circumstances hidden from all others, she could readily infer that, besides the legitimate action of his own conscience, a terrible machinery had been brought to bear, and was still operating, on Mr. Dimmesdale's well-being and repose. Knowing what this poor, fallen man had once been, her whole soul was moved by the shuddering terror with which he had appealed to her,—the outcast woman,—for support against his instinctively discovered enemy. She decided, moreover, that he had a right to her utmost aid. Little accustomed, in her long seclusion from society, to measure her ideas of right and wrong by any standard external to herself, Hester saw—or seemed to see—that there lay a responsibility upon her, in reference to the clergyman, which she owed to no other, nor to the whole world besides. The links that united her to the rest of human kind—links of flowers, or silk, or gold, or whatever the material—had all been broken. Here was the iron link of mutual crime, which neither he nor she could break. Like all other ties, it brought along with it its obligations.

Hester Prynne did not now occupy precisely the same position in which we beheld her during the earlier periods of her ignominy. Years had come and gone. Pearl was now seven years old. Her mother, with the scarlet letter on her breast, glittering in its fantastic embroidery, had long been a familiar object to the towns-people. As is apt to be the case when a person stands out in any prominence before the community, and, at the same time, interferes neither with public nor individual interests and convenience, a species of general regard had ultimately grown up in reference to Hester Prynne. It is to the credit of human nature, that, except where its selfishness is brought into play, it loves more readily than it hates. Hatred, by a gradual and quiet process, will even be transformed to love, unless the change be impeded by a continually new irritation of the original feeling of hostility. In this matter of Hester Prynne, there was neither irritation nor irksomeness. She never battled with the public, but submitted, uncomplainingly, to its worst usage; she made no claim upon it, in requital for what she suffered; she did not weigh upon its sympathies. Then, also, the blameless purity of her life during all these years in which she had been set apart to infamy, was reckoned largely in her favor. With nothing now to lose, in the sight of mankind, and with no hope, and seemingly no wish, of gaining anything, it could only be a genuine regard for virtue that had brought back the poor wanderer to its paths.

It was perceived, too, that while Hester never put forward even the humblest title to share in the world's privileges, — further than to breathe the common air, and earn daily bread for little Pearl and herself by the faithful labor of her hands, — she was quick to acknowledge her sisterhood with the race of man, whenever benefits were to be conferred. None so ready as she to give of her little substance to every demand of poverty; even though the bitter-hearted pauper threw back a gibe in requital of the food brought regularly to his door, or the garments wrought for him by the fingers that could have embroidered a monarch's robe. None so self-devoted as Hester, when pestilence stalked through the town. In all seasons of calamity, indeed, whether general or of individuals, the outcast of society at once found her place. She came, not as a guest, but as a rightful inmate, into the household that was darkened by trouble; as if its gloomy twilight were a medium in which she was entitled to hold intercourse with her fellow-creatures. There glimmered the embroidered letter, with comfort in its unearthly ray. Elsewhere the token of sin, it was the taper of the sick-chamber. It had even thrown its gleam, in the sufferer's hard extremity, across the verge of time. It had shown him where to set his foot, while the light of earth was fast becoming dim, and ere the light of futurity could reach him. In such emergencies, Hester's nature showed itself warm and rich; a well-spring of human tenderness, unfailing to every real demand, and inexhaustible by the largest. Her breast, with its badge of shame, was but the softer pillow for the head that needed one. She was self-ordained a Sister of Mercy; or, we may rather say, the world's heavy hand had so ordained her, when neither the world nor she looked forward to this result. The letter was the symbol of her calling. Such helpfulness was found in her,—so much power to do, and power to sympathize,— that many people refused to interpret the scarlet A by its original signification. They said that it meant Able; so strong was Hester Prynne, with a woman's strength.

It was only the darkened house that could contain her. When sunshine came again, she was not there. Her shadow had faded across the threshold. The helpful inmate had departed, without one backward glance to gather up the meed of gratitude, if any were in the hearts of those whom she had served so zealously. Meeting them in the street, she never raised her head to receive their greeting. If they were resolute to accost her, she laid her finger on the scarlet

173

letter, and passed on. This might be pride, but was so like humility, that it produced all the softening influence of the latter quality on the public mind. The public is despotic in its temper; it is capable of denying common justice, when too strenuously demanded as a right; but quite as frequently it awards more than justice, when the appeal is made, as despots love to have it made, entirely to its generosity. Interpreting Hester Prynne's deportment as an appeal of this nature, society was inclined to show its former victim a more benign countenance than she cared to be favored with, or, perchance, than she deserved.

The rulers, and the wise and learned men of the community, were longer in acknowledging the influence of Hester's good qualities than the people. The prejudices which they shared in common with the latter were fortified in themselves by an iron framework of reasoning, that made it a far tougher labor to expel them. Day by day, nevertheless, their sour and rigid wrinkles were relaxing into something which, in the due course of years, might grow to be an expression of almost benevolence. Thus it was with the men of rank, on whom their eminent position imposed the guardianship of the public morals. Individuals in private life, meanwhile, had quite forgiven Hester Prynne for her frailty; nay, more, they had begun to look upon the scarlet letter as the token, not of that one sin, for which she had borne so long and dreary a penance, but of her many good deeds since. "Do you see that woman with the embroidered badge?" they would say to strangers. "It is our Hester,—the town's own Hester, who is so kind to the poor, so helpful to the sick, so comfortable to the afflicted!" Then, it is true, the propensity of human nature to tell the very worst of itself, when embodied in the person of another, would constrain them to whisper the black scandal of bygone years. It was none the less a fact, however, that, in the eyes of the very men who spoke thus, the scarlet letter had the effect of the cross on a nun's bosom. It imparted to the wearer a kind of sacredness, which enabled her to walk securely amid all peril. Had she fallen among thieves, it would have kept her safe. It was reported, and believed by many, that an Indian had drawn his arrow against the badge, and that the missile struck it, but fell harmless to the ground.

The effect of the symbol—or, rather, of the position in respect to society that was indicated by it—on the mind of Hester Prynne herself, was powerful and peculiar. All the light and graceful foliage of her character had been withered up by this red-hot brand, and had long ago fallen away, leaving a bare and harsh outline, which might have been repulsive, had she possessed friends or companions to be repelled by it. Even the attractiveness of her person had undergone a similar change. It might be partly owing to the studied austerity of her dress, and partly to the lack of demonstration in her manners. It was a sad transformation, too, that her rich and luxuriant hair had either been cut off, or was so completely hidden by a cap, that not a shining lock of it ever once gushed into the sunshine. It was due in part to all these causes, but still more to something else, that there seemed to be no longer anything in Hester's face for Love to dwell upon; nothing in Hester's form, though majestic and statue-like, that Passion would ever dream of clasping in its embrace; nothing in Hester's bosom, to make it ever again the pillow of Affection. Some attribute had departed from her, the permanence of which had been essential to keep her a woman. Such is frequently the fate, and such the stern development, of the feminine character and person, when the woman has encountered, and lived through, an experience of peculiar severity. If she be all tenderness, she will die. If she survive, the tenderness will either be crushed out of her, or—and the outward semblance is the same—crushed so deeply into her heart that it can never show itself more. The latter is perhaps the truest theory. She who has once been woman, and ceased to be so, might at any moment become a woman again if there were only the magic touch to effect the transfiguration. We shall see whether Hester Prynne were ever afterwards so touched, and so transfigured.

Much of the marble coldness of Hester's impression was to be attributed to the circumstance, that her life had turned, in a great measure, from passion and feeling, to thought. Standing alone in the world, — alone, as to any dependence on society, and with little Pearl to be guided and protected, — alone, and hopeless of retrieving her position, even had she not scorned to consider it desirable, — she cast away the fragments of a broken chain. The world's law was no law for her mind. It was an age in which the human intellect, newly emancipated, had taken a more active and a wider range than for many centuries before. Men of the sword had overthrown nobles and kings. Men bolder than these had overthrown and rearranged — not actually, but within the sphere of theory, which was their most real abode — the whole system of ancient prejudice, wherewith was linked much of ancient principle. Hester Prynne imbibed this spirit. She assumed a freedom of speculation, then common enough on the other side of the Atlantic, but which our forefathers, had they known it, would have held to be a deadlier crime than that stigmatized by the scarlet letter. In her lonesome cottage, by the sea-shore, thoughts visited her, such as dared to enter no other dwelling in New England; shadowy guests, that would have been as perilous as demons to their entertainer, could they have been seen so much as knocking at her door.

It is remarkable, that persons who speculate the most boldly often conform with the most perfect quietude to the external regulations of society. The thought suffices them, without investing itself in the flesh and blood of action. So it seemed to be with Hester. Yet, had little Pearl never come to her from the spiritual world, it might have been far otherwise. Then, she might have come down to us in history, hand in hand with Ann Hutchinson, as the foundress of a religious sect. She might, in one of her phases, have been a prophetess. She might, and not improbably would, have suffered death from the stern tribunals of the period, for attempting to undermine the foundations of the Puritan establishment. But, in the education of her child, the mother's enthusiasm of thought had something to wreak itself upon. Providence, in the person of this little girl, had assigned to Hester's charge the germ and blossom of womanhood, to be cherished and developed amid a host of difficulties. Everything was against her. The world was hostile. The child's own nature had something wrong in it, which continually betokened that she had been born amiss, — the effluence of her mother's lawless passion, — and often impelled Hester to ask, in bitterness of heart, whether it were for ill or good that the poor little creature had been born at all.

Indeed, the same dark question often rose into her mind, with reference to the whole race of womanhood. Was existence worth accepting, even to the happiest among them? As concerned her own individual existence, she had long ago decided in the negative, and dismissed the point as settled. A tendency to speculation, though it may keep woman quiet, as it does man, yet makes her sad. She discerns, it may be, such a hopeless task before her. As a first step, the whole system of society is to be torn down, and built up anew. Then, the very nature of the opposite sex, or its long hereditary habit, which has become like nature, is to be essentially modified, before woman can be allowed to assume what seems a fair and suitable position. Finally, all other difficulties being obviated, woman cannot take advantage of these preliminary reforms, until she herself shall have undergone a still mightier change; in which, perhaps, the ethereal essence, wherein she has her truest life, will be found to have evaporated. A woman never overcomes these problems by any exercise of thought. They are not to be solved, or only in one way. If her heart chance to come uppermost, they vanish. Thus, Hester Prynne, whose heart had lost its regular and healthy throb, wandered without a clew in the dark labyrinth of mind; now turned aside by an insurmountable precipice; now starting back from a deep chasm. There was wild and ghastly scenery all around her, and a home and comfort nowhere. At times, a fearful doubt strove to possess her soul, whether it were not better to send Pearl at once to heaven, and go herself to such futurity as Eternal Justice should provide.

The scarlet letter had not done its office.

Now, however, her interview with the Reverend Mr. Dimmesdale, on the night of his vigil, had given her a new theme of reflection, and held up to her an object that appeared worthy of any exertion and sacrifice for its attainment. She had witnessed the intense misery beneath which the minister struggled, or, to speak more accurately, had ceased to struggle. She saw that he stood on the verge of lunacy, if he had not already stepped across it. It was impossible to doubt, that, whatever painful efficacy there might be in the secret sting of remorse, a deadlier venom had been infused into it by the hand that proffered relief. A secret enemy had been continually by his side, under the semblance of a friend and helper, and had availed himself of the opportunities thus afforded for tampering with the delicate springs of Mr. Dimmesdale's nature. Hester could not but ask herself, whether there had not originally been a defect of truth, courage, and loyalty, on her own part, in allowing the minister to be thrown into a position where so much evil was to be foreboded, and nothing auspicious to be hoped. Her only justification lay in the fact, that she had been able to discern no method of rescuing him from a blacker ruin than had overwhelmed herself, except by acquiescing in Roger Chillingworth's scheme of disguise.

Under that impulse, she had made her choice, and had chosen, as it now appeared, the more wretched alternative of the two. She determined to redeem her error, so far as it might yet be possible. Strengthened by years of hard and solemn trial, she felt herself no longer so inadequate to cope with Roger Chillingworth as on that night, abased by sin, and half maddened by the ignominy that was still new, when they had talked together in the prison-chamber. She had climbed her way, since then, to a higher point. The old man, on the other hand, had brought himself nearer to her level, or perhaps below it, by the revenge which he had stooped for.

In fine, Hester Prynne resolved to meet her former husband, and do what might be in her power for the rescue of the victim on whom he had so evidently set his gripe. The occasion was not long to seek. One afternoon, walking with Pearl in a retired part of the peninsula, she beheld the old physician, with a basket on one arm, and a staff in the other hand, stooping along the ground, in quest of roots and herbs to concoct his medicines withal.

Chapter 14

Hester bade little Pearl run down to the margin of the water, and play with the shells and tangled sea-weed, until she should have talked awhile with yonder gatherer of herbs. So the child flew away like a bird, and, making bare her small white feet, went pattering along the moist margin of the sea. Here and there she came to a full stop, and peeped curiously into a pool, left by the retiring tide as a mirror for Pearl to see her face in. Forth peeped at her, out of the pool, with dark, glistening curls around her head, and an elf-smile in her eyes, the image of a little maid, whom Pearl, having no other playmate, invited to take her hand, and run a race with her. But the visionary little maid, on her part, beckoned likewise, as if to say, — "This is a better place! Come thou into the pool!" And Pearl, stepping in, mid-leg deep, beheld her own white feet at the bottom; while, out of a still lower depth, came the gleam of a kind of fragmentary smile, floating to and fro in the agitated water.

Meanwhile, her mother had accosted the physician.

"I would speak a word with you," said she, — "a word that concerns us much."

"Aha! and is it Mistress Hester that has a word for old Roger Chillingworth?" answered he, raising himself from his stooping posture. "With all my heart! Why, Mistress, I hear good tidings of you on all hands! No longer ago than yester-eve, a magistrate, a wise and godly man, was discoursing of your affairs, Mistress Hester, and whispered me that there had been question concerning you in the council. It was debated whether or no, with safety to the common weal, yonder scarlet letter might be taken off your bosom. On my life, Hester, I made my entreaty to the worshipful magistrate that it might be done forthwith!"

"It lies not in the pleasure of the magistrates to take off this badge," calmly replied Hester. "Were I worthy to be quit of it, it would fall away of its own nature, or be transformed into something that should speak a different purport."

"Nay, then, wear it, if it suit you better," rejoined he. "A woman must needs follow her own fancy, touching the adornment of her person. The letter is gayly embroidered, and shows right bravely on your bosom!"

All this while, Hester had been looking steadily at the old man, and was shocked, as well as wonder-smitten, to discern what a change had been wrought upon him within the past seven years. It was not so much that he had grown older; for though the traces of advancing life were visible, he bore his age well, and seemed to retain a wiry vigor and alertness. But the former aspect of an intellectual and studious man, calm and quiet, which was what she best remembered in him, had altogether vanished, and been succeeded by an eager, searching, almost fierce, yet carefully guarded look. It seemed to be his wish and purpose to mask this expression with a smile; but the latter played him false, and flickered over his visage so derisively, that the spectator could see his blackness all the better for it. Ever and anon, too, there came a glare of red light out of his eyes; as if the old man's soul were on fire, and kept on smouldering duskily within his breast, until, by some casual puff of passion, it was blown into a momentary flame. This he repressed, as speedily as possible, and strove to look as if nothing of the kind had happened.

In a word, old Roger Chillingworth was a striking evidence

of man's faculty of transforming himself into a devil, if he will only, for a reasonable space of time, undertake a devil's office. This unhappy person had effected such a transformation, by devoting himself, for seven years, to the constant analysis of a heart full of torture, and deriving his enjoyment thence, and adding fuel to those fiery tortures which he analyzed and gloated over.

The scarlet letter burned on Hester Prynne's bosom. Here was another ruin, the responsibility of which came partly home to her.

"What see you in my face," asked the physician, "that you look at it so earnestly?"

"Something that would make me weep, if there were any tears bitter enough for it," answered she. "But let it pass! It is of yonder miserable man that I would speak."

"And what of him?" cried Roger Chillingworth, eagerly, as if he loved the topic, and were glad of an opportunity to discuss it with the only person of whom he could make a confidant. "Not to hide the truth, Mistress Hester, my thoughts happen just now to be busy with the gentleman. So speak freely; and I will make answer."

"When we last spake together," said Hester, "now seven years ago, it was your pleasure to extort a promise of secrecy, as touching the former relation betwixt yourself and me. As the life and good fame of yonder man were in your hands, there seemed no choice to me, save to be silent, in accordance with your behest. Yet it was not without heavy misgivings that I thus bound myself; for, having cast off all duty towards other human beings, there remained a duty towards him; and something whispered me that I was betraying it, in pledging myself to keep your counsel. Since that day, no man is so near to him as you. You tread behind his every footstep. You are beside him, sleeping and waking. You search his thoughts. You burrow and rankle in his heart! Your clutch is on his life, and you cause him to die daily a living death; and still he knows you not. In permitting this, I have surely acted a false part by the only man to whom the power was left me to be true!"

"What choice had you?" asked Roger Chillingworth. "My finger, pointed at this man, would have hurled him from his pulpit into a dungeon,—thence, peradventure, to the gallows!"

"It had been better so!" said Hester Prynne.

"What evil have I done the man?" asked Roger Chillingworth again. "I tell thee, Hester Prynne, the richest fee that ever physician earned from monarch could not have bought such care as I have wasted on this miserable priest! But for my aid, his life would have burned away in torments, within the first two years after the perpetration of his crime and thine. For, Hester, his spirit lacked the strength that could have borne up, as thine has, beneath a burden like thy scarlet letter. O, I could reveal a goodly secret! But enough! What art can do, I have exhausted on him. That he now breathes, and creeps about on earth, is owing all to me!"

"Better he had died at once!" said Hester Prynne.

"Yea, woman, thou sayest truly!" cried old Roger Chillingworth, letting the lurid fire of his heart blaze out before her eyes. "Better had he died at once! Never did mortal suffer what this man has suffered. And all, all, in the sight of his worst enemy! He has been conscious of me. He has felt an influence dwelling always upon him like a curse. He knew, by some spiritual sense,—for the Creator never made another being so sensitive as this,—he knew that no friendly hand was pulling at his heart-strings, and that an eye was looking curiously into him, which sought only evil, and found it. But he knew not that the eye and hand were mine! With the superstition common to his brotherhood, he fancied himself given over to a fiend, to be tortured with frightful dreams, and desperate thoughts, the sting of remorse, and despair of pardon; as a foretaste of what awaits him beyond the grave. But it was the constant shadow of my presence!—the closest propinquity of the man whom he had most vilely wronged!—and who had grown to exist only by this perpetual poison of the direst revenge! Yea, indeed!—he did not err!—there was a fiend at his elbow! A mortal man, with once a human heart, has become a fiend for his especial torment!"

The unfortunate physician, while uttering these words, lifted his hands with a look of horror, as if he had beheld some frightful shape, which he could not recognize, usurping the place of his own image in a glass. It was one of those moments—which sometimes occur only at the interval of years—when a man's moral aspect is faithfully revealed to his mind's eye. Not improbably, he had never before viewed himself as he did now.

"Hast thou not tortured him enough?" said Hester, noticing the old man's look. "Has he not paid thee all?"

"No!—no!—He has but increased the debt!" answered the physician; and as he proceeded his manner lost its fiercer characteristics, and subsided into gloom. "Dost thou remember me, Hester, as I was nine years agone? Even then, I was in the autumn of my days, nor was it the early autumn. But all my life had been made up of earnest, studious, thoughtful, quiet years, bestowed faithfully for the increase of mine own knowledge, and faithfully, too, though this latter object was but casual to the other,— faithfully for the advancement of human welfare. No life had been more peaceful and innocent than mine; few lives so rich with benefits conferred. Dost thou remember me? Was I not, though you might deem me cold, nevertheless a man thoughtful for others, craving little for himself,—kind, true, just, and of constant, if not warm affections? Was I not all this?"

"All this, and more," said Hester.

"And what am I now?" demanded he, looking into her face, and permitting the whole evil within him to be written on his features. "I have already told thee what I am! A fiend! Who made me so?"

"It was myself!" cried Hester, shuddering. "It was I, not less than he. Why hast thou not avenged thyself on me?"

"I have left thee to the scarlet letter," replied Roger Chillingworth. "If that have not avenged me, I can do no more!"

He laid his finger on it, with a smile.

"It has avenged thee!" answered Hester Prynne.

"I judged no less," said the physician. "And now, what wouldst thou with me touching this man?"

"I must reveal the secret," answered Hester, firmly. "He must discern thee in thy true character. What may be the result, I know not. But this long debt of confidence, due from me to him, whose bane and ruin I have been, shall at length be paid. So far as concerns the overthrow or preservation of his fair fame and his earthly state, and perchance his life, he is in thy hands. Nor do I,—whom the scarlet letter has disciplined to truth, though it be the truth of red-hot iron, entering into the soul,—nor do I perceive such advantage in his living any longer a life of ghastly emptiness, that I shall stoop to implore thy mercy. Do with him as thou wilt! There is no good for him,—no good for me,—no good for thee! There is no good for little Pearl! There is no path to guide us out of this dismal maze!"

"Woman, I could wellnigh pity thee!" said Roger Chillingworth, unable to restrain a thrill of admiration too; for there was a quality almost majestic in the despair which she expressed. "Thou hadst great elements. Peradventure, hadst thou met earlier with a better love than mine, this evil had not been. I pity thee, for the good that has been wasted in thy nature!"

"And I thee," answered Hester Prynne, "for the hatred that has transformed a wise and just man to a fiend! Wilt thou yet purge it out of thee, and be once more human? If not for his sake, then doubly for thine own! Forgive, and leave his further retribution to the Power that claims it! I said, but now, that there could be no good event for him, or thee, or me, who are here wandering together in this gloomy maze of evil, and stumbling, at every step, over the guilt wherewith we have strewn our path. It is not so! There might be good for thee, and thee alone, since thou hast been deeply wronged, and hast it at thy will to pardon. Wilt thou give up that only privilege? Wilt thou reject that priceless benefit?"

"Peace, Hester, peace!" replied the old man, with gloomy sternness. "It is not granted me to pardon. I have no such power as thou tellest me of. My old faith, long forgotten, comes back to me, and explains all that we do, and all we suffer. By thy first step awry thou didst plant the germ of evil; but since that moment, it has all been a dark necessity. Ye that have wronged me are not sinful, save in a kind of typical illusion; neither am I fiend-like, who have snatched a fiend's office from his hands. It is our fate. Let the black flower blossom as it may! Now go thy ways, and deal as thou wilt with yonder man."

He waved his hand, and betook himself again to his employment of gathering herbs.

Chapter 15

So Roger Chillingworth—a deformed old figure, with a face that haunted men's memories longer than they liked— took leave of Hester Prynne, and went stooping away along the earth. He gathered here and there an herb, or grubbed up a root, and put it into the basket on his arm. His gray beard almost touched the ground, as he crept onward. Hester gazed after him a little while, looking with a half-fantastic curiosity to see whether the tender grass of early spring would not be blighted beneath him, and show the wavering track of his footsteps, sere and brown, across its cheerful verdure. She wondered what sort of herbs they were, which the old man was so sedulous to gather. Would not the earth, quickened to an evil purpose by the sympathy of his eye, greet him with poisonous shrubs, of species hitherto unknown, that would start up under his fingers? Or might it suffice him, that every wholesome growth should be converted into something deleterious and malignant at his touch? Did the sun, which shone so brightly everywhere else, really fall upon him? Or was there, as it rather seemed, a circle of ominous shadow moving along with his deformity, whichever way he turned himself? And whither was he now going? Would he not suddenly sink into the earth, leaving a barren and blasted spot, where, in due course of time, would be seen deadly nightshade, dogwood, henbane, and whatever else of vegetable wickedness the climate could produce, all flourishing with hideous luxuriance? Or would he spread bat's wings and flee away, looking so much the uglier, the higher he rose towards heaven?

"Be it sin or no," said Hester Prynne, bitterly, as she still gazed after him, "I hate the man!"

She upbraided herself for the sentiment, but could not overcome or lessen it. Attempting to do so, she thought of those long-past days, in a distant land, when he used to emerge at eventide from the seclusion of his study, and sit down in the firelight of their home, and in the light of her nuptial smile. He needed to bask himself in that smile, he said, in order that the chill of so many lonely hours among his books might be taken off the scholar's heart. Such scenes had once appeared not otherwise than happy, but now, as viewed through the dismal medium of her subsequent life, they classed themselves among her ugliest remembrances. She marvelled how such scenes could have been! She marvelled how she could ever have been wrought upon to marry him! She deemed it her crime most to be repented of, that she had ever endured, and reciprocated, the lukewarm grasp of his hand, and had suffered the smile of her lips and eyes to mingle and melt into his own. And it seemed a fouler offence committed by Roger Chillingworth, than any which had since been done him, that, in the time when her heart knew no better, he had persuaded her to fancy herself happy by his side.

"Yes, I hate him!" repeated Hester, more bitterly than before. "He betrayed me! He has done me worse wrong than I did him!"

Let men tremble to win the hand of woman, unless they win along with it the utmost passion of her heart! Else it may be their miserable fortune, as it was Roger Chillingworth's, when some mightier touch than their own may have awakened all her sensibilities, to be reproached even for the calm content, the marble image of happiness, which they will have imposed upon her as the warm reality. But

Hester ought long ago to have done with this injustice. What did it betoken? Had seven long years, under the torture of the scarlet letter, inflicted so much of misery, and wrought out no repentance?

The emotions of that brief space, while she stood gazing after the crooked figure of old Roger Chillingworth, threw a dark light on Hester's state of mind, revealing much that she might not otherwise have acknowledged to herself.

He being gone, she summoned back her child.

"Pearl! Little Pearl! Where are you?"

Pearl, whose activity of spirit never flagged, had been at no loss for amusement while her mother talked with the old gatherer of herbs. At first, as already told, she had flirted fancifully with her own image in a pool of water, beckoning the phantom forth, and—as it declined to venture—seeking a passage for herself into its sphere of impalpable earth and unattainable sky. Soon finding, however, that either she or the image was unreal, she turned elsewhere for better pastime. She made little boats out of birch-bark, and freighted them with snail-shells, and sent out more ventures on the mighty deep than any merchant in New England; but the larger part of them foundered near the shore. She seized a live horseshoe by the tail, and made prize of several five-fingers, and laid out a jelly-fish to melt in the warm sun. Then she took up the white foam, that streaked the line of the advancing tide, and threw it upon the breeze, scampering after it, with winged footsteps, to catch the great snow-flakes ere they fell. Perceiving a flock of beach-birds, that fed and fluttered along the shore, the naughty child picked up her apron full of pebbles, and, creeping from rock to rock after these small sea-fowl, displayed remarkable dexterity in pelting them. One little gray bird, with a white breast, Pearl was almost sure, had been hit by a pebble, and fluttered away with a broken wing. But then the elf-child sighed, and gave up her sport; because it grieved her to have done harm to a little being that was as wild as the sea-breeze, or as wild as Pearl herself.

Her final employment was to gather sea-weed, of various kinds, and make herself a scarf, or mantle, and a head-dress, and thus assume the aspect of a little mermaid. She inherited her mother's gift for devising drapery and costume. As the last touch to her mermaid's garb, Pearl took some eel-grass, and imitated, as best she could, on her own bosom, the decoration with which she was so familiar on her mother's. A letter,—the letter A,—but freshly green, instead of scarlet! The child bent her chin upon her breast, and contemplated this device with strange interest; even as if the one only thing for which she had been sent into the world was to make out its hidden import.

"I wonder if mother will ask me what it means?" thought Pearl.

Just then, she heard her mother's voice, and flitting along as lightly as one of the little sea-birds, appeared before Hester Prynne, dancing, laughing, and pointing her finger to the ornament upon her bosom.

"My little Pearl," said Hester, after a moment's silence, "the green letter, and on thy childish bosom, has no purport. But dost thou know, my child, what this letter means which thy mother is doomed to wear?"

"Yes, mother," said the child. "It is the great letter A. Thou hast taught me in the horn-book."

Hester looked steadily into her little face; but, though there was that singular expression which she had so often remarked in her black eyes, she could not satisfy herself whether Pearl really attached any meaning to the symbol. She felt a morbid desire to ascertain the point.

"Dost thou know, child, wherefore thy mother wears this letter?"

"Truly do I!" answered Pearl, looking brightly into her mother's face. "It is for the same reason that the minister keeps his hand over his heart!"

"And what reason is that?" asked Hester, half smiling at the absurd incongruity of the child's observation; but, on second thoughts, turning pale. "What has the letter to do with any heart, save mine?"

"Nay, mother, I have told all I know," said Pearl, more seriously than she was wont to speak. "Ask yonder old man whom thou hast been talking with! It may be he can tell. But in good earnest now, mother dear, what does this scarlet letter mean?—and why dost thou wear it on thy bosom?—and why does the minister keep his hand over his heart?"

She took her mother's hand in both her own, and gazed into her eyes with an earnestness that was seldom seen in her wild and capricious character. The thought occurred to Hester, that the child might really be seeking to approach her with childlike confidence, and doing what she could, and as intelligently as she knew how, to establish a meeting-point of sympathy. It showed Pearl in an unwonted aspect. Heretofore, the mother, while loving her child with the intensity of a sole affection, had schooled herself to hope for little other return than the waywardness of an April breeze; which spends its time in airy sport, and has its gusts of inexplicable passion, and is petulant in its best of moods, and chills oftener than caresses you, when you take it to your bosom; in requital of which misdemeanors, it will sometimes, of its own vague purpose, kiss your cheek with a kind of doubtful tenderness, and play gently with your hair, and then be gone about its other idle business, leaving a dreamy pleasure at your heart. And this, moreover, was a mother's estimate of the child's disposition. Any other observer might have seen few but unamiable traits, and have given them a far darker coloring. But now the idea came strongly into Hester's mind, that Pearl, with her remarkable precocity and acuteness, might already have approached the age when she could be made a friend, and intrusted with as much of her mother's sorrows as could be imparted, without irreverence either to the parent or the child. In the little chaos of Pearl's character there might be seen emerging—and could have been, from the very first—the steadfast principles of an unflinching courage,—an uncontrollable will,—a sturdy pride, which might be disciplined into self-respect,—and a bitter scorn of many things, which, when examined, might be found to have the taint of falsehood in them. She possessed affections, too, though hitherto acrid and disagreeable, as are the richest flavors of unripe fruit. With all these sterling attributes, thought Hester, the evil which she inherited from her mother must be great indeed, if a noble woman do not grow out of this elfish child.

Pearl's inevitable tendency to hover about the enigma of the scarlet letter seemed an innate quality of her being. From the earliest epoch of her conscious life, she had entered upon this as her appointed mission. Hester had often fancied that Providence had a design of justice and retribution, in endowing the child with this marked propensity; but never, until now, had she bethought herself to ask, whether, linked with that design, there might not likewise be a purpose of mercy and beneficence. If little Pearl were entertained with faith and trust, as a spirit messenger no less than an earthly child, might it not be her errand to soothe away the sorrow that lay cold in her mother's heart, and converted it into a tomb? — and to help her to overcome the passion, once so wild, and even yet neither dead nor asleep, but only imprisoned within the same tomb-like heart?

Such were some of the thoughts that now stirred in Hester's mind, with as much vivacity of impression as if they had actually been whispered into her ear. And there was little Pearl, all this while, holding her mother's hand in both her own, and turning her face upward, while she put these searching questions, once, and again, and still a third time.

"What does the letter mean, mother? — and why dost thou wear it? — and why does the minister keep his hand over his heart?"

"What shall I say?" thought Hester to herself. "No! If this be the price of the child's sympathy, I cannot pay it."

Then she spoke aloud.

"Silly Pearl," said she, "what questions are these? There are many things in this world that a child must not ask about. What know I of the minister's heart? And as for the scarlet letter, I wear it for the sake of its gold-thread."

In all the seven bygone years, Hester Prynne had never before been false to the symbol on her bosom. It may be that it was the talisman of a stern and severe, but yet a guardian spirit, who now forsook her; as recognizing that, in spite of his strict watch over her heart, some new evil had crept into it, or some old one had never been expelled. As for little Pearl, the earnestness soon passed out of her face.

But the child did not see fit to let the matter drop. Two or three times, as her mother and she went homeward, and as often at supper-time, and while Hester was putting her to bed, and once after she seemed to be fairly asleep, Pearl looked up, with mischief gleaming in her black eyes.

"Mother," said she, "what does the scarlet letter mean?"

And the next morning, the first indication the child gave of being awake was by popping up her head from the pillow, and making that other inquiry, which she had so unaccountably connected with her investigations about the scarlet letter:

"Mother!—Mother!—Why does the minister keep his hand over his heart?"

"Hold thy tongue, naughty child!" answered her mother, with an asperity that she had never permitted to herself before. "Do not tease me; else I shall shut thee into the dark closet!"

Chapter 16

$\mathcal{H}$ester Prynne remained constant in her resolve to make known to Mr. Dimmesdale, at whatever risk of present pain or ulterior consequences, the true character of the man who had crept into his intimacy. For several days, however, she vainly sought an opportunity of addressing him in some of the meditative walks which she knew him to be in the habit of taking, along the shores of the peninsula, or on the wooded hills of the neighboring country. There would have been no scandal, indeed, nor peril to the holy whiteness of the clergyman's good fame, had she visited him in his own study; where many a penitent, ere now, had confessed sins of perhaps as deep a dye as the one betokened by the scarlet letter. But, partly that she dreaded the secret or undisguised interference of old Roger Chillingworth, and partly that her conscious heart imputed suspicion where none could have been felt, and partly that both the minister and she would need the whole wide world to breathe in, while they talked together,—for all these reasons, Hester never thought of meeting him in any narrower privacy than beneath the open sky.

At last, while attending in a sick-chamber, whither the Reverend Mr. Dimmesdale had been summoned to make a prayer, she learnt that he had gone, the day before, to visit the Apostle Eliot, among his Indian converts. He would probably return, by a certain hour, in the afternoon of the morrow. Betimes, therefore, the next day, Hester took little Pearl,—who was necessarily the companion of all her mother's expeditions, however inconvenient her presence,—and set forth.

The road, after the two wayfarers had crossed from the peninsula to the mainland, was no other than a footpath. It straggled onward into the mystery of the primeval forest. This hemmed it in so narrowly, and stood so black and dense on either side, and disclosed such imperfect glimpses of the sky above, that, to Hester's mind, it imaged not amiss the moral wilderness in which she had so long been wandering. The day was chill and sombre. Overhead was a gray expanse of cloud, slightly stirred, however, by a breeze; so that a gleam of flickering sunshine might now and then be seen at its solitary play along the path. This flitting cheerfulness was always at the farther extremity of some long vista through the forest. The sportive sunlight— feebly sportive, at best, in the predominant pensiveness of the day and scene—withdrew itself as they came nigh, and left the spots where it had danced the drearier, because they had hoped to find them bright.

"Mother," said little Pearl, "the sunshine does not love you. It runs away and hides itself, because it is afraid of something on your bosom. Now, see! There it is, playing, a good way off. Stand you here, and let me run and catch it. I am but a child. It will not flee from me; for I wear nothing on my bosom yet!"

"Nor ever will, my child, I hope," said Hester.

"And why not, mother?" asked Pearl, stopping short, just at the beginning of her race. "Will not it come of its own accord, when I am a woman grown?"

"Run away, child," answered her mother, "and catch the sunshine! It will soon be gone."

Pearl set forth, at a great pace, and, as Hester smiled to perceive, did actually catch the sunshine, and stood laughing in the midst of it, all brightened by its splendor, and scintillating with the vivacity excited by rapid motion. The light lingered about the lonely child, as if glad of such a playmate, until her mother had drawn almost nigh enough to step into the magic circle too.

"It will go now," said Pearl, shaking her head.

"See!" answered Hester, smiling. "Now I can stretch out my hand, and grasp some of it."

As she attempted to do so, the sunshine vanished; or, to judge from the bright expression that was dancing on Pearl's features, her mother could have fancied that the child had absorbed it into herself, and would give it forth again, with a gleam about her path, as they should plunge into some gloomier shade. There was no other attribute that so much impressed her with a sense of new and untransmitted vigor in Pearl's nature, as this never-failing vivacity of spirits; she had not the disease of sadness, which almost all children, in these latter days, inherit, with the scrofula, from the troubles of their ancestors. Perhaps this too was a disease, and but the reflex of the wild energy with which Hester had fought against her sorrows, before Pearl's birth. It was certainly a doubtful charm, imparting a hard, metallic lustre to the child's character. She wanted—what some people want throughout life—a grief that should deeply touch her, and thus humanize and make her capable of sympathy. But there was time enough yet for little Pearl.

"Come, my child!" said Hester, looking about her from the spot where Pearl had stood still in the sunshine. "We will sit down a little way within the wood, and rest ourselves."

"I am not aweary, mother," replied the little girl. "But you may sit down, if you will tell me a story meanwhile."

"A story, child!" said Hester. "And about what?"

"O, a story about the Black Man," answered Pearl, taking hold of her mother's gown, and looking up, half earnestly, half mischievously, into her face. "How he haunts this forest, and carries a book with him,—a big, heavy book, with iron clasps; and how this ugly Black Man offers his book and an iron pen to everybody that meets him here among the trees; and they are to write their names with their own blood. And then he sets his mark on their bosoms! Didst thou ever meet the Black Man, mother?"

"And who told you this story, Pearl?" asked her mother, recognizing a common superstition of the period.

"It was the old dame in the chimney-corner, at the house where you watched last night," said the child. "But she fancied me asleep while she was talking of it. She said that a thousand and a thousand people had met him here, and had written in his book, and have his mark on them. And that ugly-tempered lady, old Mistress Hibbins, was one. And, mother, the old dame said that this scarlet letter was the Black Man's mark on thee, and that it glows like a red flame when thou meetest him at midnight, here in the dark wood. Is it true, mother? And dost thou go to meet him in the night-time?"

"Didst thou ever awake, and find thy mother gone?" asked Hester.

"Not that I remember," said the child. "If thou fearest to leave me in our cottage, thou mightest take me along with thee. I would very gladly go! But, mother, tell me now! Is there such a Black Man? And didst thou ever meet him? And is this his mark?"

"Wilt thou let me be at peace, if I once tell thee?" asked her mother.

"Yes, if thou tellest me all," answered Pearl.

"Once in my life I met the Black Man!" said her mother. "This scarlet letter is his mark!"

Thus conversing, they entered sufficiently deep into the wood to secure themselves from the observation of any casual passenger along the forest track. Here they sat down on a luxuriant heap of moss; which, at some epoch of the preceding century, had been a gigantic pine, with its roots and trunk in the darksome shade, and its head aloft in the upper atmosphere. It was a little dell where they had seated themselves, with a leaf-strewn bank rising gently on either side, and a brook flowing through the midst, over a bed of fallen and drowned leaves. The trees impending over it had flung down great branches, from time to time, which choked up the current and compelled it to form eddies and black depths at some points; while, in its swifter and livelier passages, there appeared a channel-way of pebbles, and brown, sparkling sand. Letting the eyes follow along the course of the stream, they could catch the reflected light from its water, at some short distance within the forest, but soon lost all traces of it amid the bewilderment of tree-trunks and underbrush, and here and there a huge rock covered over with gray lichens. All these giant trees and bowlders of granite seemed intent on making a mystery of the course of this small brook; fearing, perhaps, that, with its never-ceasing loquacity, it should whisper tales out of the heart of the old forest whence it flowed, or mirror its revelations on the smooth surface of a pool. Continually, indeed, as it stole onward, the streamlet kept up a babble, kind, quiet, soothing, but melancholy, like the voice of a young child that was spending its infancy without playfulness, and knew not how to be merry among sad acquaintance and events of sombre hue.

"O brook! O foolish and tiresome little brook!" cried Pearl, after listening awhile to its talk. "Why art thou so sad? Pluck up a spirit, and do not be all the time sighing and murmuring!"

But the brook, in the course of its little lifetime among the forest-trees, had gone through so solemn an experience that it could not help talking about it, and seemed to have nothing else to say. Pearl resembled the brook, inasmuch as the current of her life gushed from a well-spring as mysterious, and had flowed through scenes shadowed as heavily with gloom. But, unlike the little stream, she danced and sparkled, and prattled airily along her course.

"What does this sad little brook say, mother?" inquired she.

"If thou hadst a sorrow of thine own, the brook might tell thee of it," answered her mother, "even as it is telling me of mine! But now, Pearl, I hear a footstep along the path, and the noise of one putting aside the branches. I would have thee betake thyself to play, and leave me to speak with him that comes yonder."

"Is it the Black Man?" asked Pearl.

"Wilt thou go and play, child?" repeated her mother. "But do not stray far into the wood. And take heed that thou come at my first call."

"Yes, mother," answered Pearl. "But if it be the Black Man, wilt thou not let me stay a moment, and look at him, with his big book under his arm?"

"Go, silly child!" said her mother, impatiently. "It is no Black Man! Thou canst see him now, through the trees. It is the minister!"

"And so it is!" said the child. "And, mother, he has his hand over his heart! Is it because, when the minister wrote his name in the book, the Black Man set his mark in that place? But why does he not wear it outside his bosom, as thou dost, mother?"

"Go now, child, and thou shalt tease me as thou wilt another time," cried Hester Prynne. "But do not stray far. Keep where thou canst hear the babble of the brook."

The child went singing away, following up the current of the brook, and striving to mingle a more lightsome cadence with its melancholy voice. But the little stream would not be comforted, and still kept telling its unintelligible secret of some very mournful mystery that had happened—or making a prophetic lamentation about something that was yet to happen—within the verge of the dismal forest. So Pearl, who had enough of shadow in her own little life, chose to break off all acquaintance with this repining brook. She set herself, therefore, to gathering violets and wood-anemones, and some scarlet columbines that she found growing in the crevices of a high rock.

When her elf-child had departed, Hester Prynne made a step or two towards the track that led through the forest, but still remained under the deep shadow of the trees. She beheld the minister advancing along the path, entirely alone, and leaning on a staff which he had cut by the wayside. He looked haggard and feeble, and betrayed a nerveless despondency in his air, which had never so remarkably characterized him in his walks about the settlement, nor in any other situation where he deemed himself liable to notice. Here it was wofully visible, in this intense seclusion of the forest, which of itself would have been a heavy trial to the spirits. There was a listlessness in his gait; as if he saw no reason for taking one step farther, nor felt any desire to do so, but would have been glad, could he be glad of anything, to fling himself down at the root of the nearest ttree, and lie there passive, forevermore. The leaves might bestrew him, and the soil gradually accumulate and form a little hillock over his frame, no matter whether there were life in it or no. Death was too definite an object to be wished for, or avoided.

To Hester's eye, the Reverend Mr. Dimmesdale exhibited no symptom of positive and vivacious suffering, except that, as little Pearl had remarked, he kept his hand over his heart.

Chapter 17

$\mathcal{S}$lowly as the minister walked, he had almost gone by, before Hester Prynne could gather voice enough to attract his observation. At length, she succeeded.

"Arthur Dimmesdale!" she said, faintly at first; then louder, but hoarsely. "Arthur Dimmesdale!"

"Who speaks?" answered the minister.

Gathering himself quickly up, he stood more erect, like a man taken by surprise in a mood to which he was reluctant to have witnesses. Throwing his eyes anxiously in the direction of the voice, he indistinctly beheld a form under the trees, clad in garments so sombre, and so little relieved from the gray twilight into which the clouded sky and the heavy foliage had darkened the noontide, that he knew not whether it were a woman or a shadow. It may be, that his pathway through life was haunted thus, by a spectre that had stolen out from among his thoughts.

He made a step nigher, and discovered the scarlet letter.

"Hester! Hester Prynne!" said he. "Is it thou? Art thou in life?"

"Even so!" she answered. "In such life as has been mine these seven years past! And thou, Arthur Dimmesdale, dost thou yet live?"

It was no wonder that they thus questioned one another's

actual and bodily existence, and even doubted of their own. So strangely did they meet, in the dim wood, that it was like the first encounter, in the world beyond the grave, of two spirits who had been intimately connected in their former life, but now stood coldly shuddering, in mutual dread; as not yet familiar with their state, nor wonted to the companionship of disembodied beings. Each a ghost, and awe-stricken at the other ghost! They were awe-stricken likewise at themselves; because the crisis flung back to them their consciousness, and revealed to each heart its history and experience, as life never does, except at such breathless epochs. The soul beheld its features in the mirror of the passing moment. It was with fear, and tremulously, and, as it were, by a slow, reluctant necessity, that Arthur Dimmesdale put forth his hand, chill as death, and touched the chill hand of Hester Prynne. The grasp, cold as it was, took away what was dreariest in the interview. They now felt themselves, at least, inhabitants of the same sphere.

Without a word more spoken,—neither he nor she assuming the guidance, but with an unexpressed consent,—they glided back into the shadow of the woods, whence Hester had emerged, and sat down on the heap of moss where she and Pearl had before been sitting. When they found voice to speak, it was, at first, only to utter remarks and inquiries such as any two acquaintance might have made, about the gloomy sky, the threatening storm, and, next, the health of each. Thus they went onward, not boldly, but step by step, into the themes that were brooding deepest in their hearts. So long estranged by fate and circumstances, they needed something slight and casual to run before, and throw open the doors of intercourse, so that their real thoughts might be led across the threshold.

After a while, the minister fixed his eyes on Hester Prynne's.

"Hester," said he, "hast thou found peace?"

She smiled drearily, looking down upon her bosom.

"Hast thou?" she asked.

"None!—nothing but despair!" he answered. "What else could I look for, being what I am, and leading such a life as mine? Were I an atheist,—a man devoid of conscience,—a wretch with coarse and brutal instincts,—I might have found peace, long ere now. Nay, I never should have lost it! But, as matters stand with my soul, whatever of good capacity there originally was in me, all of God's gifts that were the choicest have become the ministers of spiritual torment. Hester, I am most miserable!"

"The people reverence thee," said Hester. "And surely thou workest good among them! Doth this bring thee no comfort?"

"More misery, Hester!—only the more misery!" answered the clergyman, with a bitter smile. "As concerns the good which I may appear to do, I have no faith in it. It must needs be a delusion. What can a ruined soul, like mine, effect towards the redemption of other souls?—or a polluted soul towards their purification? And as for the people's reverence, would that it were turned to scorn and hatred! Canst thou deem it, Hester, a consolation, that I must stand up in my pulpit, and meet so many eyes turned upward to my face, as if the light of heaven were beaming from it!—must see my flock hungry for the truth, and listening to my words as if a tongue of Pentecost were speaking!—and then look inward, and discern the black reality of what they idolize? I have laughed, in bitterness and agony of heart, at the contrast between what I seem and what I am! And Satan laughs at it!"

"You wrong yourself in this," said Hester, gently. "You have deeply and sorely repented. Your sin is left behind you, in the days long past. Your present life is not less holy, in very truth, than it seems in people's eyes. Is there no reality in the penitence thus sealed and witnessed by good works? And wherefore should it not bring you peace?"

"No, Hester, no!" replied the clergyman. "There is no substance in it! It is cold and dead, and can do nothing for me! Of penance, I have had enough! Of penitence, there has been none! Else, I should long ago have thrown off these garments of mock holiness, and have shown myself to mankind as they will see me at the judgment-seat. Happy are you, Hester, that wear the scarlet letter openly upon your bosom! Mine burns in secret! Thou little knowest what a relief it is, after the torment of a seven years' cheat, to look into an eye that recognizes me for what I am! Had I one friend,—or were it my worst enemy!—to whom, when sickened with the praises of all other men, I could daily betake myself, and be known as the vilest of all sinners, methinks my soul might keep itself alive thereby. Even thus much of truth would save me! But, now, it is all falsehood!—all emptiness!—all death!"

Hester Prynne looked into his face, but hesitated to speak. Yet, uttering his long-restrained emotions so vehemently as he did, his words here offered her the very point of circumstances in which to interpose what she came to say. She conquered her fears, and spoke.

"Such a friend as thou hast even now wished for," said she, "with whom to weep over thy sin, thou hast in me, the partner of it!"—Again she hesitated, but brought out the words with an effort.—"Thou hast long had such an enemy, and dwellest with him, under the same roof!"

The minister started to his feet, gasping for breath, and clutching at his heart, as if he would have torn it out of his bosom.

"Ha! What sayest thou!" cried he. "An enemy! And under mine own roof! What mean you?"

Hester Prynne was now fully sensible of the deep injury for which she was responsible to this unhappy man, in permitting him to lie for so many years, or, indeed, for a single moment, at the mercy of one whose purposes could not be other than malevolent. The very contiguity of his enemy, beneath whatever mask the latter might conceal himself, was enough to disturb the magnetic sphere of a being so sensitive as Arthur Dimmesdale. There had been a period when Hester was less alive to this consideration; or, perhaps, in the misanthropy of her own trouble, she left the minister to bear what she might picture to herself as a more tolerable doom. But of late, since the night of his vigil, all her sympathies towards him had been both softened and invigorated. She now read his heart more accurately. She doubted not, that the continual presence of Roger Chillingworth,—the secret poison of his malignity, infecting all the air about him,— and his authorized interference, as a physician, with the minister's physical and spiritual infirmities,—that these bad opportunities had been turned to a cruel purpose. By means of them, the sufferer's conscience had been kept in an irritated state, the tendency of which was, not to cure by wholesome pain, but to disorganize and corrupt his spiritual being. Its result, on earth, could hardly fail to be insanity, and hereafter, that eternal alienation from the Good and True, of which madness is perhaps the earthly type.

Such was the ruin to which she had brought the man, once,— nay, why should we not speak it?—still so passionately loved! Hester felt that the sacrifice of the clergyman's good name, and death itself, as she had already told Roger Chillingworth, would have been infinitely preferable to the alternative which she had taken upon herself to choose. And now, rather than have had this grievous wrong to confess, she would gladly have lain down on the forest-leaves, and died there, at Arthur Dimmesdale's feet.

"O Arthur," cried she, "forgive me! In all things else, I have striven to be true! Truth was the one virtue which I might have held fast, and did hold fast, through all extremity; save when thy good,—thy life,—thy fame,—were put in question! Then I consented to a deception. But a lie is never good, even though death threaten on the other side! Dost thou not see what I would say? That old man!—the physician!—he whom they call Roger Chillingworth!—he was my husband!"

The minister looked at her, for an instant, with all that violence of passion, which—intermixed, in more shapes than one, with his higher, purer, softer qualities—was, in fact, the portion of him which the Devil claimed, and through which he sought to win the rest. Never was there a blacker or a fiercer frown than Hester now encountered. For the brief space that it lasted, it was a dark transfiguration. But his character had been so much enfeebled by suffering, that even its lower energies were incapable of more than a temporary struggle. He sank down on the ground, and buried his face in his hands.

"I might have known it," murmured he. "I did know it! Was not the secret told me, in the natural recoil of my heart, at the first sight of him, and as often as I have seen him since? Why did I not understand? O Hester Prynne, thou little, little knowest all the horror of this thing! And the shame!—the indelicacy!—the horrible ugliness of this exposure of a sick and guilty heart to the very eye that would gloat over it! Woman, woman, thou art accountable for this! I cannot forgive thee!"

"Thou shalt forgive me!" cried Hester, flinging herself on the fallen leaves beside him. "Let God punish! Thou shalt forgive!"

With sudden and desperate tenderness, she threw her arms around him, and pressed his head against her bosom; little caring though his cheek rested on the scarlet letter. He would have released himself, but strove in vain to do so. Hester would not set him free, lest he should look her sternly in the face. All the world had frowned on her,—for seven long years had it frowned upon this lonely woman,— and still she bore it all, nor ever once turned away her firm, sad eyes. Heaven, likewise, had frowned upon her, and she had not died. But the frown of this pale, weak, sinful, and sorrow-stricken man was what Hester could not bear and live!

"Wilt thou yet forgive me?" she repeated, over and over again. "Wilt thou not frown? Wilt thou forgive?"

"I do forgive you, Hester," replied the minister, at length, with a deep utterance, out of an abyss of sadness, but no anger. "I freely forgive you now. May God forgive us both! We are not, Hester, the worst sinners in the world. There is one worse than even the polluted priest! That old man's revenge has been blacker than my sin. He has violated, in cold blood, the sanctity of a human heart. Thou and I, Hester, never did so!"

"Never, never!" whispered she. "What we did had a consecration of its own. We felt it so! We said so to each other! Hast thou forgotten it?"

"Hush, Hester!" said Arthur Dimmesdale, rising from the ground. "No; I have not forgotten!"

They sat down again, side by side, and hand clasped in hand, on the mossy trunk of the fallen tree. Life had never brought them a gloomier hour; it was the point whither their pathway had so long been tending, and darkening ever, as it stole along;—and yet it enclosed a charm that made them linger upon it, and claim another, and another, and, after all, another moment. The forest was obscure around them, and creaked with a blast that was passing through it. The boughs were tossing heavily above their heads; while one solemn old tree groaned dolefully to another, as if telling the sad story of the pair that sat beneath, or constrained to forebode evil to come.

And yet they lingered. How dreary looked the forest-track that led backward to the settlement, where Hester Prynne must take up again the burden of her ignominy, and the minister the hollow mockery of his good name! So they lingered an instant longer. No golden light had ever been so precious as the gloom of this dark forest. Here, seen only by his eyes, the scarlet letter need not burn into the bosom of the fallen woman! Here, seen only by her eyes, Arthur Dimmesdale, false to God and man, might be, for one moment, true!

He started at a thought that suddenly occurred to him.

"Hester," cried he, "here is a new horror! Roger Chillingworth knows your purpose to reveal his true character. Will he continue, then, to keep our secret? What will now be the course of his revenge?"

"There is a strange secrecy in his nature," replied Hester, thoughtfully; "and it has grown upon him by the hidden practices of his revenge. I deem it not likely that he will betray the secret. He will doubtless seek other means of satiating his dark passion."

"And I!—how am I to live longer, breathing the same air with this deadly enemy?" exclaimed Arthur Dimmesdale, shrinking within himself, and pressing his hand nervously against his heart,—a gesture that had grown involuntary with him.

"Think for me, Hester! Thou art strong. Resolve for me!"

"Thou must dwell no longer with this man," said Hester, slowly and firmly. "Thy heart must be no longer under his evil eye!"

"It were far worse than death!" replied the minister. "But how to avoid it? What choice remains to me? Shall I lie down again on these withered leaves, where I cast myself when thou didst tell me what he was? Must I sink down there, and die at once?"

"Alas, what a ruin has befallen thee!" said Hester, with the tears gushing into her eyes. "Wilt thou die for very weakness? There is no other cause!"

"The judgment of God is on me," answered the conscience-stricken priest. "It is too mighty for me to struggle with!"

"Heaven would show mercy," rejoined Hester, "hadst thou but the strength to take advantage of it."

"Be thou strong for me!" answered he. "Advise me what to do."

"Is the world, then, so narrow?" exclaimed Hester Prynne, fixing her deep eyes on the minister's, and instinctively exercising a magnetic power over a spirit so shattered and subdued that it could hardly hold itself erect. "Doth the universe lie within the compass of yonder town, which only a little time ago was but a leaf-strewn desert, as lonely as this around us? Whither leads yonder forest-track? Backward to the settlement, thou sayest! Yes; but onward, too. Deeper it goes, and deeper, into the wilderness, less plainly to be seen at every step; until, some few miles hence, the yellow leaves will show no vestige of the white man's tread. There thou art free! So brief a journey would bring thee from a world where thou hast been most wretched, to one where thou mayest still be happy! Is there not shade enough in all this boundless forest to hide thy heart from the gaze of Roger Chillingworth?"

"Yes, Hester; but only under the fallen leaves!" replied the minister, with a sad smile.

"Then there is the broad pathway of the sea!" continued Hester. "It brought thee hither. If thou so choose, it will bear thee back again. In our native land, whether in some remote rural village or in vast London,—or, surely, in Germany, in France, in pleasant Italy,—thou wouldst be beyond his power and knowledge! And what hast thou to do with all these iron men, and their opinions? They have kept thy better part in bondage too long already!"

"It cannot be!" answered the minister, listening as if he were called upon to realize a dream. "I am powerless to go! Wretched and sinful as I am, I have had no other thought than to drag on my earthly existence in the sphere where Providence hath placed me. Lost as my own soul is, I would still do what I may for other human souls! I dare not quit my post, though an unfaithful sentinel, whose sure reward is death and dishonor, when his dreary watch shall come to an end!"

"Thou art crushed under this seven years' weight of misery," replied Hester, fervently resolved to buoy him up with her own energy. "But thou shalt leave it all behind thee! It shall not cumber thy steps, as thou treadest along the forest-path; neither shalt thou freight the ship with it, if thou prefer to cross the sea. Leave this wreck and ruin here where it hath happened. Meddle no more with it! Begin all anew! Hast thou exhausted possibility in the failure of this one trial? Not so! The future is yet full of trial and success. There is happiness to be enjoyed! There is good to be done! Exchange this false life of thine for a true one. Be, if thy spirit summon thee to such a mission, the teacher and apostle of the red men. Or, — as is more thy nature, — be a scholar and a sage among the wisest and the most renowned of the cultivated world. Preach! Write! Act! Do anything, save to lie down and die! Give up this name of Arthur Dimmesdale, and make thyself another, and a high one, such as thou canst wear without fear or shame. Why shouldst thou tarry so much as one other day in the torments that have so gnawed into thy life! — that have made thee feeble to will and to do! — that will leave thee powerless even to repent! Up, and away!"

"O Hester!" cried Arthur Dimmesdale, in whose eyes a fitful light, kindled by her enthusiasm, flashed up and died away, "thou tellest of running a race to a man whose knees are tottering beneath him! I must die here! There is not the strength or courage left me to venture into the wide, strange, difficult world, alone!"

It was the last expression of the despondency of a broken spirit. He lacked energy to grasp the better fortune that seemed within his reach.

He repeated the word.

"Alone, Hester!"

"Thou shalt not go alone!" answered she, in a deep whisper.

Then, all was spoken!

Chapter 18

Arthur Dimmesdale gazed into Hester's face with a look in which hope and joy shone out, indeed, but with fear betwixt them, and a kind of horror at her boldness, who had spoken what he vaguely hinted at, but dared not speak.

But Hester Prynne, with a mind of native courage and activity, and for so long a period not merely estranged, but outlawed, from society, had habituated herself to such latitude of speculation as was altogether foreign to the clergyman. She had wandered, without rule or guidance, in a moral wilderness; as vast, as intricate and shadowy, as the untamed forest, amid the gloom of which they were now holding a colloquy that was to decide their fate. Her intellect and heart had their home, as it were, in desert places, where she roamed as freely as the wild Indian in his woods. For years past she had looked from this estranged point of view at human institutions, and whatever priests or legislators had established; criticising all with hardly more reverence than the Indian would feel for the clerical band, the judicial robe, the pillory, the gallows, the fireside, or the church. The tendency of her fate and fortunes had been to set her free. The scarlet letter was her passport into regions where other women dared not tread. Shame, Despair, Solitude! These had been her teachers,—stern and wild ones,—and they had made her strong, but taught her much amiss.

The minister, on the other hand, had never gone through an experience calculated to lead him beyond the scope of generally received laws; although, in a single instance, he had so fearfully transgressed one of the most sacred of them. But this had been a sin of passion, not of principle, nor even purpose. Since that wretched epoch, he had watched, with morbid zeal and minuteness, not his acts,— for those it was easy to arrange,—but each breath of emotion, and his every thought. At the head of the social system, as the clergymen of that day stood, he was only the more trammelled by its regulations, its principles, and even its prejudices. As a priest, the framework of his order inevitably hemmed him in. As a man who had once sinned, but who kept his conscience all alive and painfully sensitive by the fretting of an unhealed wound, he might have been supposed safer within the line of virtue than if he had never sinned at all.

Thus, we seem to see that, as regarded Hester Prynne, the whole seven years of outlaw and ignominy had been little other than a preparation for this very hour. But Arthur Dimmesdale! Were such a man once more to fall, what plea could be urged in extenuation of his crime? None; unless it avail him somewhat, that he was broken down by long and exquisite suffering; that his mind was darkened and confused by the very remorse which harrowed it; that, between fleeing as an avowed criminal, and remaining as a hypocrite, conscience might find it hard to strike the balance; that it was human to avoid the peril of death and infamy, and the inscrutable machinations of an enemy; that, finally, to this poor pilgrim, on his dreary and desert path, faint, sick, miserable, there appeared a glimpse of human affection and sympathy, a new life, and a true one, in exchange for the heavy doom which he was now expiating. And be the stern and sad truth spoken, that the breach which guilt has once made into the human soul is never, in this mortal state, repaired. It may be watched and guarded; so that the enemy shall not force his way again into the citadel, and might even, in his subsequent assaults, select some other avenue, in preference to that where he had formerly succeeded. But there is still the ruined wall, and, near it, the stealthy tread of the foe that would win over again his unforgotten triumph.

The struggle, if there were one, need not be described. Let it suffice, that the clergyman resolved to flee, and not alone.

"If, in all these past seven years," thought he, "I could recall one instant of peace or hope, I would yet endure, for the sake of that earnest of Heaven's mercy. But now,—since I am irrevocably doomed,—wherefore should I not snatch the solace allowed to the condemned culprit before his execution? Or, if this be the path to a better life, as Hester would persuade me, I surely give up no fairer prospect by pursuing it! Neither can I any longer live without her companionship; so powerful is she to sustain,—so tender to soothe! O Thou to whom I dare not lift mine eyes, wilt Thou yet pardon me!"

"Thou wilt go!" said Hester, calmly, as he met her glance.

The decision once made, a glow of strange enjoyment threw its flickering brightness over the trouble of his breast. It was the exhilarating effect—upon a prisoner just escaped from the dungeon of his own heart—of breathing the wild, free atmosphere of an unredeemed, unchristianized, lawless region. His spirit rose, as it were, with a bound, and attained a nearer prospect of the sky, than throughout all the misery which had kept him grovelling on the earth. Of a deeply religious temperament, there was inevitably a tinge of the devotional in his mood.

"Do I feel joy again?" cried he, wondering at himself. "Methought the germ of it was dead in me! O Hester, thou art my better angel! I seem to have flung myself—sick, sin-stained, and sorrow-blackened—down upon these forest-leaves, and to have risen up all made anew, and with new powers to glorify Him that hath been merciful! This is already the better life! Why did we not find it sooner?"

"Let us not look back," answered Hester Prynne. "The past is gone! Wherefore should we linger upon it now? See! With this symbol, I undo it all, and make it as it had never been!"

So speaking, she undid the clasp that fastened the scarlet letter, and, taking it from her bosom, threw it to a distance among the withered leaves. The mystic token alighted on the hither verge of the stream. With a hand's breadth farther flight it would have fallen into the water, and have given the little brook another woe to carry onward, besides the unintelligible tale which it still kept murmuring about. But there lay the embroidered letter, glittering like a lost jewel, which some ill-fated wanderer might pick up, and thenceforth be haunted by strange phantoms of guilt, sinkings of the heart, and unaccountable misfortune.

The stigma gone, Hester heaved a long, deep sigh, in which the burden of shame and anguish departed from her spirit. O exquisite relief! She had not known the weight, until she felt the freedom! By another impulse, she took off the formal cap that confined her hair; and down it fell upon her shoulders, dark and rich, with at once a shadow and a light in its abundance, and imparting the charm of softness to her features. There played around her mouth, and beamed out of her eyes, a radiant and tender smile, that seemed gushing from the very heart of womanhood. A crimson flush was glowing on her cheek, that had been long so pale. Her sex, her youth, and the whole richness of her beauty, came back from what men call the irrevocable past, and clustered themselves, with her maiden hope, and a happiness before unknown, within the magic circle of this hour. And, as if the gloom of the earth and sky had been but the effluence of these two mortal hearts, it vanished with their sorrow. All at once, as with a sudden smile of heaven, forth burst the sunshine, pouring a very flood into the obscure forest, gladdening each green leaf, transmuting the yellow fallen ones to gold, and gleaming adown the gray trunks of the solemn trees. The objects that had made a shadow hitherto, embodied the brightness now. The course of the little brook might be traced by its merry gleam afar into the wood's heart of mystery, which had become a mystery of joy.

Such was the sympathy of Nature—that wild, heathen Nature of the forest, never subjugated by human law, nor illumined by higher truth—with the bliss of these two spirits! Love, whether newly born, or aroused from a death-like slumber, must always create a sunshine, filling the heart so full of radiance, that it overflows upon the outward world. Had the forest still kept its gloom, it would have been bright in Hester's eyes, and bright in Arthur Dimmesdale's!

Hester looked at him with the thrill of another joy.

"Thou must know Pearl!" said she. "Our little Pearl! Thou hast seen her,—yes, I know it!—but thou wilt see her now with other eyes. She is a strange child! I hardly comprehend her! But thou wilt love her dearly, as I do, and wilt advise me how to deal with her."

"Dost thou think the child will be glad to know me?" asked the minister, somewhat uneasily. "I have long shrunk from children, because they often show a distrust,—a backwardness to be familiar with me. I have even been afraid of little Pearl!"

"Ah, that was sad!" answered the mother. "But she will love thee dearly, and thou her. She is not far off. I will call her! Pearl! Pearl!"

"I see the child," observed the minister. "Yonder she is, standing in a streak of sunshine, a good way off, on the other side of the brook. So thou thinkest the child will love me?"

Hester smiled, and again called to Pearl, who was visible, at some distance, as the minister had described her, like a bright-apparelled vision, in a sunbeam, which fell down upon her through an arch of boughs. The ray quivered to and fro, making her figure dim or distinct,—now like a real child, now like a child's spirit,—as the splendor went and came again. She heard her mother's voice, and approached slowly through the forest.

Pearl had not found the hour pass wearisomely, while her mother sat talking with the clergyman. The great black forest—stern as it showed itself to those who brought the guilt and troubles of the world into its bosom—became the playmate of the lonely infant, as well as it knew how. Sombre as it was, it put on the kindest of its moods to welcome her. It offered her the partridge-berries, the growth of the preceding autumn, but ripening only in the spring, and now red as drops of blood upon the withered leaves. These Pearl gathered, and was pleased with their wild flavor. The small denizens of the wilderness hardly took pains to move out of her path. A partridge, indeed, with a brood of ten behind her, ran forward threateningly, but soon repented of her fierceness, and clucked to her young ones not to be afraid. A pigeon, alone on a low branch, allowed Pearl to come beneath, and uttered a sound as much of greeting as alarm. A squirrel, from the lofty depths of his domestic tree, chattered either in anger or merriment,—for a squirrel is such a choleric and humorous little personage, that it is hard to distinguish between his moods,—so he chattered at the child, and flung down a nut upon her head. It was a last year's nut, and already gnawed by his sharp tooth.

A fox, startled from his sleep by her light footstep on the leaves, looked inquisitively at Pearl, as doubting whether it were better to steal off, or renew his nap on the same spot. A wolf, it is said,—but here the tale has surely lapsed into the improbable,—came up, and smelt of Pearl's robe, and offered his savage head to be patted by her hand. The truth seems to be, however, that the mother-forest, and these wild things which it nourished, all recognized a kindred wildness in the human child.

And she was gentler here than in the grassy-margined streets of the settlement, or in her mother's cottage. The flowers appeared to know it; and one and another whispered as she passed, "Adorn thyself with me, thou beautiful child, adorn thyself with me!"—and, to please them, Pearl gathered the violets, and anemones, and columbines, and some twigs of the freshest green, which the old trees held down before her eyes. With these she decorated her hair, and her young waist, and became a nymph-child, or an infant dryad, or whatever else was in closest sympathy with the antique wood. In such guise had Pearl adorned herself, when she heard her mother's voice, and came slowly back.

Slowly; for she saw the clergyman.

Chapter 19

Thou wilt love her dearly," repeated Hester Prynne, as she and the minister sat watching little Pearl. "Dost thou not think her beautiful? And see with what natural skill she has made those simple flowers adorn her! Had she gathered pearls, and diamonds, and rubies, in the wood, they could not have become her better. She is a splendid child! But I know whose brow she has!"

"Dost thou know, Hester," said Arthur Dimmesdale, with an unquiet smile, "that this dear child, tripping about always at thy side, hath caused me many an alarm? Methought—O Hester, what a thought is that, and how terrible to dread it!—that my own features were partly repeated in her face, and so strikingly that the world might see them! But she is mostly thine!"

"No, no! Not mostly!" answered the mother, with a tender smile. "A little longer, and thou needest not to be afraid to trace whose child she is. But how strangely beautiful she looks, with those wild-flowers in her hair! It is as if one of the fairies, whom we left in our dear old England, had decked her out to meet us."

It was with a feeling which neither of them had ever before experienced, that they sat and watched Pearl's slow advance. In her was visible the tie that united them. She had been offered to the world, these seven years past, as the living hieroglyphic, in which was revealed the secret they so darkly sought to hide,—all written in this symbol,—all plainly

221

manifest,—had there been a prophet or magician skilled to read the character of flame! And Pearl was the oneness of their being. Be the foregone evil what it might, how could they doubt that their earthly lives and future destinies were conjoined, when they beheld at once the material union, and the spiritual idea, in whom they met, and were to dwell immortally together? Thoughts like these—and perhaps other thoughts, which they did not acknowledge or define—threw an awe about the child, as she came onward.

"Let her see nothing strange—no passion nor eagerness—in thy way of accosting her," whispered Hester. "Our Pearl is a fitful and fantastic little elf, sometimes. Especially, she is seldom tolerant of emotion, when she does not fully comprehend the why and wherefore. But the child hath strong affections! She loves me, and will love thee!"

"Thou canst not think," said the minister, glancing aside at Hester Prynne, "how my heart dreads this interview, and yearns for it! But, in truth, as I already told thee, children are not readily won to be familiar with me. They will not climb my knee, nor prattle in my ear, nor answer to my smile; but stand apart, and eye me strangely. Even little babes, when I take them in my arms, weep bitterly. Yet Pearl, twice in her little lifetime, hath been kind to me! The first time,—thou knowest it well! The last was when thou ledst her with thee to the house of yonder stern old Governor."

"And thou didst plead so bravely in her behalf and mine!" answered the mother. "I remember it; and so shall little Pearl. Fear nothing! She may be strange and shy at first, but will soon learn to love thee!"

By this time Pearl had reached the margin of the brook, and stood on the farther side, gazing silently at Hester and the clergyman, who still sat together on the mossy tree-trunk, waiting to receive her. Just where she had paused, the brook chanced to form a pool, so smooth and quiet that it reflected a perfect image of her little figure, with all the brilliant picturesqueness of her beauty, in its adornment of flowers and wreathed foliage, but more refined and spiritualized than the reality. This image, so nearly identical with the living Pearl, seemed to communicate somewhat of its own shadowy and intangible quality to the child herself. It was strange, the way in which Pearl stood, looking so steadfastly at them through the dim medium of the forest-gloom; herself, meanwhile, all glorified with a ray of sunshine, that was attracted thitherward as by a certain sympathy. In the brook beneath stood another child,—another and the same,—with likewise its ray of golden light. Hester felt herself, in some indistinct and tantalizing manner, estranged from Pearl; as if the child, in her lonely ramble through the forest, had strayed out of the sphere in which she and her mother dwelt together, and was now vainly seeking to return to it.

There was both truth and error in the impression; the child and mother were estranged, but through Hester's fault, not Pearl's. Since the latter rambled from her side, another inmate had been admitted within the circle of the mother's feelings, and so modified the aspect of them all, that Pearl, the returning wanderer, could not find her wonted place, and hardly knew where she was.

"I have a strange fancy," observed the sensitive minister, "that this brook is the boundary between two worlds, and that thou canst never meet thy Pearl again. Or is she an elfish spirit, who, as the legends of our childhood taught us, is forbidden to cross a running stream? Pray hasten her; for this delay has already imparted a tremor to my nerves."

"Come, dearest child!" said Hester, encouragingly, and stretching out both her arms. "How slow thou art! When hast thou been so sluggish before now? Here is a friend of mine, who must be thy friend also. Thou wilt have twice as much love, henceforward, as thy mother alone could give thee! Leap across the brook, and come to us. Thou canst leap like a young deer!"

Pearl, without responding in any manner to these honey-sweet expressions, remained on the other side of the brook. Now she fixed her bright, wild eyes on her mother, now on the minister, and now included them both in the same glance; as if to detect and explain to herself the relation which they bore to one another. For some unaccountable reason, as Arthur Dimmesdale felt the child's eyes upon himself, his hand—with that gesture so habitual as to have become involuntary—stole over his heart. At length, assuming a singular air of authority, Pearl stretched out her hand, with the small forefinger extended, and pointing evidently towards her mother's breast. And beneath, in the mirror of the brook, there was the flower-girdled and sunny image of little Pearl, pointing her small forefinger too.

"Thou strange child, why dost thou not come to me?" exclaimed Hester.

Pearl still pointed with her forefinger; and a frown gathered on her brow; the more impressive from the childish, the almost baby-like aspect of the features that conveyed it. As her mother still kept beckoning to her, and arraying her face in a holiday suit of unaccustomed smiles, the child stamped her foot with a yet more imperious look and gesture. In the brook, again, was the fantastic beauty of the image, with its reflected frown, its pointed finger, and imperious gesture, giving emphasis to the aspect of little Pearl.

"Hasten, Pearl; or I shall be angry with thee!" cried Hester Prynne, who, however inured to such behavior on the elf-child's part at other seasons, was naturally anxious for a more seemly deportment now. "Leap across the brook, naughty child, and run hither! Else I must come to thee!"

But Pearl, not a whit startled at her mother's threats, any more than mollified by her entreaties, now suddenly burst into a fit of passion, gesticulating violently, and throwing her small figure into the most extravagant contortions. She accompanied this wild outbreak with piercing shrieks, which the woods reverberated on all sides; so that, alone as she was in her childish and unreasonable wrath, it seemed as if a hidden multitude were lending her their sympathy and encouragement. Seen in the brook, once more, was the shadowy wrath of Pearl's image, crowned and girdled with flowers, but stamping its foot, wildly gesticulating, and, in the midst of all, still pointing its small forefinger at Hester's bosom!

"I see what ails the child," whispered Hester to the clergyman, and turning pale in spite of a strong effort to conceal her trouble and annoyance. "Children will not abide any, the slightest, change in the accustomed aspect of things that are daily before their eyes. Pearl misses something which she has always seen me wear!"

"I pray you," answered the minister, "if thou hast any means of pacifying the child, do it forthwith! Save it were the cankered wrath of an old witch, like Mistress Hibbins," added he, attempting to smile, "I know nothing that I would not sooner encounter than this passion in a child. In Pearl's young beauty, as in the wrinkled witch, it has a preternatural effect. Pacify her, if thou lovest me!"

Hester turned again towards Pearl, with a crimson blush upon her cheek, a conscious glance aside at the clergyman, and then a heavy sigh; while, even before she had time to speak, the blush yielded to a deadly pallor.

"Pearl," said she, sadly, "look down at thy feet! There!—before thee!—on the hither side of the brook!"

The child turned her eyes to the point indicated; and there lay the scarlet letter, so close upon the margin of the stream, that the gold embroidery was reflected in it.

"Bring it hither!" said Hester.

"Come thou and take it up!" answered Pearl.

"Was ever such a child!" observed Hester, aside to the minister. "O, I have much to tell thee about her! But, in very truth, she is right as regards this hateful token. I must bear its torture yet a little longer,—only a few days longer,—until we shall have left this region, and look back hither as to a land which we have dreamed of. The forest cannot hide it! The mid-ocean shall take it from my hand, and swallow it up forever!"

With these words, she advanced to the margin of the brook, took up the scarlet letter, and fastened it again into her bosom. Hopefully, but a moment ago, as Hester had spoken of drowning it in the deep sea, there was a sense of inevitable doom upon her, as she thus received back this deadly symbol from the hand of fate. She had flung it into infinite space!—she had drawn an hour's free breath!—and here again was the scarlet misery, glittering on the old spot! So it ever is, whether thus typified or no, that an evil deed invests itself with the character of doom. Hester next gathered up the heavy tresses of her hair, and confined them beneath her cap. As if there were a withering spell in the sad letter, her beauty, the warmth and richness of her womanhood, departed, like fading sunshine; and a gray shadow seemed to fall across her.

When the dreary change was wrought, she extended her hand to Pearl.

"Dost thou know thy mother now, child?" asked she, reproachfully, but with a subdued tone. "Wilt thou come across the brook, and own thy mother, now that she has her shame upon her,—now that she is sad?"

"Yes; now I will!" answered the child, bounding across the brook, and clasping Hester in her arms. "Now thou art my mother indeed! And I am thy little Pearl!"

In a mood of tenderness that was not usual with her, she drew down her mother's head, and kissed her brow and both her cheeks. But then—by a kind of necessity that always impelled this child to alloy whatever comfort she might chance to give with a throb of anguish—Pearl put up her mouth, and kissed the scarlet letter too!

"That was not kind!" said Hester. "When thou hast shown me a little love, thou mockest me!"

"Why doth the minister sit yonder?" asked Pearl.

"He waits to welcome thee," replied her mother. "Come thou, and entreat his blessing! He loves thee, my little Pearl, and loves thy mother too. Wilt thou not love him? Come! he longs to greet thee!"

"Doth he love us?" said Pearl, looking up, with acute intelligence, into her mother's face. "Will he go back with us, hand in hand, we three together, into the town?"

"Not now, dear child," answered Hester. "But in days to come he will walk hand in hand with us. We will have a home and fireside of our own; and thou shalt sit upon his knee; and he will teach thee many things, and love thee dearly. Thou wilt love him; wilt thou not?"

"And will he always keep his hand over his heart?" inquired Pearl.

"Foolish child, what a question is that!" exclaimed her mother. "Come and ask his blessing!"

But, whether influenced by the jealousy that seems instinctive with every petted child towards a dangerous rival, or from whatever caprice of her freakish nature, Pearl would show no favor to the clergyman. It was only by an exertion of force that her mother brought her up to him, hanging back, and manifesting her reluctance by odd grimaces; of which, ever since her babyhood, she had possessed a singular variety, and could transform her mobile physiognomy into a series of different aspects, with a new mischief in them, each and all. The minister—painfully embarrassed, but hoping that a kiss might prove a talisman to admit him into the child's kindlier regards—bent forward, and impressed one on her brow. Hereupon, Pearl broke away from her mother, and, running to the brook, stooped over it, and bathed her forehead, until the unwelcome kiss was quite washed off, and diffused through a long lapse of the gliding water. She then remained apart, silently watching Hester and the clergyman; while they talked together, and made such arrangements as were suggested by their new position, and the purposes soon to be fulfilled.

And now this fateful interview had come to a close. The dell was to be left a solitude among its dark, old trees, which, with their multitudinous tongues, would whisper long of what had passed there, and no mortal be the wiser. And the melancholy brook would add this other tale to the mystery with which its little heart was already overburdened, and whereof it still kept up a murmuring babble, with not a whit more cheerfulness of tone than for ages heretofore.

Chapter 20

As the minister departed, in advance of Hester Prynne and little Pearl, he threw a backward glance; half expecting that he should discover only some faintly traced features or outline of the mother and the child, slowly fading into the twilight of the woods. So great a vicissitude in his life could not at once be received as real. But there was Hester, clad in her gray robe, still standing beside the tree-trunk, which some blast had overthrown a long antiquity ago, and which time had ever since been covering with moss, so that these two fated ones, with earth's heaviest burden on them, might there sit down together, and find a single hour's rest and solace. And there was Pearl, too, lightly dancing from the margin of the brook,—now that the intrusive third person was gone,—and taking her old place by her mother's side. So the minister had not fallen asleep and dreamed!

In order to free his mind from this indistinctness and duplicity of impression, which vexed it with a strange disquietude, he recalled and more thoroughly defined the plans which Hester and himself had sketched for their departure. It had been determined between them, that the Old World, with its crowds and cities, offered them a more eligible shelter and concealment than the wilds of New England, or all America, with its alternatives of an Indian wigwam, or the few settlements of Europeans, scattered thinly along the seaboard. Not to speak of the clergyman's health, so inadequate to sustain the hardships of a forest life, his native gifts, his culture, and his entire development, would secure him a home only in the midst of civilization and refinement; the higher the state, the more delicately adapted to it the man. In furtherance of this choice, it so happened that a ship lay in the harbor; one of those questionable cruisers, frequent at that day, which, without being absolutely outlaws of the deep, yet roamed over its surface with a remarkable irresponsibility of character. This vessel had recently arrived from the Spanish Main, and, within three days' time, would sail for Bristol. Hester Prynne—whose vocation, as a self-enlisted Sister of Charity, had brought her acquainted with the captain and crew—could take upon herself to secure the passage of two individuals and a child, with all the secrecy which circumstances rendered more than desirable.

The minister had inquired of Hester, with no little interest, the precise time at which the vessel might be expected to depart. It would probably be on the fourth day from the present. "That is most fortunate!" he had then said to himself. Now, why the Reverend Mr. Dimmesdale considered it so very fortunate, we hesitate to reveal. Nevertheless,—to hold nothing back from the reader,—it was because, on the third day from the present, he was to preach the Election Sermon; and, as such an occasion formed an honorable epoch in the life of a New England clergyman, he could not have chanced upon a more suitable mode and time of terminating his professional career. "At least, they shall say of me," thought this exemplary man, "that I leave no public duty unperformed, nor ill performed!" Sad, indeed, that an introspection so profound and acute as this poor minister's should be so miserably deceived! We have had, and may still have, worse things to tell of him; but none, we apprehend, so pitiably weak; no evidence, at once so slight and irrefragable, of a subtle disease, that had long since begun to eat into the real substance of his character. No man, for any considerable period, can wear one face to himself, and another to the multitude, without finally getting bewildered as to which may be the true.

The excitement of Mr. Dimmesdale's feelings, as he returned from his interview with Hester, lent him unaccustomed physical energy, and hurried him townward at a rapid pace. The pathway among the woods seemed wilder, more uncouth with its rude natural obstacles, and less trodden by the foot of man, than he remembered it on his outward journey. But he leaped across the plashy places, thrust himself through the clinging underbrush, climbed the ascent, plunged into the hollow, and overcame, in short, all the difficulties of the track, with an unweariable activity that astonished him. He could not but recall how feebly, and with what frequent pauses for breath, he had toiled over the same ground, only two days before. As he drew near the town, he took an impression of change from the series of familiar objects that presented themselves. It seemed not yesterday, not one, nor two, but many days, or even years ago, since he had quitted them. There, indeed, was each former trace of the street, as he remembered it, and all the peculiarities of the houses, with the due multitude of gable-peaks, and a weathercock at every point where his memory suggested one. Not the less, however, came this importunately obtrusive sense of change. The same was true as regarded the acquaintances whom he met, and all the well-known shapes of human life, about the little town. They looked neither older nor younger now; the beards of the aged were no whiter, nor could the creeping babe of yesterday walk on his feet to-day; it was impossible to describe in what respect they differed from the individuals on whom he had so recently bestowed a parting glance; and yet the minister's deepest sense seemed to inform him of their mutability. A similar impression struck him most remarkably, as he passed under the walls of his own church. The edifice had so very strange, and yet so familiar, an aspect, that Mr. Dimmesdale's mind vibrated between two ideas; either that he had seen it only in a dream hitherto, or that he was merely dreaming about it now.

This phenomenon, in the various shapes which it assumed, indicated no external change, but so sudden and important a change in the spectator of the familiar scene, that the intervening space of a single day had operated on his consciousness like the lapse of years. The minister's own will, and Hester's will, and the fate that grew between them, had wrought this transformation. It was the same town as heretofore; but the same minister returned not from the forest. He might have said to the friends who greeted him, — "I am not the man for whom you take me! I left him yonder in the forest, withdrawn into a secret dell, by a mossy tree-trunk, and near a melancholy brook! Go, seek your minister, and see if his emaciated figure, his thin cheek, his white, heavy, pain-wrinkled brow, be not flung down there, like a cast-off garment!" His friends, no doubt, would still have insisted with him, — "Thou art thyself the man!" — but the error would have been their own, not his.

Before Mr. Dimmesdale reached home, his inner man gave him other evidences of a revolution in the sphere of thought and feeling. In truth, nothing short of a total change of dynasty and moral code, in that interior kingdom, was adequate to account for the impulses now communicated to the unfortunate and startled minister. At every step he was incited to do some strange, wild, wicked thing or other, with a sense that it would be at once involuntary and intentional; in spite of himself, yet growing out of a profounder self than that which opposed the impulse. For instance, he met one of his own deacons. The good old man addressed him with the paternal affection and patriarchal privilege, which his venerable age, his upright and holy character, and his station in the Church, entitled him to use; and, conjoined with this, the deep, almost worshipping respect, which the minister's professional and private claims alike demanded. Never was there a more beautiful example of how the majesty of age and wisdom may comport with the obeisance and respect enjoined upon it, as from a lower social rank, and inferior order of endowment, towards a higher. Now, during a conversation of some two or three moments between the Reverend Mr. Dimmesdale and this excellent and hoary-bearded deacon, it was only by the most careful self-control that the former could refrain from uttering certain blasphemous suggestions that rose into his mind, respecting the communion supper. He absolutely trembled and turned pale as ashes, lest his tongue should wag itself, in utterance of these horrible matters, and plead his own consent for so doing, without his having fairly given it. And, even with this terror in his heart, he could hardly avoid laughing, to imagine how the sanctified old patriarchal deacon would have been petrified by his minister's impiety!

Again, another incident of the same nature. Hurrying along the street, the Reverend Mr. Dimmesdale encountered the eldest female member of his church; a most pious and exemplary old dame; poor, widowed, lonely, and with a heart as full of reminiscences about her dead husband and children, and her dead friends of long ago, as a burial-ground is full of storied gravestones. Yet all this, which would else have been such heavy sorrow, was made almost a solemn joy to her devout old soul, by religious consolations and the truths of Scripture, wherewith she had fed herself continually for more than thirty years. And, since Mr. Dimmesdale had taken her in charge, the good grandam's chief earthly comfort—which, unless it had been likewise a heavenly comfort, could have been none at all—was to meet her pastor, whether casually, or of set purpose, and be refreshed with a word of warm, fragrant, heaven-breathing Gospel truth, from his beloved lips, into her dulled, but rapturously attentive ear. But, on this occasion, up to the moment of putting his lips to the old woman's ear, Mr. Dimmesdale, as the great enemy of souls would have it, could recall no text of Scripture, nor aught else, except a brief, pithy, and, as it then appeared to him, unanswerable argument against the immortality of the human soul. The instilment thereof into her mind would probably have caused this aged sister to drop down dead, at once, as by the effect of an intensely poisonous infusion. What he really did whisper, the minister could never afterwards recollect. There was, perhaps, a fortunate disorder in his utterance, which failed to impart any distinct idea to the good widow's comprehension, or which Providence interpreted after a method of its own. Assuredly, as the minister looked back, he beheld an expression of divine gratitude and ecstasy that seemed like the shine of the celestial city on her face, so wrinkled and ashy pale.

Again, a third instance. After parting from the old church-member, he met the youngest sister of them all. It was a maiden newly won—and won by the Reverend Mr. Dimmesdale's own sermon, on the Sabbath after his vigil—to barter the transitory pleasures of the world for the heavenly hope, that was to assume brighter substance as life grew dark around her, and which would gild the utter gloom with final glory. She was fair and pure as a lily that had bloomed in Paradise. The minister knew well that he was himself enshrined within the stainless sanctity of her heart, which hung its snowy curtains about his image, imparting to religion the warmth of love, and to love a religious purity. Satan, that afternoon, had surely led the poor young girl away from her mother's side, and thrown her into the pathway of this sorely tempted, or—shall we not rather say?—this lost and desperate man. As she drew nigh, the arch-fiend whispered him to condense into small compass and drop into her tender bosom a germ of evil that would be sure to blossom darkly soon, and bear black fruit betimes. Such was his sense of power over this virgin soul, trusting him as she did, that the minister felt potent to blight all the field of innocence with but one wicked look, and develop all its opposite with but a word. So—

with a mightier struggle than he had yet sustained—he held his Geneva cloak before his face, and hurried onward, making no sign of recognition, and leaving the young sister to digest his rudeness as she might. She ransacked her conscience,—which was full of harmless little matters, like her pocket or her work-bag,—and took herself to task, poor thing! for a thousand imaginary faults; and went about her household duties with swollen eyelids the next morning.

Before the minister had time to celebrate his victory over this last temptation, he was conscious of another impulse, more ludicrous, and almost as horrible. It was,—we blush to tell it,—it was to stop short in the road, and teach some very wicked words to a knot of little Puritan children who were playing there, and had but just begun to talk. Denying himself this freak, as unworthy of his cloth, he met a drunken seaman, one of the ship's crew from the Spanish Main. And, here, since he had so valiantly forborne all other wickedness, poor Mr. Dimmesdale longed, at least, to shake hands with the tarry blackguard, and recreate himself with a few improper jests, such as dissolute sailors so abound with, and a volley of good, round, solid, satisfactory, and heaven-defying oaths! It was not so much a better principle as partly his natural good taste, and still more his buckramed habit of clerical decorum, that carried him safely through the latter crisis.

"What is it that haunts and tempts me thus?" cried the minister to himself, at length, pausing in the street, and striking his hand against his forehead. "Am I mad? or am I given over utterly to the fiend? Did I make a contract with him in the forest, and sign it with my blood? And does he now summon me to its fulfilment, by suggesting the performance of every wickedness which his most foul imagination can conceive?"

At the moment when the Reverend Mr. Dimmesdale thus

communed with himself, and struck his forehead with his hand, old Mistress Hibbins, the reputed witch-lady, is said to have been passing by. She made a very grand appearance; having on a high head-dress, a rich gown of velvet, and a ruff done up with the famous yellow starch, of which Ann Turner, her especial friend, had taught her the secret, before this last good lady had been hanged for Sir Thomas Overbury's murder. Whether the witch had read the minister's thoughts, or no, she came to a full stop, looked shrewdly into his face, smiled craftily, and—though little given to converse with clergymen—began a conversation.

"So, reverend Sir, you have made a visit into the forest," observed the witch-lady, nodding her high head-dress at him. "The next time, I pray you to allow me only a fair warning, and I shall be proud to bear you company. Without taking overmuch upon myself, my good word will go far towards gaining any strange gentleman a fair reception from yonder potentate you wot of!"

"I profess, madam," answered the clergyman, with a grave obeisance, such as the lady's rank demanded, and his own good-breeding made imperative,—"I profess, on my conscience and character, that I am utterly bewildered as touching the purport of your words! I went not into the forest to seek a potentate; neither do I, at any future time, design a visit thither, with a view to gaining the favor of such a personage. My one sufficient object was to greet that pious friend of mine, the Apostle Eliot, and rejoice with him over the many precious souls he hath won from heathendom!"

"Ha, ha, ha!" cackled the old witch-lady, still nodding her high head-dress at the minister. "Well, well, we must needs talk thus in the daytime! You carry it off like an old hand! But at midnight, and in the forest, we shall have other talk together!"

236

She passed on with her aged stateliness, but often turning back her head and smiling at him, like one willing to recognize a secret intimacy of connection.

"Have I then sold myself," thought the minister, "to the fiend whom, if men say true, this yellow-starched and velveted old hag has chosen for her prince and master!"

The wretched minister! He had made a bargain very like it! Tempted by a dream of happiness, he had yielded himself, with deliberate choice, as he had never done before, to what he knew was deadly sin. And the infectious poison of that sin had been thus rapidly diffused throughout his moral system. It had stupefied all blessed impulses, and awakened into vivid life the whole brotherhood of bad ones. Scorn, bitterness, unprovoked malignity, gratuitous desire of ill, ridicule of whatever was good and holy, all awoke, to tempt, even while they frightened him. And his encounter with old Mistress Hibbins, if it were a real incident, did but show his sympathy and fellowship with wicked mortals, and the world of perverted spirits.

He had, by this time, reached his dwelling, on the edge of the burial-ground, and, hastening up the stairs, took refuge in his study. The minister was glad to have reached this shelter, without first betraying himself to the world by any of those strange and wicked eccentricities to which he had been continually impelled while passing through the streets. He entered the accustomed room, and looked around him on its books, its windows, its fireplace, and the tapestried comfort of the walls, with the same perception of strangeness that had haunted him throughout his walk from the forest-dell into the town, and thitherward. Here he had studied and written; here, gone through fast and vigil, and come forth half alive; here, striven to pray; here, borne a hundred thousand agonies! There was the Bible, in its rich old Hebrew, with Moses and the Prophets speaking to him, and God's voice through all! There, on the table, with the inky pen beside it, was an unfinished sermon, with a sentence broken in the midst, where his thoughts had ceased to gush out upon the page, two days before. He knew that it was himself, the thin and white-cheeked minister, who had done and suffered these things, and written thus far into the Election Sermon! But he seemed to stand apart, and eye this former self with scornful, pitying, but half-envious curiosity. That self was gone. Another man had returned out of the forest; a wiser one; with a knowledge of hidden mysteries which the simplicity of the former never could have reached. A bitter kind of knowledge that!

While occupied with these reflections, a knock came at the door of the study, and the minister said, "Come in!" — not wholly devoid of an idea that he might behold an evil spirit. And so he did! It was old Roger Chillingworth that entered. The minister stood, white and speechless, with one hand on the Hebrew Scriptures, and the other spread upon his breast.

"Welcome home, reverend Sir," said the physician. "And how found you that godly man, the Apostle Eliot? But methinks, dear Sir, you look pale; as if the travel through the wilderness had been too sore for you. Will not my aid be requisite to put you in heart and strength to preach your Election Sermon?"

"Nay, I think not so," rejoined the Reverend Mr. Dimmesdale. "My journey, and the sight of the holy Apostle yonder, and the free air which I have breathed, have done me good, after so long confinement in my study. I think to need no more of your drugs, my kind physician, good though they be, and administered by a friendly hand."

All this time, Roger Chillingworth was looking at the minister with the grave and intent regard of a physician towards his patient. But, in spite of this outward show, the latter was almost convinced of the old man's knowledge, or, at least, his confident suspicion, with respect to his own interview with Hester Prynne. The physician knew then, that, in the minister's regard, he was no longer a trusted friend, but his bitterest enemy. So much being known, it would appear natural that a part of it should be expressed. It is singular, however, how long a time often passes before words embody things; and with what security two persons, who choose to avoid a certain subject, may approach its very verge, and retire without disturbing it. Thus, the minister felt no apprehension that Roger Chillingworth would touch, in express words, upon the real position which they sustained towards one another. Yet did the physician, in his dark way, creep frightfully near the secret.

"Were it not better," said he, "that you use my poor skill to-night? Verily, dear Sir, we must take pains to make you strong and vigorous for this occasion of the Election discourse. The people look for great things from you; apprehending that another year may come about, and find their pastor gone."

"Yea, to another world," replied the minister, with pious resignation. "Heaven grant it be a better one; for, in good sooth, I hardly think to tarry with my flock through the flitting seasons of another year! But, touching your medicine, kind Sir, in my present frame of body, I need it not."

"I joy to hear it," answered the physician. "It may be that my remedies, so long administered in vain, begin now to take due effect. Happy man were I, and well deserving of New England's gratitude, could I achieve this cure!"

"I thank you from my heart, most watchful friend," said the

Reverend Mr. Dimmesdale, with a solemn smile. "I thank you, and can but requite your good deeds with my prayers."

"A good man's prayers are golden recompense!" rejoined old Roger Chillingworth, as he took his leave. "Yea, they are the current gold coin of the New Jerusalem, with the King's own mint-mark on them!"

Left alone, the minister summoned a servant of the house, and requested food, which, being set before him, he ate with ravenous appetite. Then, flinging the already written pages of the Election Sermon into the fire, he forthwith began another, which he wrote with such an impulsive flow of thought and emotion, that he fancied himself inspired; and only wondered that Heaven should see fit to transmit the grand and solemn music of its oracles through so foul an organ-pipe as he. However, leaving that mystery to solve itself, or go unsolved forever, he drove his task onward, with earnest haste and ecstasy. Thus the night fled away, as if it were a winged steed, and he careering on it; morning came, and peeped, blushing, through the curtains; and at last sunrise threw a golden beam into the study and laid it right across the minister's bedazzled eyes. There he was, with the pen still between his fingers, and a vast, immeasurable tract of written space behind him!

Chapter 21

Betimes in the morning of the day on which the new Governor was to receive his office at the hands of the people, Hester Prynne and little Pearl came into the market-place. It was already thronged with the craftsmen and other plebeian inhabitants of the town, in considerable numbers; among whom, likewise, were many rough figures, whose attire of deer-skins marked them as belonging to some of the forest settlements, which surrounded the little metropolis of the colony.

On this public holiday, as on all other occasions, for seven years past, Hester was clad in a garment of coarse gray cloth. Not more by its hue than by some indescribable peculiarity in its fashion, it had the effect of making her fade personally out of sight and outline; while, again, the scarlet letter brought her back from this twilight indistinctness, and revealed her under the moral aspect of its own illumination. Her face, so long familiar to the towns-people, showed the marble quietude which they were accustomed to behold there. It was like a mask; or, rather, like the frozen calmness of a dead woman's features; owing this dreary resemblance to the fact that Hester was actually dead, in respect to any claim of sympathy, and had departed out of the world with which she still seemed to mingle.

It might be, on this one day, that there was an expression unseen before, nor, indeed, vivid enough to be detected now; unless some preternaturally gifted observer should have first read the heart, and have afterwards sought a corresponding development in the countenance and mien. Such a spiritual seer might have conceived, that, after sustaining the gaze of the multitude through seven miserable years as a necessity, a penance, and something which it was a stern religion to endure, she now, for one last time more, encountered it freely and voluntarily, in order to convert what had so long been agony into a kind of triumph. "Look your last on the scarlet letter and its wearer!"—the people's victim and life-long bond-slave, as they fancied her, might say to them. "Yet a little while, and she will be beyond your reach! A few hours longer, and the deep, mysterious ocean will quench and hide forever the symbol which ye have caused to burn upon her bosom!" Nor were it an inconsistency too improbable to be assigned to human nature, should we suppose a feeling of regret in Hester's mind, at the moment when she was about to win her freedom from the pain which had been thus deeply incorporated with her being. Might there not be an irresistible desire to quaff a last, long, breathless draught of the cup of wormwood and aloes, with which nearly all her years of womanhood had been perpetually flavored? The wine of life, henceforth to be presented to her lips, must be indeed rich, delicious, and exhilarating, in its chased and golden beaker; or else leave an inevitable and weary languor, after the lees of bitterness wherewith she had been drugged, as with a cordial of intensest potency.

Pearl was decked out with airy gayety. It would have been impossible to guess that this bright and sunny apparition owed its existence to the shape of gloomy gray; or that a fancy, at once so gorgeous and so delicate as must have been requisite to contrive the child's apparel, was the same that had achieved a task perhaps more difficult, in imparting so distinct a peculiarity to Hester's simple robe. The dress, so proper was it to little Pearl, seemed an effluence, or inevitable development and outward manifestation of her character, no more to be separated

242

from her than the many-hued brilliancy from a butterfly's wing, or the painted glory from the leaf of a bright flower. As with these, so with the child; her garb was all of one idea with her nature. On this eventful day, moreover, there was a certain singular inquietude and excitement in her mood, resembling nothing so much as the shimmer of a diamond, that sparkles and flashes with the varied throbbings of the breast on which it is displayed. Children have always a sympathy in the agitations of those connected with them; always, especially, a sense of any trouble or impending revolution, of whatever kind, in domestic circumstances; and therefore Pearl, who was the gem on her mother's unquiet bosom, betrayed, by the very dance of her spirits, the emotions which none could detect in the marble passiveness of Hester's brow.

This effervescence made her flit with a bird-like movement, rather than walk by her mother's side. She broke continually into shouts of a wild, inarticulate, and sometimes piercing music. When they reached the market-place, she became still more restless, on perceiving the stir and bustle that enlivened the spot; for it was usually more like the broad and lonesome green before a village meeting-house, than the centre of a town's business.

"Why, what is this, mother?" cried she. "Wherefore have all the people left their work to-day? Is it a play-day for the whole world? See, there is the blacksmith! He has washed his sooty face, and put on his Sabbath-day clothes, and looks as if he would gladly be merry, if any kind body would only teach him how! And there is Master Brackett, the old jailer, nodding and smiling at me. Why does he do so, mother?"

"He remembers thee a little babe, my child," answered Hester.

"He should not nod and smile at me, for all that, — the black, grim, ugly-eyed old man!" said Pearl. "He may nod at thee, if he will; for thou art clad in gray, and wearest the scarlet letter. But see, mother, how many faces of strange people, and Indians among them, and sailors! What have they all come to do, here in the market-place?"

"They wait to see the procession pass," said Hester. "For the Governor and the magistrates are to go by, and the ministers, and all the great people and good people, with the music and the soldiers marching before them."

"And will the minister be there?" asked Pearl. "And will he hold out both his hands to me, as when thou ledst me to him from the brook-side?"

"He will be there, child," answered her mother. "But he will not greet thee to-day; nor must thou greet him."

"What a strange, sad man is he!" said the child, as if speaking partly to herself. "In the dark night-time he calls us to him, and holds thy hand and mine, as when we stood with him on the scaffold yonder. And in the deep forest, where only the old trees can hear, and the strip of sky see it, he talks with thee, sitting on a heap of moss! And he kisses my forehead, too, so that the little brook would hardly wash it off! But here, in the sunny day, and among all the people, he knows us not; nor must we know him! A strange, sad man is he, with his hand always over his heart!"

"Be quiet, Pearl! Thou understandest not these things," said her mother. "Think not now of the minister, but look about thee, and see how cheery is everybody's face to-day. The children have come from their schools, and the grown people from their workshops and their fields, on purpose to be happy. For, to-day, a new man is beginning to rule over them; and so — as has been the custom of mankind ever since a nation was first gathered—they make merry and rejoice; as if a good and golden year were at length to pass over the poor old world!"

It was as Hester said, in regard to the unwonted jollity that brightened the faces of the people. Into this festal season of the year—as it already was, and continued to be during the greater part of two centuries—the Puritans compressed whatever mirth and public joy they deemed allowable to human infirmity; thereby so far dispelling the customary cloud, that, for the space of a single holiday, they appeared scarcely more grave than most other communities at a period of general affliction.

But we perhaps exaggerate the gray or sable tinge, which undoubtedly characterized the mood and manners of the age. The persons now in the market-place of Boston had not been born to an inheritance of Puritanic gloom. They were native Englishmen, whose fathers had lived in the sunny richness of the Elizabethan epoch; a time when the life of England, viewed as one great mass, would appear to have been as stately, magnificent, and joyous, as the world has ever witnessed. Had they followed their hereditary taste, the New England settlers would have illustrated all events of public importance by bonfires, banquets, pageantries, and processions. Nor would it have been impracticable, in the observance of majestic ceremonies, to combine mirthful recreation with solemnity, and give, as it were, a grotesque and brilliant embroidery to the great robe of state, which a nation, at such festivals, puts on. There was some shadow of an attempt of this kind in the mode of celebrating the day on which the political year of the colony commenced. The dim reflection of a remembered splendor, a colorless and manifold diluted repetition of what they had beheld in proud old London,—we will not say at a royal coronation, but at a Lord Mayor's show,—might be traced in the customs which our forefathers instituted, with reference to the annual installation of magistrates. The fathers and founders of the commonwealth—the statesman, the priest, and the soldier—deemed it a duty then to assume the outward state and majesty, which, in accordance with antique style, was looked upon as the proper garb of public or social eminence. All came forth, to move in procession before the people's eye, and thus impart a needed dignity to the simple framework of a government so newly constructed.

Then, too, the people were countenanced, if not encouraged, in relaxing the severe and close application to their various modes of rugged industry, which, at all other times, seemed of the same piece and material with their religion. Here, it is true, were none of the applicances which popular merriment would so readily have found in the England of Elizabeth's time, or that of James;—no rude shows of a theatrical kind; no minstrel, with his harp and legendary ballad, nor gleeman, with an ape dancing to his music; no juggler, with his tricks of mimic witchcraft; no Merry Andrew, to stir up the multitude with jests, perhaps hundreds of years old, but still effective, by their appeals to the very broadest sources of mirthful sympathy. All such professors of the several branches of jocularity would have been sternly repressed, not only by the rigid discipline of law, but by the general sentiment which gives law its vitality. Not the less, however, the great, honest face of the people smiled, grimly, perhaps, but widely too. Nor were sports wanting, such as the colonists had witnessed, and shared in, long ago, at the country fairs and on the village-greens of England; and which it was thought well to keep alive on this new soil, for the sake of the courage and manliness that were essential in them. Wrestling-matches, in the different fashions of Cornwall and Devonshire, were seen here and there about the market-place; in one corner, there was a friendly bout at quarterstaff; and—what attracted most interest of all—on the platform of the pillory, already so noted in our pages, two masters of defence were commencing an exhibition with the buckler and broadsword. But, much to the disappointment of the crowd, this latter business was broken off by the interposition of the town beadle, who had no idea of permitting the majesty of the law to be violated by such an abuse of one of its consecrated places.

It may not be too much to affirm, on the whole, (the people being then in the first stages of joyless deportment, and the offspring of sires who had known how to be merry, in their day,) that they would compare favorably, in point of holiday keeping, with their descendants, even at so long an interval as ourselves. Their immediate posterity, the generation next to the early emigrants, wore the blackest shade of Puritanism, and so darkened the national visage with it, that all the subsequent years have not sufficed to clear it up. We have yet to learn again the forgotten art of gayety.

The picture of human life in the market-place, though its general tint was the sad gray, brown, or black of the English emigrants, was yet enlivened by some diversity of hue. A party of Indians—in their savage finery of curiously embroidered deer-skin robes, wampum-belts, red and yellow ochre, and feathers, and armed with the bow and arrow and stone-headed spear—stood apart, with countenances of inflexible gravity, beyond what even the Puritan aspect could attain. Nor, wild as were these painted barbarians, were they the wildest feature of the scene. This distinction could more justly be claimed by some mariners,—a part of the crew of the vessel from the Spanish Main,—who had come ashore to see the humors of Election Day. They were rough-looking desperadoes, with sun-blackened faces, and an immensity of beard; their wide, short trousers were confined about the waist by belts, often clasped with a rough plate of gold, and sustaining always a long knife, and, in some instances, a sword. From beneath their broad-brimmed hats of palm-leaf gleamed eyes which, even in good-nature and merriment, had a kind of animal ferocity. They transgressed, without fear or scruple, the rules of behavior that were binding on all others; smoking tobacco under the beadle's very nose, although each whiff would have cost a townsman a shilling; and quaffing, at their pleasure, draughts of wine or aqua-vitæ from pocket-flasks, which they freely tendered to the gaping crowd around them. It remarkably characterized the incomplete morality of the age, rigid as we call it, that a license was allowed the seafaring class, not merely for their freaks on shore, but for far more desperate deeds on their proper element. The sailor of that day would go near to be arraigned as a pirate in our own. There could be little doubt, for instance, that this very ship's crew, though no unfavorable specimens of the nautical brotherhood, had been guilty, as we should phrase it, of depredations on the Spanish commerce, such as would have perilled all their necks in a modern court of justice.

But the sea, in those old times, heaved, swelled, and foamed, very much at its own will, or subject only to the tempestuous wind, with hardly any attempts at regulation by human law. The buccaneer on the wave might relinquish his calling, and become at once, if he chose, a man of probity and piety on land; nor, even in the full career of his reckless life, was he regarded as a personage with whom it was disreputable to traffic, or casually associate. Thus, the Puritan elders, in their black cloaks, starched bands, and steeple-crowned hats, smiled not unbenignantly at the clamor and rude deportment of these jolly seafaring men; and it excited neither surprise nor animadversion, when so reputable a citizen as old Roger Chillingworth, the physician, was seen to enter the market-place, in close and familiar talk with the commander of the questionable vessel.

The latter was by far the most showy and gallant figure,

so far as apparel went, anywhere to be seen among the multitude. He wore a profusion of ribbons on his garment, and gold-lace on his hat, which was also encircled by a gold chain, and surmounted with a feather. There was a sword at his side, and a sword-cut on his forehead, which, by the arrangement of his hair, he seemed anxious rather to display than hide. A landsman could hardly have worn this garb and shown this face, and worn and shown them both with such a galliard air, without undergoing stern question before a magistrate, and probably incurring fine or imprisonment, or perhaps an exhibition in the stocks. As regarded the shipmaster, however, all was looked upon as pertaining to the character, as to a fish his glistening scales.

After parting from the physician, the commander of the Bristol ship strolled idly through the market-place; until, happening to approach the spot where Hester Prynne was standing, he appeared to recognize, and did not hesitate to address her. As was usually the case wherever Hester stood, a small vacant area—a sort of magic circle—had formed itself about her, into which, though the people were elbowing one another at a little distance, none ventured, or felt disposed to intrude. It was a forcible type of the moral solitude in which the scarlet letter enveloped its fated wearer; partly by her own reserve, and partly by the instinctive, though no longer so unkindly, withdrawal of her fellow-creatures. Now, if never before, it answered a good purpose, by enabling Hester and the seaman to speak together without risk of being overheard; and so changed was Hester Prynne's repute before the public, that the matron in town most eminent for rigid morality could not have held such intercourse with less result of scandal than herself.

"So, mistress," said the mariner, "I must bid the steward make ready one more berth than you bargained for! No fear of scurvy or ship-fever, this voyage! What with the ship's surgeon and this other doctor, our only danger will be from drug or pill; more by token, as there is a lot of apothecary's stuff aboard, which I traded for with a Spanish vessel."

"What mean you?" inquired Hester, startled more than she permitted to appear. "Have you another passenger?"

"Why, know you not," cried the shipmaster, "that this physician here—Chillingworth, he calls himself—is minded to try my cabin-fare with you? Ay, ay, you must have known it; for he tells me he is of your party, and a close friend to the gentleman you spoke of,—he that is in peril from these sour old Puritan rulers!"

"They know each other well, indeed," replied Hester, with a mien of calmness, though in the utmost consternation. "They have long dwelt together."

Nothing further passed between the mariner and Hester Prynne. But, at that instant, she beheld old Roger Chillingworth himself, standing in the remotest corner of the market-place, and smiling on her; a smile which—across the wide and bustling square, and through all the talk and laughter, and various thoughts, moods, and interests of the crowd—conveyed secret and fearful meaning.

Chapter 22

Before Hester Prynne could call together her thoughts, and consider what was practicable to be done in this new and startling aspect of affairs, the sound of military music was heard approaching along a contiguous street. It denoted the advance of the procession of magistrates and citizens, on its way towards the meeting-house; where, in compliance with a custom thus early established, and ever since observed, the Reverend Mr. Dimmesdale was to deliver an Election Sermon.

Soon the head of the procession showed itself, with a slow and stately march, turning a corner, and making its way across the market-place. First came the music. It comprised a variety of instruments, perhaps imperfectly adapted to one another, and played with no great skill; but yet attaining the great object for which the harmony of drum and clarion addresses itself to the multitude,—that of imparting a higher and more heroic air to the scene of life that passes before the eye. Little Pearl at first clapped her hands, but then lost, for an instant, the restless agitation that had kept her in a continual effervescence throughout the morning; she gazed silently, and seemed to be borne upward, like a floating sea-bird, on the long heaves and swells of sound. But she was brought back to her former mood by the shimmer of the sunshine on the weapons and bright armor of the military company, which followed after the music, and formed the honorary escort of the procession. This body of soldiery—which still sustains a corporate existence, and marches down from past ages with an ancient and honorable fame—was composed of no mercenary materials. Its ranks were filled with gentlemen, who felt the stirrings of martial impulse, and sought to establish a kind of College of Arms, where, as in an association of Knights Templars, they might learn the science, and, so far as peaceful exercise would teach them, the practices of war. The high estimation then placed upon the military character might be seen in the lofty port of each individual member of the company. Some of them, indeed, by their services in the Low Countries and on other fields of European warfare, had fairly won their title to assume the name and pomp of soldiership. The entire array, moreover, clad in burnished steel, and with plumage nodding over their bright morions, had a brilliancy of effect which no modern display can aspire to equal.

And yet the men of civil eminence, who came immediately behind the military escort, were better worth a thoughtful observer's eye. Even in outward demeanor, they showed a stamp of majesty that made the warrior's haughty stride look vulgar, if not absurd. It was an age when what we call talent had far less consideration than now, but the massive materials which produce stability and dignity of character a great deal more. The people possessed, by hereditary right, the quality of reverence; which, in their descendants, if it survive at all, exists in smaller proportion, and with a vastly diminished force, in the selection and estimate of public men. The change may be for good or ill, and is partly, perhaps, for both. In that old day, the English settler on these rude shores—having left king, nobles, and all degrees of awful rank behind, while still the faculty and necessity of reverence were strong in him—bestowed it on the white hair and venerable brow of age; on long-tried integrity; on solid wisdom and sad-colored experience; on endowments of that grave and weighty order which gives the idea of permanence, and comes under the general definition of respectability. These primitive statesmen, therefore,—Bradstreet, Endicott, Dudley, Bellingham, and their compeers,—who were elevated to power by the early choice of the people, seem to have been not often brilliant, but distinguished by a ponderous sobriety, rather than activity of intellect. They had fortitude and self-reliance, and, in time of difficulty or peril, stood up for the welfare of the state like a line of cliffs against a tempestuous tide. The traits of character here indicated were well represented in the square cast of countenance and large physical development of the new colonial magistrates. So far as a demeanor of natural authority was concerned, the mother country need not have been ashamed to see these foremost men of an actual democracy adopted into the House of Peers, or made the Privy Council of the sovereign.

Next in order to the magistrates came the young and eminently distinguished divine, from whose lips the religious discourse of the anniversary was expected. His was the profession, at that era, in which intellectual ability displayed itself far more than in political life; for—leaving a higher motive out of the question—it offered inducements powerful enough, in the almost worshipping respect of the community, to win the most aspiring ambition into its service. Even political power—as in the case of Increase Mather—was within the grasp of a successful priest.

It was the observation of those who beheld him now, that never, since Mr. Dimmesdale first set his foot on the New England shore, had he exhibited such energy as was seen in the gait and air with which he kept his pace in the procession. There was no feebleness of step, as at other times; his frame was not bent; nor did his hand rest ominously upon his heart. Yet, if the clergyman were rightly viewed, his strength seemed not of the body. It might be spiritual, and imparted to him by angelic ministrations. It might be the exhilaration of that potent cordial, which is distilled only in the furnace-glow of earnest and long-continued thought. Or, perchance, his sensitive temperament was invigorated by the loud and piercing music, that swelled heavenward, and uplifted him on its ascending wave. Nevertheless, so abstracted was his look, it might be questioned whether Mr. Dimmesdale even heard the music. There was his body, moving onward, and with an unaccustomed force. But where was his mind? Far and deep in its own region, busying itself, with preternatural activity, to marshal a procession of stately thoughts that were soon to issue thence; and so he saw nothing, heard nothing, knew nothing, of what was around him; but the spiritual element took up the feeble frame, and carried it along, unconscious of the burden, and converting it to spirit like itself. Men of uncommon intellect, who have grown morbid, possess this occasional power of mighty effort, into which they throw the life of many days, and then are lifeless for as many more.

Hester Prynne, gazing steadfastly at the clergyman, felt a dreary influence come over her, but wherefore or whence she knew not; unless that he seemed so remote from her own sphere, and utterly beyond her reach. One glance of recognition, she had imagined, must needs pass between them. She thought of the dim forest, with its little dell of solitude, and love, and anguish, and the mossy tree-trunk, where, sitting hand in hand, they had mingled their sad and passionate talk with the melancholy murmur of the brook. How deeply had they known each other then! And was this the man? She hardly knew him now! He, moving proudly past, enveloped, as it were, in the rich music, with the procession of majestic and venerable fathers; he, so unattainable in his worldly position, and still more so in that far vista of his unsympathizing thoughts, through which she now beheld him! Her spirit sank with the idea that all must have been a delusion, and that, vividly as she had dreamed it, there could be no real bond betwixt the clergyman and herself. And thus much of woman was there in Hester, that she could scarcely forgive him, — least of all now, when the heavy footstep of their approaching Fate might be heard, nearer, nearer, nearer! — for being able so completely to withdraw himself from their mutual world; while she groped darkly, and stretched forth her cold hands, and found him not.

Pearl either saw and responded to her mother's feelings, or

herself felt the remoteness and intangibility that had fallen around the minister. While the procession passed, the child was uneasy, fluttering up and down, like a bird on the point of taking flight. When the whole had gone by, she looked up into Hester's face.

"Mother," said she, "was that the same minister that kissed me by the brook?"

"Hold thy peace, dear little Pearl!" whispered her mother. "We must not always talk in the market-place of what happens to us in the forest."

"I could not be sure that it was he; so strange he looked," continued the child. "Else I would have run to him, and bid him kiss me now, before all the people; even as he did yonder among the dark old trees. What would the minister have said, mother? Would he have clapped his hand over his heart, and scowled on me, and bid me be gone?"

"What should he say, Pearl," answered Hester, "save that it was no time to kiss, and that kisses are not to be given in the market-place? Well for thee, foolish child, that thou didst not speak to him!"

Another shade of the same sentiment, in reference to Mr. Dimmesdale, was expressed by a person whose eccentricities—or insanity, as we should term it—led her to do what few of the towns-people would have ventured on; to begin a conversation with the wearer of the scarlet letter, in public. It was Mistress Hibbins, who, arrayed in great magnificence, with a triple ruff, a broidered stomacher, a gown of rich velvet, and a gold-headed cane, had come forth to see the procession. As this ancient lady had the renown (which subsequently cost her no less a price than her life) of being a principal actor in all the works of necromancy that were continually going forward, the crowd gave way before her, and seemed to fear the touch of her garment, as if it carried the plague among its gorgeous folds. Seen in conjunction with Hester Prynne,—kindly as so many now felt towards the latter,—the dread inspired by Mistress Hibbins was doubled, and caused a general movement from that part of the market-place in which the two women stood.

"Now, what mortal imagination could conceive it!" whispered the old lady, confidentially, to Hester. "Yonder divine man! That saint on earth, as the people uphold him to be, and as—I must needs say—he really looks! Who, now, that saw him pass in the procession, would think how little while it is since he went forth out of his study,—chewing a Hebrew text of Scripture in his mouth, I warrant,—to take an airing in the forest! Aha! we know what that means, Hester Prynne! But, truly, forsooth, I find it hard to believe him the same man. Many a church-member saw I, walking behind the music, that has danced in the same measure with me, when Somebody was fiddler, and, it might be, an Indian powwow or a Lapland wizard changing hands with us! That is but a trifle, when a woman knows the world. But this minister! Couldst thou surely tell, Hester, whether he was the same man that encountered thee on the forest path?"

"Madam, I know not of what you speak," answered Hester Prynne, feeling Mistress Hibbins to be of infirm mind; yet strangely startled and awe-stricken by the confidence with which she affirmed a personal connection between so many persons (herself among them) and the Evil One. "It is not for me to talk lightly of a learned and pious minister of the Word, like the Reverend Mr. Dimmesdale!"

"Fie, woman, fie!" cried the old lady, shaking her finger at Hester. "Dost thou think I have been to the forest so many times, and have yet no skill to judge who else has been there? Yea; though no leaf of the wild garlands, which they wore while they danced, be left in their hair! I know thee, Hester; for I behold the token. We may all see it in the sunshine; and it glows like a red flame in the dark. Thou wearest it openly; so there need be no question about that. But this minister! Let me tell thee, in thine ear! When the Black Man sees one of his own servants, signed and sealed, so shy of owning to the bond as is the Reverend Mr. Dimmesdale, he hath a way of ordering matters so that the mark shall be disclosed in open daylight to the eyes of all the world! What is it that the minister seeks to hide, with his hand always over his heart? Ha, Hester Prynne!"

"What is it, good Mistress Hibbins?" eagerly asked little Pearl. "Hast thou seen it?"

"No matter, darling!" responded Mistress Hibbins, making Pearl a profound reverence. "Thou thyself wilt see it, one time or another. They say, child, thou art of the lineage of the Prince of the Air! Wilt thou ride with me, some fine night, to see thy father? Then thou shalt know wherefore the minister keeps his hand over his heart!"

Laughing so shrilly that all the market-place could hear her, the weird old gentlewoman took her departure.

By this time the preliminary prayer had been offered in the meeting-house, and the accents of the Reverend Mr. Dimmesdale were heard commencing his discourse. An irresistible feeling kept Hester near the spot. As the sacred edifice was too much thronged to admit another auditor, she took up her position close beside the scaffold of the pillory. It was in sufficient proximity to bring the whole sermon to her ears, in the shape of an indistinct, but varied, murmur and flow of the minister's very peculiar voice.

This vocal organ was in itself a rich endowment; insomuch that a listener, comprehending nothing of the language in which the preacher spoke, might still have been swayed to and fro by the mere tone and cadence. Like all other music, it breathed passion and pathos, and emotions high or tender, in a tongue native to the human heart, wherever educated. Muffled as the sound was by its passage through the church-walls, Hester Prynne listened with such intentness, and sympathized so intimately, that the sermon had throughout a meaning for her, entirely apart from its indistinguishable words. These, perhaps, if more distinctly heard, might have been only a grosser medium, and have clogged the spiritual sense. Now she caught the low undertone, as of the wind sinking down to repose itself; then ascended with it, as it rose through progressive gradations of sweetness and power, until its volume seemed to envelop her with an atmosphere of awe and solemn grandeur. And yet, majestic as the voice sometimes became, there was forever in it an essential character of plaintiveness. A loud or low expression of anguish,—the whisper, or the shriek, as it might be conceived, of suffering humanity, that touched a sensibility in every bosom! At times this deep strain of pathos was all that could be heard, and scarcely heard, sighing amid a desolate silence. But even when the minister's voice grew high and commanding,—when it gushed irrepressibly upward,—when it assumed its utmost breadth and power, so overfilling the church as to burst its way through the solid walls, and diffuse itself in the open air,—still, if the auditor listened intently, and for the purpose, he could detect the same cry of pain. What was it? The complaint of a human heart, sorrow-laden, perchance guilty, telling its secret, whether of guilt or sorrow, to the great heart of mankind; beseeching its sympathy or forgiveness,—at every moment,—in each accent,—and never in vain! It was this profound and continual undertone that gave the clergyman his most appropriate power.

During all this time, Hester stood, statue-like, at the foot of the scaffold. If the minister's voice had not kept her there, there would nevertheless have been an inevitable magnetism in that spot, whence she dated the first hour of her life of ignominy. There was a sense within her,—too ill-defined to be made a thought, but weighing heavily on her mind, —that her whole orb of life, both before and after, was connected with this spot, as with the one point that gave it unity.

Little Pearl, meanwhile, had quitted her mother's side, and was playing at her own will about the market-place. She made the sombre crowd cheerful by her erratic and glistening ray; even as a bird of bright plumage illuminates a whole tree of dusky foliage, by darting to and fro, half seen and half concealed amid the twilight of the clustering leaves. She had an undulating, but, oftentimes, a sharp and irregular movement. It indicated the restless vivacity of her spirit, which to-day was doubly indefatigable in its tiptoe dance, because it was played upon and vibrated with her mother's disquietude. Whenever Pearl saw anything to excite her ever-active and wandering curiosity, she flew thitherward and, as we might say, seized upon that man or thing as her own property, so far as she desired it; but without yielding the minutest degree of control over her motions in requital. The Puritans looked on, and, if they smiled, were none the less inclined to pronounce the child a demon offspring, from the indescribable charm of beauty and eccentricity that shone through her little figure, and sparkled with its activity. She ran and looked the wild Indian in the face; and he grew conscious of a nature wilder than his own. Thence, with native audacity, but still with a reserve as characteristic, she flew into the midst of a group of mariners, the swarthy-cheeked wild men of the ocean, as the Indians were of the land; and they gazed wonderingly and admiringly at Pearl, as if a flake of the sea-foam had taken the shape of a little maid, and were gifted with a soul of the sea-fire, that flashes beneath the prow in the night-time.

One of these seafaring men—the shipmaster, indeed, who had spoken to Hester Prynne—was so smitten with Pearl's aspect, that he attempted to lay hands upon her, with purpose to snatch a kiss. Finding it as impossible to touch her as to catch a humming-bird in the air, he took from his hat the gold chain that was twisted about it, and threw it to the child. Pearl immediately twined it around her neck and waist, with such happy skill, that, once seen there, it became a part of her, and it was difficult to imagine her without it.

"Thy mother is yonder woman with the scarlet letter," said the seaman. "Wilt thou carry her a message from me?"

"If the message pleases me, I will," answered Pearl.

"Then tell her," rejoined he, "that I spake again with the black-a-visaged, hump-shouldered old doctor, and he engages to bring his friend, the gentleman she wots of, aboard with him. So let thy mother take no thought, save for herself and thee. Wilt thou tell her this, thou witch-baby?"

"Mistress Hibbins says my father is the Prince of the Air!" cried Pearl, with a naughty smile. "If thou callest me that ill name, I shall tell him of thee; and he will chase thy ship with a tempest!"

Pursuing a zigzag course across the market-place, the child returned to her mother, and communicated what the mariner had said. Hester's strong, calm, steadfastly enduring spirit almost sank, at last, on beholding this dark and grim countenance of an inevitable doom, which—at the moment when a passage seemed to open for the minister and herself out of their labyrinth of misery—showed itself, with an unrelenting smile, right in the midst of their path.

With her mind harassed by the terrible perplexity in which the shipmaster's intelligence involved her, she was also subjected to another trial. There were many people present, from the country round about, who had often heard of the scarlet letter, and to whom it had been made terrific by a hundred false or exaggerated rumors, but who had never beheld it with their own bodily eyes. These, after exhausting other modes of amusement, now thronged about Hester Prynne with rude and boorish intrusiveness. Unscrupulous as it was, however, it could not bring them nearer than a circuit of several yards. At that distance they accordingly stood, fixed there by the centrifugal force of the repugnance which the mystic symbol inspired. The whole gang of sailors, likewise, observing the press of spectators, and learning the purport of the scarlet letter, came and thrust their sunburnt and desperado-looking faces into the ring. Even the Indians were affected by a sort of cold shadow of the white man's curiosity, and, gliding through the crowd, fastened their snake-like black eyes on Hester's bosom; conceiving, perhaps, that the wearer of this brilliantly embroidered badge must needs be a personage of high dignity among her people. Lastly the inhabitants of the town (their own interest in this worn-out subject languidly reviving itself, by sympathy with what they saw others feel) lounged idly to the same quarter, and tormented Hester Prynne, perhaps more than all the rest, with their cool, well-acquainted gaze at her familiar shame. Hester saw and recognized the selfsame faces of that group of matrons, who had awaited her forthcoming from the prison-door, seven years ago; all save one, the youngest and only compassionate among them, whose burial-robe she had since made. At the final hour, when she was so soon to fling aside the burning letter, it had strangely become the centre of more remark and excitement, and was thus made to sear her breast more painfully, than at any time since the first day she put it on.

While Hester stood in that magic circle of ignominy, where the cunning cruelty of her sentence seemed to have fixed her forever, the admirable preacher was looking down from the sacred pulpit upon an audience whose very inmost spirits had yielded to his control. The sainted minister in the church! The woman of the scarlet letter in the market-place! What imagination would have been irreverent enough to surmise that the same scorching stigma was on them both!

261

Chapter 23

The eloquent voice, on which the souls of the listening audience had been borne aloft as on the swelling waves of the sea, at length came to a pause. There was a momentary silence, profound as what should follow the utterance of oracles. Then ensued a murmur and half-hushed tumult; as if the auditors, released from the high spell that had transported them into the region of another's mind, were returning into themselves, with all their awe and wonder still heavy on them. In a moment more, the crowd began to gush forth from the doors of the church. Now that there was an end, they needed other breath, more fit to support the gross and earthly life into which they relapsed, than that atmosphere which the preacher had converted into words of flame, and had burdened with the rich fragrance of his thought.

In the open air their rapture broke into speech. The street and the market-place absolutely babbled, from side to side, with applauses of the minister. His hearers could not rest until they had told one another of what each knew better than he could tell or hear. According to their united testimony, never had man spoken in so wise, so high, and so holy a spirit, as he that spake this day; nor had inspiration ever breathed through mortal lips more evidently than it did through his. Its influence could be seen, as it were, descending upon him, and possessing him, and continually lifting him out of the written discourse that lay before him, and filling him with ideas that must have been as marvellous to himself as to his audience. His subject, it appeared, had been the relation between the Deity and the communities of mankind, with a special reference to the New England which they were here planting in the wilderness. And, as he drew towards the close, a spirit as of prophecy had come upon him, constraining him to its purpose as mightily as the old prophets of Israel were constrained; only with this difference, that, whereas the Jewish seers had denounced judgments and ruin on their country, it was his mission to foretell a high and glorious destiny for the newly gathered people of the Lord. But, throughout it all, and through the whole discourse, there had been a certain deep, sad undertone of pathos, which could not be interpreted otherwise than as the natural regret of one soon to pass away. Yes; their minister whom they so loved—and who so loved them all, that he could not depart heavenward without a sigh—had the foreboding of untimely death upon him, and would soon leave them in their tears! This idea of his transitory stay on earth gave the last emphasis to the effect which the preacher had produced; it was as if an angel, in his passage to the skies, had shaken his bright wings over the people for an instant,—at once a shadow and a splendor,—and had shed down a shower of golden truths upon them.

Thus, there had come to the Reverend Mr. Dimmesdale—as to most men, in their various spheres, though seldom recognized until they see it far behind them—an epoch of life more brilliant and full of triumph than any previous one, or than any which could hereafter be. He stood, at this moment, on the very proudest eminence of superiority, to which the gifts of intellect, rich lore, prevailing eloquence, and a reputation of whitest sanctity, could exalt a clergyman in New England's earliest days, when the professional character was of itself a lofty pedestal. Such was the position which the minister occupied, as he bowed his head forward on the cushions of the pulpit, at the close of his Election Sermon. Meanwhile Hester Prynne was standing beside the scaffold of the pillory, with the scarlet letter still burning on her breast!

Now was heard again the clangor of the music, and the measured tramp of the military escort, issuing from the church-door. The procession was to be marshalled thence to the town-hall, where a solemn banquet would complete the ceremonies of the day.

Once more, therefore, the train of venerable and majestic fathers was seen moving through a broad pathway of the people, who drew back reverently, on either side, as the Governor and magistrates, the old and wise men, the holy ministers, and all that were eminent and renowned, advanced into the midst of them. When they were fairly in the market-place, their presence was greeted by a shout. This—though doubtless it might acquire additional force and volume from the childlike loyalty which the age awarded to its rulers—was felt to be an irrepressible outburst of enthusiasm kindled in the auditors by that high strain of eloquence which was yet reverberating in their ears. Each felt the impulse in himself, and, in the same breath, caught it from his neighbor. Within the church, it had hardly been kept down; beneath the sky, it pealed upward to the zenith. There were human beings enough, and enough of highly wrought and symphonious feeling, to produce that more impressive sound than the organ tones of the blast, or the thunder, or the roar of the sea; even that mighty swell of many voices, blended into one great voice by the universal impulse which makes likewise one vast heart out of the many. Never, from the soil of New England, had gone up such a shout! Never, on New England soil, had stood the man so honored by his mortal brethren as the preacher!

How fared it with him then? Were there not the brilliant particles of a halo in the air about his head? So etherealized by spirit as he was, and so apotheosized by worshipping admirers, did his footsteps, in the procession, really tread upon the dust of earth?

As the ranks of military men and civil fathers moved onward, all eyes were turned towards the point where the minister was seen to approach among them. The shout died into a murmur, as one portion of the crowd after another obtained a glimpse of him. How feeble and pale he looked, amid all his triumph! The energy—or say, rather, the inspiration which had held him up, until he should have delivered the sacred message that brought its own strength along with it from heaven—was withdrawn, now that it had so faithfully performed its office. The glow, which they had just before beheld burning on his cheek, was extinguished, like a flame that sinks down hopelessly among the late-decaying embers. It seemed hardly the face of a man alive, with such a death-like hue; it was hardly a man with life in him, that tottered on his path so nervelessly, yet tottered, and did not fall!

One of his clerical brethren,—it was the venerable John Wilson,—observing the state in which Mr. Dimmesdale was left by the retiring wave of intellect and sensibility, stepped forward hastily to offer his support. The minister tremulously, but decidedly, repelled the old man's arm. He still walked onward, if that movement could be so described, which rather resembled the wavering effort of an infant, with its mother's arms in view, outstretched to tempt him forward. And now, almost imperceptible as were the latter steps of his progress, he had come opposite the well-remembered and weather-darkened scaffold, where, long since, with all that dreary lapse of time between, Hester Prynne had encountered the world's ignominious stare. There stood Hester, holding little Pearl by the hand! And there was the scarlet letter on her breast! The minister here made a pause; although the music still played the stately and rejoicing march to which the procession moved. It summoned him onward,—onward to the festival!—but here he made a pause.

Bellingham, for the last few moments, had kept an anxious eye upon him. He now left his own place in the procession, and advanced to give assistance; judging, from Mr. Dimmesdale's aspect, that he must otherwise inevitably fall. But there was something in the latter's expression that warned back the magistrate, although a man not readily obeying the vague intimations that pass from one spirit to another. The crowd, meanwhile, looked on with awe and wonder. This earthly faintness was, in their view, only another phase of the minister's celestial strength; nor would it have seemed a miracle too high to be wrought for one so holy, had he ascended before their eyes, waxing dimmer and brighter, and fading at last into the light of heaven.

He turned towards the scaffold, and stretched forth his arms.

"Hester," said he, "come hither! Come, my little Pearl!"

It was a ghastly look with which he regarded them; but there was something at once tender and strangely triumphant in it. The child, with the bird-like motion which was one of her characteristics, flew to him, and clasped her arms about his knees. Hester Prynne—slowly, as if impelled by inevitable fate, and against her strongest will—likewise drew near, but paused before she reached him. At this instant, old Roger Chillingworth thrust himself through the crowd,—or, perhaps, so dark, disturbed, and evil, was his look, he rose up out of some nether region,—to snatch back his victim from what he sought to do! Be that as it might, the old man rushed forward, and caught the minister by the arm.

"Madman, hold! what is your purpose?" whispered he. "Wave back that woman! Cast off this child! All shall be

266

well! Do not blacken your fame, and perish in dishonor! I can yet save you! Would you bring infamy on your sacred profession?"

"Ha, tempter! Methinks thou art too late!" answered the minister, encountering his eye, fearfully, but firmly. "Thy power is not what it was! With God's help, I shall escape thee now!"

He again extended his hand to the woman of the scarlet letter.

"Hester Prynne," cried he, with a piercing earnestness, "in the name of Him, so terrible and so merciful, who gives me grace, at this last moment, to do what—for my own heavy sin and miserable agony—I withheld myself from doing seven years ago, come hither now, and twine thy strength about me! Thy strength, Hester; but let it be guided by the will which God hath granted me! This wretched and wronged old man is opposing it with all his might!—with all his own might, and the fiend's! Come, Hester, come! Support me up yonder scaffold!"

The crowd was in a tumult. The men of rank and dignity, who stood more immediately around the clergyman, were so taken by surprise, and so perplexed as to the purport of what they saw,—unable to receive the explanation which most readily presented itself, or to imagine any other,—that they remained silent and inactive spectators of the judgment which Providence seemed about to work. They beheld the minister, leaning on Hester's shoulder, and supported by her arm around him, approach the scaffold, and ascend its steps; while still the little hand of the sin-born child was clasped in his. Old Roger Chillingworth followed, as one intimately connected with the drama of guilt and sorrow in which they had all been actors, and well entitled, therefore, to be present at its closing scene.

"Hadst thou sought the whole earth over," said he, looking darkly at the clergyman, "there was no one place so secret,—no high place nor lowly place, where thou couldst have escaped me,—save on this very scaffold!"

"Thanks be to Him who hath led me hither!" answered the minister.

Yet he trembled, and turned to Hester with an expression of doubt and anxiety in his eyes, not the less evidently betrayed, that there was a feeble smile upon his lips.

"Is not this better," murmured he, "than what we dreamed of in the forest?"

"I know not! I know not!" she hurriedly replied. "Better? Yea; so we may both die, and little Pearl die with us!"

"For thee and Pearl, be it as God shall order," said the minister; "and God is merciful! Let me now do the will which he hath made plain before my sight. For, Hester, I am a dying man. So let me make haste to take my shame upon me!"

Partly supported by Hester Prynne, and holding one hand of little Pearl's, the Reverend Mr. Dimmesdale turned to the dignified and venerable rulers; to the holy ministers, who were his brethren; to the people, whose great heart was thoroughly appalled, yet overflowing with tearful sympathy, as knowing that some deep life-matter—which, if full of sin, was full of anguish and repentance likewise—was now to be laid open to them. The sun, but little past its meridian, shone down upon the clergyman, and gave a distinctness to his figure, as he stood out from all the earth, to put in his plea of guilty at the bar of Eternal Justice.

"People of New England!" cried he, with a voice that rose over them, high, solemn, and majestic,—yet had always a tremor through it, and sometimes a shriek, struggling up out of a fathomless depth of remorse and woe,—"ye, that have loved me!—ye, that have deemed me holy!—behold me here, the one sinner of the world! At last!—at last!—I stand upon the spot where, seven years since, I should have stood; here, with this woman, whose arm, more than the little strength wherewith I have crept hitherward, sustains me, at this dreadful moment, from grovelling down upon my face! Lo, the scarlet letter which Hester wears! Ye have all shuddered at it! Wherever her walk hath been,—wherever, so miserably burdened, she may have hoped to find repose,—it hath cast a lurid gleam of awe and horrible repugnance round about her. But there stood one in the midst of you, at whose brand of sin and infamy ye have not shuddered!"

It seemed, at this point, as if the minister must leave the remainder of his secret undisclosed. But he fought back the bodily weakness,—and, still more, the faintness of heart,—that was striving for the mastery with him. He threw off all assistance, and stepped passionately forward a pace before the woman and the child.

"It was on him!" he continued, with a kind of fierceness; so determined was he to speak out the whole. "God's eye beheld it! The angels were forever pointing at it! The Devil knew it well, and fretted it continually with the touch of his burning finger! But he hid it cunningly from men, and walked among you with the mien of a spirit, mournful, because so pure in a sinful world!—and sad, because he missed his heavenly kindred! Now, at the death-hour, he stands up before you! He bids you look again at Hester's scarlet letter! He tells you, that, with all its mysterious horror, it is but the shadow of what he bears on his own breast, and that even this, his own red stigma, is no more than the type of what has seared his inmost heart! Stand any here that question God's judgment on a sinner? Behold! Behold a dreadful witness of it!"

With a convulsive motion, he tore away the ministerial band from before his breast. It was revealed! But it were irreverent to describe that revelation. For an instant, the gaze of the horror-stricken multitude was concentred on the ghastly miracle; while the minister stood, with a flush of triumph in his face, as one who, in the crisis of acutest pain, had won a victory. Then, down he sank upon the scaffold! Hester partly raised him, and supported his head against her bosom. Old Roger Chillingworth knelt down beside him, with a blank, dull countenance, out of which the life seemed to have departed.

"Thou hast escaped me!" he repeated more than once. "Thou hast escaped me!"

"May God forgive thee!" said the minister. "Thou, too, hast deeply sinned!"

He withdrew his dying eyes from the old man, and fixed them on the woman and the child.

"My little Pearl," said he, feebly,—and there was a sweet and gentle smile over his face, as of a spirit sinking into deep repose; nay, now that the burden was removed, it seemed almost as if he would be sportive with the child,—"dear little Pearl, wilt thou kiss me now? Thou wouldst not, yonder, in the forest! But now thou wilt?"

Pearl kissed his lips. A spell was broken. The great scene of grief, in which the wild infant bore a part, had developed all her sympathies; and as her tears fell upon her father's cheek, they were the pledge that she would grow up amid human joy and sorrow, nor forever do battle with the world, but be a woman in it. Towards her mother, too, Pearl's errand as a messenger of anguish was all fulfilled.

"Hester," said the clergyman, "farewell!"

"Shall we not meet again?" whispered she, bending her face down close to his. "Shall we not spend our immortal life together? Surely, surely, we have ransomed one another, with all this woe! Thou lookest far into eternity, with those bright dying eyes! Then tell me what thou seest?"

"Hush, Hester, hush!" said he, with tremulous solemnity. "The law we broke!—the sin here so awfully revealed!—let these alone be in thy thoughts! I fear! I fear! It may be, that, when we forgot our God,—when we violated our reverence each for the other's soul,—it was thenceforth vain to hope that we could meet hereafter, in an everlasting and pure reunion. God knows; and He is merciful! He hath proved his mercy, most of all, in my afflictions. By giving me this burning torture to bear upon my breast! By sending yonder dark and terrible old man, to keep the torture always at red-heat! By bringing me hither, to die this death of triumphant ignominy before the people! Had either of these agonies been wanting, I had been lost forever! Praised be his name! His will be done! Farewell!"

That final word came forth with the minister's expiring breath. The multitude, silent till then, broke out in a strange, deep voice of awe and wonder, which could not as yet find utterance, save in this murmur that rolled so heavily after the departed spirit.

Chapter 24

After many days, when time sufficed for the people to arrange their thoughts in reference to the foregoing scene, there was more than one account of what had been witnessed on the scaffold.

Most of the spectators testified to having seen, on the breast of the unhappy minister, a SCARLET LETTER—the very semblance of that worn by Hester Prynne—imprinted in the flesh. As regarded its origin, there were various explanations, all of which must necessarily have been conjectural. Some affirmed that the Reverend Mr. Dimmesdale, on the very day when Hester Prynne first wore her ignominious badge, had begun a course of penance,—which he afterwards, in so many futile methods, followed out,—by inflicting a hideous torture on himself. Others contended that the stigma had not been produced until a long time subsequent, when old Roger Chillingworth, being a potent necromancer, had caused it to appear, through the agency of magic and poisonous drugs. Others, again,—and those best able to appreciate the minister's peculiar sensibility, and the wonderful operation of his spirit upon the body,—whispered their belief, that the awful symbol was the effect of the ever-active tooth of remorse, gnawing from the inmost heart outwardly, and at last manifesting Heaven's dreadful judgment by the visible presence of the letter. The reader may choose among these theories. We have thrown all the light we could acquire upon the portent, and would gladly, now that it has done its office, erase its deep print out of our own brain; where long meditation has fixed it in very undesirable distinctness.

It is singular, nevertheless, that certain persons, who were spectators of the whole scene, and professed never once to have removed their eyes from the Reverend Mr. Dimmesdale, denied that there was any mark whatever on his breast, more than on a new-born infant's. Neither, by their report, had his dying words acknowledged, nor even remotely implied, any, the slightest connection, on his part, with the guilt for which Hester Prynne had so long worn the scarlet letter. According to these highly respectable witnesses, the minister, conscious that he was dying,— conscious, also, that the reverence of the multitude placed him already among saints and angels,— had desired, by yielding up his breath in the arms of that fallen woman, to express to the world how utterly nugatory is the choicest of man's own righteousness. After exhausting life in his efforts for mankind's spiritual good, he had made the manner of his death a parable, in order to impress on his admirers the mighty and mournful lesson, that, in the view of Infinite Purity, we are sinners all alike. It was to teach them, that the holiest among us has but attained so far above his fellows as to discern more clearly the Mercy which looks down, and repudiate more utterly the phantom of human merit, which would look aspiringly upward. Without disputing a truth so momentous, we must be allowed to consider this version of Mr. Dimmesdale's story as only an instance of that stubborn fidelity with which a man's friends—and especially a clergyman's—will sometimes uphold his character, when proofs, clear as the mid-day sunshine on the scarlet letter, establish him a false and sin-stained creature of the dust.

The authority which we have chiefly followed,—a manuscript of old date, drawn up from the verbal testimony of individuals, some of whom had known Hester Prynne, while others had heard the tale from contemporary witnesses,—fully confirms the view taken in the foregoing pages. Among many morals which press upon us from the poor minister's miserable experience, we put only this into a sentence: — "Be true! Be true! Be true! Show freely to the world, if not your worst, yet some trait whereby the worst may be inferred!"

Nothing was more remarkable than the change which took place, almost immediately after Mr. Dimmesdale's death, in the appearance and demeanor of the old man known as Roger Chillingworth. All his strength and energy — all his vital and intellectual force — seemed at once to desert him; insomuch that he positively withered up, shrivelled away, and almost vanished from mortal sight, like an uprooted weed that lies wilting in the sun. This unhappy man had made the very principle of his life to consist in the pursuit and systematic exercise of revenge; and when, by its completest triumph and consummation, that evil principle was left with no further material to support it, when, in short, there was no more Devil's work on earth for him to do, it only remained for the unhumanized mortal to betake himself whither his Master would find him tasks enough, and pay him his wages duly. But, to all these shadowy beings, so long our near acquaintances, — as well Roger Chillingworth as his companions, — we would fain be merciful. It is a curious subject of observation and inquiry, whether hatred and love be not the same thing at bottom. Each, in its utmost development, supposes a high degree of intimacy and heart-knowledge; each renders one individual dependent for the food of his affections and spiritual life upon another; each leaves the passionate lover, or the no less passionate hater, forlorn and desolate by the withdrawal of his subject. Philosophically considered, therefore, the two passions seem essentially the same, except that one happens to be seen in a celestial radiance, and the other in a dusky and lurid glow. In the spiritual world, the old physician and the minister — mutual victims as they have been—may, unawares, have found their earthly stock of hatred and antipathy transmuted into golden love.

Leaving this discussion apart, we have a matter of business to communicate to the reader. At old Roger Chillingworth's decease, (which took place within the year,) and by his last will and testament, of which Governor Bellingham and the Reverend Mr. Wilson were executors, he bequeathed a very considerable amount of property, both here and in England, to little Pearl, the daughter of Hester Prynne.

So Pearl—the elf-child,—the demon offspring, as some people, up to that epoch, persisted in considering her,—became the richest heiress of her day, in the New World. Not improbably, this circumstance wrought a very material change in the public estimation; and, had the mother and child remained here, little Pearl, at a marriageable period of life, might have mingled her wild blood with the lineage of the devoutest Puritan among them all. But, in no long time after the physician's death, the wearer of the scarlet letter disappeared, and Pearl along with her. For many years, though a vague report would now and then find its way across the sea,—like a shapeless piece of drift-wood tost ashore, with the initials of a name upon it,—yet no tidings of them unquestionably authentic were received. The story of the scarlet letter grew into a legend. Its spell, however, was still potent, and kept the scaffold awful where the poor minister had died, and likewise the cottage by the sea-shore, where Hester Prynne had dwelt. Near this latter spot, one afternoon, some children were at play, when they beheld a tall woman, in a gray robe, approach the cottage-door. In all those years it had never once been opened; but either she unlocked it, or the decaying wood and iron yielded to her hand, or she glided shadow-like through these impediments,—and, at all events, went in.

On the threshold she paused,—turned partly round,—for, perchance, the idea of entering all alone, and all so changed, the home of so intense a former life, was more dreary and desolate than even she could bear. But her hesitation was only for an instant, though long enough to display a scarlet letter on her breast.

And Hester Prynne had returned, and taken up her long-forsaken shame! But where was little Pearl? If still alive, she must now have been in the flush and bloom of early womanhood. None knew—nor ever learned, with the fulness of perfect certainty—whether the elf-child had gone thus untimely to a maiden grave; or whether her wild, rich nature had been softened and subdued, and made capable of a woman's gentle happiness. But, through the remainder of Hester's life, there were indications that the recluse of the scarlet letter was the object of love and interest with some inhabitant of another land. Letters came, with armorial seals upon them, though of bearings unknown to English heraldry. In the cottage there were articles of comfort and luxury such as Hester never cared to use, but which only wealth could have purchased, and affection have imagined for her. There were trifles, too, little ornaments, beautiful tokens of a continual remembrance, that must have been wrought by delicate fingers, at the impulse of a fond heart. And, once, Hester was seen embroidering a baby-garment, with such a lavish richness of golden fancy as would have raised a public tumult, had any infant, thus apparelled, been shown to our sober-hued community.

In fine, the gossips of that day believed,—and Mr. Surveyor Pue, who made investigations a century later, believed,—and one of his recent successors in office, moreover, faithfully believes,—that Pearl was not only alive, but married, and happy, and mindful of her mother, and that she would most joyfully have entertained that sad and lonely mother at her fireside.

But there was a more real life for Hester Prynne here, in New England, than in that unknown region where Pearl had found a home. Here had been her sin; here, her sorrow; and here was yet to be her penitence. She had returned, therefore, and resumed,—of her own free will, for not the sternest magistrate of that iron period would have imposed it,—resumed the symbol of which we have related so dark a tale. Never afterwards did it quit her bosom. But, in the lapse of the toilsome, thoughtful, and self-devoted years that made up Hester's life, the scarlet letter ceased to be a stigma which attracted the world's scorn and bitterness, and became a type of something to be sorrowed over, and looked upon with awe, yet with reverence too. And, as Hester Prynne had no selfish ends, nor lived in any measure for her own profit and enjoyment, people brought all their sorrows and perplexities, and besought her counsel, as one who had herself gone through a mighty trouble. Women, more especially,—in the continually recurring trials of wounded, wasted, wronged, misplaced, or erring and sinful passion,—or with the dreary burden of a heart unyielded, because unvalued and unsought,—came to Hester's cottage, demanding why they were so wretched, and what the remedy! Hester comforted and counselled them as best she might. She assured them, too, of her firm belief, that, at some brighter period, when the world should have grown ripe for it, in Heaven's own time, a new truth would be revealed, in order to establish the whole relation between man and woman on a surer ground of mutual happiness. Earlier in life, Hester had vainly imagined that she herself might be the destined prophetess, but had long since recognized the impossibility that any mission of divine and mysterious truth should be confided to a woman stained with sin, bowed down with shame, or even burdened with a life-long sorrow. The angel and apostle of the coming revelation must be a woman, indeed, but lofty, pure, and beautiful; and wise, moreover, not through dusky grief, but the ethereal medium of joy; and showing how sacred love should make us happy, by the truest test of a life successful to such an end!

So said Hester Prynne, and glanced her sad eyes downward at the scarlet letter. And, after many, many years, a new grave was delved, near an old and sunken one, in that burial-ground beside which King's Chapel has since been built. It was near that old and sunken grave, yet with a space between, as if the dust of the two sleepers had no right to mingle. Yet one tombstone served for both. All around, there were monuments carved with armorial bearings; and on this simple slab of slate—as the curious investigator may still discern, and perplex himself with the purport—there appeared the semblance of an engraved escutcheon. It bore a device, a herald's wording of which might serve for a motto and brief description of our now concluded legend; so sombre is it, and relieved only by one ever-glowing point of light gloomier than the shadow:—

"On a field, sable, the letter A, gules."

THE HARVARD CLASSICS
EDITED BY CHARLES W ELIOT LL D

THE PILGRIM'S PROGRESS
BY JOHN BUNYAN

"DR ELIOT'S FIVE-FOOT SHELF OF BOOKS"

P F COLLIER & SON
NEW YORK

Chapter 1

As I walked through the wilderness of this world, I lighted on a certain place where was a den, and laid me down in that place to sleep; and as I slept, I dreamed a dream. I dreamed, and behold, I saw a man clothed with rags, standing in a certain place, with his face from his own house, a book in his hand, and a great burden upon his back. I looked, and saw him open the book, and read therein; and as he read, he wept and trembled; and, not being able longer to contain, he brake out with a lamentable cry, saying, "What shall I do?"

In this plight, therefore, he went home, and restrained himself as long as he could, that his wife and children should not perceive his distress; but he could not be silent long, because that his trouble increased. Wherefore at length he brake his mind to his wife and children; and thus he began to talk to them: "Oh my dear wife," said he, "and you my sweet children, I, your dear friend, am in myself undone by reason of a burden that lieth hard upon me; moreover, I am told to a certainty that this our city will be burned with fire from heaven; in which fearful overthrow, both myself, with thee, my wife, and you, my sweet babes, shall miserably come to ruin, except some way of escape can be found whereby we may be delivered." At this all his family were sore amazed; not for that they believed that what he had said to them was true, but because they thought that some frenzy or madness had got into his head; therefore, it drawing towards night, and they hoping that sleep might settle his brain, with all haste they got him to bed. But the night was as troublesome to him as the day; wherefore, instead of sleeping, he spent it in sighs and tears. So when the morning was come, they would know how he did. He told them, Worse and worse: he also set to talking to them again; but they began to be hardened. They also thought to drive away his madness by harsh and surly treatment of him: sometimes they would ridicule, sometimes they would chide, and sometimes they would quite neglect him. Wherefore he began to retire himself to his chamber, to pray for and pity them, and also to sorrow over his own misery; he would also walk solitary in the fields, sometimes reading, and sometimes praying; and thus for some days he spent his time.

Now, I saw, upon a time, when he was walking in the fields, that he was (as he was wont) reading in his book, and greatly distressed in his mind; and as he read, he burst out as he had done before, crying, "What shall I do to be saved?"

I saw also that he looked this way and that way, as if he would run; yet he stood still, because (as I perceived) he could not tell which way to go. I looked then, and saw a man named Evangelist coming to him, who asked, "Wherefore dost thou cry?"

He answered, "Sir, I read in the book in my hand, that I am condemned to die, and after that to come to judgment; and I find that I am not willing to do the first, nor able to do the second."

Then said Evangelist, "Why not willing to die, since this life is troubled with so many evils?" The man answered, "Because I fear that this burden that is upon my back will sink me lower than the grave, and I shall fall into Tophet.And, sir, if I be not fit to go to prison, I am not fit to go to judgment, and from thence to death; and the thoughts of these things make me cry."

Then said Evangelist, "If this be thy condition, why standest thou still?"

He answered, "Because I know not whither to go." Then he gave him a parchment roll, and there was written within, "Flee from the wrath to come."

The man, therefore, read it, and looking upon Evangelist very carefully, said, "Whither must I fly?" Then said Evangelist (pointing with his finger over a very wide field), "Do you see yonder wicket-gate?" The man said, "No." Then said the other, "Do you see yonder shining light?" He said, "I think I do." Then said Evangelist, "Keep that light in your eye, and go up directly thereto; so shalt thou see the gate; at which, when thou knockest, it shall be told thee what thou shalt do." So I saw in my dream that the man began to run. Now, he had not run far from his own door, when his wife and children perceiving it, began to cry after him to return; but the man put his fingers in his ears, and ran on, crying, "Life! life! eternal life!" So he looked not behind him, but fled towards the middle of the plain.

The neighbors also came out to see him run; and as he ran, some mocked, others threatened, and some cried after him to return; and among those that did so there were two that resolved to fetch him back by force. The name of the one was Obstinate, and the name of the other Pliable. Now, by this time the man was got a good distance from them; but, however, they were resolved to pursue him, which they did, and in a little time they overtook him. Then said the man, "Neighbors, wherefore are ye come?" They said, "To persuade you to go back with us." But he said, "That can by no means be: you dwell," said he, "in the City of Destruction, the place also where I was born: I see it to be so; and, dying there, sooner or later, you will sink lower than the grave, into a place that burns with fire and brimstone. Be content, good neighbors, and go along with me."

Obst. "What!" said Obstinate, "and leave our friends and comforts behind us?"

Chris. "Yes," said Christian (for that was his name), "because that all which you forsake is not worthy to be compared with a little of that I am seeking to enjoy; and if you would go along with me, and hold it, you shall fare as I myself; for there, where I go, is enough and to spare. Come away, and prove my words."

Obst. What are the things you seek, since you leave all the world to find them?

Chris. I seek a place that can never be destroyed, one that is pure, and that fadeth not away, and it is laid up in heaven, and safe there, to be given, at the time appointed, to them that seek it with all their heart. Read it so, if you will, in my book.

Obst. "Tush!" said Obstinate, "away with your book; will you go back with us or no?"

Chris. "No, not I," said the other, "because I have put my hand to the plough."

Obst. Come, then, neighbor Pliable, let us turn again, and go home without him: there is a company of these crazy-headed fools, that, when they take a fancy by the end, are wiser in their own eyes than seven men that can render a reason.

Pli. Then said Pliable, "Don't revile; if what the good Christian says is true, the things he looks after are better than ours; my heart inclines to go with my neighbor."

Obst. What! more fools still? Be ruled by me, and go back; who knows whither such a brain-sick fellow will lead you? Go back, go back, and be wise.

Chris. Nay, but do thou come with thy neighbor Pliable; there are such things to be had which I spoke of, and many more glories besides. If you believe not me, read here in this book; and for the truth of what is told therein, behold, all is made by the blood of Him that made it.

Pli. "Well, neighbor Obstinate," said Pliable, "I begin to come to a point; I intend to go along with this good man, and to cast in my lot with him. But, my good companion, do you know the way to this desired place?"

Chris. I am directed by a man, whose name is Evangelist, to speed me to a little gate that is before us, where we shall receive directions about the way.

Pli. Come, then, good neighbor, let us be going. Then they went both together.

"And I will go back to my place," said Obstinate; "I will be no companion of such misled, fantastical fellows."

Now, I saw in my dream, that, when Obstinate was gone back, Christian and Pliable went talking over the plain; and thus they began:

Chris. Come, neighbor Pliable, how do you do? I am glad you are persuaded to go along with me. Had even Obstinate himself but felt what I have felt of the powers and terrors of what is yet unseen, he would not thus lightly have given us the back.

Pli. Come, neighbor Christian, since there are none but us two here, tell me now further what the things are, and how to be enjoyed, whither we are going.

Chris. I can better understand them with my mind than speak of them with my tongue; but yet, since you are desirous to know, I will read of them in my book.

Pli. And do you think that the words of your book are certainly true?

Chris. Yes, verily; for it was made by Him that cannot lie.

Pli. Well said; what things are they?

Chris. There is an endless kingdom to be enjoyed, and everlasting life to be given us, that we may live in that kingdom forever.

Pli. Well said; and what else?

Chris. There are crowns of glory to be given us, and garments that will make us shine like the sun in the sky.

Pli. This is very pleasant; and what else?

Chris. There shall be no more crying, nor sorrow; for he that is owner of the place will wipe all tears from our eyes.

Pli. And what company shall we have there?

Chris. There we shall be with seraphims and cherubims, creatures that shall dazzle your eyes to look on them. There also you shall meet with thousands and ten thousands that have gone before us to that place; none of them are hurtful, but all loving and holy; every one walking in the sight of God, and standing in His presence with acceptance for ever. In a word, there we shall see the elders with their golden crowns; there we shall see the holy women with their golden harps; there we shall see men that by the world were cut in pieces, burnt in flames, eaten of beasts, drowned in the seas, for the love they bear to the Lord of the place, all well, and clothed with everlasting life as with a garment.

Pli. The hearing of this is enough to delight one's heart. But are these things to be enjoyed? How shall we get to be sharers thereof?

Chris. The Lord, the Governor of the country, hath written that in this book; the substance of which is, If we be truly willing to have it, He will bestow it upon us freely.

Pli. Well, my good companion, glad am I to hear of these things; come on, let us mend our pace.

Chris. I cannot go so fast as I would, by reason of this burden that is on my back.

Now, I saw in my dream, that just as they had ended this talk, they drew nigh to a very miry slough or swamp, that was in the midst of the plain; and they, being heedless, did both fall suddenly into the bog. The name of the slough was Despond. Here, therefore, they wallowed for a time, being grievously bedaubed with the dirt; and Christian, because of the burden that was on his back, began to sink into the mire.

Pli. Then said Pliable, "Ah! neighbor Christian where are you now?"

Chris. "Truly," said Christian, "I do not know."

Pli. At this Pliable began to be offended, and angrily said to his fellow, "Is this the happiness you have told me all this while of? If we have such ill speed at our first setting out, what may we expect between this and our journey's end? May I get out again with my life, you shall possess the brave country alone for me." And with that, he gave a desperate struggle or two, and got out of the mire on that side of the swamp which was next to his own house: so away he went, and Christian saw him no more.

Wherefore Christian was left to tumble in the Slough of Despond alone; but still he tried to struggle to that side of the slough which was farthest from his own house, and next to the wicket-gate; the which, he did but could not get out because of the burden that was upon his back; but I beheld in my dream, that a man came to him whose name was Help, and asked him, What he did there?

Chris. "Sir," said Christian, "I was bid to go this way by a man called Evangelist, who directed me also to yonder gate, that I might escape the wrath to come; and as I was going there I fell in here."

Help. But why did you not look for the steps?

Chris. Fear followed me so hard, that I fled the next way and fell in.

Help. Then said he, "Give me thine hand." So he gave him his hand, and he drew him out, and set him upon solid ground, and bade him go on his way.

Then I stepped to him that plucked him out, and said, "Sir, wherefore, since over this place is the way from the City of Destruction to yonder gate, is it that this place is not mended, that poor travelers might go thither with more safety?" And he said unto me, "This miry slough is such a place as cannot be mended; it is the hollow whither the scum and filth that go with the feeling of sin, do continually run, and therefore it is called the Slough of Despond; for still, as the sinner is awakened by his lost condition, there arise in his soul many fears, and doubts, and discouraging alarms, which all of them get together and settle in this place; and this is the reason of the badness of the ground.

"It is not the pleasure of the King that this place should remain so bad. His laborers also have, by the direction of His Majesty's surveyors, been for about these sixteen hundred years employed about this patch of ground, if perhaps it might have been mended; yea, and to my knowledge," said he, "here have been swallowed up at least twenty thousand cart-loads, yea, millions, of wholesome teachings, that have at all seasons been brought from all places of the King's dominions (and they that can tell say they are the best materials to make good ground of the place), if so be it might have been mended; but it is the Slough of Despond still, and so will be when they have done what they can.

"True, there are, by the direction of the Lawgiver, certain good and substantial steps, placed even through the very midst of this slough; but at such time as this place doth much spew out its filth, as it doth against change of weather, these steps are hardly seen; or, if they be, men, through the dizziness of their heads, step aside, and then they are bemired to purpose, notwithstanding the steps be there; but the ground is good when they are got in at the gate."

Now, I saw in my dream, that by this time Pliable was got home to his house. So his neighbors came to visit him; and some of them called him wise man for coming back, and some called him a fool for risking himself with Christian; others again did mock at his cowardliness, saying "Surely since you began to venture, I would not have been so base to have given out for a few difficulties;" so Pliable sat sneaking among them. But at last he got more confidence; and then they all turned their tales, and began to abuse poor Christian behind his back. And thus much concerning Pliable.

Now, as Christian was walking solitary by himself, he espied one afar off come crossing over the field to meet him; and their hap was to meet just as they were crossing the way of each other. The gentleman's name that met him was Mr. Worldly Wiseman: he dwelt in the town of Carnal Policy, a very great town, and also hard by from whence Christian came. This man, then, meeting with Christian, and having heard about him—(for Christian's setting forth from the City of Destruction was much noised abroad, not only in the town where he dwelt, but also it began to be the town-talk in some other places)—Mr. Worldly Wiseman therefore, having some guess of him, by beholding his laborious going, by noticing his sighs and groans, and the like, began thus to enter into some talk with Christian:

World. How now, good fellow! whither away after this burdened manner?

Chris. A burdened manner indeed, as ever I think poor creature had! And whereas you ask me, Whither away? I tell you, sir, I am going to yonder wicket-gate before me; for there, as I am informed, I shall be put into a way to be rid of my heavy burden.

World. Hast thou a wife and children?

Chris. Yes; but I am so laden with this burden, that I cannot take that pleasure in them as formerly; methinks I am as if I had none.

World. Wilt thou hearken to me, if I give thee counsel?

Chris. If it be good, I will; for I stand in need of good counsel.

World. I would advise thee, then, that thou with all speed get thyself rid of thy burden; for thou wilt never be settled in thy mind till then; nor canst thou enjoy the blessings which God hath bestowed upon thee till then.

Chris. That is that which I seek for, even to be rid of this heavy burden; but get it off myself I cannot; nor is there any man in our country that can take it off my shoulders; therefore am I going this way, as I told you, that I may be rid of my burden.

World. Who bid thee go this way to be rid of thy burden?

Chris. A man that appeared to me to be a very great and honorable person; his name, as I remember, is Evangelist.

World. I curse him for his counsel! there is not a more dangerous and troublesome way in the world than is that into which he hath directed thee; and that thou shalt find, if thou wilt be ruled by his advice. Thou hast met with something, as I perceive, already; for I see the dirt of the Slough of Despond is upon thee; but that slough is the beginning of the sorrows that do attend those that go on in that way. Hear me: I am older than thou: thou art like to meet with, in the way which thou goest, wearisomeness, painfulness, hunger, perils, nakedness, sword, lions, dragons, darkness, and, in a word, death, and what not. These things are certainly true, having been proved by the words of many people. And why should a man so carelessly cast away himself, by giving heed to a stranger?

Chris. Why, sir, this burden upon my back is more terrible to me than all these things which you have mentioned; nay, methinks I care not what I meet with in the way, if so be I can also meet with deliverance from my burden.

World. How camest thou by the burden at first?

Chris. By reading this book in my hand.

World. I thought so. And it has happened unto thee as unto other weak men, who, meddling with things too high for them, do suddenly fall into thy crazy thoughts, which thoughts do not only unman men, as thine I perceive have done thee, but they run them upon desperate efforts to obtain they know not what.

Chris. I know what I would obtain; it is ease for my heavy burden.

World. But why wilt thou seek for ease this way, seeing so many dangers attend it? Especially since (hadst thou but patience to hear me,) I could direct thee to the getting of what thou desirest, without the dangers that thou in this way wilt run thyself into. Yea, and the remedy is at hand. Besides, I will add that, instead of those dangers, thou shalt meet with much safety, friendship, and content.

Chris. Sir, I pray, open this secret to me.

World. Why, in yonder village (the village is named Morality), there dwells a gentleman whose name is Legality, a very wise man, and a man of very good name, that has skill to help men off with such burdens as thine is from their shoulders; yea, to my knowledge he hath done a great deal of good this way; aye, and besides, he hath skill to cure those that are somewhat crazed in their wits with their burdens. To him, as I said, thou mayest go, and be helped presently. His house is not quite a mile from this place; and if he should not be at home himself, he hath a pretty young man as his son, whose name is Civility, that can do it (to speak on) as well as the old gentleman himself. There, I say, thou mayest be eased of thy burden; and if thou art not minded to go back to thy former habitation (as indeed I would not wish thee), thou mayest send for thy wife and children to thee in this village, where there are houses now standing empty, one of which thou mayest have at a reasonable rate; provision is there also cheap and good; and that which will make thy life the more happy is, to be sure there thou shalt live by honest neighbors, in credit and good fashion.

Now was Christian somewhat at a stand; but presently he concluded, "If this be true which this gentleman hath said, my wisest course is to take his advice;" and with that, he thus further spake:

Chris. Sir, which is my way to this honest man's house?

World. Do you see yonder high hill?

Chris. Yes, very well.

World. By that hill you must go, and the first house you come at is his.

So Christian turned out of his way to go to Mr. Legality's house for help; but, behold, when he was got now hard by the hill, it seemed so high, and also that side of it that was next the wayside did hang so much over, that Christian was afraid to venture farther, lest the hill should fall on his head; wherefore there he stood still, and knew not what to do. Also his burden now seemed heavier to him than while he was in his way. There came also flashes of fire out of the hill, that made Christian afraid that he should be burnt: here, therefore, he sweat and did quake for fear. And now he began to be sorry that he had taken Mr. Worldly Wiseman's counsel; and with that, he saw Evangelist coming to meet him, at the sight also of whom he began to blush for shame. So Evangelist drew nearer and nearer; and, coming up to him, he looked upon him with a severe and dreadful countenance, and thus began to reason with Christian:

Evan. "What dost thou here, Christian?" said he; at which words Christian knew not what to answer; wherefore at present he stood speechless before him. Then said Evangelist further, "Art thou not the man that I found crying, without the walls of the City of Destruction?"

Chris. Yes, dear sir, I am the man.

Evan. Did not I direct thee the way to the little wicket-gate?

Chris. "Yes, dear sir," said Christian.

Evan. How is it, then, that thou art so quickly turned aside? For thou art now out of the way.

Chris. I met with a gentleman as soon as I had got over the Slough of Despond, who persuaded me that I might, in the village before me, find a man that could take off my burden.

Evan. What was he?

Chris. He looked like a gentleman, and talked much to me, and got me at last to yield: so I came hither, but when I beheld this hill, and how it hangs over the way, I suddenly made a stand, lest it should fall on my head.

Evan. What said that gentleman to you?

Chris. Why, he asked me whither I was going, and I told him.
Evan. And what said he then?

Chris. He asked me if I had a family, and I told him. But, said I, I am so laden with the burden that is on my back, that I cannot take pleasure in them as formerly.

Evan. And what said he then?

Chris. He bid me with speed get rid of my burden; and I told him it was ease that I sought. And, said I, I am therefore going to yonder gate to receive further direction how I may get to the place of deliverance. So he said that he would show me a better way, and short, not so hard as the way, sir, that you sent me in; which way, said he, will direct you to a gentleman's house that hath skill to take off these burdens. So I believed him, and turned out of that way into this, if haply I might soon be eased of my burden. But, when I came to this place, and beheld things as they are, I stopped for fear (as I said) of danger; but I now know not what to do.

Evan. Then said Evangelist, "Stand still a little, that I may show thee the words of God." So he stood trembling. Then said Evangelist, "God says in his book, 'See that ye refuse not him that speaketh; for if they escaped not who refused him that spake on earth, much more shall not we escape, if we turn away from Him that speaketh from heaven.' He said, moreover, 'Now, the righteous man shall live by faith in God, but if any man draw back, my soul shall have no pleasure in him.'" He also did thus apply them: "Thou art the man that art running into misery; thou hast begun to reject the counsel of the Most High, and to draw back thy foot from the way of peace, even almost to the danger of thy everlasting ruin."

Then Christian fell down at his feet as dead, crying, "Woe is me, for I am undone!" At the sight of which Evangelist caught him by the right hand, saying, "All manner of sin and evil words shall be forgiven unto men." "Be not faithless, but believing." Then did Christian again a little revive, and stood up trembling, as at first, before Evangelist.

Then Evangelist proceeded, saying, "Give more earnest heed to the things that I shall tell thee of. I will now show thee who it was that led thee astray, and who it was also to whom he sent thee. That man that met thee is one Worldly Wiseman; and rightly is he so called; partly because he seeks only for the things of this world (therefore he always goes to the town of Morality to church), and partly because he loveth that way best, for it saveth him from the Cross; and because he is of this evil temper, therefore he seeketh to turn you from my way though it is the right way.

"He to whom thou wast sent for ease, being by name Legality, is not able to set thee free from thy burden. No man was as yet ever rid of his burden by him; no, nor ever is like to be: ye cannot be set right by any such plan. Therefore, Mr. Worldly Wiseman is an enemy, and Mr. Legality is a cheat; and, for his son Civility, notwithstanding his simpering looks, he is but a fraud and cannot help thee. Believe me, there is nothing in all this noise that thou hast heard of these wicked men, but a design to rob thee of thy salvation, by turning thee from the way in which I had set thee." After this, Evangelist called aloud to the heavens for proof of what he had said; and with that there came words and fire out of the mountain under which poor Christian stood, which made the hair of his flesh stand up. The words were thus spoken: "As many as are of the works of the law are under the curse."

Now, Christian looked for nothing but death, and began to cry out lamentably; even cursing the time in which he met with Mr. Worldly Wiseman; still calling himself a thousand fools for listening to his counsel. He also was greatly ashamed to think that this gentleman's arguments should have the power with him so far as to cause him to forsake the right way. This done, he spoke again to Evangelist, in words and sense as follows:

Chris. Sir, what think you? Is there any hope? May I now go back, and go up to the wicket-gate? Shall I not be abandoned for this, and sent back from thence ashamed? I am sorry I have hearkened to this man's counsel; but may my sins be forgiven?

Evan. Then said Evangelist to him, "Thy sin is very great, for by it thou hast committed two evils; thou hast forsaken the way that is good, to tread in forbidden paths. Yet will the man at the gate receive thee, for he has good will for men; only," said he, "take heed that thou turn not aside again, lest thou perish from the way, when his anger is kindled but a little."

Chapter 2

Then did Christian begin to go back to the right road; and Evangelist, after he had kissed him, gave him one smile, and bid him God speed; so he went on with haste, neither spake he to any man by the way; nor, if any asked him, would he give them an answer. He went like one that was all the while treading on forbidden ground, and could by no means think himself safe, till again he was got in the way which he had left to follow Mr. Worldly Wiseman's counsel: so after a time, Christian got up to the gate. Now, over the gate there was written, "Knock, and it shall be opened unto you."

He knocked, therefore, more than once or twice, saying:

> "May I now enter here? Will He within
> Open to sorry me, though I have been
> An undeserving rebel? Then shall I
> Not fail to sing His lasting praise on high."

At last there came a grave person to the gate named Goodwill, who asked who was there, and whence he came, and what he would have?

Chris. Here is a poor burdened sinner. I come from the City of Destruction, but am going to Mount Zion, that I may be set free from the wrath to come; I would therefore, sir, since I am told that by this gate is the way thither, know, if you are willing to let me in.

Good. "I am willing with all my heart," said he; and, with that, he opened the gate.

So, when Christian was stepping in, the other gave him a pull. Then said Christian, "What means that?" The other told him, "A little distance from this gate there is erected a strong castle, of which Beelzebub, the Evil One, is the captain; from whence both he and they that are with him shoot arrows at those that come up to this gate, if haply they may die before they can enter in." Then said Christian, "I rejoice and tremble." So when he was got in, the man of the gate asked him who directed him thither.

Chris. Evangelist bid me come hither and knock, as I did; and he said that you, sir, would tell me what I must do.

Good. An open door is set before thee, and no man can shut it.

Chris. Now I begin to reap the benefit of the trouble which I have taken.

Good. But how is it that you came alone?

Chris. Because none of my neighbors saw their danger, as I saw mine.

Good. Did any of them know you were coming?

Chris. Yes, my wife and children saw me at the first, and called after me to turn again; also some of my neighbors stood crying and calling after me to return; but I put my fingers in my ears, and so came on my way.

Good. But did none of them follow you, to persuade you to go back?

Chris. Yes, both Obstinate and Pliable: but, when they saw that they could not prevail, Obstinate went railing back, but Pliable came with me a little way.

Good. But why did he not come through?

Chris. We indeed came both together until we came to the Slough of Despond, into the which we also suddenly fell. And then was my neighbor Pliable discouraged, and would not venture farther. Wherefore, getting out again on the side next his own house, he told me I should win the brave country alone for him: so he went his way, and I came mine; he after Obstinate, and I to this gate.

Good. Then said Goodwill, "Alas, poor man! is the heavenly glory of so little worth with him, that he counteth it not worth running the risk of a few difficulties to obtain it?"

Chris. "Truly," said Christian, "I have said the truth of Pliable; and if I should also say the truth of myself, it will appear there is not betterment betwixt him and myself. 'Tis true, he went on back to his own house; but I also turned aside to go into the way of death, being persuaded thereto by the words of one Mr. Worldly Wiseman."

Good. Oh! did he light upon you? What! he would have had you seek for ease at the hands of Mr. Legality! They are both of them a very cheat. But did you take his counsel?

Chris. Yes, as far as I durst. I went to find out Mr. Legality, until I thought that the mountain that stands by his house would have fallen upon my head: wherefore there I was forced to stop.

Good. That mountain has been the death of many, and will be the death of many more; it is well you escaped being by it dashed in pieces.

Chris. Why, truly, I do not know what had become of me there, had not Evangelist happily met me again as I was musing in the midst of my dumps; but it was God's mercy that he came to me again, for else I had never come hither. But now I am come, such a one as I am, more fit indeed for death by that mountain, than thus to stand talking with my Lord. But, oh! what a favor this is to me, that yet I am to enter here!

Good. We make no objections against any, notwithstanding all that they have done before they come hither; they in no wise are cast out. And therefore, good Christian, come a little with me, and I will teach thee about the way thou must go. Look before thee: dost thou see this narrow way? That is the way thou must go. It was cast up by the men of old, prophets, Christ and His apostles, and it is as straight as a rule can make it: this is the way thou must go.

Chris. "But," said Christian, "are there no turnings nor windings by which a stranger may lose his way?"

Good. "Yes, there are many ways butt down upon this, and they are crooked and wide; but thus thou mayest distinguish the right from the wrong, the right only being straight and narrow."

Then I saw in my dream, that Christian asked him further if he could not help him off with his burden that was upon his back. For as yet he had not got rid thereof, nor could he by any means get it off without help.

He told him, "As to thy burden, be content to bear it until thou comest to the place of deliverance; for there it will fall from thy back of itself."

Then Christian began to gird up his loins, and to turn again to his journey.

So the other told him that as soon as he was gone some distance from the gate, he would come at the house of the Interpreter, at whose door he should knock, and he would show him excellent things. Then Christian took his leave of his friend, and he again bid him God speed.

Then he went on till he came to the house of the Interpreter, where he knocked over and over. At last one came to the door, and asked who was there.

Chris. Sir, here is a traveler who was bid by a friend of the good man of this house to call here for his benefit; I would therefore speak with the master of the house.

So he called for the master of the house, who, after a little time, came to Christian, and asked him what he would have.

Chris. "Sir," said Christian, "I am a man that am come from the City of Destruction, and am going to Mount Zion; and I was told by the man that stands at the gate at the head of this way, that, if I called here, you would show me excellent things, such as would be helpful to me on my journey."

Inter. Then said the Interpreter, "Come in; I will show thee that which will be profitable to thee." So he commanded his man to light the candle, and bid Christian follow him; so he led him into a private room, and bid his man open a door; the which when he had done, Christian saw the picture of a very grave person hung up against the wall; and this was the fashion of it: it had eyes lifted up to heaven, the best of books in its hand, the law of truth was written upon its lips, the world was behind its back; it stood as if it pleaded with men, and a crown of gold did hang over its head.

Chris. Then said Christian, "What meaneth this?"

Inter. The man whose picture this is, is one of a thousand. He can say, in the words of the apostle Paul, "Though ye have ten thousand teachers in Christ, yet have you not many fathers; for in Christ Jesus I have been your father through the Gospel." And whereas thou seest him with his eyes lifted up to heaven, the best of books in his hand, and the law of truth writ on his lips, it is to show thee that his work is to know and unfold dark things to sinners; even as also thou seest him stand as if he pleaded with men. And whereas thou seest the world is cast behind him, and that a crown hangs over his head; that is to show thee that, slighting and despising the things that are in the world, for the love that he hath to his Master's service, he is sure in the world that comes next to have glory for his reward. Now, said the Interpreter, I have showed thee this picture first, because the man whose picture this is, is the only man whom the Lord of the place whither thou art going hath chosen to be thy guide, in all difficult places thou mayest meet with in thy way; wherefore take good heed to what I have showed thee, and bear well in thy mind what thou hast seen, lest in thy journey thou meet with some that pretend to lead thee right, but their way goes down to death.

Then he took him by the hand, and led him into a very large parlor, that was full of dust, because never swept; the which after he had looked at it a little while, the Interpreter called for a man to sweep. Now, when he began to sweep, the dust began so abundantly to fly about that Christian had almost therewith been choked. Then said the Interpreter to a girl that stood by, "Bring hither water, and sprinkle the room;" the which when she had done, it was swept and cleansed with ease.

Chris. Then said Christian, "What means this?"

Inter. The Interpreter answered, "This parlor is the heart of a man that was never made pure by the sweet grace of the Gospel. The dust is his sin, and inward evils that have defiled the whole man. He that began to sweep at first is the law; but she that brought water, and did sprinkle it, is the Gospel. Now, whereas thou sawest that, as soon as the first began to sweep, the dust did fly so about that the room could not by him be cleansed, but that thou wast almost choked therewith; this is to show thee, that the law, instead of cleansing the heart (by its working) from sin, doth revive, put strength into, and increase it in the soul, even as it doth discover and forbid it, for it doth not give power to overcome. Again, as thou sawest the girl sprinkle the room with water, upon which it was cleansed with ease; this is to show thee, that when the Gospel comes, in the sweet and gracious power thereof, to the heart, then, I say, even as thou sawest the maiden lay the dust by sprinkling the floor with water, so is sin vanquished and subdued, and the soul made clean through the faith of it, and, consequently, fit for the King of Glory to dwell in."

I saw moreover in my dream, that the Interpreter took him by the hand, and led him into a little room where sat two little children, each one in his own chair. The name of the eldest was Passion, and the name of the other Patience. Passion seemed to be much discontented, but Patience was very quiet. The Christian asked, "What is the reason of the discontent of Passion?" The Interpreter answered, "The governor of them would have him stay for his best things till the beginning of next year; but he will have all now. Patience is willing to wait."

Then I saw that one came to Passion, and brought him a bag of treasure, and poured it down at his feet; the which he took up, and rejoiced therein, and withal laughed Patience to scorn. But I beheld but awhile, and he had wasted all away, and had nothing left him but rags.

Chris. Then said Christian to the Interpreter, "Explain this matter more fully to me."

Inter. So he said, "These two lads are pictures: Passion, of the men of this world; and Patience, of the men of that which is to come: for, as here thou seest, Passion will have all now, this year, that is to say in this world; so are the men of this world; they must have all their good things now; they cannot stay till the next year, that is, until the next world, for their portion of good. That proverb, 'A bird in the hand is worth two in the bush,' is of more weight with them than all the words in the Bible of the good of the world to come. But, as thou sawest that he had quickly wasted all away, and had presently left him nothing but rags, so will it be with all such men at the end of this world."

Chris. Then said Christian, "Now I see that Patience has the best wisdom, and that upon many accounts. 1. Because he stays for the best things. 2. And also because he will have the glory of his when the other has nothing but rags."

Inter. Nay, you may add another; this, the glory of the next world will never wear out; but these are suddenly gone. Therefore Passion had not so much reason to laugh at Patience because he had his good things at first, as Patience will have to laugh at Passion, because he had his best things last; for first must give place to last, because last must have his time to come; but last gives place to nothing, for there is not another to succeed: he, therefore, that hath his portion first, must needs have a time to spend it; but he that hath his portion last, must have it lastingly.

Chris. Then I see it is not best to covet things that are now, but to wait for things to come.

Inter. You say truth; "for the things that are seen soon pass away, but the things that are not seen endure forever."

Then I saw in my dream, that the Interpreter took Christian by the hand and led him into a place where was a fire burning against a wall, and one standing by it, always casting much water upon it, to quench it; yet did the fire burn higher and hotter.

Chris. Then said Christian, "What means this?"

Inter. The Interpreter answered, "This fire is the work of God that is wrought in the heart: he that casts water upon it to extinguish and put it out, is the devil; but, in that thou seest the fire notwithstanding burn higher and hotter, thou shalt also see the reason of that." So then he led him about to the other side of the wall, where he saw a man with a vessel of oil in his hand, of the which he did also continually cast, but secretly, into the fire.

Chris. Then said Christian, "What means this?"

Inter. The Interpreter answered, "This is Christ, who continually, with the oil of His grace, helps the work already begun in the heart; by the means of which notwithstanding what the devil can do, the souls of His people prove gracious still. And in that thou sawest that the man stood behind the wall to keep up the fire; this is to teach thee, that it is hard for the tempted to see how this work of grace is kept alive in the soul."

I saw also that the Interpreter took him again by the hand, and led him into a pleasant place, where was built a stately palace, beautiful to behold, at the sight of which Christian was greatly delighted. He saw also upon the top thereof certain persons walking, who were clothed all in gold.

Then said Christian, "May we go in thither?"

Then the Interpreter took him and led him up toward the door of the palace; and behold, at the door stood a great company of men, as desirous to go in, but durst not. There also sat a man at a little distance from the door, at a table-side, with a book and his ink-horn before him, to take the name of him that should enter therein; he saw also that in the doorway stood many men in armor to keep it, being resolved to do to the men that would enter what hurt and mischief they could. Now was Christian somewhat in amaze. At last, when every man started back for fear of the armed men, Christian saw a man of a very stout countenance come up to the man that sat there to write, saying, "Set down my name, sir:" the which when he had done, he saw the man draw his sword, and put a helmet upon his head, and rush toward the door upon the armed men, who laid upon him with deadly force; but the man, not at all discouraged, fell to cutting and hacking most fiercely. So that, after he had received and given many wounds to those that attempted to keep him out, he cut his way through them all and pressed forward into the palace; at which there was a pleasant voice heard from those that were within, even of those that walked upon the top of the palace, saying:

"Come in, come in;
Eternal glory thou shalt win."
So he went in, and was clothed in such garments as they. Then Christian smiled, and said, "I think verily I know the meaning of this."

"Now," said Christian, "let me go hence." "Nay, stay," said the Interpreter, "until I have showed thee a little more; and after that thou shalt go on thy way." So he took him by the hand again, and led him into a very dark room, where there sat a man in an iron cage.

Now, the man, to look on, seemed very sad. He sat with his eyes looking down to the ground, his hands folded together; and he sighed as if he would break his heart. Then said Christian, "What means this?" At which the Interpreter bid him talk with the man.

Then said Christian to the man, "What art thou?" The man answered, "I am what I was not once."

Chris. What wast thou once?

Man. The man said, "I was once a fair and flourishing Christian, both in mine own eyes, and also in the eyes of others; I was once, as I thought, fair for the Celestial City, and had even joy at the thoughts that I should get thither."

Chris. Well, but what art thou now?

Man. I am now a man of despair, and am shut up in it, as in this iron cage. I cannot get out. Oh, now I cannot!

Chris. But how camest thou in this condition?

Man. I left off to watch and be sober. I gave free reins to sin; I sinned against the light of the Word and the goodness of God; I have grieved the Spirit, and He is gone; I tempted the devil, and he has come to me; I have provoked God to anger, and He has left me; I have so hardened my heart that I cannot turn.

Then said Christian to the Interpreter, "But are there no hopes for such a man as this?" "Ask him," said the Interpreter.

Chris. Then said Christian, "Is there no hope, but you must be kept in the iron cage of despair?"

Man. No, none at all.

Chris. Why? the Son of the Blessed is very pitiful.

Man. I have crucified Him to myself afresh. I have despised His person. I have despised His holiness; I have counted His blood an unholy thing; I have shown contempt to the Spirit of mercy. Therefore I have shut myself out of all the promises of God, and there now remains to me nothing but threatenings, dreadful threatenings, fearful threatenings of certain judgment and fiery anger, which shall devour me as an enemy.

Chris. For what did you bring yourself into this condition?

Man. For the desires, pleasures, and gains of this world; in the enjoyment of which I did then promise myself much delight; but now every one of those things also bite me, and gnaw me, like a burning worm.

Chris. But canst thou not now turn again to God?

Man. God no longer invites me to come to Him. His Word gives me no encouragement to believe; yea, Himself hath shut me up in this iron cage; nor can all the men in the world let me out. O eternity! eternity! how shall I grapple with the misery that I must meet with in eternity?

Inter. Then said the Interpreter to Christian, "Let this man's misery be remembered by thee, and be an everlasting caution to thee."

Chris. "Well," said Christian, "this is fearful! God help me to watch and be sober, and to pray, that I may shun the cause of this man's misery. Sir, is it not time for me to go on my way now?"

Inter. Tarry till I show thee one thing more, and then thou shalt go on thy way.

So he took Christian by the hand again, and led him into a chamber, where there was one rising out of bed; and, as he put on his clothing, he shook and trembled. Then said Christian, "Why doth this man thus tremble?" The Interpreter then bid him tell to Christian the reason of his so doing. So he began, and said, "This night, as I was in my sleep, I dreamed, and behold, the heavens grew exceeding black; also it thundered and lightened in most fearful manner, that it put me into an agony. So I looked up in my dream, and saw the clouds rack at an unusual rate; upon which I heard a great sound of a trumpet, and saw also a Man sitting upon a cloud, attended with the thousands of heaven; they were all in flaming fire; also the heavens were in a burning flame. I heard then a great voice saying, 'Arise, ye dead, and come to judgment.' And with that the rocks rent, the graves opened, and the dead that were therein came forth: some of them were exceeding glad, and looked upward; and some thought to hide themselves under the mountains. Then I saw the Man that sat upon the cloud open the book and bid the world draw near. Yet there was, by reason of a fierce flame that issued out and came before Him, a certain distance betwixt Him and them, as betwixt the judge and the prisoners at the bar. I heard it also called out to them that stood around on the Man that sat on the cloud, 'Gather together the tares, the chaff, and stubble, and cast them into the burning lake. And, with that, the bottomless pit opened, just whereabout I stood; out of the mouth of which there came, in an abundant manner, smoke and coals of fire, with hideous noises. It was also said to the same persons, 'Gather my wheat into the garner.' And, with that, I saw many catched up and carried away into the clouds; but I was left behind. I also sought to hide myself, but I could not; for the Man that sat upon the cloud still kept His eye upon me; my sins also came into my mind, and my conscience did accuse me on every side. Upon this I awakened from my sleep."

Chris. But what was it that made you so afraid of this sight?

Man. Why I thought that the day of judgment was come, and that I was not ready for it. But this affrighted me most, that the angels gathered up several, and left me behind; also the pit of hell opened her mouth just where I stood. My conscience, too, troubled me; and, as I thought, the judge had always His eye upon me, showing anger in His countenance.

Inter. Then said the Interpreter to Christian, "Hast thou considered these things?"

Chris. Yes; and they put me in hope and fear.

Inter. Well, keep all things so in thy mind, that they may be as a goad in thy sides, to prick thee forward in the way thou must go.

Then Christian began to gird up his loins, and to address himself to his journey. Then said the Interpreter, "The Comforter be always with thee, good Christian, to guide thee into the way that leads to the city."

So Christian went on his way, saying:

"Here have I seen things rare and profitable;
Things pleasant, dreadful; things to make me stable
In what I have begun to take in hand:
Then let me think on them, and understand
Wherefore they showed me where; and let me be
Thankful, O good Interpreter, to thee."

Chapter 3

Now, I saw in my dream that the highway up which Christian was to go was fenced on either side with a wall that was called Salvation. Up this way, therefore, did burdened Christian run, but not without great difficulty, because of the load on his back.

He ran thus till he came to a place somewhat ascending; and upon that place stood a Cross, and a little below, in the bottom, a tomb. So I saw in my dream, that just as Christian came up with the cross, his burden loosed from off his shoulders, and fell from off his back, and began to tumble, and so continued to do till it came to the mouth of the tomb, where it fell in, and I saw it no more. Then was Christian glad and lightsome, and said with a merry heart, "He hath given me rest by His sorrow, and life by His death." Then he stood still awhile to look and wonder; for it was very surprising to him that the sight of the cross should thus ease him of his burden. He looked, therefore, and looked again, even till the springs that were in his head sent the water down his cheeks. Now, as he stood looking and weeping, behold, three Shining Ones came to him, and saluted him with "Peace be to thee." So the first said to him, "Thy sins be forgiven thee;" the second stripped him of his rags, and clothed him with a change of garments; the third also set a mark on his forehead, and gave him a roll with a seal upon it, which he bade him look on as he ran, and that he should give it in at the heavenly gate; so they went their way. Then Christian gave three leaps for joy, and went on, singing:

"Thus far did I come laden with my sin;
Nor could aught ease the grief that I was in,
Till I came hither; what a place is this!
Must here be the beginning of my bliss?
Must here the burden fall from off my back?
Must here the strings that bound it to me crack?
Blest cross! blest sepulchre! blest rather be
The Man that was there put to shame for me!"

I saw then in my dream that he went on thus, even until he came to the bottom, where he saw, a little out of the way, three men fast asleep, with fetters upon their heels. The name of one was Simple, of another Sloth, and of the third Presumption.

Christian, then, seeing them lie in this case, went to them, if perhaps he might awake them, and cried, "You are like them that sleep on the top of a mast; for the deep sea is under you, a gulf that hath no bottom: awake, therefore, and come away; be willing, also, and I will help you off with your irons." He also told them, "If he that goeth about like a roaring lion comes by, you will certainly become a prey to his teeth." With that they looked upon him, and began to reply in this sort: Simple said, "I see no danger." Sloth said, "Yet a little more sleep." And Presumption said, "Every tub must stand upon his own bottom." And so they lay down to sleep again, and Christian went on his way.

Yet was he troubled to think that men in that danger should so little care for the kindness of him that so offered to help them, both by awakening of them, advising them, and offering to help them off with their irons. And, as he was troubled thereabout, he espied two men come tumbling over the wall on the left hand of the narrow way; and they made up apace to him. The name of one was Formalist, and the name of the other was Hypocrisy. So, as I said, they drew up unto him, who thus began talking with them:

Chris. Gentlemen, whence came you, and whither go you?

Form. and Hyp. We were born in the land of Vain-glory, and are going for praise to Mount Zion.

Chris. Why came you not in at the gate which standeth at the beginning of the way? Know ye not that it is written, "He that cometh not in by the door, but climbeth up some other way, the same is a thief and a robber?"

Form. and Hyp. They said that to go to the gate for entrance was, by all their countrymen, counted too far about; and that therefore their usual way was to make a short cut of it, and to climb over the wall as they had done.

Chris. But will it not be counted a trespass against the Lord of the city whither we are bound, thus to disobey His will?

Form. and Hyp. They told him, that as for that, he needed not trouble his head thereabout; for what they did they had custom for, and could show, if need were, testimony that could prove it for more than a thousand years.

Chris. "But," said Christian, "will it stand a trial at law?"

Form. and Hyp. They told him that custom, it being of so long standing as above a thousand years, would doubtless now be admitted as a thing according to law by a fair judge. "And besides," said they, "if we get into the way, what matter is it which way we may get in? If we are in, we are in: thou art but in the way, who, as we perceive, came in at the gate; and we are also in the way, that came tumbling over the wall: wherein, now, is thy condition better than ours?"

Chris. I walk by the rule of my Master; you walk by the rude working of your fancies. You are counted thieves already by the Lord of the way; therefore I doubt you will not be found true men at the end of the way. You come in by yourselves without His word, and shall go out by yourselves without His mercy.

To this they made him but little answer; only they bid him look to himself. Then I saw that they went on every man in his way, without much talking one with another; save that these two men told Christian, that, as to law and rules, they doubted not but that they should as carefully do them as he. "Therefore," said they, "we see not wherein thou differest from us, but by the coat which is on thy back, which was, as we believe given thee by some of thy neighbors to hide the shame of thy nakedness."

Chris. By laws and rules you will not be saved, since you came not in by the door. And as for this coat that is on my back, it was given to me by the Lord of the place whither I go; and that, as you say, to cover my nakedness with. And I take it as a token of His kindness to me; for I had nothing but rags before. And besides, thus I comfort myself as I go. Surely, think I, when I come to the gate of the city, the Lord thereof will know me for good, since I have His coat on my back; a coat that He gave me freely in the day that He stripped me of my rags. I have moreover, a mark in my forehead, of which perhaps you have taken no notice, which one of my Lord's most intimate friends fixed there the day that my burden fell off my shoulders. I will tell you, moreover, that I had then given me a roll sealed, to comfort me by reading as I go in the way; I was also bid to give it in at the heavenly gate, in token of my certain going in after it; all which things, I doubt, you want, and want them because you came not in at the gate.

To these things they gave him no answer; only they looked upon each other, and laughed. Then I saw that they went on all, save that Christian kept before, who had no more talk but with himself, and sometimes sighingly, and sometimes comfortably; also he would be often reading in the roll that one of the Shining Ones gave him, by which he was refreshed.

I beheld then that they all went on till they came to the foot of the Hill Difficulty, at the bottom of which was a spring. There were also in the same place two other ways, besides that which came straight from the gate; one turned to the left hand, and the other to the right, at the bottom of the hill; but the narrow way lay right up the hill, and the name of that going up the side of the hill is called Difficulty. Christian now went to the spring, and drank thereof to refresh himself, and then began to go up the hill, saying:

> "The hill, though high, I covet to ascend;
> The difficulty will not me offend,
> For I perceive the way to life lies here.
> Come, pluck up, heart, let's neither faint nor fear.
> Better, though difficult, the right way to go,
> Than wrong, though easy, where the end is woe."

The other two also came to the foot of the hill. But when they saw that the hill was steep and high, and that there were two other ways to go; and supposing also that these two ways might meet again with that up which Christian went, on the other side of the hill; therefore they were resolved to go in those ways. Now, the name of one of those ways was Danger, and the name of the other Destruction. So the one took the way which is called Danger, which led him into a great wood; and the other took directly up the way to destruction, which led him into a wide field, full of dark mountains, where he stumbled and fell, and rose no more.

I looked then after Christian, to see him go up the hill, where I perceived he fell from running to going, and from going to clambering upon his hands and his knees, because of the steepness of the place. Now, about the midway to the top of the hill was a pleasant arbor, made by the Lord of the hill for the refreshment of weary travelers. Thither, therefore, Christian got, where also he sat down to rest him; then he pulled his roll out of his bosom, and read therein to his comfort; he also now began afresh to take a review of the coat or garment that was given him as he stood by the cross. Thus pleasing himself a while, he at last fell into a slumber, and thence into a fast sleep, which detained him in that place until it was almost night; and in his sleep his roll fell out of his hand. Now, as he was sleeping, there came one to him, and awaked him, saying, "Go to the ant, thou sluggard; consider her ways, and be wise." And, with that, Christian suddenly started up, and sped on his way, and went apace till he came to the top of the hill.

Now, when he was got up to the top of the hill, there came two men running amain: the name of the one was Timorous, and of the other Mistrust; to whom Christian said, "Sirs, what's the matter? You run the wrong way." Timorous answered, that they were going to the city of Zion, and had got up that difficult place: "but," said he, "the farther we go, the more danger we meet with; wherefore we turned, and are going back again."

"Yes," said Mistrust, "for just before us lie a couple of lions in the way, whether sleeping or waking we know not; and we could not think, if we came within reach, but they would presently pull us in pieces."

Chris. Then said Christian, "You make me afraid; but whither shall I fly to be safe? If I go back to my own country, that is prepared for fire and brimstone, and I shall certainly perish there; if I can get to the Celestial City, I am sure to be in safety there: I must venture. To go back is nothing but death; to go forward is fear of death, and life everlasting beyond it. I will yet go forward." So Mistrust and Timorous ran down the hill, and Christian went on his way. But, thinking again of what he heard from the men, he felt in his bosom for his roll, and found it not. Then was Christian in great distress, and knew not what to do; for he wanted that which used to comfort him, and that which should have been his pass into the Celestial City. Here, therefore, he began to be greatly troubled, and knew not what to do. At last he bethought himself that he had slept in the arbor that is on the side of the hill; and, falling down upon his knees, he asked God's forgiveness for that his foolish act, and then went back to look for his roll. But all the way he went back, who can sufficiently set forth the sorrow of Christian's heart? Sometimes he sighed, sometimes he wept, and oftentimes he blamed himself for being so foolish to fall asleep in that place, which was erected only for a little refreshment from his weariness. Thus, therefore, he went back, carefully looking on this side and on that, all the way as he went, if happily he might find his roll that had been his comfort so many times in his journey. He went thus till he came again within sight of the arbor where he sat and slept; but that sight renewed his sorrow the more, by bringing again, even afresh, his evil of sleeping into his mind. Thus, therefore, he now went on, bewailing his sinful sleep, saying, "O wretched man that I am, that I should sleep in the day-time; that I should sleep in the midst of difficulty! that I should so indulge myself, as to use that rest for ease to my flesh which the Lord of the hill hath builded only for the relief of the spirits of pilgrims! How many steps have I taken in vain! Thus it happened to Israel; for their sin they were sent back again by the way of the Red Sea; and I am made to tread those steps with sorrow which I might have trod with delight, had it not been for this sinful sleep. How far might I have been on my way by this time! I am made to tread those steps thrice over which

I needed not to have trod but once; yea, also, now I am like to be benighted, for the day is almost spent. Oh that I had not slept!"

Now, by this time he was come to the arbor again, where for awhile he sat down and wept; but at last (as Providence would have it), looking sorrowfully down under the settle, there he espied his roll, the which he, with trembling and haste, caught up, and put it into his bosom. But who can tell how joyful this man was when he had got his roll again? for this roll was the assurance of his life and acceptance at the desired haven. Therefore he laid it up in his bosom, giving thanks to God for directing his eye to the place where it lay, and with joy and tears betook himself again to his journey. But oh, how nimbly now did he go up the rest of the hill! Yet, before he got up, the sun went down upon Christian; and this made him again recall the folly of his sleeping to his remembrance; and thus he began again to condole with himself, "Oh, thou sinful sleep! how for thy sake am I like to be benighted in my journey. I must walk without the sun, darkness must cover the path of my feet, and I must hear the noise of the doleful creatures, because of my sinful sleep." Now also he remembered the story that Mistrust and Timorous told him, of how they were frighted with the sight of the lions. Then said Christian to himself again, "These beasts range in the night for their prey; and if they should meet with me in the dark, how should I avoid them? how should I escape being torn in pieces?" Thus he went on his way. But, while he was thus bewailing his unhappy mistake, he lifted up his eyes, and behold there was a very stately palace before him, the name of which was Beautiful, and it stood just by the highway side.

So I saw in my dream that he made haste, and went forward, that, if possible, he might get lodging there. Now, before he had gone far, he entered into a very narrow passage, which was about a furlong off the Porter's lodge; and looking very narrowly before him as he went, he espied two lions in the way. Now, thought he, I see the dangers by which Mistrust and Timorous were driven back. (The lions were chained, but he saw not the chains). Then he was afraid, and thought also himself to go back after them; for he thought nothing but death was before him. But the Porter at the lodge, whose name is Watchful, perceiving that Christian made a halt as if he would go back, cried out unto him, saying, "Is thy strength so small? fear not the lions, for they are chained, and are placed there for the trial of faith where it is, and for the finding out of those that have none: keep in the midst of the path, and no hurt shall come unto thee."

Then I saw that he went on trembling for fear of the lions; but, taking good heed to the words of the Porter, he heard them roar, but they did him no harm. Then he clapped his hands, and went on till he came and stood before the gate where the Porter was. Then said Christian to the Porter, "Sir, what house is this? and may I lodge here to-night?"

The Porter answered, "This house was built by the Lord of the hill, and He built it for the relief and security of pilgrims." The Porter also asked whence he was, and whither he was going.

Chris. I am come from the City of Destruction, and am going to Mount Zion; but, because the sun is now set, I desire, if I may, to lodge here to-night.

Port. What is your name?

Chris. My name is now Christian, but my name at the first was Graceless.

Port. But how doth it happen that you come so late? The sun is set.

Chris. I had been here sooner, but that, wretched man that I am, I slept in the arbor that stands on the hill-side. Nay, I had, notwithstanding that, been here much sooner, but that in my sleep I lost my roll, and came without it to the brow of the hill; and then, feeling for it and finding it not, I was forced with sorrow of heart to go back to the place where I slept my sleep, where I found it; and now I am come.

Port. Well, I will call out one of the women of this place, who will, if she likes your talk, bring you in to the rest of the family, according to the rules of the house.

So Watchful the Porter rang a bell, at the sound of which came out of the door of the house a grave and beautiful young woman, named Discretion, and asked why she was called.

The Porter answered, "This man is on a journey from the City of Destruction to Mount Zion; but, being weary and benighted, he asked me if he might lodge here to-night; so I told him I would call for thee, who, after speaking with him, mayest do as seemeth thee good, even according to the law of the house."

Then she asked him whence he was, and whither he was going; and he told her. She asked him also how he got into the way; and he told her. Then she asked him what he had seen and met with on the way; and he told her. And at last she asked his name. So he said, "It is Christian; and I have so much the more a desire to lodge here to-night, because, by what I perceive, this place was built by the Lord of the hill for the relief and safety of pilgrims." So she smiled, but the water stood in her eyes; and after a little pause, she said, "I will call forth two or three of my family." So she ran to the door, and called out Prudence, Piety, and Charity, who, after a little more discourse with him brought him in to the family; and many of them, meeting him at the threshold of the house, said, "Come in, thou blessed of the Lord: this house was built by the Lord of the hill on purpose to entertain such pilgrims in." Then he bowed his head, and followed them into the house. So, when he was come in and sat down, they gave him something to drink, and agreed together, that, until supper was ready, some of them should talk with Christian, for the best use of the time; and they appointed Piety, Prudence, and Charity to talk with him; and thus they began:

Piety. Come, good Christian since we have been so loving to you to receive you into our house this night, let us, if perhaps we may better ourselves thereby, talk with you of all things that have happened to you in your pilgrimage.

Chris. With a very good will, and I am glad that you are so well disposed.

Piety. What moved you at first to betake yourself to a pilgrim's life?

Chris. I was driven out of my native country by a dreadful sound that was in mine ears; to wit, that certain destruction did await me, if I abode in that place where I was.

Piety. But how did it happen that you came out of your country this way?

Chris. It was as God would have it; for, when I was under the fears of destruction, I did not know whither to go; but by chance there came a man even to me, as I was trembling and weeping, whose name is Evangelist, and he directed me to the wicket-gate, which else I should never have found, and so set me in the way that hath led me directly to this house.

Piety. But did you not come by the house of the Interpreter?

Chris. Yes, and did see such things there, the remembrance of which will stick by me as long as I live, especially three things; to wit, how Christ, in despite of Satan, the Evil One maintains His work of grace in the heart; how the man had sinned himself quite out of hopes of God's mercy; and also the dream of him that thought in his sleep the day of judgment was come.

Piety. Why? did you hear him tell his dream?

Chris. Yes, and a dreadful one it was, I thought it made my heart ache as he was telling of it; but yet I am glad I heard of it.

Piety. Was that all you saw at the house of the Interpreter?

Chris. No; he took me, and had me where he showed me a stately palace; and how the people were clad in gold that were in it; and how there came a venturous man, and cut his way through the armed men that stood in the door to keep him out; and how he was bid to come in and win eternal glory. Methought those things did delight my heart. I would have stayed at that good man's house a twelvemonth, but that I knew I had farther to go.

Piety. And what saw you else in the way?

Chris. Saw? Why, I went but a little farther, and I saw One, as I thought in my mind, hang bleeding upon a tree; and the very sight of Him made my burden fall off my back; for I groaned under a very heavy burden, and then it fell down from off me. It was a strange thing to me, for I never saw such a thing before; yea, and while I stood looking up (for then I could not forbear looking), three Shining Ones came to me. One of them told me that my sins were forgiven me; another stripped me of my rags, and gave me this broidered coat which you see; and the third set the mark which you see in my forehead, and gave me this sealed roll. (And, with that, he plucked it out of his bosom.)

Piety. But you saw more than this, did you not?

Chris. The things that I have told you were the best; yet some other matters I saw; as namely I saw three men, Simple, Sloth, and Presumption, lie asleep, a little out of the way as I came, with irons upon their heels; but do you think I could wake them? I also saw Formalist and Hypocrisy come tumbling over the wall, to go, as they pretended, to Zion; but they were quickly lost, even as I myself did tell them, but they would not believe. But, above all, I found it hard work to get up this hill, and as hard to come by the lions' mouths; and truly, if it had not been for the good man the Porter, that stands at the gate, I do not know but that, after all, I might have gone back again; but now I thank God I am here, and I thank you for receiving of me.

Then Prudence thought good to ask him a few questions, and desired his answer to them.

Pru. Do you think sometimes of the country from whence you came?

Chris. Yes, but with much shame and detestation. Truly, if I had been mindful of that country from whence I came out, I might have had an opportunity to have returned; but now I desire a better country, that is, a heavenly one.

Pru. Do you not yet bear away with you in your thoughts some of the things that you did in the former time?

Chris. Yes, but greatly against my will; especially my inward and sinful thoughts, with which all my countrymen, as well as myself, were delighted. But now all those things are my grief; and, might I but choose mine own things, I would choose never to think of those things more; but when I would be doing that which is best, that which is worst is with me.

Pru. Do you not find sometimes as if those things were overcome, which at other times are your trouble?

Chris. Yes, but that is but seldom; but they are to me golden hours in which such things happen to me.

Pru. Can you remember by what means you find your annoyances, at times, as if they were overcome?

Chris. Yes; when I think what I saw at the cross, that will do it; and when I look upon my broidered coat, that will do it; also when I look into the roll that I carry in my bosom, that will do it; and when my thoughts wax warm about whither I am going, that will do it.

Pru. And what makes you so desirous to go to Mount Zion?

Chris. Why, there I hope to see Him alive that did hang dead on the cross; and there I hope to be rid of all these things that to this day are in me an annoyance to me. There, they say, there is no death; and there I shall dwell with such company as I like best. For, to tell you the truth, I love Him because I was by Him eased of my burden; and I am weary of my inward sickness. I would fain be where I shall die no more, and with the company that shall continually cry, "Holy, holy, holy!"

Char. Then said Charity to Christian, "Have you a family? are you a married man?"

Chris. I have a wife and four small children.

Char. And why did you not bring them along with you?

Chris. Then Christian wept, and said, "Oh, how willingly would I have done it! but they were all of them utterly against my going on pilgrimage."

Char. But you should have talked to them, and endeavored to have shown them the danger of staying behind.

Chris. So I did, and told them also what God had shown to me of the destruction of our city; but I seemed to them as one that mocked, and they believed me not.

Char. And did you pray to God that He would bless your words to them?

Chris. Yes, and that with much affection; for you must think that my wife and poor children are very dear unto me.

Char. But did you tell them of your own sorrow and fear of destruction? for I suppose that you could see your destruction before you.

Chris. Yes, over, and over, and over. They might also see my fears in my countenance, in my tears, and also in my trembling under the fear of the judgment that did hang over our heads: but all was not enough to prevail with them to come with me.

Char. But what could they say for themselves why they came not?

Chris. Why, my wife was afraid of losing this world, and my children were given to the foolish delights of youth; so, what by one thing, and what by another, they left me to wander in this manner alone.

Char. But did you not, with your vain life, hinder all that you by words used by way of persuasion to bring them away with you?

324

Chris. Indeed, I cannot commend my life, for I am conscious to myself of many failings therein. I know also, that a man, by his actions may soon overthrow what, by proofs or persuasion, he doth labor to fasten upon others for their good. Yet this I can say, I was very wary of giving them occasion, by any unseemly action, to make them averse to going on pilgrimage. Yea, for this very thing they would tell me I was too precise, and that I denied myself of things (for their sakes) in which they saw no evil. Nay, I think I may say that, if what they saw in me did hinder them, it was my great tenderness in sinning against God, or of doing any wrong to my neighbor.

Char. Indeed, Cain hated his brother because his own works were evil, and his brother's righteous; and, if thy wife and children have been offended with thee for this, they thereby show themselves to be resolutely opposed to good: thou hast freed thy soul from their blood.

Now I saw in my dream, that thus they sat talking together till supper was ready. So, when they had made ready, they sat down to meat. Now, the table was furnished with fat things, and wine that was well refined; and all their talk at the table was about the Lord of the hill; as, namely, about what He had done, and wherefore He did what He did, and why He had builded that house; and by what they said, I perceived that He had been a great warrior, and had fought with and slain him that had the power of death, but not without great danger to Himself, which made me love Him the more.

For, as they said, and as I believe (said Christian), He did it with the loss of much blood. But that which puts the glory of grace into all He did, was, that He did it out of pure love to this country. And, besides, there were some of them of the household that said they had seen and spoken with Him since He did die on the cross; and they have declared that they had it from His own lips, that He is such a lover of poor pilgrims, that the like is not to be found from the east to the west. They moreover gave an instance of what they affirmed; and that was, He had stripped Himself of His glory, that He might do this for the poor; and that they had heard Him say and affirm that He would not dwell in the mountains of Zion alone. They said, moreover, that He had made many pilgrims princes, though by nature they were beggars born, and their home had been the dunghill.

Thus they talked together till late at night; and after they had committed themselves to their Lord for protection, they betook themselves to rest. The Pilgrim they laid in a large upper chamber, whose window opened towards the sunrising. The name of the chamber was Peace, where he slept till break of day, and then he awoke and sang:

"Where am I now? Is this the love and care
Of Jesus, for the men that pilgrims are,
Thus to provide that I should be forgiven,
And dwell already the next door to heaven?"

So in the morning they all got up; and after some more talking together, they told him that he should not depart till they had shown him the rarities of that place. And first they took him into the study, where they showed him records of the greatest age; in which, as I remember in my dream, they showed him first the history of the Lord of the hill, that He was the son of the Ancient of Days, and had lived from the beginning. Here also were more fully written the acts that He had done, and the names of many hundreds that He had taken into his service; and how he had placed them in such houses that could neither by length of days nor decays of nature be destroyed.

Then they read to him some of the worthy acts that some of His servants had done; as, how they had conquered kingdoms, wrought righteousness, obtained promises, stopped the mouths of lions, quenched the violence of fire, escaped the edge of the sword, out of weakness were made strong, waxed valiant in fight, and turned to flight the armies of the enemies.

They then read again in another part of the records of the house, where it was shown how willing their Lord was to receive into His favor any even any, though they in time past had done great wrongs to His person and rule. Here also were several other histories of many other famous things, of all which Christian had a view; as of things both ancient and modern, together with prophecies and foretellings of things that surely come to pass, both to the dread and wonder of enemies, and the comfort and happiness of pilgrims.

The next day they took him and led him into the armory, where they showed him all manner of weapons which their Lord had provided for pilgrims; as sword, shield, helmet, breast-plate, all-prayer, and shoes that would not wear out. And there was here enough of this to harness out as many men for the service of their Lord as there be stars in the heaven for multitude.

They also showed him some of the things with which some of His servants had done wonderful things. They showed him Moses' rod; the hammer and nail with which Jael slew Sisera; the pitchers, trumpets, and lamps too, with which Gideon put to flight the armies of Midian. Then they showed him the ox's goad wherewith Shamgar slew six hundred men. They showed him also the jaw-bone with which Samson did such mighty feats. They showed him, moreover, the sling and stone with which David slew Goliath of Gath, and the sword also with which their Lord will kill the Man of Sin, in the day that He shall rise up to the battle. They showed him, besides, many excellent things, with which Christian was much delighted. This done, they went to their rest again.

Then I saw in my dream that on the morrow he got up to go forward, but they desired him to stay till the next day also; "and then," said they, "we will, if the day be clear, show you the Delectable Mountains;" which they said would yet further add to his comfort, because they were nearer the desired haven than the place where at present he was. So he consented and stayed. When the morning was up, they led him to the top of the house, and bid him look south. So he did, and behold, at a great distance he saw a most pleasant mountainous country, beautified with woods, vineyards, fruits of all sorts, flowers also, with springs and fountains, very lovely to behold. Then he asked the name of the country. They said it was Immanuel's Land; "and it is as common," said they, "as this hill is, to and for all the pilgrims. And when thou comest there, from thence thou mayest see to the gate of the Celestial City, as the shepherds that live there will make appear."

Now he bethought himself of setting forward, and they were willing he should. "But first," said they, "let us go again into the armory." So they did; and when he came there, they dressed him from head to foot with armor of proof, lest perhaps he should meet with assaults in the way. He being, therefore, thus armed, walked out with his friends to the gate; and there he asked the Porter if he saw any pilgrim pass by. Then the Porter answered, "Yes."

Chris. "Pray, did you know him?" said he.

Port. I asked his name, and he told me it was Faithful.

Chris. "Oh," said Christian, "I know him, he is my townsman, my near neighbor; he comes from the place where I was born. How far do you think he may be before?"

Port. He has got by this time below the hill.

Chris. "Well," said Christian, "good Porter, the Lord be with thee, and add to all thy blessings much increase for the kindness thou has shown to me!"

Then he began to go forward; but Discretion, Piety, Charity, and Prudence would accompany him down to the foot of the hill. So they went on together repeating their former discourses, till they came to go down the hill. Then said Christian, "As it was difficult coming up, so far so as I can see, it is dangerous going down." "Yes," said Prudence, "so it is; for it is a hard matter for a man to go down the Valley of Humiliation, as thou art now, and to catch no slip by the way; therefore," said they, "are we come out to accompany thee down the hill." So he began to go down, but very warily; yet he caught a slip or two.

Then I saw in my dream that these good companions, when Christian was gone down to the bottom of the hill, gave him a loaf of bread, a bottle of wine, and a cluster of raisins; and then he went his way.

Chapter 4

$\mathfrak{B}$ut now, in this Valley of Humiliation, poor Christian was hard put to it; for he had gone but a little way before he espied a foul fiend coming over the field to meet him: his name is Apollyon. Then did Christian begin to be afraid, and to cast in his mind whether to go back or to stand his ground. But he considered again that he had no armor for his back, and therefore thought that to turn the back to him might give him greater advantage with ease to pierce him with darts; therefore he resolved to venture and stand his ground; for, thought he, had I no more in mine eye than the saving of my life, it would be the best way to stand. So he went on, and Apollyon met him. Now, the monster was hideous to behold: he was clothed with scales like a fish, and they are his pride; he had wings like a dragon, and feet like a bear, and out of his belly came fire and smoke; and his mouth was as the mouth of a lion. When he was come up to Christian, he beheld him with a disdainful countenance, and thus began to question with him:

Apollyon. Whence come you, and whither are you bound?

Chris. I am come from the City of Destruction, which is the place of all evil, and am going to the City of Zion.

Apol. By this I perceive that thou art one of my subjects; for all that country is mine, and I am the prince and God of it. How is it then that thou hast run away from thy king? Were it not that I hope that thou mayest do me more service, I would strike thee now at one blow to the ground.

Chris. I was indeed born in your kingdom; but your service was hard, and your wages such as a man could not live on; for the wages of sin is death; therefore, when I was come to years, I did as other thoughtful persons do, look out, if perhaps I might mend myself.

Apol. There is no prince that will thus lightly lose his subjects, neither will I as yet lose thee; but, since thou complainest of thy service and wages, be content to go back, and what our country will afford I do here promise to give thee.

Chris. But I have let myself to another, even to the King of princes; and how can I with fairness go back with thee?

Apol. Thou hast done in this according to the proverb, "changed a bad for a worse;" but it is common for those that have called themselves His servants, after awhile to give Him the slip, and return again to me. Do thou so too, and all shall be well.

Chris. I have given Him my faith, and sworn my service to Him; how, then, can I go back from this, and not be hanged as a traitor?

Apol. Thou didst the same to me, and yet I am willing to pass by all, if now thou wilt yet turn again and go back.

Chris. What I promised thee was in my youth, and besides, I count that the Prince under whose banner I now stand is able to set me free, yea, and to pardon also what I did as to my service with thee. And besides, O thou destroying Apollyon, to speak the truth, I like His service, His wages, His servants, His government, His company, and country, better than thine; therefore leave off to persuade me further: I am His servant, and I will follow Him.

Apol. Consider again when thou art in cold blood, what thou art likely to meet with in the way that thou goest. Thou knowest that for the most part His servants come to an ill end, because they are disobedient against me and my ways. How many of them have been put to shameful deaths! And besides, thou countest His service better than mine; whereas He never came yet from the place where He is, to deliver any that served Him out of their hands; but as for me, how many times, as all the world very well knows, have I delivered, either by power or fraud, those that have faithfully served me, from Him and His, though taken by them! And so I will deliver thee.

Chris. His forbearing at present to deliver them is on purpose to try their love, whether they will cleave to Him to the end; and, as for the ill end thou sayest they come to, that is most glorious in their account. For, for present deliverance, they do not much expect it; for they stay for their glory, and then they shall have it when their prince comes in His and the glory of the angels.

Apol. Thou hast already been unfaithful in thy service to Him; and how dost thou think to receive wages of Him?

Chris. Wherein, O Apollyon, have I been unfaithful to Him?

Apol. Thou didst faint at first setting out, when thou wast almost choked in the Gulf of Despond. Thou didst attempt wrong ways to be rid of thy burden, whereas thou shouldst have stayed till thy Prince had taken it off. Thou didst sinfully sleep and lose thy choice things. Thou wast almost persuaded to go back at the sight of the lions. And when thou talkest of thy journey, and of what thou hast seen and heard, thou art inwardly desirous of glory to thyself in all that thou sayest or doest.

Chris. All this is true, and much more which thou hast left out; but the Prince whom I serve and honor is merciful and ready to forgive. But besides, these infirmities possessed me in thy own country; for there I sucked them in, and I have groaned under them, been sorry for them, and have obtained pardon of my Prince.

Apol. Then Apollyon broke out into a grievous rage, saying, "I am an enemy to this Prince; I hate His person, His laws, and people. I am come out on purpose to withstand thee."

Chris. Apollyon, beware what you do, for I am in the King's highway, the way of holiness: therefore take heed to yourself.

Apol. Then Apollyon straddled quite over the whole breadth of the way, and said, "I am void of fear in this matter. Prepare thyself to die; for I swear by my infernal den, that thou shalt go no farther: here will I spill thy soul." And, with that, he threw a flaming dart at his breast; but Christian held a shield in his hand, with which he caught, and so prevented the danger of that.

Then did Christian draw, for he saw it was time to bestir him; and Apollyon as fast made at him, throwing darts as thick as hail, by the which, notwithstanding all that Christian could do to avoid it, Apollyon wounded him in his head, his hand, and foot. This made Christian give a little back; Apollyon, therefore, followed his work amain, and Christian again took courage, and resisted as manfully as he could. This sore combat lasted for above half a day, even till Christian was almost quite spent. For you must know that Christian, by reason of his wounds, must needs grow weaker and weaker.

Then Apollyon, espying his opportunity, began to gather up close to Christian, and, wrestling with him, gave him a dreadful fall; and, with that, Christian's sword flew out of his hand. Then said Apollyon, "I am sure of thee now." And, with that, he had almost pressed him to death, so that Christian began to despair of life. But, as God would have it, while Apollyon was fetching his last blow, thereby to make a full end of this good man, Christian nimbly reached out his hand for his sword, and caught it, saying, "Rejoice not against me, O mine enemy: when I fall I shall arise;" and, with that, gave him a deadly thrust, which made him give back, as one that had received his mortal wound. Christian, perceiving that, made at him again, saying, "Nay, in all these things we are more than conquerors through Him that loved us." And, with that, Apollyon spread forth his dragon's wings, and sped him away, that Christian for a season saw him no more.

In this combat no man can imagine, unless he had seen and heard, as I did, what yelling and hideous roaring Apollyon made all the time of the fight: he spake like a dragon; and, on the other side, what sighs and groans burst from Christian's heart. I never saw him all the while give so much as one pleasant look, till he perceived he had wounded Apollyon with his two-edged sword; then, indeed, he did smile and look upward; but it was the dreadfullest sight that ever I saw.

Chris. So, when the battle was over, Christian said, "I will here give thanks to Him that hath delivered me out of the mouth of the lion; to Him that did help me against Apollyon." And so he did, saying:

"Great Satan, the captain of this fiend,
Designed my ruin; therefore to this end
He sent him harnessed out: and he with rage
That hellish was, did fiercely me engage;
But blessed angels helped me; and I,
By dint of sword, did quickly make him fly:

Therefore to God let me give lasting praise,
And thank and bless His holy name always."

Then there came to him a hand with some of the leaves of the tree of life; the which Christian took, and laid upon the wounds that he had received in the battle, and was healed immediately. He also sat down in that place to eat bread, and to drink of the bottle that was given to him a little before: so, being refreshed, he went forth on his journey, with his sword drawn in his hand; "For," he said, "I know not but some other enemy may be at hand." But he met with no other harm from Apollyon quite through this valley.

Now, at the end of this valley was another, called the Valley of the Shadow of Death; and Christian must needs go through it, because the way to the Celestial City lay through the midst of it. Now this valley is a very solitary place; the prophet Jeremiah thus describes it: "A wilderness, a land of deserts and pits, a land of drought, and of the shadow of death, a land that no man" but a Christian "passeth through, and where no man dwelt."

Now here Christian was worse put to it than in his fight with Apollyon, as in the story you shall see.

I saw then in my dream, that when Christian was got to the borders of the Shadow of Death, there met him two men, children of them that brought up an evil report of the good land, making haste to go back; to whom Christian spake as follows:

Chris. Whither are you going?

Men. They said, "Back, back! and we would have you to do so too, if either life or peace is prized by you."

Chris. "Why, what's the matter?" said Christian.

Men. "Matter!" said they: "we were going that way as you are going, and went as far as we durst: and indeed we were almost past coming back; for had we gone a little farther, we had not been here to bring the news to thee."

Chris. "But what have you met with?" said Christian.

Men. Why, we were almost in the Valley of the Shadow of Death, but that by good hap we looked before us, and saw the danger before we came to it.

Chris. "But what have you seen?" said Christian.

Men. Seen! why, the valley itself, which is as dark as pitch: we also saw there the hobgoblins, satyrs, and dragons of the pit; we heard also in that valley a continual howling and yelling, as of a people under unutterable misery, who there sat bound in affliction and irons; and over that hung the discouraging clouds of confusion; Death also does always spread his wings over it. In a word, it is every whit dreadful, being utterly without order.

Chris. Then said Christian, "I perceive not yet, by what you have said, but that this is my way to the desired haven."

Men. Be it thy way, we will not choose it for ours.

So they parted, and Christian went on his way, but still with his sword drawn in his hand, for fear lest he should be attacked.

I saw then in my dream, as far as this valley reached, there was on the right hand a very deep ditch; that ditch is it into which the blind have led the blind in all ages, and have both there miserably perished. Again, behold, on the left hand there was a very dangerous quag, or marsh, into which, if even a good man falls, he finds no bottom for his foot to stand on: into that quag King David once did fall, and had no doubt there been smothered, had not He that is able plucked him out.

The pathway was here also exceedingly narrow, and therefore good Christian was the more put to it; for when he sought, in the dark, to shun the ditch, on the one hand he was ready to tip over into the mire on the other; also when he sought to escape the mire, without great carefulness he would be ready to fall into the ditch. Thus he went on, and I heard him here sigh bitterly, for besides the danger mentioned above, the pathway was here so dark, that ofttimes, when he lifted up his foot to go forward, he knew not where or upon what he should set it next.

About the midst of this valley I perceived the mouth of hell to be, and it stood also hard by the wayside. Now, thought Christian, what shall I do? And ever and anon the flame and smoke would come out in such abundance, with sparks and hideous noises (things that cared not for Christian's sword, as did Apollyon before), that he was forced to put up his sword, and betake himself to another weapon, called "All-Prayer." So he cried in my hearing, "O Lord, I beseech Thee, deliver my soul." Thus he went on a great while, yet still the flames would be reaching towards him; also he heard doleful voices, and rushings to and fro, so that sometimes he thought he should be torn in pieces, or trodden down like mire in the streets. This frightful sight was seen, and those dreadful noises were heard by him, for several miles together, and, coming to a place where he thought he heard a company of fiends coming forward to meet him, he stopped, and began to muse what he had best to do. Sometimes he had half a thought to go back; then again he thought he might be half-way through the valley. He remembered, also, how he had already vanquished many a danger, and that the danger of going back might be much more than going forward. So he resolved to go on; yet the fiends seemed to come nearer and nearer. But, when they were come even almost at him, he cried out with a most vehement voice, "I will walk in the strength of the Lord God." So they gave back, and came no farther.

One thing I would not let slip: I took notice that now poor Christian was so confounded that he did not know his own voice; and thus I perceived it: just when he was come over against the mouth of the burning pit, one of the wicked ones got behind him, and stepped up softly to him, and whisperingly suggested many wicked words to him, which he verily thought had proceeded from his own mind. This put Christian more to it than anything he had met with before, even to think that he should now speak evil of Him that he had so much loved before. Yet, if he could have helped it, he would not have done it; but he had not the wisdom either to stop his ears, or to know from whence those wicked words came.

When Christian had traveled in this sorrowful condition some considerable time he thought he heard the voice of a man, as going before him, saying, "Though I walk through the Valley of the Shadow of Death I will fear no evil; for Thou art with me."

Then he was glad, and that for these reasons:

First,—Because he gathered from thence, that some who feared God were in this valley as well as himself.

Secondly,—For that he perceived God was with them, though in that dark and dismal state. And why not, thought he, with me, though by reason of the kindness that attends this place, I cannot perceive it?

Thirdly,—For that he hoped (could he overtake them) to have company by-and-by. So he went on, and called to him that was before; but he knew not what to answer, for that he also thought himself to be alone. And by-and-by the day broke. Then said Christian, "He hath turned the shadow of death into the morning."

Now, morning being come, he looked back, not out of desire to return, but to see, by the light of the day, what dangers he had gone through in the dark. So he saw more perfectly the ditch that was on the one hand, and the quag that was on the other; also how narrow the way which led betwixt them both. Also now he saw the hobgoblins, and satyrs, and dragons of the pit, but all afar off; for after break of day they came not nigh; yet they were shown to him according to that which is written, "He showeth deep things out of darkness, and bringeth out to light the shadow of death."

Now was Christian much affected with his deliverance from all the dangers of his solitary way; which dangers, though he feared them much before, yet he saw them more clearly now, because the light of the day made them plain to him. And about this time the sun was rising, and this was another mercy to Christian; for you must note that, though the first part of the Valley of the Shadow of Death was dangerous, yet this second part, which he was yet to go, was if possible far more dangerous; for, from the place where he now stood, even to the end of the valley, the way was all along set so full of snares, traps, gins, and nets here, and so full of pits, pitfalls, deep holes, and shelvings down there, that, had it now been dark, as it was when he came the first part of the way, had he had a thousand souls, they had in reason been cast away. But, as I said just now the sun was rising. Then said he, "His candle shineth on my head, and by His light I go through darkness."

In this light, therefore, he came to the end of the valley. Now, I saw in my dream that at the end of the valley lay blood, bones, ashes, and mangled bodies of men, even of pilgrims that had gone this way formerly; and, while I was musing what should be the reason, I espied a little before me a cave, where two giants, POPE and PAGAN, dwelt in old time; by whose power and tyranny, the men whose bones, blood, ashes, etc., lay there, were cruelly put to death. But by this place Christian went without danger, whereat I somewhat wondered; but I have learnt since, that Pagan has been dead many a day; and, as for the other, though he be yet alive, he is, by reason of age, also of the many shrewd brushes that he met with in his younger days, grown so crazy and stiff in his joints, that he can now do little more than sit in his cave's mouth, grinning at pilgrims as they go by, and biting his nails because he cannot come to them.

So I saw that Christian went on his way; yet, at the sight of the old man that sat at the mouth of the cave, he could not tell what to think, especially because he spoke to him, though he could not go after him, saying, "You will never mend till more of you be burned." But he held his peace, and set a good face on it, and so went by and caught no hurt. Then sang Christian:

> "O, world of wonders (I can say no less),
> That I should be preserved in that distress
> That I have met with here! Oh, blessed be
> That hand that from it hath delivered me!
> Dangers in darkness, devils, hell, and sin,
> Did compass me, while I this vale was in;
> Yes, snares, and pits, and traps, and nets did lie
> My path about, that worthless, silly I
> Might have been catched, entangled, and cast down;
> But, since I live, let Jesus wear the crown."

Chapter 5

Now as Christian went on his way, he came to a little ascent which was cast up on purpose that pilgrims might see before them: up there, therefore, Christian went; and looking forward, he saw Faithful before him upon his journey. Then said Christian aloud, "Ho, ho! so-ho! stay, and I will be your companion." At that Faithful looked behind him; to whom Christian cried, "Stay, stay, till I come up to you." But Faithful answered, "No, I am upon my life, and the avenger of blood is behind me."

At this Christian was somewhat moved; and putting to all his strength, he quickly got up with Faithful, and did also overrun him: so the last was first. Then did Christian boastfully smile, because he had gotten the start of his brother; but, not taking good heed to his feet, he suddenly stumbled and fell, and could not rise again until Faithful came up to help him.

Then I saw in my dream, they went very lovingly on together, and had sweet talk together of all things that had happened to them in their pilgrimage; and thus Christian began:

Chris. My honored and well-beloved brother Faithful, I am glad that I have overtaken you, and that God has so tempered our spirits that we can walk as companions in this so pleasant a path.

Faith. I had thought, dear friend, to have had your company quite from our town; but you did get the start of me, wherefore I was forced to come thus much of the way alone.

Chris. How long did you stay in the City of Destruction before you set out after me on your pilgrimage?

Faith. Till I could stay no longer; for there was great talk, presently after you were gone out, that our city would, in a short time, with fire from heaven, be burned down to the ground.

Chris. What! did your neighbors talk so?

Faith. Yes, it was for a while in everybody's mouth.

Chris. What! and did no more of them but you come out to escape the danger?

Faith. Though there was, as I said, a great talk thereabout, yet I do not think they did firmly believe it. For, in the heat of the talking I heard some of them deridingly speak of you, and of your desperate journey; for so they called this your pilgrimage. But I did believe, and do still, that the end of our city will be with fire and brimstone from above; and therefore I have made my escape.

Chris. Did you hear no talk of neighbor Pliable?

Faith. Yes, Christian; I heard that he followed you till he came to the Slough of Despond, where, as some said, he fell in; but he would not be known to have so done; but I am sure he was soundly bedabbled with that kind of dirt.

Chris. And what said the neighbors to him?

Faith. He hath, since his going back, been held greatly in derision, and that among all sorts of people: some do mock and despise him, and scarce any will set him on work. He is now seven times worse than if he had never gone out of the city.

Chris. But why should they be set so against him, since they also despise the way that he forsook?

Faith. "Oh," they say, "hang him; he is a turncoat! he was not true to his profession!" I think God has stirred up even his enemies to hiss at him and laugh at him, because he hath forsaken the way.

Chris. Had you no talk with him before you came out?

Faith. I met him once in the streets, but he leered away on the other side, as one ashamed of what he had done; so I spake not to him.

Chris. Well, at my first setting out, I had hopes of that man, but now I fear he will perish in the overthrow of the city. For it has happened to him according to the true proverb, "The dog is turned to his vomit again, and the sow that was washed to her wallowing in the mire."

Faith. These are my fears of him too; but who can hinder that which will be?

Chris. "Well, neighbor Faithful," said Christian, "let us leave him, and talk of things that more immediately concern ourselves. Tell me now what you have met with in the way as you came; for I know you have met with some things, or else it may be writ for a wonder."

Faith. I escaped the slough that I perceive you fell into, and got up to the gate without that danger; only I met with one whose name was Wanton, that had like to have done me a mischief.

Chris. It was well you escaped her net: Joseph was hard put to it by her, and he escaped her as you did; but it had like to have cost him his life. But what did she do to you?

Faith. You cannot think (but that you know something) what a flattering tongue she had; she lay at me hard to turn aside with her, promising me all manner of enjoyment.

Chris. Nay, she did not promise you the enjoyment of a good conscience.

Faith. You know what I mean—not the enjoyment of the soul, but of the body.

Chris. Thank God you have escaped her: the abhorred of the Lord shall fall into her ditch.

Faith. Nay, I know not whether I did wholly escape her or no.

Chris. Why, I suppose you did not consent to her desires?

Faith. No, not to defile myself; for I remembered an old writing that I had seen which saith, "Her steps take hold of hell." So I shut mine eyes, because I would not be bewitched with her looks. Then she railed on me, and I went my way.

Chris. Did you meet with no other assault as you came?

Faith. When I came to the foot of the hill called Difficulty, I met with a very aged man, who asked me what I was and whither bound. I told him that I was a pilgrim, going to the Celestial City. Then said the old man, "Thou lookest like an honest fellow: wilt thou be content to dwell with me, for the wages that I shall give thee?" Then I asked him his name, and where he dwelt. He said his name was Adam the First, and that he dwelt in the town of Deceit. I asked him then what was his work, and what the wages that he would give. He told me that his work was many delights; and his wages, that I should be his heir at last. I further asked him what house he kept, and what other servants he had. So he told me that his house was filled with all the dainties of the world, and that his servants were his own children. Then I asked him how many children he had. He said that he had but three daughters, the Lust of the Flesh, the Lust of the Eyes, and the Pride of Life, and that I should marry them if I would. Then I asked, how long time he would have me live with him? And he told me, As long as he lived himself.

Chris. Well, and what conclusion came the old man and you to at last?

Faith. Why, at first I found myself somewhat inclinable to go with the man, for I thought he spake very fair; but looking in his forehead, as I talked with him, I saw there written, "Put off the old man with his deeds."

Chris. And how then?

Faith. Then it came burning hot into my mind, whatever he said, and however he flattered, when he got home to his house he would sell me for a slave. So I bid him forbear, for I would not come near the door of his house. Then he reviled me, and told me that he would send such a one after me that should make my way bitter to my soul. So I turned to go away from him; but, just as I turned myself to go thence, I felt him take hold of my flesh, and give me such a deadly twitch back, that I thought he had pulled part of me after himself: this made me cry, "O wretched man!" So I went on my way up the hill. Now, when I had got about half-way up, I looked behind me, and saw one coming after me, swift as the wind; so he overtook me just about the place where the settle stands.

Chris. "Just there," said Christian, "did I sit down to rest me; but being overcome with sleep, I there lost this roll out of my bosom."

Faith. But, good brother, hear me out. So soon as the man overtook me, he was but a word and a blow; for down he knocked me, and laid me for dead. But, when I was a little come to myself again, I asked him wherefore he served me so. He said, because of my secret inclining to Adam the First. And, with that, he struck me another deadly blow on the breast, and beat me down backwards; so I lay at his feet as dead as before. So, when I came to myself again, I cried him mercy; but he said, "I know not how to show mercy;" and, with that, he knocked me down again. He had doubtless made an end of me, but that One came by, and bid him forbear.

Chris. Who was that that bid him forbear?

Faith. I did not know him at first; but, as He went by, I perceived the holes in His hands and His side; then I concluded that He was our Lord. So I went up the hill.

Chris. That man that overtook you was Moses. He spareth none, neither knoweth he how to show mercy to those that disobey his law.

Faith. I know it very well: it was not the first time that he has met with me. It was he that came to me when I dwelt securely at home, and that told me he would burn my house over my head if I stayed there.

Chris. But did not you see the house that stood there, on the top of that hill on the side of which Moses met you?

Faith. Yes, and the lions too, before I came at it. But, for the lions, I think they were asleep, for it was about noon; and because I had so much of the day before me I passed by the Porter, and came down the hill.

Chris. He told me, indeed, that he saw you go by; but I wished you had called at the house, for they would have showed you so many rarities, that you would scarce have forgot them to the day of your death. But pray tell me, did you meet nobody in the Valley of Humility?

Faith. Yes, I met with one Discontent, who would willingly have persuaded me to go back again with him: his reason was, for that the valley was altogether without honor. He told me, moreover, that there to go was the way to disoblige all my friends, as Pride, Arrogancy, Self-Conceit, Worldly-Glory, with others, who he knew, as he said, would be very much offended if I made such a fool of myself as to wade through this valley.

Chris. Well, and how did you answer him?

Faith. I told him that, although all these that he named might claim kindred of me, and that rightly (for, indeed, they were my relations according to the flesh), yet, since I became a pilgrim, they have disowned me, as I also have rejected them; and therefore they were to me now no more than if they had never been of my lineage. I told him, moreover, that as to this valley, he had quite misrepresented the thing; for before honor is humility, and a haughty spirit before a fall. "Therefore," said I, "I had rather go through this valley to the honor that was so accounted by the wisest, than choose that which he esteemed most worthy of our affections."

Chris. Met you with nothing else in that valley?

Faith. Yes, I met with Shame; but, of all the men that I met with in my pilgrimage, he I think, bears the wrong name. The others would take "No" for an answer, at least after some words of denial; but this bold-faced Shame would never have done.

Chris. Why, what did he say to you?

Faith. What? why, he objected against religion itself. He said it was a pitiful, low, sneaking business for a man to mind religion. He said that a tender conscience was an unmanly thing; and that for a man to watch over his words and ways, so as to tie up himself from that liberty that the brave spirits of the times accustom themselves unto, would make him the ridicule of all the people in our time. He objected also, that but a few of the mighty, rich, or wise were ever of my opinion; nor any of them neither, before they were persuaded to be fools, to venture the loss of all for nobody else knows what. He, moreover, objected the base and low estate and condition of those that were chiefly the pilgrims of the times in which they lived; also their ignorance, and want of understanding in all worldly knowledge. Yea, he did hold me to it at that rate also, about a great many more things than here I relate; as, that it was a shame to sit whining and mourning under a sermon, and a shame to come sighing and groaning home; that it was a shame to ask my neighbor forgiveness for petty faults, or to give back what I had taken from any. He said also that religion made a man grow strange to the great, because of a few vices (which he called by finer names), and because religion made him own and respect the base, who were of the same religious company; "and is not this," said he, "a shame?"

Chris. And what did you say to him?

Faith. Say? I could not tell what to say at first. Yea, he put me so to it that my blood came up in my face; even this Shame fetched it up, and had almost beat me quite off. But at last I began to consider that that which is highly esteemed among men is had in abomination with God. And I thought again, This Shame tells me what men are, but it tells me nothing what God, or the Word of God is. And I thought, moreover, that at the day of doom we shall not be doomed to death or life according to the spirits of the world, but according to the wisdom and law of the Highest. Therefore, thought I, what God says is best—is best, though all the men in the world are against it. Seeing, then, that God prefers His religion; seeing God prefers a tender conscience; seeing they that make themselves fools for the kingdom of heaven are wisest, and that the poor man that loveth Christ is richer than the greatest man in the world that hates Him; Shame, depart! thou art an enemy to my salvation. Shall I listen to thee against my sovereign Lord? how, then, shall I look Him in the face at His coming? Should I now be ashamed of His way and servants how can I expect the blessing? But, indeed, this Shame was a bold villain: I could scarce shake him out of my company; yea, he would be haunting of me, and continually whispering me in the ear with some one or other of the weak things that attend religion. But at last I told him it was in vain to attempt further in this business; for those things that he despised, in those did I see most glory; and so, at last, I got past this persistent one. And when I had shaken him off, then I began to sing,

> "The trials that those men do meet withal,
> That are obedient to the heavenly call,
> Are manifold, and suited to the flesh,
> And come, and come, and come again afresh;
> That now, or some time else, we by them may

Be taken, overcome, and cast away.
Oh, let the pilgrims, let the pilgrims then,
Be vigilant and quit themselves like men!"

Chris. I am glad, my brother, that thou didst withstand this villain so bravely: for of all, as thou sayest, I think he has the wrong name; for he is so bold as to follow us in the streets, and to attempt to put us to shame before all men; that is, to make us ashamed of that which is good. But, if he was not himself bold, he would never attempt to do as he does. But let us still resist him; for, notwithstanding all his bold words, he promoteth the fool, and none else. "The wise shall inherit glory," said Solomon; "but shame shall be the promotion of fools."

Faith. I think we must cry to Him for help against Shame who would have us to be valiant for truth upon the earth.

Chris. You say true. But did you meet nobody else in that valley?

Faith. No, not I; for I had sunshine all the rest of the way through that, and also through the Valley of the Shadow of Death.

Chris. It was well for you! I am sure it fared far otherwise with me. I had for a long season, as soon almost as I entered into that valley, a dreadful combat with that foul fiend Apollyon; yea, I thought verily he would have killed me, especially when he got me down, and crushed me under him, as if he would have crushed me to pieces. For, as he threw me, my sword flew out of my hand; nay, he told me he was sure of me; and I cried to God, and He heard me, and delivered me out of all my troubles. Then I entered into the Valley of the Shadow of Death, and had no light for almost half the way through it. I thought I should have been killed there over and over: but at last day broke, and the sun rose, and I went through that which was behind with far more ease and quiet.

Moreover, I saw in my dream that, as they went on, Faithful, as he chanced to look on one side, saw a man whose name is Talkative walking at a distance beside them; for in this place there was room enough for them all to walk. He was a tall man, and something better looking at a distance than near at hand. To this man Faithful spoke himself in this manner:

Faith. Friend, whither away? Are you going to the heavenly country?

Talk. I am going to that same place.

Faith. That is well; then I hope we may have your good company.

Talk. With a very good will, will I be your companion.

Faith. Come on, then, and let us go together, and let us spend our time in talking of things that are profitable.

Talk. To talk of things that are good, to me is very acceptable, with you or with any other; and I am glad that I have met with those that incline to so good a work; for, to speak the truth, there are but few who care thus to spend their time as they are in their travels, but choose much rather to be speaking of things to no profit; and this has been a trouble to me.

Faith. That is, indeed, a thing to be lamented; for what things so worthy of the use of the tongue and mouth of men on earth, as are the things of the God of heaven?

Talk. I like you wonderfully well, for your saying is full of the truth; and I will add, What thing is so pleasant, and what so profitable, as to talk of the things of God? What things so pleasant? that is, if a man hath any delight in things that are wonderful. For instance, if a man doth delight to talk of the history or the mystery of things, or if a man doth love to talk of miracles, wonders, or signs, where shall he find things written so delightful, or so sweetly penned, as in the Holy Scripture?

Faith. That's true; but to be profited by such things in our talk should be that which we design.

Talk. That is it that I said; for to talk of such things is most profitable; for, by so doing, a man may get knowledge of many things; as of the folly of earthly things, and the benefit of things above. Besides, by this a man may learn what it is to turn from sin, to believe, to pray, to suffer, or the like; by this, also, a man may learn what are the great promises and comforts of the Gospel, to his own enjoyment. Further, by this a man may learn to answer false opinions, to prove the truth, and also to teach the ignorant.

Faith. All this is true; and glad am I to hear these things from you.

Talk. Alas! the want of this is the cause that so few understand the need of faith, and the necessity of a work of grace in their soul, in order to eternal life.

Faith. But, by your leave, heavenly knowledge of these is the gift of God; no man attaineth to them by human working, or only by the talk of them.

Talk. All that I know very well, for a man can receive nothing except it be given him from heaven; I could give you a hundred scriptures for the confirmation of this.

Faith. "Well, then," said Faithful, "what is that one thing that we shall at this time found our talk upon?"

Talk. What you will. I will talk of things heavenly or things earthly; things in life or things in the gospel; things sacred or things worldly; things past or things to come; things foreign or things at home; things necessary or things accidental, provided that all be done to our profit.

Faith. Now did Faithful begin to wonder; and, stepping to Christian (for he walked all this while by himself), he said to him, but softly, "What a brave companion have we got! Surely this man will make a very excellent pilgrim."

Chris. At this Christian modestly smiled, and said, "This man with whom you are so taken will deceive with this tongue of his twenty of them that know him not."

Faith. Do you know him, then?

Chris. Know him? Yes, better than he knows himself.

Faith. Pray what is he?

Chris. His name is Talkative; he dwelleth in our town. I wonder that you should be a stranger to him: only I consider that our town is large.

Faith. Whose son is he? and whereabout doth he dwell?

Chris. He is the son of one Say-well. He dwelt in Prating Row, and is known to all that are acquainted with him by the name of Talkative of Prating Row; and notwithstanding his fine tongue, he is but a sorry fellow.

Faith. Well, he seems to be a very pretty man.

Chris. That is, to them that have not a thorough acquaintance with him, for he is best abroad; near home he is ugly enough. Your saying that he is a pretty man brings to my mind what I have observed in the work of the painter, whose pictures show best at a distance, but very near more unpleasing.

Faith. But I am ready to think you do but jest, because you smiled.

Chris. God forbid that I should jest (though I smiled) in this matter, or that I should accuse any falsely. I will give you a further discovery of him. This man is for any company, and for any talk. As he talketh now with you, so will he talk when he is on the ale-bench; and the more drink he hath in his crown, the more of these things he hath in his mouth. Religion hath no place in his heart, or house, or conversation: all he hath lieth in his tongue, and his religion is to make a noise therewith.

Faith. Say you so? Then am I in this man greatly deceived.

Chris. Deceived! you may be sure of it. Remember the proverb, "They say, and do not;" but the kingdom of God is not in word, but in power. He talketh of prayer, of turning to God, of faith, and of the new birth; but he knows but only to talk of them. I have been in his family, and have seen him both at home and abroad, and I know what I say of him is the truth. His house is as empty of religion as the white of an egg is of savor. There is there neither prayer nor sign of turning from sin; yea, the brute, in his kind, serves God far better than he. He is the very stain, reproach, and shame of religion to all that know him. It can hardly have a good word in all that end of the town where he dwells, through him. Thus say the common people that know him: "A saint abroad, and a devil at home." His poor family finds it so: he is such a fault-finder, such a railer at, and so unreasonable with his servants, that they neither know how to do for or speak to him. Men that have any dealings with him say, it is better to deal with a Turk than with him, for fairer dealing they shall have at their hands. This Talkative, if it be possible, will go beyond them, cheat, beguile, and overreach them. Besides, he brings up his sons to follow his steps; and, if he findeth in any of them a foolish timorousness (for so he calls the first appearance of a tender conscience), he calls them fools and blockheads, and by no means will employ them in much, or speak to their commendation before others. For my part, I am of opinion that he has, by his wicked life, caused many to stumble and fall, and will be, if God prevent not, the ruin of many more.

Faith. Well, my brother, I am bound to believe you, not only because you say you know him, but also because like a Christian you make your reports of men. For I cannot think you speak these things of ill-will, but because it is even so as you say.

Chris. Had I known him no more than you, I might, perhaps, have thought of him as at first you did; yea, had he received this report only from those that are enemies to religion, I should have thought it had been a slander, a lot that often falls from bad men's mouths upon good men's names and professions. But all these things, yea, and a great many more as bad, of my own knowledge I can prove him guilty of. Besides, good men are ashamed of him: they can neither call him brother nor friend; the very naming of him among them makes them blush, if they know him.

Faith. Well, I see that saying and doing are two things, and hereafter I shall better observe the difference between them.

Chris. They are two things, indeed, and are as diverse as

are the soul and the body; for, as the body without the soul is but a dead carcase, so saying, if it be alone, is but a dead carcase also. The soul of religion is the practical part. "Pure religion and undefiled before God and the Father is this, to visit the fatherless and the widows in their affliction, and to keep himself unspotted from the world." This, Talkative is not aware of: he thinks that hearing and saying will make a good Christian, and thus he deceiveth his own soul. Hearing is but as the sowing of the seed; talking is not sufficient to prove that fruit is indeed in the heart and life. And let us assure ourselves that, at the day of doom, men shall be judged according to their fruits.

Faith. Well, I was not so fond of his company at first, but I am as sick of it now. What shall we do to be rid of him?

Chris. Take my advice, and do as I bid you, and you shall find that he will soon be sick of your company too, except God shall touch his heart and turn it.

Faith. What would you have me to do?

Chris. Why, go to him, and enter into some serious conversation about the power of religion and ask him plainly (when he has approved of it, for that he will) whether this thing be set up in his heart, house or conduct.

Faith. Then Faithful stepped forward again, and said to Talkative, "Come, what cheer? How is it now?"

Talk. Thank you, well: I thought we should have had a great deal of talk by this time.

Faith. Well, if you will, we will fall to it now; and, since you left it with me to state the question, let it be this: How doth the saving grace of God show itself when it is in the heart of man?

Talk. I perceive, then, that our talk must be about the power of things. Well, it is a very good question, and I shall be willing to answer you. And take my answer in brief, thus. First, where the grace of God is in the heart, it causeth there a great outcry against sin. Secondly, —

Faith. Nay, hold; let us consider of one at once. I think you should rather say, it shows itself by inclining the soul to hate its sin.

Talk. Why, what difference is there between crying out against and hating sin?

Faith. Oh! a great deal. A man may cry out against sin in order to appear good; but he cannot hate it except by a real dislike for it. I have heard many cry out against sin in the pulpit, who yet can abide it well enough in the heart, house, and life. Some cry out against sin, even as the mother cries out against her child in her lap, when she calleth it a naughty girl, and then falls to hugging and kissing it.

Talk. You are trying to catch me, I perceive.

Faith. No, not I; I am only for setting things right. But what is the second thing whereby you would prove a discovery of a work of God in the heart?

Talk. Great knowledge of hard things in the Bible.

Faith. This sign should have been first; but, first or last, it is also false; for knowledge, great knowledge, may be obtained in the mysteries of the Gospel, and yet no work of grace in the soul. Yea, if a man have all knowledge, he may yet be nothing, and so, consequently, be no child of God. When Christ said, "Do ye know all these things?" and the disciples had answered, "Yes," He added, "Blessed are ye if ye do them." He doth not lay the blessing in the knowledge of them, but in the doing of them. For there is a knowledge that is not attended with doing: "He that knoweth his master's will, and doeth it not." A man may know like an angel, and yet be no Christian; therefore your sign of it is not true. Indeed, to know, is a thing that pleaseth talkers and boasters; but to do is that which pleaseth God.

Talk. You are trying to catch me again: this is not profitable.

Faith. Well, if you please, name another sign how this work of grace showeth itself where it is.

Talk. Not I; for I see we shall not agree.

Faith. Well, if you will not, will you give me leave to do it?

Talk. You may say what you please.

Faith. God's work in the soul showeth itself either to him that hath it or to standers by. To him that has it, it is shown by making him see and feel his own sins. To others who are standing by it is shown by his life, a life of doing right in the sight of God. And now, sir, as to this brief account of the work of grace, and also the showing of it, if you have aught to object, object; if not, then give me leave to ask you a second question.

Talk. Nay, my part is not now to object, but to hear; let me, therefore, have your second question.

Faith. It is this: Have you felt your own sins, and have you turned from them? And do your life and conduct show it the same? Or is your religion in word or in tongue, and not in deed and truth? Pray, if you incline to answer me in this, say no more than you know the God above will say Amen to, and also nothing but what your conscience can approve you in; for not he that commendeth himself is approved, but whom the Lord commendeth. Besides, to say I am thus and thus, when my conduct and all my neighbors tell me I lie, is great wickedness.

Talk. Then Talkative at first began to blush; but, recovering himself, thus he replied: "This kind of discourse I did not expect; nor am I disposed to give an answer to such questions, because I count not myself bound thereto, unless you take upon you to be a questioner; and though you should do so, yet I may refuse to make you my judge. But, I pray, will you tell me why you ask me such questions?"

Faith. Because I saw you forward to talk, and because I knew not that you had aught else but notion. Besides, to tell you all the truth, I have heard of you that you are a man whose religion lies in talk, and that your life gives this your mouth-profession the lie. They say you are a spot among Christians, and that religion fareth the worse for your ungodly conduct; that some already have stumbled at your wicked ways, and that more are in danger of being destroyed thereby: your religion, and an alehouse, and greed for gain, and uncleanness, and swearing, and lying, and vain company-keeping, etc., will stand together. You are a shame to all who are members of the church.

Talk. Since you are ready to take up reports, and to judge so rashly as you do, I cannot but conclude you are some peevish or cross man, not fit to be talked with; and so adieu.

Chris. Then came up Christian, and said to his brother, "I told you how it would happen; your words and his heart could not agree. He had rather leave your company than reform his life. But he is gone, as I said: let him go; the loss is no man's but his own: he has saved us the trouble of going from him; for he continuing (as I suppose he will do) as he is, he would have been but a blot in our company.

Besides, the Apostle says, 'From such withdraw thyself.'"

Faith. But I am glad we had this little talk with him; it may happen that he will think of it again: however, I have dealt plainly with him, and so am clear of his blood, if he perisheth.

Chris. You did well to talk so plainly to him as you did. There is but little of this faithful dealing with men now-a-days; and that makes religion to be despised by so many; for they are these talkative fools, whose religion is only in word, and are vile and vain in their life, that, being so much admitted into the fellowship of the godly, do puzzle the world, blemish Christianity, and grieve the sincere. I wish that all men would deal with such as you have done; then should they either be made more suitable to religion, or the company of saints would be too hot for them.

Faith. Then did Faithful say,

> "How Talkative at first lifts up his plumes!
> How bravely doth he speak! How he presumes
> To drive down all before him! But so soon
> As Faithful talks of heart-work, like the moon
> That's past the full, into the wane he goes;
> And so will all but he who heart-work knows."

Thus they went on, talking of what they had seen by the way, and so made that way easy, which would otherwise, no doubt, have been tedious to them; for now they went through a wilderness.

Chapter 6

Now, when they were got almost quite out of this wilderness, Faithful chanced to cast his eye back, and espied one coming after him, and he knew him. "Oh!" said Faithful to his brother, "who comes yonder?" Then Christian looked, and said, "It is my good friend Evangelist." "Ay, and my good friend, too," said Faithful; "for it was he that set me the way to the gate." Now was Evangelist come up unto them, and thus saluted them:

Evan. Peace be with you, dearly beloved, and peace be to your helpers.

Chris. Welcome, welcome, my good Evangelist: the sight of thy face brings to my thought thy former kindness and unwearied laboring for my eternal good.

Faith. "And a thousand times welcome," said good Faithful: "thy company, O sweet Evangelist, how desirable is it to us poor pilgrims!"

Evan. Then said Evangelist, "How hath it fared with you, my friends, since the time of our last parting? What have you met with, and how have you behaved yourselves?"

Then Christian and Faithful told him of all things that had happened to them in the way; and how, and with what difficulty, they had arrived to that place.

Evan. "Right glad am I," said Evangelist, "not that you met with trials, but that you have been victors, and for that you have, notwithstanding many weaknesses, continued in the way to this very day. I say, right glad am I of this thing, and that for my own sake and yours. I have sowed, and you have reaped; and the day is coming when 'both he that sowed and they that reaped shall rejoice together;' that is, if you faint not. The crown is before you, and it is an uncorruptible one: so run that you may obtain it. Some there be that set out for this crown, and after they have gone far for it, another comes in and takes it from them: 'Hold fast, therefore, that you have; let no man take your crown.'"

Then Christian thanked him for his words, but told him withal that they would have him speak further to them, for their help the rest of the way; and the rather, for that they well knew that he was a prophet, and could tell them of things that might happen unto them, and also how they might resist and overcome them. To which request Faithful also consented. So Evangelist began as followeth:

Evan. My sons, you have heard, in the words of the truth of the Gospel, that you must "through many trials enter into the kingdom of heaven;" and again, that "in every city bonds and afflictions await you;" and therefore you cannot expect that you should go long on your pilgrimage without them in some sort or other. You have found something of the truth of these words upon you already, and more will immediately follow; for now, as you see, you are almost out of this wilderness, and therefore you will soon come into a town that you will by-and-by see before you; and in that town you will be hardly beset with enemies who will strain hard but they will kill you; and be you sure that one or both of you must seal the truth which you hold with blood: but be you faithful unto death, and the King will give you a crown of life. He that shall die there, although his death will be unnatural, and his pain, perhaps, great, he will yet have the better of his fellow; not only because he will be arrived at the Celestial City soonest, but because he will escape many miseries that the other will meet with in the rest of his journey. But when you are come to the town, and shall find fulfilled what I have here related, then remember your friend, and quit yourselves like men, and commit the keeping of your souls to God in well-doing, as unto a faithful Creator.

Then I saw in my dream, that, when they were got out of the wilderness, they presently saw a town before them, and the name of that town is Vanity; and at the town there is a fair kept, called Vanity Fair. It is kept all the year long. It beareth the name of Vanity Fair, because the town where it is kept is lighter than vanity, and also because all that is there sold, or that cometh thither, is vanity; as is the saying of the Wise, "All that cometh is vanity."

This is no newly begun business, but a thing of ancient standing. I will show you the original of it.

Almost five thousand years ago, there were pilgrims walking to the Celestial City, as these two honest persons are; and Beelzebub, Apollyon, and Legion, with their companions, perceiving by the path that the pilgrims made that their way to the city lay through this town of Vanity, they contrived here to set up a fair; a fair wherein should be sold all sorts of vanity, and that it should last all the year long. Therefore at this fair are all such things sold as houses, lands, trades, places, honors, preferments, titles, countries, kingdoms, lusts, pleasures, and delights of all sorts, as wives, husbands, children, masters, servants, lives, blood, bodies, souls, silver, gold, pearls, precious stones, and what not.

And, moreover, at this fair there are at all times to be seen jugglings, cheats, games, plays, fools, apes, knaves, and rogues, and that of every kind.

Here are to be seen, too, and that for nothing, thefts, murders, false swearers, and that of a blood-red color.

And, as in other fairs of less moment there are several rows and streets under their proper names, where such and such wares are vended; so here likewise you have the proper places, rows, streets (namely, countries and kingdoms), where the wares of this fair are soonest to be found. Here are the Britain Row, the French Row, the Italian Row, the Spanish Row, the German Row, where several sorts of vanities are to be sold. But, as in other fairs some one commodity is as the chief of all the fair, so the ware of Rome and her goods are greatly promoted in this fair; only our English nation, with some others, have taken dislike thereat.

Now, as I said, the way to the Celestial City lies just through this town where this lusty fair is kept; and he that would go to the city, and yet not go through this town, "must needs go out of the world." The Prince of princes Himself, when here, went through this town to His own country, and that upon a fair day too; yea, and as I think, it was Beelzebub, the chief lord of this fair, that invited Him to buy of his vanities; yea, would have made Him lord of the fair, would He but have done him reverence as He went through the town. Yea, because He was such a person of honor, Beelzebub had Him from street to street, and showed Him all the kingdoms of the world in a little time, that he might, if possible, allure that Blessed One to ask for and buy some of his vanities; but He had no mind to the merchandise, and therefore left the town without laying out so much as one farthing upon these vanities. This fair, therefore, is an ancient thing of long-standing, and a very great fair.

Now, these pilgrims, as I said, must needs go through this fair. Well, so they did; but, behold, even as they entered into the fair, all the people in the fair were moved and the town itself, as it were, in a hubbub about them, and that for several reasons; for,

First,—The pilgrims were clothed with such kind of garments as were different from the raiment of any that traded in that fair. The people, therefore, of the fair, made a great gazing upon them: some said they were fools; some, they were bedlams; and some, they were outlandish men.

Secondly,—And, as they wondered at their apparel, so they did likewise at their speech; for few could understand what they said. They naturally spoke the language of Canaan; but they that kept the fair were the men of this world. So that from one end of the fair to the other, they seemed barbarians each to the other.

Thirdly,—But that which did not a little amuse the store-keepers was, that these pilgrims set very light by all their wares. They cared not so much as to look upon them; and if they called upon them to buy, they would put their fingers in their ears, and cry, "Turn away mine eyes from beholding vanity," and look upwards, signifying that their trade and traffic were in heaven.

One chanced, mockingly, beholding the actions of the men, to say unto them, "What will you buy?" But they, looking gravely upon him, said, "We buy the truth." At that there was an occasion taken to despise the men the more: some mocking, some taunting, some speaking reproachfully, and some calling on others to smite them. At last things came to a hubbub and great stir in the fair, insomuch that all order was confounded. Now was word presently brought to the great one of the fair, who quickly came down, and deputed some of his most trusty friends to take these men for trial about whom the fair was almost overturned. So the men were brought to trial, and they that sat upon them asked them whence they came, whither they went, and what they did there in such an unusual garb. The men told them that they were pilgrims and strangers in the world, and that they were going to their own country, which was the heavenly Jerusalem, and that they had given no occasion to the men of the town, nor yet to the merchants, thus to abuse them, and to hinder them in their journey, except it was for that, when one asked them what they would buy, they said they would buy the truth. But they that were appointed to examine them did not believe them to be any other than crazy people and mad, or else such as came to put all things into a confusion in the fair. Therefore they took them and beat them, and besmeared them with dirt, and then put them into the cage, that they might be made a spectacle to all the men of the fair. There, therefore, they lay for some time, and were made the objects of any man's sport, or malice, or revenge; the great one of the fair laughing still at all that befell them. But, the men being patient, and "not rendering railing for railing, but contrariwise blessing," and giving good words for bad, and kindness for injuries done, some men in the fair that were more observing and less opposed than the rest, began to check and blame the baser sort for their continual abuses done by them to the men. They, therefore, in an angry manner, let fly at them again, counting them as bad as the men in the cage, and telling them that they seemed to be in league with them, and should be made partakers of their misfortunes. The others replied, that, for aught they could see, the men were quiet and sober, and intended nobody any harm; and that there were many that traded in their fair that were more worthy to be put into the cage, yea, and pillory too, than were the men that they had abused. Thus, after divers words had passed on both sides (the men behaving themselves all the while very wisely and soberly before them,) they fell to some blows, and did harm to one another. Then were these two poor men brought before the court again, and there charged as being guilty of the late hubbub that had been in the fair. So they beat them pitifully, and hanged irons upon them, and led them in chains up and down the fair, for an example and terror to others, lest any should speak in their behalf, or join themselves unto them. But Christian and Faithful behaved themselves yet more wisely, and received the wrongs and shame that were cast upon them with so much meekness and patience, that it won to their side (though but few in comparison of the rest) several of the men in the fair. This put the other party in yet a greater rage, insomuch that they resolved upon the death of these two men. Wherefore they threatened that neither cage nor irons should serve their turn, but that they should die for the abuse they had done, and for deceiving the men of the fair.

Then were they remanded to the cage again, until further order should be taken with them. So they put them in, and made their feet fast in the stocks.

Here, therefore, they called again to mind what they had heard from their faithful friend Evangelist, and were more confirmed in their way and sufferings, by what he told them would happen to them. They also now comforted each other, that whose lot it was to suffer, even he should have the best of it; therefore each man secretly wished he might have that privilege. But, committing themselves to the all-wise disposal of Him that ruleth all things, with much content they abode in the condition in which they were, until they should be otherwise disposed of.

Then a convenient time being appointed, they brought them forth to their trial, in order to their being condemned. When the time was come, they were brought before their enemies, and placed on trial. The judge's name was Lord Hate-good: the charges against both were one and the same in substance, though somewhat varying in form; the contents whereof were this: "That they were enemies to and disturbers of their trade; that they had made riots and divisions in the town, and had won a party to their own most dangerous opinions, in contempt of the law of their prince."

Then Faithful began to answer, that he had only set himself against that which had set itself against Him that is higher than the highest. "And," said he, "as for disturbances, I make none, being myself a man of peace; the parties that were won to us, were won by beholding our truth and innocence, and they are only turned from the worse to the better. And, as to the king you talk of, since he is Beelzebub, the enemy of our Lord, I defy him and all his angels."

Then it was made known that they that had aught to say for their lord the king against the prisoner at the bar should forthwith appear and give in their evidence. So there came in three witnesses; to wit, Envy, Superstition, and Pickthank. They were then asked if they knew the prisoner at the bar, and what they had to say for their lord the king against him.

Then stood forth Envy, and said to this effect: "My lord, I have known this man a long time, and will attest upon my oath before this honorable bench that he is — "

Judge. Hold! Give him his oath.

Envy. So they sware him. Then said he, "My lord, this man, notwithstanding his name, Faithful is one of the vilest men in our country. He cares for neither prince nor people, law nor custom, but doth all that he can to possess all men with certain of his disloyal notions, which he in the general calls principles of faith and holiness. And in particular, I heard him once myself affirm that Christianity and the customs of our town of Vanity were opposite, and could not be reconciled. By which saying, my lord, he doth at once not only condemn all our laudable doings, but us in the doing of them."

Judge. Then did the judge say to him, "Hast thou any more to say?"

Envy. My lord, I could say much more, only I would not be tiresome to the court. Yet, if need be, when the other gentlemen have given in their evidence, rather than anything shall be wanting that will dispatch him, I will have more to speak against him. So he was bid stand by.

Then they called Superstition, and bade him look upon the prisoner. They also asked what he could say for their lord the king against him. Then they sware him: so he began:

Super. My lord, I have no great acquaintance with this man, nor do I desire to have further knowledge of him. However, this I know, that he is a very pestilent fellow, from some discourse the other day that I had with him in this town; for then, talking with him, I heard him say that our religion was naught, and such by which a man could by no means please God. Which saying of his, my lord, your lordship very well knows what necessarily thence will follow; to wit, that we still do worship in vain, are yet in our sins, and finally shall be destroyed: and this is that which I have to say.

Then was Pickthank sworn, and bid say what he knew, in behalf of their lord the king, against the prisoner at the bar.

Pick. My lord, and you gentlemen all, this fellow I have known a long time, and have heard him speak things that ought not to be spoken, for he hath railed on our noble prince Beelzebub, and hath spoken contemptuously of his honorable friends, whose names are, the Lord Old-man, the Lord Carnal-Delight, the Lord Luxurious, the Lord Desire-of-Vain-Glory, my old Lord Lust, Sir Having Greedy, with all the rest of our nobility and he hath said, moreover, that, if all men were of his mind, if possible there is not one of these noblemen should have any longer a being in this town. Besides, he has not been afraid to rail on you, my lord, who are now appointed to be his judge, calling you an ungodly villain, with many other such-like abusive terms, with which he hath bespattered most of the gentry of our town.

Judge. When this Pickthank had told his tale, the judge directed his speech to the prisoner at the bar, saying, "Thou runagate, heretic, and traitor! hast thou heard what these honest gentlemen have witnessed against thee?"

Faith. May I speak a few words in my own defense?

Judge. Sirrah, sirrah, thou deservest to live no longer, but to be slain immediately upon the place; yet, that all men may see our gentleness towards thee, let us hear what thou, vile runagate, hast to say.

Faith. 1. I say, then, in answer to what Mr. Envy hath spoken, I have never said aught but this, that what rule, or laws, or custom, or people were flat against the Word of God, are opposite to Christianity. If I have said amiss in this, convince me of my error, and I am ready here before you to take back my words.

2. As to the second, to wit, Mr. Superstition and his charge against me, I said only this, that in the worship of God there is required true faith. But there can be no true faith without a knowledge of the will of God. Therefore, whatever is thrust into the worship of God that is not agreeable to the word of God will not profit to eternal life.

3. As to what Mr. Pickthank hath said, I say (avoiding terms, as that I am said to rail, and the like), that the prince of this town, with all the rabblement his attendants, by this gentleman named, are more fit for a being in hell than in this town and country. And so the Lord have mercy upon me!

Then the judge called to the jury (who all this while stood by to hear and observe), "Gentlemen of the jury, you see this man about whom so great an uproar hath been made in this town; you have also heard what these worthy gentlemen have witnessed against him; also you have heard his reply and confession. It lieth now in your breast to hang him or to save his life; but yet I think meet to instruct you into our law.

"There was an act made in the days of Pharaoh, the great servant to our prince, that, lest those of a contrary religion should multiply and grow too strong for him, their males should be thrown into the river. There was also an act made in the days of Nebuchadnezzar the Great, another of his servants, that whoever would not fall down and worship his golden image should be thrown into a fiery furnace. There was also an act made in the days of Darius, that whoso for some time called upon any god but him should be cast into the lions' den. Now, the substance of these laws this rebel has broken, not only in thought (which is not to be borne,) but also in word and deed, which must, therefore, needs be intolerable. You see he disputeth against our religion; and for the reason that he hath confessed he deserveth to die the death."

Then went the jury out, whose names were Mr. Blind-man, Mr. No-good, Mr. Malice, Mr. Love-lust, Mr. Live-loose, Mr. Heady, Mr. High-mind, Mr. Enmity, Mr. Liar, Mr. Cruelty, Mr. Hate-light, and Mr. Implacable, who every one gave in his private voice against him among themselves, and afterwards unanimously concluded to bring him in guilty before the Judge. And first among themselves, Mr. Blind-man, the foreman, said, "I see clearly that this man is a heretic." Then said Mr. No-good, "Away with such a fellow from the earth!" "Ay," said Mr. Malice, "for I hate the very look of him." Then said Mr. Love-lust, "I could never endure him." "Nor I," said Mr. Live-loose; "for he would always be condemning my way." "Hang him, hang him!" said Mr. Heady. "A sorry scrub," said Mr. High-mind. "My heart riseth against him," said Mr. Enmity. "He is a rogue," said Mr. Liar. "Hanging is too good for him," said Mr. Cruelty. "Let us dispatch him out of the way," said Mr. Hate-light.

Then said Mr. Implacable, "Might I have all the world given to me, I could not be reconciled to him; therefore let us forthwith bring him in guilty of death."

And so they did: therefore he was presently condemned to be had from the place where he was, to the place from whence he came, and there to be put to the most cruel death that could be invented.

They therefore brought him out, to do with him according to their law; and first they scourged him, then they buffeted him, then they lanced his flesh with knives; after that they stoned him with stones, then pricked him with their swords, and, last of all, they burned him to ashes at the stake. Thus came Faithful to his end.

Now, I saw that there stood behind the multitude a chariot and a couple of horses waiting for Faithful, who (so soon as his enemies had slain him) was taken up into it, and straightway was carried up through the clouds with sound of trumpet the nearest way to the Celestial Gate. But as for Christian, he had some delay, and was sent back to prison; so he there remained for a space. But He who overrules all things, having the power of their rage in his own hand, so wrought it about that Christian for that time escaped them, and went his way. And as he went, he sang, saying,

> "Well, Faithful, thou hast faithfully professed
> Unto thy Lord, with whom thou shalt be blest,
> When faithless ones, with all their vain delights,
> Are crying out under their hellish plights.
> Sing, Faithful, sing, and let thy name survive;
> For though they killed thee, thou art yet alive."

Chapter 7

Now, I saw in my dream, that Christian went forth not alone; for there was one whose name was Hopeful (being so made by looking upon Christian and Faithful in their words and behavior in their sufferings at the fair,) who joined himself unto him, and, entering into a brotherly pledge told him that he would be his companion. Thus one died to show faithfulness to the truth, and another rises out of his ashes to be a companion with Christian in his pilgrimage. This Hopeful also told Christian that there were many more of the men in the fair that would take their time and follow after.

So I saw that, quickly after they were got out of the fair, they overtook one that was going before them, whose name was By-ends; so they said to him, "What countryman, sir? and how far go you this way?" He told them that he came from the town of Fair-speech, and he was going to the Celestial City; but told them not his name.

Chris. "From Fair-speech! are there any that be good live there?"

By. "Yes," said By-ends, "I hope."

Chris. Pray, sir, what may I call you?

By. I am a stranger to you, and you to me: if you be going this way, I shall be glad of your company; if not, I must be content.

Chris. This town of Fair-speech, I have heard of it; and, as I remember, they say it's a wealthy place.

By. Yes, I will assure you that it is; and I have very many rich kindred there.

Chris. Pray, who are your kindred there? if a man may be so bold.

By. Almost the whole town; but in particular my Lord Turnabout, my Lord Timeserver, my Lord Fair-speech, from whose ancestors that town first took its name; also Mr. Smooth-man, Mr. Facing-both-ways, Mr. Anything; and the parson of our parish, Mr. Two-tongues, was my mother's own brother by father's side; and to tell you the truth, I am become a gentleman of good quality; yet my great-grandfather was but a waterman, looking one way and rowing another, and I got most of my estate by the same occupation.

Chris. Are you a married man?

By. Yes, and my wife is a very virtuous woman, the daughter of a virtuous woman; she was my Lady Feigning's daughter: therefore she came of a very honorable family, and is arrived to such a pitch of breeding, that she knows how to carry it to all, even to prince and peasant. 'Tis true we somewhat differ in religion from those of the stricter sort, yet but in two small points: First, we never strive against wind and tide; secondly, we are always most zealous when Religion is well dressed and goes in his silver slippers: we love much to walk with him in the street if the sun shines and the people praise him.

Then Christian stepped a little aside to his fellow Hopeful, saying, "It runs in my mind that this is one By-ends, of Fair-speech; and if it be he, we have as very a knave in our company as dwelleth in all these parts." Then said Hopeful, "Ask him; methinks he should not be ashamed of his name." So Christian came up with him again, and said, "Sir, you talk as if you knew something more than all the world doth; and if I take not my mark amiss, I deem I have half a guess of you. Is not your name Mr. By-ends, of Fair-speech?"

By. This is not my name; but, indeed, it is a nickname that is given me by some that cannot abide me, and I must be content to bear it as a reproach, as other good men have borne theirs before me.

Chris. But did you never give an occasion to men to call you by this name?

By. Never, never! The worst that ever I did to give them an occasion to give me this name was, that I had always the luck to jump in my judgment with the present way of the times, whatever it was, and my chance was to gain thereby. But if things are thus cast upon me, let me count them a blessing; but let not the malicious load me therefore with reproach.

Chris. I thought, indeed, that you were the man that I heard of; and, to tell you what I think, I fear this name belongs to you more properly than you are willing we should think it doth.

By. Well, if you will thus imagine, I cannot help it: you shall find me a fair company-keeper if you still admit me your companion.

Chris. If you will go with us, you must go against wind and tide; the which, I perceive, is against your opinion; you must also own Religion in his rags, as well as when in his silver slippers; and stand by him, too, when bound in irons, as well as when he walketh the streets with applause.

By. You must not impose or lord it over my faith; leave it to my liberty, and let me go with you.

Chris. Not a step farther, unless you will do in what I declare as we do.

By. Then said By-ends, "I never desert my old principles, since they are harmless and profitable. If I may not go with you, I must do as I did before you overtook me, even go by myself, until some overtake me that will be glad of my company."

Now, I saw in my dream that Christian and Hopeful forsook him, and kept their distance before him; but one of them, looking back, saw three men following Mr. By-ends; and, behold, as they came up with him, he made them a very low bow, and they also gave him a compliment. The men's names were Mr. Hold-the-world, Mr. Money-love, and Mr. Save-all; men that Mr. By-ends had been formerly acquainted with; for in their boyhood they were schoolfellows, and taught by one Mr. Gripe-man a schoolmaster in Love-gain, which is a market town in the county of Coveting, in the North. This schoolmaster taught them the art of getting, either by violence, cheating, flattery, lying, or by putting on a pretence of religion; and these four gentlemen had learned much of the art of their master, so that they could each of them have kept such a school themselves.

Well, when they had, as I said, thus saluted each other, Mr. Money-love said to Mr. By-ends, "Who are they upon the road before us?" for Christian and Hopeful were yet within view.

By. They are a couple of far countrymen, that, after their

mode, are going on pilgrimage.

Money. Alas! why did they not stay, that we might have had their good company? for they, and we, and you, sir, I hope, are all going on pilgrimage.

By. We are so, indeed; but the men before us are so rigid, and love so much their own notions, and do also so lightly esteem the opinions of others, that, let a man be ever so godly, yet, if he agrees not with them in all things, they thrust him quite out of their company.

Save. That is bad; but we read of some that are righteous overmuch, and such men's rigidness makes them to judge and condemn all but themselves. But I pray, what and how many were the things wherein you differed?

By. Why, they, after their headstrong manner conclude that it is their duty to rush on their journey all weathers; and I am for waiting for wind and tide. They are for taking the risk of all for God at a clap; and I am for taking all advantages to secure my life and property. They are for holding their notions, though all other men be against them; but I am for religion in what and so far as, the times and my safety will bear it. They are for Religion when in rags and contempt; but I am for him when he walks in his golden slippers, in the sunshine, and with applause.

Hold. Ay, and hold you there still, good Mr. By-ends; for, for my part, I can count him but a fool, that, having the liberty to keep what he has, shall be so unwise as to lose it. Let us be wise as serpents. It is best to make hay while the sun shines. You see how the bee lieth still all winter, and bestirs her only when she can have profit and pleasure. God sends sometimes rain and sometimes sunshine; if they be such fools to go through the rain, yet let us be content to take fair weather along with us. For my part, I like that religion best that will stand with the safety of God's good blessings unto us; for who can imagine, that is ruled by his reason, since God has bestowed upon us the good things of this life, but that He would have us keep them for His sake? Abraham and Solomon grew rich in religion; and Job says that "a good man should lay up gold as dust;" but he must not be such as the men before us, if they be as you have described them.

Save. I think that we are all agreed in this matter, and therefore there needs no more words about it.

Money. No, there needs no more words about this matter, indeed; for he that believes neither Scripture nor reason (and you see we have both on our side), neither knows his own liberty nor seeks his own safety.

And so these four men, Mr. By-ends, Mr. Money-love, Mr. Save-all, and old Mr. Hold-the-world, walked on together, while Christian and Hopeful were far in advance.

Then Christian and Hopeful went on till they came to a delicate plain, called Ease, where they went with much content; but that plain was but narrow, so they were quickly got over it. Now at the farther side of that plain was a little hill, called Lucre, and in that hill a silver mine, which some of them that had formerly gone that way, because of the rarity of it, had turned aside to see; but going too near the brink of the pit, the ground, being deceitful under them, broke, and they were slain; some also had been maimed there, and could not to their dying day be their own men again.

Then I saw in my dream that a little off the road, over against the silver mine, stood Demas (gentleman-like) to call to passengers to come and see; who said to Christian and his fellow, "Ho! turn aside hither, and I will show you a thing."

Chris. What thing so deserving as to turn us out of the way?

Demas. Here is a silver mine, and some digging in it for treasure; if you will come, with a little pains you may richly provide for yourselves.

Hope. Then said Hopeful, "Let us go see."

Chris. "Not I," said Christian. "I have heard of this place before now, and how many have there been slain; and besides, that treasure is a snare to those that seek it, for it hindereth them in their pilgrimage."

Chris. Then Christian called to Demas, saying, "Is not the place dangerous? Hath it not hindered many in their pilgrimage?"

Demas. Not very dangerous, except to those that are careless. But withal, he blushed as he spake.

Chris. Then said Christian to Hopeful, "Let us not stir a step, but still keep on our way."

Hope. I will warrant you, when By-ends comes up, if he hath the same invitation as we, he will turn in thither to see.

Chris. No doubt thereof, for his principles lead him that way; and a hundred to one but he dies there.

Demas. Then Demas called out again, saying, "But will you not come over and see?"

Chris. Then Christian roundly answered, saying, "Demas, thou art an enemy to the right ways of the Lord of this way, and hast been already condemned for thine own turning aside, by one of His Majesty's judges; and why seekest thou to have us condemned also? Besides, if we at all turn aside, our Lord the King will certainly hear thereof, and will there put us to shame where we should stand with boldness before Him."

Demas cried again that he also was one of their company, a pilgrim like themselves, and that, if they would tarry a little, he also himself would walk with them.

Chris. Then said Christian, "What is thy name? Is it not the same by the which I have called thee?"

Demas. Yes, my name is Demas; I am the son of Abraham.

Chris. I know you: Gehazi was your great-grandfather, and Judas your father, and you have trod in their steps. It is but a devilish prank that thou usest: thy father was hanged for a traitor, and thou deservest no better reward. Assure thyself that when we come to the King, we will tell him of this thy behavior. Thus they went their way.

By this time By-ends and his companions were come again within sight, and they at the first beck went over to Demas. Now, whether they fell into the pit by looking over the brink thereof, or whether they went down to dig, or whether they were smothered in the bottom by the damps that commonly arise, of these things I am not certain; but this I observed, that they never were seen again in the way. Then sang Christian:

> "By-ends and silver Demas both agree;
> One calls; the other runs, that he may be
> A sharer in his lucre; so these two
> Take up in this world, and no farther go."

Now, I saw that just on the other side of the plain the pilgrims came to a place where stood an old monument hard by the highway-side; at the sight of which they were both concerned, because of the strangeness of the form thereof; for it seemed to them as if it had been a woman changed into the shape of a pillar. Here, therefore, they stood looking and looking upon it, but could not for a time tell what they should make thereof. At last Hopeful espied written above, upon the head thereof, a writing in an unusual hand; but he, being no scholar, called to Christian (for he was learned,) to see if he could pick out the meaning; so he came, and after a little laying of letters together, he found the same to be this, "Remember Lot's wife." So he read it to his fellow; after which, they both concluded that that was the pillar of salt into which Lot's wife was turned, for her looking back with a covetous heart when she was going from Sodom. Which sudden and amazing sight gave them occasion for speaking thus:

Chris. Ah, my brother! this is a seasonable sight. It came just in time to us after the invitation which Demas gave us to come over to view the hill Lucre; and, had we gone over, as he desired us, and as thou wast inclining to do, my brother, we had, for aught I know, been made ourselves, like this woman, a spectacle for those that shall come after to behold.

Hope. I am sorry that I was so foolish, and am made to wonder that I am not now as Lot's wife; for wherein was the difference betwixt her sin and mine? She only looked back, and I had a desire to go see. Let God's goodness be praised; and let me be ashamed that ever such a thing should be in mine heart.

Chris. Let us take notice of what we see here, for our help for time to come. This woman escaped one judgment, for she fell not by the destruction of Sodom; yet she was destroyed by another, as we see: she is turned into a pillar of salt.

Hope. What a mercy is it that neither thou, but especially I, am not made myself this example! This gives reason to us to thank God, to fear before Him and always to remember Lot's wife.

I saw, then, that they went on their way to a pleasant river, which David the King called "the river of God," but John, "the river of the water of life." Now their way lay just upon the bank of this river; here, therefore, Christian and his companion walked with great delight; they drank also of the water of the river, which was pleasant and enlivening to their weary spirits. Besides, on the banks of this river on either side were green trees that bore all manner of fruit; and the leaves of the trees were good for medicine; with the fruit of these trees they were also much delighted; and the leaves they ate to prevent illness, especially such diseases that come to those that heat their blood by travels. On either side of the river was also a meadow, curiously beautified with lilies, and it was green all the year long. In this meadow they lay down and slept, for here they might lie down safely. When they awoke, they gathered again of the fruit of the trees and drank again of the water of the river, and they lay down again to sleep. This they did several days and nights. Then they sang:

> "Behold ye, how these crystal streams do glide,
> To comfort pilgrims by the highway-side;
> The meadows green, besides their fragrant smell,
> Yield dainties for them; and he who can tell
> What pleasant fruit, yea, leaves, these trees do yield,
> Will soon sell all, that he may buy this field."
> So when they were disposed to go on (for they were
> not as yet at their journey's end,) they ate and drank,
> and departed.

Now, I beheld in my dream that they had not journeyed far, but the river and the way for a time parted, at which they were not a little sorry; yet they durst not go out of the way. Now the way from the river was rough, and their feet tender by reason of their travels; so the souls of the pilgrims were much discouraged because of the way. Wherefore, still as they went on they wished for a better way. Now, a little before them there was, on the left hand of the road, a meadow, and a stile to go over into it, and that meadow is called By-path Meadow. Then said Christian to his fellow, "If this meadow lieth along by our wayside, let's go over it." Then he went to the stile to see; and behold, a path lay along by the way on the other side of the fence. "It is according to my wish," said Christian; "here is the easiest going. Come, good Hopeful, and let us go over."

Hope. But how if this path should lead us out of the way?

Chris. "That is not likely," said the other. "Look, doth it not go along by the wayside?" So Hopeful, being persuaded by his fellow, went after him over the stile. When they were gone over, and were got into the path, they found it very easy to their feet; and withal, they, looking before them, espied a man walking as they did, and his name was Vain-Confidence: so they called after him, and asked him whither that way led. He said, "To the Celestial Gate." "Look," said Christian, "did not I tell you so? By this you may see we are right." So they followed, and he went before them. But, behold, the night came on, and it grew very dark; so that they that were behind lost sight of him that went before. He, therefore, that went before (Vain-Confidence by name) not seeing the way before him, fell into a deep pit, which was on purpose there made by the prince of those grounds to catch careless fools, withal and was dashed in pieces with his fall.

Now Christian and his fellow heard him fall. So they called to know the matter; but there was none to answer, only they heard a groaning. Then said Hopeful, "Where are we now?"

Then was his fellow silent, as mistrusting that he had led him out of the way; and now it began to rain, and thunder, and lighten in a most dreadful manner, and the water rose amain.

Then Hopeful groaned in himself, saying, "Oh that I had kept on my way!"

Chris. Who could have thought that this path should have led us out of the way?

Hope. I was afraid on't at the very first, and therefore gave you that gentle caution. I would have spoken plainer, but that you are older than I.

Chris. Good brother, be not offended. I am very sorry I have brought thee out of the way, and that I have put thee into such great danger. Pray, my brother, forgive me: I did not do it of any evil intent.

Hope. Be comforted, my brother, for I forgive thee, and believe, too, that this shall be for our good.

Chris. I am glad I have with me a merciful brother; but we must not stand still: let us try to go back again.

Hope. But, good brother, let me go before.

Chris. No, if you please; let me go first, that, if there be any danger, I may be first therein, because by my means we are both gone out of the way.

Hope. "No, you shall not go first; for your mind being troubled may lead you out of the way again." Then for their encouragement they heard the voice of one saying, "Let thine heart be towards the highway, even the way that thou wentest; turn again." But by this time the waters were greatly risen, by reason of which the way of going back was very dangerous. (Then I thought that it is easier going out of the way when we are in, than going in when we are out.) Yet they undertook to go back; but it was so dark, and the flood so high, that, in their going back, they had like to have been drowned nine or ten times.

Neither could they, with all the skill they had, get again to the stile that night. Wherefore, at last lighting under a little shelter, they sat down there until daybreak; but, being weary, they fell asleep. Now, there was, not far from the place where they lay, a castle, called Doubting Castle the owner whereof was Giant Despair, and it was in his grounds they now were sleeping; wherefore he, getting up in the morning early, and walking up and down in his fields, caught Christian and Hopeful asleep in his grounds. Then, with a grim and surly voice, he bid them awake, and asked them whence they were, and what they did in his grounds. They told him they were pilgrims, and that they had lost their way. Then said the giant, "You have this night trespassed on me by trampling in and lying on my grounds, and therefore you must go along with me." So they were forced to go, because he was stronger than they. They had also but little to say, for they knew themselves in fault. The giant, therefore, drove them before him, and put them into his castle, into a very dark dungeon, nasty and smelling vilely to the spirits of these two men. Here, then, they lay from Wednesday morning till Saturday night, without one bit of bread or drop of drink, or light, or any to ask how they did; they were, therefore, here in evil case, and were far from friends and people whom they knew. Now, in this place Christian had double sorrow, because it was through his thoughtless haste that they were brought into this distress.

Now, Giant Despair had a wife, and her name was Diffidence. So, when he was gone to bed, he told his wife what he had done; to wit, that he had taken a couple of prisoners and cast them into his dungeon for trespassing on his grounds. Then he asked her also what he had best to do further to them. So she asked him what they were, whence they came, and whither they were bound; and he told her. Then she advised him, that when he arose in the morning, he should beat them without any mercy. So, when he arose, he getteth him a grievous crab-tree cudgel, and goes down into the dungeon to them, and there first fell to abusing them as if they were dogs, although they never gave him a word of distaste. Then he falls upon them, and beats them fearfully, in such sort that they were not able to help themselves, or to turn them upon the floor. This done, he withdraws and leaves them there to sorrow over their misery and to mourn under their distress. So all that day they spent their time in nothing but sighs and bitter grief. The next night she, talking with her husband about them further, and understanding that they were yet alive, did advise him to tell them to make away with themselves. So, when morning was come, he goes to them in a surly manner, as before and, perceiving them to be very sore with the stripes that he had given them the day before, he told them that, since they were never like to come out of that place, their only way would be forthwith to make an end of themselves, either with knife, halter, or poison: "For why," said he, "should you choose life, seeing it is attended with so much bitterness?" But they desired him to let them go. With that, he looked ugly upon them, and rushing to them, had doubtless made an end of them himself, but that he fell into one of his fits (for he sometimes, in sunshiny weather, fell into fits), and lost for a time the use of his hands, wherefore he withdrew, and left them as before to consider what to do. Then did the prisoners consult between themselves, whether it was best to take his advice or no; and thus they began to discourse:

Chris. "Brother," said Christian, "what shall we do? The life we now live is miserable. For my part, I know not whether is best, to live thus, or to die out of hand. My soul chooseth strangling rather than life, and the grave is more easy for me than this dungeon. Shall we be ruled by the giant?"

Hope. Indeed, our present condition is dreadful; and death would be far more welcome to me than thus for ever to abide. But yet, let us think: the Lord of the country to which we are going hath said, "Thou shalt do no murder," no, not to another man's person; much more, then, are we forbidden to take his advice to kill ourselves. Besides, he that kills another can but commit murder upon his body; but for one to kill himself is to kill body and soul at once. And, moreover, my brother, thou talkest of ease in the grave; but hast thou forgotten the hell, whither, for certain, the murderers go? for "no murderer hath eternal life." And let us consider again, that all the law is not in the hand of Giant Despair: others, so far as I can understand, have been taken by him as well as we, and yet have escaped out of his hand. Who knows but that God, who made the world, may cause that Giant Despair may die? or that, at some time or other, he may forget to lock us in? or that he may, in a short time, have another of his fits before us, and he may lose the use of his limbs? and if ever that should come to pass again, for my part, I am resolved to pluck up the heart of a man, and try to my utmost to get from under his hand. I was a fool that I did not try to do it before. But however, my brother, let us be patient, and endure awhile: the time may come that may give us a happy release; but let us not be our own murderers.

With these words, Hopeful at present did calm the mind of his brother; so they continued together in the dark that day, in their sad and doleful condition.

Well, towards evening, the giant goes down into the dungeon again, to see if his prisoners had taken his counsel. But, when he came there, he found them alive; and truly, alive was all; for now, what for want of bread and water, and by reason of the wounds they received when he beat them, they could do little but breathe. But, I say, he found them alive; at which he fell into a grievous rage, and told them that, seeing they had disobeyed his counsel, it should be worse with them than if they had never been born.

At this they trembled greatly, and I think that Christian fell into a swoon; but, coming a little to himself again, they renewed their discourse about the giant's advice and whether yet they had best to take it or no. Now, Christian again seemed for doing it; but Hopeful made his second reply as followeth:

Hope. "My brother," said he, "rememberest thou not how valiant thou hast been heretofore? Apollyon could not crush thee, nor could all that thou didst hear, or see, or feel in the Valley of the Shadow of Death. What hardship, terror, and amazement hast thou already gone through! and art thou now nothing but fear? Thou seest that I am in the dungeon with thee, a far weaker man by nature than thou art; also this giant has wounded me as well as thee, and hath also cut off the bread and water from my mouth; and, with thee, I mourn without the light. But let us have a little more patience. Remember how thou showedst thyself the man at Vanity Fair, and wast neither afraid of the chain, nor cage, nor yet of bloody death. Wherefore, let us (at least to avoid the shame that it becomes not a Christian to be found in) bear up with patience as well as we can."

Now, night being come again, and the giant and his wife being in bed, she asked him concerning the prisoners, and if they had taken his advice: to which he replied, "They are sturdy rogues; they choose rather to bear all hardship than to make away with themselves." Then said she, "Take them unto the castle-yard to-morrow, and show them the bones and skulls of those that thou hast already killed;

and make them believe, ere a week comes to an end, thou wilt tear them also in pieces, as thou hast done their fellows before them."

So when the morning was come, the giant goes to them again, and takes them into the castle-yard and shows them as his wife had bidden him. "These," said he, "were pilgrims, as you are, once, and they trespassed in my grounds as you have done; and when I thought fit, I tore them in pieces; and so within ten days I will do you. Go, get you down to your den again." And, with that, he beat them all the way thither. They lay, therefore, all day on Saturday in a lamentable case, as before. Now, when night was come, and when Mrs. Diffidence and her husband, the giant were got to bed, they began to renew their talking of their prisoners; and withal, the old giant wondered that he could neither by his blows nor counsel bring them to an end. And, with that, his wife replied, "I fear," said she, "that they live in hope that some will come to relieve them; or that they have picklocks about them, by the means of which they hope to escape." "And sayest thou so, my dear?" said the giant: "I will therefore search them in the morning."

Well, on Saturday about midnight, they began to pray, and continued in prayer till almost break of day.

Now, a little before it was day, good Christian, as one half amazed, brake out into this earnest speech: "What a fool," quoth he, "am I to lie in a foul-smelling dungeon, when I may as well walk at liberty! I have a key in my bosom called Promise, that will, I am sure, open any lock in Doubting Castle." Then said Hopeful, "That is good news, good brother: pluck it out of thy bosom, and try."

Then Christian pulled it out of his bosom, and began to try at the dungeon door, whose bolt, as he turned the key, gave back, and the door flew open with ease, and Christian and

Hopeful both came out. Then he went to the outward door that leads into the castle-yard, and with his key opened that door also. After, he went to the iron gate, for that must be opened too; but that lock went exceedingly hard, yet the key did open it. Then they thrust open the gate to make their escape with speed; but that gate, as it opened, made such a creaking, that it waked Giant Despair who, hastily rising to pursue his prisoners, felt his limbs to fail; for his fits took him again, so that he could by no means go after them. Then they went on, and came to the King's highway again, and so were safe because they were out of Giant Despair's rule.

Now, when they were gone over the stile, they began to contrive with themselves what they should do at that stile to prevent those that should come after from falling into the hands of Giant Despair. So they agreed to build there a pillar, and to engrave upon the side thereof this sentence: "Over this stile is the way to Doubting Castle, which is kept by Giant Despair, who despiseth the King of the Celestial Country, and seeks to destroy His holy pilgrims." Many, therefore, that followed after, read what was written, and escaped the danger. This done, they sang as follows:

> "Out of the way we went, and then we found
> What 'twas to tread upon forbidden ground:
> And let them that come after have a care,
> Lest heedlessness make them as we to fare;
> Lest they for trespassing his prisoners are
> Whose Castle's Doubting, and whose
> name's Despair."

Chapter 8

They went then till they came to the Delectable Mountains, which mountains belong to the Lord of that hill of which we have spoken before. So they went up to the mountains to behold the gardens and orchards, the vineyards and fountains of water, where also they drank and washed themselves, and did freely eat of the vineyards. Now there were on the tops of these mountains shepherds feeding their flocks, and they stood by the highway-side. The pilgrims, therefore, went to them, and leaning upon their staves (as is common with weary pilgrims when they stand to talk with any by the way), they asked, "Whose delightful mountains are these, and whose be the sheep that feed upon them?"

Shep. These mountains are Immanuel's Land, and they are within sight of His city; and the sheep also are His, and He laid down His life for them.

Chris. Is this the way to the Celestial City?

Shep. You are just in your way.

Chris. How far is it thither?

Shep. Too far for any but those who shall get thither indeed.

Chris. Is the way safe or dangerous?

Shep. Safe for those for whom it is to be safe; but sinners shall fall therein.

Chris. Is there in this place any relief for pilgrims that are weary and faint in the way?

Shep. The Lord of these mountains hath given us a charge not to be forgetful to care for strangers; therefore the good of the place is before you.

I saw also in my dream that when the shepherds perceived that they were wayfaring men, they also put questions to them (to which they made answer as in other places), as, "Whence came you?" and "How got you into the way?" and, "By what means have you so persevered therein? for but few of them that begin to come hither do show their faces on these mountains." But when the shepherds heard their answers, being pleased therewith they looked very lovingly upon them, and said, "Welcome to the Delectable Mountains!"

The shepherds, I say, whose names were Knowledge, Experience, Watchful, and Sincere, took them by the hand and took them to their tents, and made them partake of what was ready at present. They said moreover, "We would that you should stay here awhile, to be acquainted with us, and yet more to cheer yourselves with the good of these Delectable Mountains." They then told them that they were content to stay. So they went to rest that night, because it was very late.

Then I saw in my dream that in the morning the shepherds called up Christian and Hopeful to walk with them upon the mountains. So they went forth with them and walked a while, having a pleasant prospect on every side. Then said the shepherds one to another, "Shall we show these pilgrims some wonders?" So, when they had concluded to do it, they had them first to the top of the hill called Error, which was very steep on the farthest side, and bid them look down to the bottom. So Christian and Hopeful looked down, and saw at the bottom several men dashed all to pieces by a fall they had had from the top. Then said Christian, "What meaneth this?" Then the shepherds answered, "Have you not heard of them that were made to err, by hearkening to Hymeneus and Philetus, as concerning the faith of the rising from the dead?" They answered, "Yes." Then said the shepherds, "Those you see lie dashed to pieces at the bottom of this mountain are they; and they have continued to this day unburied, as you see, for an example to others to take heed how they clamber too high, or how they come too near the brink of this mountain."

Then I saw that they had them to the top of another mountain, and the name of that is Caution and bid them look afar off; and when they did, they perceived, as they thought, several men walking up and down among the tombs that were there; and they perceived that the men were blind, because they stumbled sometimes upon the tombs, and because they could not get out from among them. Then said Christian, "What means this?"

The shepherds then answered, "Did you not see a little below these mountains a stile that led into a meadow on the left hand side of this way?" They answered, "Yes." Then said the shepherds, "From that stile there goes a path that leads directly to Doubting Castle, which is kept by Giant Despair; and these men" (pointing to them among the tombs) "came once on pilgrimage, as you do now, even until they came to that same stile. And because the right way was rough in that place, they chose to go out of it into that meadow, and there were taken by Giant Despair, and cast into Doubting Castle, where, after they had been kept a while in the dungeon, he at last did put out their eyes, and led them among those tombs, where he has left them to wander to this very day, that the saying of the Wise Man might be fulfilled, 'He that wandereth out of the way of knowledge, shall remain in the congregation of the dead.'" Then Christian and Hopeful looked upon one another with tears gushing out, but yet said nothing to the shepherds.

Then I saw in my dream, that the shepherds had them to another place in a bottom, where was a door on the side of a hill; and they opened the door, and bid them look in. They looked in, therefore, and saw that within it was very dark and smoky; they also thought that they heard there a rumbling noise, as of fire, and a cry of some tormented, and that they smelt the scent of brimstone. Then said Christian, "What means this?" The shepherds told them, "This is a by-way to hell, a way that hypocrites go in at: namely, such as sell their birthright, with Esau; such as sell their master, with Judas; such as blaspheme the Gospel, with Alexander; and that lie and deceive with Ananias and Sapphira his wife."

Hope. Then said Hopeful to the shepherds, "I perceive that these had on them, even every one, a show of pilgrimage, as we have now; had they not?"

Shep. Yes, and held it a long time too.

Hope. How far might they go on in pilgrimage in their day, since they notwithstanding were thus miserably cast away?

Shep. Some farther, and some not so far as these mountains.

Then said the pilgrims one to another, "We have need to cry to the Strong for strength."

Shep. Ay, and you will have need to use it when you have it, too.

By this time the pilgrims had a desire to go forward, and the shepherds a desire they should; so they walked together towards the end of the mountains. Then said the shepherds one to another, "Let us here show to the pilgrims the gate of the Celestial City, if they have skill to look through our perspective glass." The pilgrims then lovingly accepted the motion; so they had them to the top of a high hill called Clear, and gave them their glass to look.

Then they tried to look; but the remembrance of that last thing, that the shepherds had showed them, made their hands shake, by means of which hindrance they could not look steadily through the glass; yet they thought they saw something like the gate, and also some of the glory of the place. Thus they went away, and sang this song:

"Thus by the shepherds secrets are revealed,
Which from all other men are kept concealed.
Come to the shepherds, then, if you would see
Things deep, things hid, and that mysterious be."

When they were about to depart, one of the shepherds gave them a note of the way. Another of them bid them beware of the Flatterer. The third bid them take heed that they slept not upon the Enchanted Ground. And the fourth bid them God speed.

So I awoke from my dream.

Chapter 9

And I slept, and dreamed again, and saw the same two pilgrims going down the mountains along the highway towards the city. Now, a little below these mountains, on the left hand, lieth the country of Conceit; from which country there comes into the way in which the pilgrims walked a little crooked lane. Here, therefore, they met with a very brisk lad, that came out of that country, and his name was Ignorance. So Christian asked him from what parts he came, and whither he was going.

Ignor. Sir, I was born in the country that lieth off there a little on the left hand, and I am going to the Celestial City.

Chris. But how do you think to get in at the gate? for you may find some difficulty there.

Ignor. As other people do.

Chris. But what have you to show at the gate, that may cause that the gate should be opened to you?

Ignor. I know my Lord's will, and have been a good liver; I pay every man his own; I pray, fast, pay money to the church and give to the poor, and have left my country for whither I am going.

Chris. But thou camest not in at the wicket-gate that is at the head of this way: thou camest in hither through that same crooked lane; and therefore I fear, however thou mayest think of thyself, when the reckoning day shall come, thou wilt have laid to thy charge that thou art a thief and a robber, instead of getting admittance into the city.

Ignor. Gentlemen, ye be utter strangers to me: I know you not: be content to follow the custom of your country, and I will follow the custom of mine. I hope all will be well. And, as for the gate that you talk of, all the world knows that that is a great way off of our country. I cannot think that any man in all our parts doth so much as know the way to it; nor need they matter whether they do or no, since we have, as you see, a fine, pleasant green lane, that comes down from our country, the next way into the way.

When Christian saw that the man was wise in his own opinion, he said to Hopeful, whisperingly, "There is more hope of a fool than of him." And said, moreover "When he that is a fool walketh by the way, his wisdom faileth him, and he saith to every one that he is a fool. What! shall we talk further with him, or outgo him at present, and so leave him to think of what he hath heard already, and then stop again for him afterwards, and see if by degrees we can do any good to him?"

Then said Hopeful:

> "Let Ignorance a little while now muse
> On what is said, and let him not refuse
> Good counsel to embrace, lest he remain
> Still ignorant of what's the chiefest gain.
> God saith, those that no understanding have
> (Although He made them), them He will not save."

Hope. He further added, "It is not good, I think, to say all to him at once: let us pass him by, if you will, and talk to him by and by, even as he is able to bear it."

So they both went on, and Ignorance he came after. Now, when they had passed him a little way, they entered into a very dark lane, where they met a man whom seven devils had bound with seven strong cords, and were carrying of him back to the door that they saw on the side of the hill. Now good Christian began to tremble, and so did Hopeful his companion; yet, as the devils led away the man, Christian looked to see if he knew him; and he thought it might be one Turn-away, that dwelt in the town of Apostasy. But he did not perfectly see his face, for he did hang his head like a thief that is found; but being gone past, Hopeful looked after him, and espied on his back a paper with this inscription, "One who was wicked while claiming to be good, and turned away from God."

Then said Christian to his fellow, "Now I call to remembrance that which was told of a thing that happened to a good man hereabout. The name of that man was Little-Faith, but a good man, and dwelt in the town of Sincere. The thing was this: At the entering in at this passage, there comes down from Broad-way Gate a lane called Dead Man's Lane; so-called because of the murders that are commonly done there; and this Little-Faith, going on pilgrimage as we do now, chanced to sit down there, and slept. Now, there happened at that time to come down that lane, from Broad-way Gate, three sturdy rogues, and their names were Faint-heart, Mistrust, and Guilt, three brothers; and they espying Little-Faith, where he was, came galloping up with speed. Now, the good man was just awaked from his sleep, and was getting up to go on his journey. So they came up all to him, and with threatening language bid him stand. At this, Little-Faith looked as white as a sheet and had neither power to fight nor fly. Then said Faint-heart, 'Deliver thy purse;' but, he making no haste to do it (for he was loth to lose his money) Mistrust ran up to him, and, thrusting his hand into his pocket, pulled out thence a bag of silver. Then he cried out, 'Thieves! thieves!' With that, Guilt, with a great club that was in his hand, struck Little-Faith on the head, and with that blow felled him flat to the ground, where he lay bleeding as one that would bleed to death. All this while the thieves stood by. But, at last, they hearing that some were upon the road, and fearing lest it should be one Great-Grace, that dwells in the city of Good-Confidence, they betook themselves to their heels, and left this good man to shift for himself. Now, after a while, Little-Faith came to himself, and, getting up, made shift to scramble on his way. This was the story."

Hope. But did they take from him all that ever he had?

Chris. No; the place where his jewels were they never ransacked; so those he kept still. But as I was told, the good man was much afflicted for his loss, for the thieves got most of his spending money. That which they got not, as I said, were jewels; also he had a little odd money left, but scarce enough to bring him to his journey's end. Nay, if I was not misinformed, he was forced to beg as he went, to keep himself alive, for his jewels he might not sell; but, beg and do what he could, he went, as we say, often with a hungry stomach the most part of the rest of the way.

Hope. But is it not a wonder they got not from him his certificate, by which he was to receive admission at the Celestial Gate?

Chris. It is a wonder; but they got not that, though they missed it not through any cunning of his; for he, being dismayed by their coming upon him, had neither power nor skill to hide anything; so it was more by good providence than by his endeavor, that they missed of that good thing.

Hope. But it must needs be a comfort to him that they got not his jewels from him.

Chris. It might have been great comfort to him, had he used it as he should; but they that told me the story said, that he made but little use of it all the rest of the way, and that because of the alarm that he had in their taking away his money. Indeed, he forgot it a great part of the rest of his journey; and besides, when at any time it came into his mind, and he began to be comforted therewith, then would fresh thoughts of his loss come again upon him, and those thoughts would swallow up all.

Hope. Alas, poor man! this could not but be a great grief unto him.

Chris. Grief! ay, a grief indeed. Would it not have been so to any of us, had we been used as he, to be robbed and wounded too, and that in a strange place, as he was? It is a wonder he did not die with grief, poor heart! I was told that he scattered almost all the rest of the way with nothing but doleful and bitter complaints; telling also to all that overtook him, or that he overtook in the way as he went, where he was robbed, and how; who they were that did it, and what he had lost; how he was wounded, and that he hardly escaped with life.

Hope. But it is a wonder that his necessities did not put him upon selling or pawning some of his jewels, that he might have wherewith to relieve himself in his journey.

Chris. Thou talkest like one whose head is thick to this very day. For what should he pawn them, or to whom should he sell them? In all that country where he was robbed, his jewels were not accounted of; nor did he want that relief which could from thence be administered to him. Besides, had his jewels been missing at the gate of the Celestial City, he had (and that he knew well enough) been shut out from an inheritance there; and that would have been worse to him than the coming and villany of ten thousand thieves.

Hope. But, Christian, these three fellows, I am persuaded in my heart, are but a company of cowards: would they have run else, think you, as they did at the noise of one that was coming on the road? Why did not Little-Faith pluck up a greater heart? He might, methinks, have stood one brush with them, and have yielded when there had been no remedy.

Chris. That they are cowards many have said, but few have found it so in the time of trial. As for a great heart, Little-Faith had none; and I perceive by thee, my brother, hadst thou been the man concerned, thou art but for a brush, and then to yield. And, verily, since this is the height of thy courage now they are at a distance from us, should they appear to thee as they did to him, they might put thee to second thoughts. But consider again, they are but journeymen-thieves; they serve under the king of the bottomless pit, who, if need be, will come in to their aid himself, and his voice is as the roaring of a lion. I myself have been engaged as this Little-Faith was, and I found it a terrible thing. These three villains set upon me: and I beginning like a Christian to resist, they gave but a call, and in came their master. I would, as the saying is, have given my life for a penny, but that, as God would have it, I was clothed with armor of proof. Ay, and yet, though I was so protected, I found it hard work to quit myself like a man. No man can tell what in that combat attends us, but he that hath been in the battle himself.

Hope. Well, but they ran, you see, when they did but suppose that one Great-Grace was in the way.

Chris. True, they have often fled, both they and their master, when Great-Grace hath but appeared; and no marvel, for he is the King's champion. But I trow you will put some difference between Little-Faith and the King's champion? All the King's subjects are not His champions, nor can they when tried do such feats of war as he. Is it meet to think that a little child should handle Goliath as David did? or that there should be the strength of an ox in a wren? Some are strong, some are weak; some have great faith, some have little: this man was one of the weak, and therefore he went to the wall.

Hope. I would it had been Great-Grace for their sakes.

Chris. If it had been he, he might have had his hands full; for

401

I must tell you that though Great-Grace is excellent good at his weapons, and has, and can, so long as he keeps them at sword's point, do well enough with them; yet, if they get within him, even Faint-heart, Mistrust, or the other, it shall go hard but they will throw up his heels. And when a man is down, you know, what can he do?

Whoso looks well upon Great-Grace's face will see those scars and cuts there, that shall easily give proof of what I say. Yea, once I heard that he should say (and that when he was in the combat), "We despaired even of life." How did these sturdy rogues and their fellows make David groan, mourn, and roar! Yea, Heman, and Hezekiah too, though champions in their days, were forced to bestir when by these attacked; and yet, notwithstanding, they had their coats soundly brushed by them. Peter, upon a time, would go try what he could do; but though some do say of him that he is the prince of the apostles, they handled him so that they made him at last afraid of a sorry girl.

Besides, their king is at their whistle—he is never out of hearing; and if at any time they be put to the worst, he, if possible, comes in to help them; and of him it is said, "The sword of him that layeth at him cannot hold; the spear, the dart, nor the habergeon. He esteemeth iron as straw, and brass as rotten wood. The arrow cannot make him flee; sling-stones are turned with him into stubble. Darts are counted as stubble: he laugheth at the shaking of a spear." What can a man do in this case? It is true, if a man could at every turn have Job's horse, and had skill and courage to ride him, he might do notable things. For his neck is clothed with thunder. He will not be afraid as the grasshopper: "the glory of his nostrils is terrible. He paweth in the valley, and rejoiceth in his strength: he goeth on to meet the armed men. He mocketh at fear, and is not affrighted, neither turneth he his back from the sword. The quiver rattleth against him, the glittering spear and the shield. He swalloweth the ground with fierceness and rage; neither believeth he that it is the sound of the trumpet. He saith among the trumpets, Ha! ha! and he smelleth the battle afar off, the thunder of the captains, and the shouting."

But for such footmen as thee and I are, let us never desire to meet with an enemy, nor vaunt as if we could do better, when we hear of others that have been foiled, nor be tickled at the thoughts of our manhood; for such commonly come by the worst when tried. Witness Peter, of whom I made mention before: he would swagger, ay, he would; he would, as his vain mind prompted him to say, do better and stand more for his Master than all men; but who so foiled and run down by those villains as he?

Then Christian sang:

> "Poor Little-Faith! hast been among the thieves?
> Wast robbed? Remember this: whoso believes
> And gets more faith, shall then a victor be
> Over ten thousand; else, scarce over three."

So they went on, and Ignorance followed. They went then till they came to a place where they saw a way put itself into their way, and seemed withal to lie as straight as the way which they should go; and here they knew not which of the two to take, for both seemed straight before them; therefore here they stood still to consider. And, as they were thinking about the way, behold, a man, black of flesh, but covered with a very light robe, came to them, and asked them why they stood there. They answered they were going to the Celestial City, but knew not which of these ways to take. "Follow me," said the man; "it is thither that I am going." So they followed him to the way that but now came into the road, which by degrees turned and turned them so from the city that they desired to go to, that, in a little time, their faces were turned away from it; yet they followed him. But by-and-by, before they were aware, he led them both within the folds of a net, in which they were both so entangled that they knew not what to do; and with that, the white robe fell off the black man's back. Then they saw where they were. Wherefore, there they lay crying some time, for they could not get themselves out.

Chris. Then said Christian to his fellow, "Now do I see myself in an error. Did not the shepherds bid us beware of flatterers? As is the saying of the Wise Man, so we have found it this day: 'A man that flattereth his neighbor, spreadeth a net at his feet.'"

Hope. They also gave us a note of directions about the way, for our more sure finding thereof; but therein we have also forgotten to read, and have not kept ourselves from the paths of the destroyer. Thus they lay bewailing themselves in the net. At last they espied a Shining One coming towards them with a whip of small cord in his hand. When he was come to the place where they were, he asked them whence they came, and what they did there. They told him that they were poor pilgrims going to Zion, but were led out of their way by a black man clothed in white, "Who bid us," said they, "follow him, for he was going thither too." Then said he with the whip, "It is Flatterer, a false prophet, that hath changed himself into an angel of light." So he rent the net, and let the men out. Then said he to them, "Follow me, that I may set you in your way again." So he led them back to the way which they had left to follow the Flatterer. Then he asked them, saying, "Where did you lie the last night?" They said, "With the shepherds upon the Delectable Mountains." He asked them then if they had not of those shepherds a note of direction for the way. They answered, "Yes." "But did you not," said he, "when you were at a stand, pluck out and read your note?" They answered, "No." He asked them, "Why?" They said they forgot. He asked them, moreover, if the shepherds did not bid them beware of the Flatterer. They answered, "Yes; but we did not imagine," said they, "that this fine-spoken man had been he."

Then I saw in my dream, that he commanded them to lie down; which when they did, he whipped them sore, to teach them the good way wherein they should walk; and, as he whipped them, he said, "As many as I love, I rebuke and chasten; be zealous, therefore, and repent." This done, he bid them go on their way, and take good heed to the other directions of the shepherds. So they thanked him for all his kindness, and went softly along the right way, singing:

"Come hither, you that walk along the way,
See how the pilgrims fare that go astray;
They catchèd are in an entangling net,
'Cause they good counsel lightly did forget;
'Tis true, they rescued were; but yet, you see,
They're scourged to boot: let this your caution be."
Now, after awhile they perceived afar off, one coming softly and alone, all along the highway, to meet them. Then said Christian to his fellow, "Yonder is a man with his back towards Zion, and he is coming to meet us."

Hope. I see him: let us take heed to ourselves lest he should prove a flatterer also.

So he drew nearer and nearer, and at last came up to them. His name was Atheist, and he asked them whither they were going.

Chris. We are going to Mount Zion.

Then Atheist fell into a very great laughter.

Chris. What is the meaning of your laughter?

Atheist. I laugh to see what ignorant persons you are, to take upon yourselves so tedious a journey, and yet are like to have nothing but your travel for your pains.

Chris. Why, man, do you think we shall not be received?

Atheist. Received! There is no such a place as you dream of in all this world.

Chris. But there is in the world to come.

Atheist. When I was at home in mine own country, I heard as you now affirm, and, from that hearing, went out to see, and have been seeking this city these twenty years, but find no more of it than I did the first day I set out.

Chris. We have both heard and believe that there is such a place to be found.

Atheist. Had not I, when at home, believed I had not come thus far to seek; but, finding none (and yet I should had there been such a place to be found, for I have gone to seek it farther than you), I am going back again, and will seek to refresh myself with the things that I then cast away for hopes of that which I now see is not.

Chris. Then said Christian to Hopeful his fellow, "Is it true which this man hath said?"

Hope. Take heed; he is one of the flatterers. Remember what it hath cost us once already for hearkening to such kind of fellows. What! no Mount Zion? Did we not see from the Delectable Mountains the gate of the city? Also, are we not now to walk by faith? Let us go on, lest the man with the whip overtake us again. I say, my brother, cease to hear him, and let us believe to the saving of the soul.

Chris. My brother, I did not put the question to thee for that I doubted of the truth of our belief myself, but to prove thee, and to fetch from thee a fruit of the honesty of thy heart. As for this man, I know that he is blinded. Let thee and me go on, knowing that we have belief of the truth, and no lie is of the truth.

Hope. Now do I rejoice in hope of the glory of God.

So they turned away from the man, and he, laughing at them, went his way.

I then saw in my dream that they went till they came into a certain country, whose air naturally tended to make one drowsy if he came a stranger into it. And here Hopeful began to be very dull and heavy of sleep; wherefore he said unto Christian, "I do now begin to grow so drowsy, that I can scarcely hold up mine eyes; let us lie down here, and take one nap."

Chris. "By no means," said the other, "lest sleeping, we never awake more."

Hope. Why, my brother? sleep is sweet to the laboring man: we may be refreshed if we take a nap.

Chris. Do not you remember that one of the shepherds bid us beware of the Enchanted Ground? He meant by that that we should beware of sleeping; wherefore let us not sleep as others, but let us watch and be sober.

Hope. I acknowledge myself in fault; and had I been here alone, I had, by sleeping, run the danger of death. I see it is true that the Wise Man saith, "Two are better than one." Hitherto hath thy company been my help; and thou shalt have a good reward for thy labor.

Chris. "Now, then," said Christian, "to prevent drowsiness in this place, let us talk about something profitable."

Hope. With all my heart.

Chris. Where shall we begin?

Hope. Where God began with us. But do you begin, if you please.

Chris. I will sing you first this song:

"When saints do sleepy grow, let them come hither,
And hear how these two pilgrims talk together;
Yea, let them learn of them, in any wise,
Thus to keep ope their drowsy, slumbering eyes.
Saints' fellowship, if it be managed well,
Keeps them awake, and that in spite of hell."
Chris. Then Christian began, and said, "I will ask you a question. How came you to think at first of doing as you do now?"

Hope. Do you mean, how came I at first to look after the good of my soul?

Chris. Yes, that is my meaning.

Hope. I continued a great while in the delight of those things which were seen and sold at our fair; things which I believe now would have, had I continued in them still, drowned me in ruin and destruction.

Chris. What things were they?

Hope. All the treasures and riches of the world. Also I delighted much in rioting, revelling, drinking, swearing, lying, uncleanness, Sabbath-breaking, and what not, that tended to destroy the soul. But I found at last, by hearing and considering of things that are holy, which indeed I heard of you, as also of beloved Faithful, that was put to death for his faith, and good living in Vanity Fair, that the end of these things is death; and that, for these things' sake, the wrath of God cometh upon those who disobey him.

Chris. And did you presently fall under the power of this feeling?

Hope. No; I was not willing presently to know the evil of sin, nor the destruction that follows upon the doing of it; but tried, when my mind at first began to be shaken with the Word, to shut mine eyes against the light thereof.

Chris. But what was the cause of your waiting so long?

Hope. The causes were, — Firstly, I was ignorant that this was the work of God upon me. Secondly, Sin was yet very sweet to my flesh, and I was loth to leave it. Thirdly, I could not tell how to part with mine old companions, their presence and actions were so desirable unto me. Fourthly, The hours in which these feelings were upon me, were such troublesome and such heart-affrighting hours, that I could not bear, no, not so much as the remembrance of them upon my heart.

Chris. Then, as it seems, sometimes you got rid of your trouble?

Hope. Yes, verily, but it would come into my mind again, and then I should be as bad, nay, worse than I was before.

Chris. Why, what was it that brought your sins to mind again?

Hope. Many things; as,

1. If I did but meet a good man in the streets; or,

2. If I have heard any read in the Bible; or,

3. If mine head did begin to ache; or,

4. If I were told that some of my neighbors were sick; or,

5. If I heard the bell toll for some that were dead; or,

6. If I thought of dying myself; or,

7. If I heard that sudden death happened to others;

8. But especially when I thought of myself that I must quickly come to judgment.

Chris. And could you at any time with ease get off the guilt of sin, when by any of these ways it came upon you?

Hope. No, not I; for then they got faster hold of my conscience; and then, if I did but think of going back to sin (though my mind was turned against it,) it would be double torment to me.

Chris. And how did you do then?

Hope. I thought I must endeavor to mend my life; for else, thought I, I am sure to be lost forever.

Chris. And did you endeavor to mend?

Hope. Yes, and fled from not only my sins, but sinful company too, and betook me to religious duties, as praying, reading, weeping for sin, speaking truth to my neighbors, etc. These things did I, with many others, too much here to tell.

Chris. And did you think yourself well then?

Hope. Yes, for a while; but, at the last, my trouble came tumbling upon me again, and that over the neck of all my trying to do right.

Chris. How came that about, since you were now doing right, as far as you knew?

Hope. There were several things brought it upon me; especially such sayings as these: "All our righteousness are as filthy rags;" "By the works of the law shall no flesh be made righteous;" "When ye shall have done all those things which are commanded you, say, We are unprofitable;" with many more such like. From whence I began to reason with myself thus: If all my righteousness are filthy rags, if by the deeds of the law no man can be made righteous, and if, when we have done all, we are yet unprofitable, then it is but a folly to think of heaven by the law. I further thought thus; If a man runs a hundred pounds into the shopkeeper's debt, and after that shall pay for all that he shall buy; yet his old debt stands still in the book uncrossed; for the which the shopkeeper may sue him, and cast him into prison till he shall pay the debt.

Chris. Well, and how did you apply this to yourself?

Hope. Why, I thought thus with myself: I have by my sins run a great way into God's book, and my now reforming will not pay off that score. Therefore I should think still, under all my present trying. But how shall I be freed from that punishment that I have brought myself in danger of by my former sins.

Chris. A very good application; but pray go on.

Hope. Another thing that hath troubled me ever since my late turning from sin is, that if I look narrowly into the best of what I do now, I still see sin, new sin, mixing itself with the best of that I do; so that now I am forced to conclude that, notwithstanding my former fond opinion of myself and duties, I have committed sin enough in one duty to send me to hell, though my former life had been faultless.

Chris. And what did you do then?

Hope. Do! I could not tell what to do, till I brake my mind to Faithful; for he and I were well acquainted. And he told me, that unless I could obtain the righteousness of a Man that never had sinned, neither mine own nor all the righteousness of the world could save me.

Chris. And did you think he spake true?

Hope. Had he told me so when I was pleased and satisfied with mine own trying, I had called him fool for his pains; but now, since I see mine own weakness and the sin which cleaves to my best performance, I have been forced to be of his opinion.

Chris. But did you think, when at first he suggested it to you, that there was such a Man to be found, of whom it might justly be said that He never committed sin?

Hope. I must confess the words at first sounded strangely; but after a little more talk and company with him I had full certainty about it.

Chris. And did you ask him what Man this was, and how you must be made righteous by Him?

Hope. Yes, and he told me it was the Lord Jesus, that dwelleth on the right hand of the Most High. And thus, said he, you must be made right by Him, even by trusting what He hath done by Himself in the days of His flesh, and suffered when He did hang on the tree. I asked him further, How that Man's righteousness could be of that power to help another before God? And he told me He was the mighty God, and did what He did, and died the death also, not for Himself, but for me; to whom His doings, and the worthiness of them, should be given if I believed on Him.

Chris. And what did you do then?

Hope. I made my objections against my believing, for that I thought He was not willing to save me.

Chris. And what said Faithful to you then?

Hope. He bid me go to Him and see. Then I said it was too much for me to ask for. But he said No, for I was invited to come. Then he gave me a book of Jesus' own writing to encourage me the more freely to come; and he said concerning that book, that every word and letter thereof stood firmer than heaven and earth. Then I asked him what I must do when I came; and he told me I must entreat on my knees, with all my heart and soul, the Father to reveal Him to me. Then I asked him further how I must make my prayer to Him; and he said, Go, and thou shalt find Him upon a mercy-seat, where He sits all the year long to give pardon and forgiveness to them that come. I told him that I knew not what to say when I came; and he bid me say to this effect: God be merciful to me a sinner, and make me to know and believe in Jesus Christ; for I see that if His righteousness had not been, or I have not faith in that righteousness, I am utterly cast away. Lord, I have heard that Thou art a merciful God, and hast given that Thy Son Jesus Christ should be the Saviour of the world; and, moreover, that Thou art willing to bestow Him upon such a poor sinner as I am. And I am a sinner indeed. Lord, take therefore this opportunity, and show Thy grace in the salvation of my soul, through Thy Son Jesus Christ. Amen.

Chris. And did you do as you were bidden?

Hope. Yes, over, and over, and over.

Chris. And did the Father show His son to you?

Hope. Not at the first, nor second, nor third, nor fourth, nor fifth; no, nor at the sixth time neither.

Chris. What did you do then?

Hope. What! why, I could not tell what to do.

Chris. Had you no thoughts of leaving off praying?

Hope. Yes; a hundred times twice told.

Chris. And what was the reason you did not?

Hope. I believed that that was true which had been told me; to wit, that without the righteousness of this Christ, all the world could not save me; and therefore, thought I with myself, if I leave off I die, and I can but die at the throne of grace. And withal, this came into my mind: "Though it tarry, wait for it; because it will surely come, it will not tarry." So I continued praying until the Father showed me His Son.

Chris. And how was He shown unto you?

Hope. I did not see Him with my bodily eyes, but with the eyes of my heart, and thus it was: One day I was very sad, I think sadder than at any one time in my life; and this sadness was through a fresh sight of the greatness and vileness of my sins. And, as I was then looking for nothing but hell and the everlasting loss of my soul, suddenly, as I thought, I saw the Lord Jesus look down from heaven upon me, and saying, "Believe on the Lord Jesus Christ, and thou shalt be saved."

But I replied, "Lord, I am a great, a very great sinner." And He answered, "My grace is sufficient for thee." Then I said, "But, Lord, what is believing?" And then I saw from that saying, "He that cometh to me shall never hunger, and he that believeth on me shall never thirst," that believing and coming was all one; and that he that came, that is, ran out in his heart and desire after salvation by Christ, he indeed believed in Christ. Then the water stood in mine eyes, and I asked further, "But, Lord, may such a great sinner as I am be indeed accepted of Thee, and be saved by thee?" and I heard Him say, "And him that cometh to me I will in no wise cast out." Then said I, "But how Lord, must I consider of Thee in my coming to Thee, that my faith may be placed aright upon Thee?" Then he said, "Christ Jesus came into the world to save sinners. He is the end of the law for righteousness to every one that believes. He died for our sins, and rose again for our righteousness. He loved us, and washed us from our sins in His own blood. He is Mediator between God and us. He ever liveth to plead for us." From all which I gathered that I must look for righteousness in His person, and for satisfaction for my sins by His blood; that what He did in obedience to His Father's law, and in submitting to the penalty thereof, was not for Himself, but for him that will accept it for his salvation, and be thankful. And now was my heart full of joy, mine eyes full of tears, and mine affections running over with love to the name, people, and ways of Jesus Christ.

Chris. This was a revelation of Christ to your soul indeed. But tell me particularly what effect this had upon your spirit.

Hope. It made me see that all the world, notwithstanding all the righteousness thereof, is in a state of condemnation. It made me see that God the Father, though He be just, can justly forgive the coming sinner. It made me greatly ashamed of the vileness of my former life, and confounded me with the sense of my own ignorance; for there never came thought into my heart before now, that showed me so the beauty of Jesus Christ. It made me love a holy life, and long to do something for the honor and glory of the name of the Lord Jesus. Yea, I thought that had I now a thousand gallons of blood in my body, I could spill it all for the sake of the Lord Jesus.

Chapter 10

I saw then in my dream that Hopeful looked back, and saw Ignorance, whom they had left behind, coming after. "Look," said he to Christian, "how far yonder youngster loitereth behind."

Chris. Ay, ay, I see him: he careth not for our company.

Hope. But I think it would not have hurt him, had he kept pace with us hitherto.

Chris. That is true; but I warrant you he thinks otherwise.

Hope. That I think he doth; but, however, let us tarry for him. So they did.

Chris. Then Christian said to him, "Come away, man; why do you stay so behind?"

Ignor. I take my pleasure in walking alone, even more a great deal than in company, unless I like it the better.

Then said Christian to Hopeful (but softly), "Did I not tell you he cared not for our company? But, however," said he, "come up, and let us talk away the time in this solitary place." Then, directing his speech to Ignorance, he said, "Come how do you? How stands it between God and your soul now?"

Ignor. I hope well; for I am always full of good thoughts, that come into my mind to comfort me as I walk.

Chris. What good motions? pray tell us.

Ignor. Why, I think of God and heaven.

Chris. So do the devils and lost souls.

Ignor. But I think of them and desire them.

Chris. So do many that are never like to come there. "The soul of the sluggard desireth and hath nothing."

Ignor. But I think of them, and leave all for them.

Chris. That I doubt, for leaving of all is a very hard matter; yea, a harder matter than many are aware of. But why, or by what, art thou persuaded that thou hast left all for God and heaven?

Ignor. My heart tells me so.

Chris. The Wise Man says, "He that trusteth in his own heart is a fool."

Ignor. This is spoken of an evil heart; but mine is a good one.

Chris. But how dost thou prove that?

Ignor. It comforts me in the hopes of heaven.

Chris. That may be through its deceitfulness; for a man's heart may minister comfort to him in the hopes of that thing for which he has yet no ground to hope.

Ignor. But my heart and life agree together; and therefore my hope is well grounded.

Chris. Who told thee that thy heart and life agree together?

Ignor. My heart tells me so.

Chris. Ask my fellow if I be a thief! Thy heart tells thee so! Except the Word of God telleth thee in this matter, other testimony is of no value.

Ignor. But is it not a good heart that hath good thoughts? and is not that a good life that is according to God's commandments?

Chris. Yes, that is a good heart that hath good thoughts, and that is a good life that is according to God's commandments; but it is one thing, indeed, to have these, and another thing only to think so.

Ignor. Pray, what count you good thoughts, and a life according to God's commandments?

Chris. There are good thoughts of many kinds: some respecting ourselves, some God, some Christ, and some other things.

Ignor. You go so fast, I cannot keep pace with you. Do you go on before: I must stay awhile behind.

Then they said:

"Well, Ignorance, wilt thou yet foolish be,
To slight good counsel, ten times given thee?
And if thou yet refuse it, thou shalt know,
Ere long, the evil of thy doing so.
Remember, man, in time; stoop, do not fear;
Good counsel, taken well, saves; therefore hear:
But, if thou yet shalt slight it, thou wilt be
The loser, Ignorance, I'll warrant thee."
Then Christian addressed himself thus to his fellow:

Chris. Well, come, my good Hopeful; I perceive that thou and I must walk by ourselves again.

So I saw in my dream that they went on apace before, and Ignorance he came hobbling after. Then said Christian to his companion, "It pities me much for this poor man: it will certainly go ill with him at last."

Hope. Alas! there are abundance in our town in his condition, whole families, yea, whole streets, and that of pilgrims, too; and if there be so many in our parts, how many, think you, must there be in the place where he was born?

Chris. Indeed, the Word saith, "He hath blinded their eyes, lest they should see."

Hope. Well said; I believe you have said the truth. Are we now almost got past the Enchanted Ground?

Chris. Why, art thou weary of our talking?

Hope. No, verily; but that I would know where we are.

Chris. We have not now above two miles farther to go thereon. Well, we will leave at this time our neighbor Ignorance by himself, and fall upon another subject.

Hope. With all my heart; but you shall still begin.

Chris. Well, then, did you not know, about ten years ago, one Temporary in your parts, who was a forward man in religion then?

Hope. Know him! yes; he dwelt in Graceless, a town about two miles off of Honesty, and he dwelt next door to one Turnback.

Chris. Right, he dwelt under the same roof with him. Well, that man was much awakened once: I believe that then he had some sight of his sins, and of the punishment that was due thereto.

Hope. I am of your mind; for (my house not being above three miles from him) he would ofttimes come to me, and that with many tears. Truly, I pitied the man, and was not altogether without hope of him; but one may see, it is not every one that cries "Lord! Lord!"

Chris. He told me once that he was resolved to go on pilgrimage as we do now; but all of a sudden he grew acquainted with one Save-self, and then he became a stranger to me, for at that time he gave up going on pilgrimage.

Chapter 11

Now I saw in my dream, that by this time the pilgrims were got over the Enchanted Ground, and entering into the country of Beulah, whose air was very sweet and pleasant: the way lying directly through it, they enjoyed themselves there for a season. Yea, here they heard continually the singing of birds and saw every day the flowers appear on the earth, and heard the voice of the turtle in the land. In this country the sun shineth night and day; wherefore this was beyond the Valley of the Shadow of Death, and also out of the reach of Giant Despair; neither could they from this place so much as see Doubting Castle. Here they were within sight of the City they were going to; also here met them some of the inhabitants thereof; for in this land the Shining Ones commonly walked, because it was upon the borders of heaven. Here they had no want of corn and wine; for in this place they met with abundance of what they had sought for in all their pilgrimage. Here they heard voices from out of the City, loud voices, saying, "Say ye to the daughter of Zion, Behold, thy salvation cometh! Behold, His reward is with Him!" Here all the inhabitants of the country called them "The holy people, and redeemed of the Lord, sought out," etc.

Now, as they walked in this land, they had more rejoicing than in parts more remote from the kingdom to which they were bound; and drawing near to the City, they had yet a more perfect view thereof. It was builded of pearls and precious stones, also the streets thereof were paved with gold; so that by reason of the natural glory of the City, and the reflection of the sunbeams upon it, Christian with desire fell sick; Hopeful also had a fit or two of the same disease, wherefore here they lay by it awhile, crying out because of their pangs, "If you see my Beloved tell Him that I am sick of love."

But being a little strengthened, and better able to bear their sickness, they walked on their way, and came yet nearer and nearer, where were orchards, vineyards, and gardens, and their gates opened into the highway. Now, as they came up to these places, behold, the gardener, stood in the way; to whom the pilgrims said, "Whose goodly vineyards and gardens are these?" He answered, "They are the King's, and are planted here for His own delight, and also for the solace of pilgrims." So the gardener had them into the vineyards, and bid them refresh themselves with the dainties. He also showed them there the King's walks, and the arbors where He delighted to be; and here they tarried and slept.

Now I beheld in my dream, that they talked more in their sleep at this time than ever they did in all their journey; and being in thought thereabout, the gardener said even to me, "Wherefore dost thou meditate at the matter? It is the nature of the fruit of the grapes of these vineyards to go down so sweetly as to cause the lips of them that are asleep to speak."

So I saw, when they awoke they undertook to go up to the City. But, as I said, the reflection of the sun upon the City (for the City was pure gold) was so extremely glorious, that they could not, as yet, with open face behold it, but through a glass made for that purpose. So I saw that, as they went on, there met them two men in raiment that shone like gold, also their faces shone as the light.

These men asked the pilgrims whence they came; and they told them. They also asked them where they had lodged, what difficulties and dangers, what comforts and pleasures, they had met in the way; and they told them. Then said the men that met them, "You have but two difficulties more to meet with, and then you are in the City."

Christian, then, and his companion, asked the men to go along with them; so they told them that they would. "But," said they, "you must obtain it by your own faith." So I saw in my dream that they went on together till they came in sight of the gate.

Now I further saw, that betwixt them and the gate was a river; but there was no bridge to go over, and the river was very deep. At the sight, therefore, of this river, the pilgrims were much stunned; but the men that went with them said, "You must go through, or you cannot come at the gate."

The pilgrims then began to inquire if there was no other way to the gate; to which they answered, "Yes; but there hath not any save two, to wit, Enoch and Elijah, been permitted to tread that path since the foundation of the world, nor shall until the last trumpet shall sound." The pilgrims then, especially Christian, began to be anxious in his mind, and looked this way and that; but no way could be found by them by which they might escape the river. Then they asked the men if the waters were all of a depth. They said, "No," yet they could not help them in that case; "for," said they, "you shall find it deeper or shallower as you believe in the King of the place."

They then addressed themselves to the water; and, entering, Christian began to sink, and crying out to his good friend Hopeful, he said, "I sink in deep waters; the billows go over my head; all His waves go over me."

Then said the other, "Be of good cheer, my brother; I feel the bottom, and it is good." Then said Christian, "Ah! my friend, the sorrows of death have compassed me about; I shall not see the land that flows with milk and honey." And with that, a great darkness and horror fell upon Christian, so that he could not see before him. Also here he in a great measure lost his senses, so that he could neither remember nor orderly talk of any of those sweet refreshments that he had met with in the way of his pilgrimage. But all the words that he spake still tended to show that he had horror of mind, and heart-fears that he should die in that river, and never obtain entrance in at the gate. Here also, as they that stood by perceived, he was much in the troublesome thoughts of the sins that he had committed, both since and before he began to be a pilgrim. It was also observed that he was troubled with the sight of demons and evil spirits; for ever and anon he would intimate so much by words.

Hopeful, therefore, here had much ado to keep his brother's head above water; yea, sometimes he would be quite gone down, and then, ere a while he would rise up again half dead. Hopeful would also endeavor to comfort him, saying, "Brother, I see the gate, and men standing by to receive us;" but Christian would answer, "It is you, it is you they wait for: you have been hopeful ever since I knew you." "And so have you," said he to Christian. "Ah, brother," said he, "surely, if I were right, He would now arise to help me; but for my sins He hath brought me into this snare, and hath left me." Then said Hopeful, "My brother, these troubles and distresses that you go through in these waters are no sign that God hath forsaken you; but are sent to try you, whether you will call to mind that which hitherto you have received of His goodness, and live upon Him in your distresses."

Then I saw in my dream that Christian was in thought awhile. To whom also Hopeful added these words, "Be of good cheer, Jesus Christ maketh thee whole." And, with that, Christian brake out with a loud voice, "Oh, I see Him again; and He tells me, 'When thou passest through the waters, I will be with thee; and through the rivers, they shall not overflow thee.'" Then they both took courage; and the enemy was, after that, as still as a stone, until they were gone over.

Christian, therefore, presently found ground to stand upon; and so it followed that the rest of the river was but shallow. Thus they got over.

Now, upon the bank of the river, on the other side, they saw the two Shining Men again, who there waited for them. Wherefore, being come out of the river, they saluted them, saying, "We are heavenly spirits, sent forth to help those that shall be heirs of salvation." Thus they went along towards the gate. Now, you must note that the City stood upon a mighty hill; but the pilgrims went up that hill with ease, because they had these two men to lead them up by the arms; also they had left their mortal garments behind them in the river; for though they went in with them, they came out without them. They therefore went up here with much activity and speed, though the foundation upon which the City was framed was higher than the clouds. They therefore went up through the regions of the air, sweetly talking as they went, being comforted because they had safely got over the river, and had such glorious companions to attend them.

The talk they had with the Shining Ones, was about the glory of the place; who told them that the beauty and glory of it were such as could not be put into words. "There," said they, "is the Mount Zion, the heavenly Jerusalem, the innumerable company of angels, and the spirits of good men made perfect. You are going now," said they, "to the Paradise of God, wherein you shall see the tree of life, and eat of the never-fading fruits thereof; and when you come there, you shall have white robes given you, and your walk and talk shall be every day with the King, even all the days of an eternal life. There you shall not see again such things as you saw when you were in the lower region upon the earth; to wit, sorrow, sickness, affliction, and death; 'for the former things are passed away.' You are going now to Abraham, to Isaac, and to Jacob, and to the prophets, men that God hath taken away from the evil to come, and that are now resting upon their beds, each one walking in his righteousness." The men then asked, "What must we do in the holy place?" To whom it was answered, "You must there receive the comfort of all your toil, and have joy for all your sorrow; you must reap what you have sown, even the fruit of all your prayers, and tears, and sufferings for the King by the way. In that place you must wear crowns of gold, and enjoy the perpetual sight and visions of the Holy One; for there you shall see Him as He is. There also you shall serve Him continually with praise, with shouting and thanksgiving, whom you desired to serve in the world, though with much difficulty, because of the weakness of your bodies. There your eyes shall be delighted with seeing and your ears with hearing the pleasant voice of the Mighty One. There you shall enjoy your friends again that are gone thither before you; and there you shall with joy receive even every one that follows into the holy place after you. There also you shall be clothed with glory and majesty, and put into a state fit to ride out with the King of Glory. When He shall come with sound of trumpet in the clouds, as upon the wings of the wind, you shall come with Him; and when He shall sit upon the throne of judgment, you shall sit by Him; yea, and when He shall pass sentence upon all the workers of evil, let them be angels or men, you also shall have a voice in that judgment because they were His and your enemies. Also, when He shall again return to the City, you shall go too, with sound of trumpet, and be ever with Him."

Now, while they were thus drawing towards the gate, behold, a company of the heavenly host came out to meet them; to whom it was said by the other two Shining Ones, "These are the men that have loved our Lord when in the world, and that have left all for His holy name; and He hath sent us to fetch them, and we have brought them thus far on their desired journey, that they may go in and look their Redeemer in the face with joy." Then the heavenly host gave a great shout, saying, "Blessed are they which are called to the marriage supper of the Lamb." There came out also at this time to meet them several of the King's trumpeters, clothed in white and shining raiment who, with melodious noises and loud, made even the heavens to echo with their sound. These trumpeters saluted Christian and his fellow with ten thousand welcomes from the world; and this they did with shouting and sound of trumpet.

This done, they compassed them round on every side; some went before, some behind, and some on the right hand, some on the left (as it were to guard them through the upper regions), continually sounding as they went, with melodious noise, in notes on high: so that the very sight was to them that could behold it as if heaven itself was come down to meet them. Thus, therefore, they walked on together; and, as they walked, ever and anon these trumpeters, even with joyful sound, would, by mixing their music, with looks and gestures, still signify to Christian and his brother how welcome they were into their company, and with what gladness they came to meet them. And now were these two men as it were in heaven before they came at it, being swallowed up with the sight of angels, and with hearing of their melodious notes. Here also they had the City itself in view, and thought they heard all the bells therein to ring, and welcome them thereto. But, above all, the warm and joyful thoughts that they had about their own dwelling there with such company, and that for ever and ever, oh! by what tongue or pen can their glorious joy be expressed?

And thus they came up to the gate. Now, when they were come up to the gate, there was written over it in letters of gold, "Blessed are they that do His commandments, that they may have right to the tree of life, and may enter in through the gates into the city."

Then I saw in my dream, that the Shining Men bid them

call at the gate: the which when they did, some from above looked over the gate: such as Enoch, Moses, and Elijah, and others, to whom it was said, "These pilgrims are come from the City of Destruction, for the love that they bear to the King of this place." And then the pilgrims gave in unto them each man his certificate, which they had received in the beginning; those therefore were carried in to the King, who, when He had read them, said, "Where are the men?" To whom it was answered, "They are standing without the gate." The King then commanded to open the gate, "that the righteous nation," said He, "which keepeth the truth, may enter in."

Now, I saw in my dream, that these two men went in at the gate; and lo! as they entered, their looks were changed so that their faces became bright; and they had garments put on that shone like gold. There were also that met them with harps and crowns, and gave them to them—the harps to praise withal, and the crowns in token of honor. Then I heard in my dream that all the bells in the City rang again for joy, and that it was said unto them, "Enter ye into the joy of your Lord." I also heard the men themselves, that they sang with a loud voice, saying, "Blessing, and honor, and glory, and power, be unto Him that sitteth upon the throne, and unto the Lamb, for ever and ever!"

Now, just as the gates were opened to let in the men, I looked in after them, and behold, the City shone like the sun; the streets also were paved with gold; and in them walked many men with crowns on their heads, palms in their hands, and golden harps to sing praises withal.

There were also of them that had wings, and they answered one another without ceasing, saying, "Holy, holy, holy is the Lord!" And, after that, they shut up the gates; which when I had seen, I wished myself among them.

Now while I was gazing upon all these things, I turned my head to look back, and saw Ignorance come up to the river-side; but he soon got over, and that without half the difficulty which the other two men met with. For it happened that there was then in the place one Vain-Hope, a ferryman, that with his boat helped him over; so he, as the others I saw, did ascend the hill, to come up to the gate; only he came alone, neither did any man meet him with the least encouragement. When he was come up to the gate, he looked up to the writing that was above, and then began to knock, supposing that entrance should have been quickly given to him; but he was asked by the men that looked over the top of the gate, "Whence came you? and what would you have?" He answered, "I have eaten and drunk in the presence of the King, and He has taught in our streets." Then they asked him for his certificate, that they might go in and show it to the King: so he fumbled in his bosom for one, and found none. Then said they, "Have you none?" But the man answered never a word. So they told the King; but He would not come down to see him, but commanded the two Shining Ones that conducted Christian and Hopeful to the City, to go out and take Ignorance, and bind him hand and foot, and have him away. Then they took him up, and carried him through the air to the door that I saw in the side of the hill, and put him in there. Then I saw that there was a way to hell, even from the gates of heaven, as well as from the City of Destruction!

So I awoke, and behold, it was a dream.

Conclusion

Now, reader, I have told my dream to thee,
See if thou canst interpret it to me,
Or to thyself or neighbor; but take heed
Of misinterpreting; for that, instead
Of doing good, will but thyself abuse:
By misinterpreting, evil ensues.
Take heed also that thou be not extreme
In playing with the outside of my dream;
Nor let my figure or similitude
Put thee into a laughter or a feud.
Leave this for boys and fools; but as for thee,
Do thou the substance of my matter see.
Put by the curtains, look within my veil;
Turn up my metaphors, and do not fail,
There, if thou seekest them, such things to find
As will be helpful to an honest mind.
What of my dross thou findest there, be bold
To throw away; but yet preserve the gold.
What if my gold be wrapped up in ore? —
None throws away the apple for the core.
But if thou shalt cast all away as vain,
I know not but t'will make me dream again.

Do you have freedom?

Those struggling with drug and alcohol addiction are not free and desperately need the help of Jesus to save them, free them, and restore them! If you don't know Jesus, you too, need freedom from sin and its weight.

Why do I need to know Jesus?

God created us to be in relationship with Him. Adam and Eve enjoyed a beautiful closeness with their Creator, but something tragic happened. They chose to disobey and sin against God. This caused separation between God and man. "All have sinned and fall short of the glory of God." Romans 3:23.

What does this mean for me?

God loves us so much that He sent His son, Jesus, to live a sinless life on earth, and then to die as a sacrifice for the sin that we deserve punishment for. Now our hearts can be made new and we can be reconciled back into a right relationship with God. This is Good News! Will you accept this free gift of salvation from your Father who loves you unrelentingly?
Romans 6:23 John 3:16

Where do I go from here?

To heaven when your life is over! Until then, walk with God, live right, read the Bible, get involved in a Bible believing church, and tell people about this great news in your life.

"For Christ also suffered once for sins, the righteous for the unrighteous, that He might bring us to God." - 1 Peter 3:18 [ESV]

CHANGED LIVES

Ten True Stories: *From Addiction to Freedom*

CHANGED LIVES books series is a compilation of miraculous stories of people who were addicted to drugs and alcohol and with no hope. But now through an encounter with God and the Teen Challenge Program, their lives have been changed. Is there a power stronger than the power of addiction? Can you or your loved one become FREE from the control of addiction and live a productive life? Absolutely yes! These books are a must read, the true stories will touch your heart, and give you and your loved ones HOPE!

Book 1   Book 2   Book 3   Book 4

Book 5   Book 6   Book 7   365 Day Devotional

TEEN CHALLENGE NEW ENGLAND & NEW JERSEY PROGRAM LOCATIONS

RHODE ISLAND WOMEN'S CENTER
572 ELMWOOD AVENUE PROVIDENCE, RI 02907
P: 401-467-2970
F: 401-461-3510
DIRECTOR@TCRHODEISLAND.ORG
TCRHODEISLAND.ORG

BLOOM ADOLESCENT GIRLS' HOME
P.O. BOX 603 BUZZARDS BAY, MA 02532
P: 774-300-8070
DIRECTOR@TCNEBLOOM.ORG
TCNEBLOOM.ORG

VERMONT WOMEN'S CENTER
130 HIGHLAND AVENUE HARDWICK, VT 05843
P: 802-635-7807
F: 802-635-7029
DIRECTOR@TCVERMONT.ORG
TCVERMONTWOMEN.ORG

FUTURE NEW JERSEY WOMEN'S CENTER
5 N 2ND STREET PLEASANTVILLE, NJ
P: 973-374-2206
F: 973-374-5866
DIRECTOR@TCNEWJERSEYWOMEN.ORG
TCNEWJERSEYWOMEN.ORG

GREATER BOSTON MEN'S CENTER
81 CHATHAM STREET WORCESTER, MA 01609
P: 617-318-1380
F: 617-318-1385
DIRECTOR@TCGREATERBOSTON.ORG
TCGREATERBOSTON.ORG

MASSACHUSETTS MEN'S CENTER
20 CLIFTON AVENUE BROCKTON, MA 02301
P: 508-586-1494
F: 508-586-0667
DIRECTOR@TCMASSACHUSETTS.ORG
TCMASSACHUSETTS.ORG

CONNECTICUT MEN'S CENTER
P.O. BOX 9492 NEW HAVEN, CT 06534
P: 203-789-6172
F: 203-789-1127
DIRECTOR@TCCONNECTICUT.ORG
TCCONNECTICUT.ORG

VERMONT MEN'S CENTER
1296 COLLINS HILL ROAD JOHNSON, VT 05656
P: 802-635-7807
F: 802-635-7029
DIRECTOR@TCVERMONT.ORG
TCVERMONT.ORG

NEW HAMPSHIRE MEN'S CENTER
147 LAUREL STREET MANCHESTER, NH 03103
P: 603-647-7770
F: 603-647-7570
DIRECTOR@TCNEWHAMPSHIRE.ORG
TCNEWHAMPSHIRE.ORG

NEW JERSEY MEN'S CENTER
245 STANTON MOUNTAIN ROAD LEBANON, NJ 08838
P: 973-374-2206
F: 973-374-5866
DIRECTOR@TCNEWJERSEY.ORG
TCNEWJERSEY.ORG

MAINE MEN'S CENTER
11 HUDSON LANE WINTHROP, ME 04364
P: 207-377-2801
F: 207-377-2806
DIRECTOR@TCMAINE.ORG
TCMAINE.ORG

VERMONT TRANSITIONAL REFERRAL CENTER
197 WEST STREET RUTLAND, VT 05656
P: 802-635-7807
DIRECTOR@TCVERMONT.ORG
TCVERMONT.ORG

MASSACHUSETTS TC CLINICAL GROUP CSS
1311 MAIN STREET BROCKTON, MA 02301
P: 744-480-5897
F: 508-256-3242
JPOSEY@TCCLINICALGROUP.ORG
TCCLINICALGROUP.ORG

MASSACHUSETTS TC CLINICAL GROUP OUTPATIENT
1305 MAIN STREET BROCKTON, MA 02301
P: 744-480-5897
F: 508-256-3242
JPOSEY@TCCLINICALGROUP.ORG
TCCLINICALGROUP.ORG